AMPHIBIOUS WARFARE
An Illustrated History

Below: Marine LVT(A)(4) amphibious tractors approach the beachhead at Okinawa. These "amtracs" carried an M-8 75-mm howitzer which could be fired while the craft was in the water or on land. There is an anti-aircraft machine-gun mounted on the open turret and another fitted in a ball mount forward. Sand-bags are attached for added protection against enemy fire. (U.S. Navy)

NORMAN POLMAR | PETER B. MERSKY

AMPHIBIOUS WARFARE

An Illustrated History

BLANDFORD PRESS

London New York Sydney

First published in Great Britain in 1988 by
Blandford Press, Artillery House, Artillery Row,
London SW1P 1RT.

Distributed in the USA by Sterling Publishing Co. Inc.,
2 Park Avenue, New York, NY 10016.

Distributed in Australia by Capricorn Link (Australia)
Pty. Ltd., P.O. Box 665, Lane Cove, New South Wales
2066, Australia.

British Library Cataloguing in Publication Data:
Polmar, Norman
Amphibious warfare: an illustrated history.
1. Amphibious operations, 1900–1987
I. Title II. Mersky, Peter B., *1945-*
359.4'09
ISBN 0-7137-1827-7

Jacket illustration: The US Marines landing at Tarawa.
A painting by Colonel Charles Waterhouse, U.S.M.C.R.
(U.S. Marine Corps Museum Art Collection)

Designed and edited by DAG Publications Ltd. Designed
by David Gibbons; edited by Michael Boxall; layout by
Anthony A. Evans; typeset by Typesetters (Birmingham)
Ltd., camerawork by M&E Graphics, North Fambridge,
Essex; printed and bound in Great Britain by The Bath
Press, Avon.

ACKNOWLEDGMENTS

The authors are in debt to many individuals for their assistance on this project, especially Dr. Dean C. Allard and Edward J. Marolda of the Navy Historical Center; Commander P. R. Compton-Hall, RN (Retired), Director, Royal Navy Submarine Museum; Russell Egnor and Patricia Toombs of the Office of Information, Department of the Navy; Intelligence Specialist 1st class Steven Haight, USN, curator of the Little Creek Amphibious Museum; Kohji Ishiwata, Editor, *Ships of the Word*; Chief Warrant Officer Joseph Leo, USN, Navy Audio-Visual Command; Paul J. Kemp, Department of Photographs, Imperial War Museum; Misses Patty Maddocks and Linda Cullen, Photographic Library, U.S. Naval Institute; Colonel Brooke Nihart, USMC (Retired), and Major Charles D. Melson, USMC, the Marine History and Museum Division; and Lieutenant Commander David Parsons, USN, Editor of *Approach* magazine.

Norman Polmar
Peter B. Mersky

GLOSSARY

Note: Amphibious and landing ship and craft designations are listed in Appendix C.

AGER	environmental research ship (e.g., USS *Pueblo*)
ARG	Amphibious Ready Group
ASW	Anti-Submarine Warfare
AVG	aircraft escort vessel (later CVE)
BB	battleship
BLT	Battalion Landing Team
CA	heavy cruiser
COS	Chiefs of Staff (British)
COSSAC	Chief of Staff to the Supreme Allied Commander
CV	aircraft carrier
CVE	escort aircraft carrier
CVL	light (small) aircraft carrier
DD	destroyer
FAC	Forward Air Control
FMF	Fleet Marine Force
JCS	Joint Chiefs of Staff (U.S.)
MAF	Marine Amphibious Force
RAF	Royal Air Force
RM	Royal Marines
RN	Royal Navy
SAS	Special Air Service
SEAL	Sea-Air-Land
SHAEF	Supreme Headquarters Allied Expeditionary Forces
SM	submarine minelayer
SS	submarine
UDT	Underwater Demolition Team
USA	U.S. Army
USAAF	U.S. Army Air Forces
USMC	U.S. Marine Corps
VSTOL	Vertical/Short Take-Off and Landing

CONTENTS

Preface   6
1. Before America   8
2. The American Experience   16
3. The Japanese Experience   23
4. European Interlude   31
5. The First Pacific Assaults   38
6. The First Atlantic Assaults   45
7. Landing Ships and Craft   55
8. The Mediterranean   72
9. "Overlord": The Greatest Assault   79
10. Submarine Operations   91
11. On the Offensive in the Pacific   96
12. Across the Pacific, 1943   102
13. Across the Pacific, 1944   109
14. Across the Pacific, 1945   122
15. Vertical Assault   132
16. Amphibious Rejuvenation   142
17. The Other Navies   160
18. Future Concepts and Requirements   171
Notes   180
Appendix A. Churchill Memorandum, June 4, 1940   183
Appendix B. Churchill Memorandum, June 15, 1942   183
Appendix C. Amphibious Warfare Ships and Craft   184
Selected Bibliography   186
Index   189

PREFACE

MAN'S earliest travel on the sea was to carry trade and also to carry troops to hostile shores. The earliest recorded amphibious landings – some 2,500 years ago – have much in common with those of the Argentinian and then the British in the Falklands conflict in 1982, and with the U.S. landings on Grenada in the Caribbean in 1983. During that long period amphibious operations have become the hallmark of major naval powers. British military historian and analyst B. H. Liddell Hart, wrote that "Amphibious flexibility is the greatest strategic asset that a sea power possesses."

Amphibious Warfare is the most complex of military operations. From the outset, amphibious operations must bridge the difficult transition from sea to land, involving naval and ground forces, and – since the 1930s – air forces. One

of the most complex aspects of amphibious or "combined" operations are the command and control of such multi-service, multi-environment activities.

Because landing ships must enter restricted waters for amphibious operations, they are highly vulnerable to hostile attack, as are the landing troops during the early phases of a landing when they reach the beach without support of their own heavy weapons. The complexity of landing operations and the potential for massive disaster was demonstrated during the 1915 landings by British and French forces in the Dardanelles, the southern entrance to the Turkish Straits. This costly failure and the unsuccessful effort to close German U-boat bases on the Belgian coast by a combination of raids and blockships convinced many military and political leaders that

Below: The U.S. amphibious assault ship *Tarawa* (LHA-1), a 39,300-ton, multi-function ship, was lead ship of the largest amphibious warfare ships ever built. An AV-8A Harrier VSTOL aircraft hovers overhead while other Harriers and helicopters are on deck; the stern gate is opening to unload landing craft from the docking well. (U.S. Navy)

amphibious assaults against defended positions were impossible. But neither the U.S. Marines nor the Japanese Army and Navy drew that lesson from the Dardanelles; rather, those services concluded that specialized training, ships, landing craft, and techniques would be needed for successful assaults.

On the eve of the war in Europe the British came to understand the need for specialized training and landing craft in amphibious operations. The Soviets also adopted specialized forces, but on a much smaller scale than the Western allies, being employed almost exclusively in restricted sea areas and for river crossings.

Some 600 amphibious landings took place during World War II, ranging in size and complexity from river crossings to raids (some carried out from submarines), to small-scale landings, to massive, multi-division assaults.

Virtually all of these landings were successful. A few did fail: The British raid-in-force at Dieppe on the English Channel coast, the British attempt to capture the French port of Dakar on the African coast, and the Japanese efforts to land at Port Moresby in New Guinea and then at Midway Island. The most dramatic failure, however, was the amphibious landing that was never begun: "Sealion," the planned German crossing of the English Channel. This assault was carefully planned, landing craft were assembled, and the troops partially trained. The failure of the German Air Force to gain control of the skies over the English Channel and south eastern England led to the delay and then aborting of that planned assault.

Four years later the largest amphibious assault in history did cross the English Channel, this the mighty Anglo-American force going to France in the Normandy or D-Day landings. This landing, like most of those carried out by the United States and Great Britain, was completely at the mercy of the availability of specialized landing ships and small craft, especially the ubiquitous Landing Ship Tank or LST. As Britain's wartime prime minister, Winston Churchill, telegraphed to the U.S. Army Chief of Staff, General George C. Marshall, in 1944: "The whole of this difficult [strategy] question only arises out of the absurd shortage of the L.S.T.s. How it is that the plans

of two great empires like Britain and the United States should be so much hamstrung and limited by a hundred or two of the particular vessels will never be understood by history."

General Marshall himself is said to have earlier remarked, "Prior to the present war I never heard of any landing craft except a rubber boat. Now I think of little else."

World War II was in large part an amphibious war, first by Japan, from operations in China in the 1930s through 1942, and then by the United States and Britain. (And, in the period 1942–1945, by the Soviet Union on a more limited scale.)

The atomic bombs exploded in 1945 heralded to many the end of amphibious landings, much as the Dardanelles campaign had three decades earlier. In 1949, the Chairman of the U.S. Joint Chiefs of Staff, General of the Army Omar Bradley, told a congressional committee, "I am wondering if we shall ever have another large-scale amphibious operation. Frankly, the atomic bomb, properly delivered, about precludes such a possibility."

But one year later, in the Korean War, another U.S. Army five-star general, Douglas MacArthur, demonstrated again that he was a master of amphibious warfare by the brilliant landing in the port of Inchon, which turned the course of the conflict. At a planning conference for that operation, MacArthur remarked, "The amphibious landing is the most powerful tool we have."

Subsequently, numerous landings have been considered and several carried out, a number by French and then U.S. forces in the 25 years of conflict in Indochina, and, of course, the Anglo-French assault at Suez, the previously cited British landings in the Falklands conflict, and the U.S. landings in Grenada.

This book seeks to provide an overview of the development of amphibious warfare – the leadership, tactics, operations, amphibious ships, and landing craft. Limitations of space prevent a complete account. But it is hoped that the descriptions and analysis that are provided will permit the reader to grasp the character, the complexity, and the importance of Amphibious Warfare.

1.
BEFORE AMERICA

HISTORIANS can identify major amphibious operations – troops being landed from ships against opposing forces – in the wars fought between Greeks and Persians 2,500 years ago.

When Themistocles, the Athenian statesman and general, mobilized Athens to fight the invading Persians in 480 B.C., he ordered the enlistment of troops called Epibatae or "heavily armed sea soldiers" to fight in the Greek fleet. In the battle at Salamis this Athenian fleet defeated the Persian ruler Xerxes and saved Athens.

Ten years earlier, in the summer of 490 B.C., a Persian fleet of 600 *triremes* sailed toward Greek shores with at least 9,000 troops for landing (in addition to the ships' crews and several thousand ship soldiers intended for fighting the ships). This fleet successfully assaulted several Greek coastal cities. Their principal and most famous landing was at Marathon, on the Attic coast, some 60 miles by sea (and 25 miles by road) from Athens. While there was no resistance to the landing, an Athenian army was marching to give battle to the Persians. Apparently, the Persians re-embarked part of their army for a direct attack on Athens while the remainder waited on the beach to prevent the Athenian force from returning to defend their city. In the ensuing battle at the Marathon beachhead the Greeks won an overwhelming victory. The Greek force then returned (by road) to Athens, where it was joined by a Spartan army, jointly to confront the arriving Persian amphibious force.

The Persian amphibious assault failed. In part as a result of that failure, a decade later the decisive naval battle at Salamis was fought. That battle, in turn, was followed a year later by an important land battle at Plataea. The Persians were again defeated in these battles, which saved that part of Europe from being conquered by Asians.

More amphibious operations followed. In general, these were *landings* and not *assaults* – that is, troops and often their horses were landed from ship onto a beach, and then went forward into battle. The term *assault* implies a landing in the face of an opposing force. Thus, the famed Norman landing in England in 1066, which would win the sobriquet William the Conqueror for the Norman leader after he defeated Harold at Hastings, was not an amphibious assault but a landing. Duke William brought some 11,000 troops across the English Channel, about 3,600 of them mounted knights, embarked in about 700 ships.

During the ensuing centuries there were many more such landings of armies – in Europe, the Middle East, and the Far East. Among the more famous efforts were the Mongol attempts to invade Japan in 1274 and 1281, the latter being defeated by a hurricane that would become known as the *kamikaze* or "divine wind," a term that would come to have significance in later plans for amphibious assaults on Japan. Halfway around the world and three centuries later, a Spanish invasion fleet – known as the Armada – sought to invade England. This fleet of only 132 vessels embarked more than 21,000 soldiers. It was to have been joined by barges setting out from the French coast with additional troops. An Anglo-Dutch blockade stopped the barges from coming out while audacious English seamen, attacking the Spanish ships in port and at sea, assisted by storms, destroyed the "invincible" Armada.

The British and Dutch navies formally organized marines, to fight on board ships and to land on hostile beaches, in 1664 and 1665, respectively. Both navies, fighting in home waters and seizing and protecting far-flung colonies, found many uses for their "soldiers of the sea." After the Peace of Utrecht in 1713, which ended the War of the Spanish Succession (1701–14), the British marines were practically disbanded; only four small companies remained. However, on the outbreak of war with Spain in 1739, King George II re-established the marines, with six regiments each to number 1,100 men. (It is interesting to note that three of the regiments were to be organized in the American colonies under command of Colonel Alexander Spotswood of Virginia. These colonial marines served at sea, chiefly in the West Indies. One of their officers was Lawrence Washington, half-brother of George.)

In many respects modern amphibious warfare began with Peter the Great, tsar of Russia from 1682 to 1725. Peter developed an early interest in ships and sailing, and developed a navy to help capture the Neva marshes from the Swedes. In 1703 he established his capital city of St. Petersburg (now Leningrad) at the mouth of the Neva river and built a fleet to control the Gulf of Finland at the eastern end of the Baltic Sea.

In 1705, Peter established a naval infantry regiment for his newly created Baltic fleet. Consisting of 45 officers and 1,320 soldiers, this "marine" regiment fought at sea against the Swedes and, from 1707, were landed in raids against offshore islands and, eventually, the coast of Sweden. The scope of these amphibious operations grew until, by the spring of 1713, according to the popular biography *Peter the Great* by Robert K. Massie:

". . . Peter sailed from Kronstadt with a fleet of ninety-three galleys and 110 other large boats carrying between them more than 16,000 soldiers. [General-Admiral Fedor] Apraxin commanded the whole fleet; the Tsar commanded the vanguard. The campaign was an overwhelming success. Using the galleys to leapfrog the troops from one point on the coast to another, the Russian army worked its way steadily westward along the Finnish coast. It was a classic example of amphibious warfare: Whenever the Swedish General Lybecker positioned his force in a strong defensive position, the Russian galleys, hugging the coastline, would slip around behind him, row into a harbor and disembark hundreds or thousands of men, unfatigued by marching, with cannon and supplies. There was nothing the Swedes could do to stop them and nothing Lybecker could do except retreat."[1]

By September 1713, the Russian amphibious advance had carried as far as Abo, and a month later the Russians held all of southern Finland. Further, this was accomplished with the more powerful Swedish fleet holding control of the open waters of the Baltic.

In September 1714, after Peter's fleet had won a major victory over the Swedes, 60 galleys landed 16,000 Russian troops in the Aland Islands. The galleys continued to shift troops westward, and just before ice closed that part of the Baltic, Admiral Apraxin sent nine galleys in a raid against a town within Sweden's historic borders.

When negotiations for peace with Sweden came to a standstill in the summer of 1719, the Russians mounted yet another major amphibious assault. This time the Russian battle fleet was accompanied by 130 galleys carrying 30,000

soldiers who wreaked havoc on the eastern coast of Sweden. Two efforts to land troops to attack the capital of Stockholm, however, were repulsed by Swedish ships in Stockholm harbor.

More amphibious operations were carried out against the Swedish coast in the summer of 1720 and again in 1721. These final landings influenced the Swedish government to capitulate to Peter's terms, ending the lengthy war between the two nations.

Peter's amphibious campaigns in the Baltic were large in size and scope, and had a direct effect upon Swedish policies for coming to terms with the Tsar – the father of the Russian navy. The interest of Peter's successors in naval matters varied considerably. But from 1770, Russian fleets periodically sailed the Mediterranean; that year Russian marines helped to capture Navarino and, in 1773, the fortress of Beirut, and in 1798–1800 they made successful landings on several islands in the Ionian Sea and at the fortress of Corfu.

In the subsequent European wars the Royal Navy became a frequent practitioner of amphibious landings. In some respects the British master of "forcible entry," as amphibious assault was known at that time, was Lieutenant-General Sir Ralph Abercromby. He was recalled to active duty at the age of 60 to command the 1799 landing of 10,000 troops in North Holland.

Although the Dutch had a large opposing force behind the beach, there was little effort to interfere with the initial landing. And, yet, as time would tell, in the landing phase an amphibious assault is at its greatest vulnerability. Sir Henry Brunbury described the confusion of amphibious landings of that era when he wrote:

". . . a strong squadron of frigates and small two-deckers drawing little water (Admiral [Lord] Duncan was in the offing with the heavier men-of-war), was able to anchor near enough to the shore to protect the transports, and throw a storm of shot upon the beach, while the boats, heavy with soldiers, were rowing to their landing place. But the only boats were those of the men-of-war, ill calculated for such a service and incapable of conveying more than 3,000 men at a time. To the officers of our navy this kind of operation was entirely new; nor did they understand the details, or feel the importance of arrangement on which military order and military success must greatly depend. Thus parts of regiments were conveyed to the shore, while parts were left behind. Battalions were intermixed; and companies had to find their proper places after they had landed and were under fire of the enemy. The soldiers had to wade and scramble out of the surf as well as they could, and look out for their comrades, and run to their stations in the line which was growing slowly into shape along the beach."[2]

Despite these difficulties and under light fire from the enemy, Abercromby got his force safely ashore and began to advance. Then he made the mistake of halting, having overestimated his own difficulties and underestimated those of his opponents. He ordered his troops to dig in and await reinforcements. Russian reinforcements were landed with overall command being taken by the Duke of York. The expedition then came to a halt and in the fall, when over-the-beach resupply became impossible, the invasion force was withdrawn.

But the success of the initial amphibious assault led to Abercromby's being given command of an even more ambitious landing in late 1801, this time at far greater distance from bases in Britain. In October of that year, under Abercromby's command, a force of 22,000 soldiers sailed from Gibraltar to attack the Spanish fortress of Cadiz, one of the most heavily defended ports of Europe. This was the height of the hurricane season and when Abercromby could not obtain unequivocal assurance of logistic support from the naval commander, he abandoned the expedition. Upon return to England, he was given orders to attack the French army which Napoleon had left at Aboukir beach, adjacent to Alexandria, Egypt.

This time Abercromby had but 16,000 soldiers, and they were poorly equipped, the War Ministry having underestimated the strength of the French force. Twenty-eight transports sailed with Abercromby's troops under a naval escort. While waiting for horses and horse transports at the island of Rhodes, Abercromby put his soldiers through realistic rehearsals, giving the assault troops and the sailors who would row them to the beach invaluable training.

Although the British were forced to wait offshore for a week because the weather made landings impracticable, the French took no preparations to oppose the landings. The amphibious tactics developed by Abercromby are described by Professor E. B. Potter and Fleet Admiral Chester W. Nimitz in the U.S. Naval Academy textbook *Sea Power*:

"Active British operations were initiated by a signal rocket ... at 2 am. From the transports,

anchored seven miles out in deep water, the soldiers of the first division were rowed to the line of departure, marked by two shallow-draft vessels moored two miles offshore. By 9 o'clock the landing force was aligned in three waves facing the mile-wide beach, with gunboats at their flanks and rear. On signal, the gunboats opened fire on the shore as the landing craft started in. The first wave consisted of 58 flatboats, carrying 3,000 infantrymen, with 50-foot intervals between boats; carrying 2,700 infantrymen; the third, of 37 launches in which seamen towed fourteen more launches bearing field guns and gunners. As the three waves advanced they were met first by a cross-fire of shot and shell that did but little damage, then by grape and langridge which caused numerous casualties, and finally by musketry.

As the first wave touched bottom, the second and third slipped into the intervals, and 6,000 men stepped ashore already organized in companies and battalions. Thrusting aside attacks by infantrymen and by mounted dragoons, the British followed Major-General Sir John Moore up the sandhills. By nightfall [of March 8] they had advanced two miles along the peninsula toward Alexandria, and the rest of Abercromby's army had landed."[3]

The British troops moved on to capture Cairo and then Alexandria. In capturing Egypt the British army won a major victory over the superior French troops. Abercromby, who was killed in the fighting in Egypt, thus joins Peter the Great as a founding master of amphibious assault. All of the elements of modern amphibious assault – except for the use of aircraft and submarines – can be found in their "forcible entry" operations.

There were additional amphibious landings during the 1800s and into the early 1900s, especially by the British, Japanese, Russians, and Americans. In general, troops landed from ships were successful in overcoming opposition. The doctrine which held that assault from the sea would always succeed received a rude shock at Gallipoli, the peninsula on the western European shore of the Dardanelles, the passage between the Mediterranean and the Sea of Marmora, just below the Black Sea.

By the winter of 1914 the fighting on the Western Front in Europe had stagnated into a grinding war of attrition characterized by trench warfare. From the fertile mind of Winston Churchill, First Lord of the Admiralty, came proposals for British forces to undertake actions on the flanks of the German and Austro-Hungarian forces. Turkey was on the enemy's side and Churchill believed that forcing the Dardanelles with warships and capturing Constantinople and opening the passage through to the Black Sea would (1) cause Turkey to leave the war and (2) open a route from the Mediterranean to help speed the flow of arms to the Russians, who were fighting on the Eastern Front against Austria and Germany.

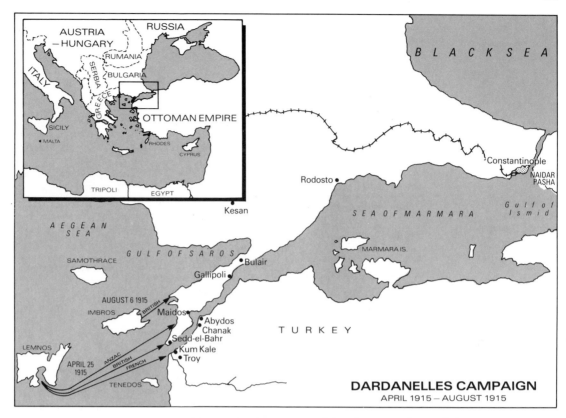

DARDANELLES CAMPAIGN
APRIL 1915 – AUGUST 1915

An amphibious landing would be made along the Dardanelles to prevent the Turks from using artillery against the warships passing through. The assault on Gallipoli was to be carried out by a British battle fleet, reinforced by four obsolete French battleships, with two battalions of Royal Marines.[4] Pre-warned of the coming attack, Turkish troops, under command of a German admiral, had artillery ready to fire on the assaulting ships, and defensive sea mines were planted. The headlands through which the warships were to steam into the Dardanelles were only 2¼ miles apart.

From February 15, 1915, the British warships took the Turkish forts on the headlands under fire. The British continued the attack, intermittently, while wooden minesweepers cleared the mines. The campaign was slow and tortuous. In early March the British Marines were sent ashore in an effort to destroy the Turkish guns. The outnumbered Marines were thrown back and withdrew to their ships.

Spurred on by a stream of messages from an irate Churchill, the British admiral forced the straits on March 7 but was unable to make sufficient progress. The British were simply not trained for such close-in work. Finally, the decision was made to land a full army on Gallipoli to open the route to Constantinople. A massive British and Empire force was assembled for the assault. Most were British soldiers, but there was an Australian-New Zealand Corps (ANZAC) of some 30,000 men, the first armies to have been raised by those members of the British Empire; a Royal Navy infantry division of 10,000 men; and a French contingent – a grand total of more than 70,000 men.

The troops were brought to the area by transports and had to be re-embarked in small boats at the fishing village of Mudros on the island of Lemnos, 40 miles south west of the Dardanelles. It was an awkward and complex maneuver.

The main landing, by the Australian and New Zealand Corps (ANZAC) and a British army division, would take place on the southern end of Gallipoli, at two separate beaches, one on each side of Cape Helles. The naval division would make a feint landing farther north. Only 15,000 Turks held the heights of southern Gallipoli, but the assault beaches were small, the British troops unpractised in the intricacies of "forcible entry," British intelligence was faulty, and the British commanders were inept and overly secret in informing their own commanders of their intentions.

The assault began at first light on April 25 – more than two months after British warships had first appeared on the scene. Warships began bombarding the Turkish positions while the tugs, pulling troop-laden boats from Mudros, approached the beaches. The troops would row the last 300 yards to the beach, having been in small craft for several hours for the voyage from Mudros.

For the landing to the east of Cape Helles (the beach designated by the letter "V") a steel-hulled collier, the *River Clyde*, was converted to a

Right: British troops in a lighter pass the battleship *Implacable* during the Gallipoli landings on April 25, 1915. A variety of coastal cargo ships, tugs, lighters, and other small craft were used to land troops, plus the steel-hulled collier *River Clyde*, which was converted to a landing ship. The *Implacable* was a pre-*Dreadnought* battleship, whose four 12-inch guns and twelve 6-inch guns joined those of other British and French warships in bombarding Turkish positions ashore prior to the landings. (Imperial War Museum)

Right: The landing of the 4th Battalion at Gallipoli from the steamer *Lake Michigan*. The officers in the left foreground include the commander and staff of the 1st Infantry Brigade. Although the troops landed rather easily on this narrow beach, they had to surmount the steep hillsides before attacking the strongly fortified Turkish positions at the top. (IWM)

Right: The *River Clyde* – the first specialized amphibious ship of this century – moored at "V" Beach after the bloody landing of April 25, 1915. Carrying some 2,000 troops, she grounded under the guns of a Turkish fortress. Visible are the holes cut into her side and the attached gangways to permit troops to run ashore. Raked by Turkish gunfire, the *River Clyde* became a charnel-house for British soldiers. (IWM)

landing ship: gangways were fitted to her sides and "sally ports" were cut in her sides, and sandbags were mounted to protect her superstructure. Some 2,000 troops from the 29th Division – the 1st Dublin Fusiliers, 1st Munster Fusiliers, and 2nd Hampshires – were embarked in the ship. Eight steam pinnaces towed additional boatloads of troops (the remainder of the Dublin Fusiliers) in company with the *River Clyde*. Their landing site was but ten miles across the Dardanelles from the ancient site of Troy, which caused the troop-laden *River Clyde* to be referred to as the "Trojan Horse." But she would be far less successful than the wooden structure used by the Greeks more than three thousand years earlier.

At 5 a.m. on April 25, off "V" Beach and the destroyed fort of Sedd-el-Bahr, the British battleship *Albion* commenced a heavy bombardment of supposed Turkish positions with her four 12-inch guns and twelve 6-inch guns. There was no response from the shore, which led the British commanders to believe that the defending Turks had either been killed or thoroughly demoralized by the British guns. But there were no forward observers to see where the British shot was falling. More serious, there were no gunboats to provide close covering fire for the assault troops, as Abercromby had used for his landing in Egypt more than a century earlier. In reality the Turkish defenders were resolute. Armed with Maxim machine-guns and rapid-fire (pom-pom) cannon as well as rifles, they withheld their fire.

Currents made it difficult for the approaching British landing craft – towed by steam tugs – to reach the planned landing beaches. At 6:22 a.m. the *River Clyde* grounded at Cape Helles, immediately west of Sedd-el-Bahr, just below the rubble of a Turkish fortress. As soon as the *River Clyde* had run aground, the Turks came to life, pouring rifle and Maxim fire down on the converted collier and the approaching landing craft. The pom-poms joined in.

The thousand troops of the Dublin Fusiliers brought in by boats at "V" Beach had to dash through the shallows with only their rifles for covering fire. Many troops died in the boats as they stood shoulder-to-shoulder awaiting their turn to climb over the sides and into the water. Those who managed to wade ashore had to force three lines of barbed-wire entanglements and a network of trenches, all under intensive fire from the Turks. Only a bank of sand four- or five-feet high on the beach provided cover for the survivors. Sailors and midshipmen who had rowed the boats up to the beach also died under the Turkish fire, and several of the boats, laden with dead and wounded, drifted away in the swift current.

The *River Clyde* lowered her ramps, the steel doors in her side were opened, and the troops poured forth. But the water was too deep for them to wade ashore. This situation had been foreseen and, under Turkish fire, a steam craft and a barge were brought alongside to bridge

Right: Troops in small boats being brought ashore with the *River Clyde* were similarly slaughtered in this, one of the many examples of costly stupidity in World War I operations. This photograph shows a corpse-strewn lighter. From the ruins of the fort and castle of Sidd-el-Bahr (background), which had been devastated by naval gunfire and other positions the Turks poured gunfire down onto the attacking troops, trapped between the water and barbed-wire entanglements. The slaughter led to the belief in the West that amphibious landings against fortified positions were impossible. (IWM)

the gap. Hundreds of British troops were killed outright on the ship and ramps. The *River Clyde*'s decks were awash with the blood of some 700 casualties to Turkish fire before they could leave the ship. A dozen Maxim machine-guns mounted on the ship gave some covering fire, but it was ineffective in the face of the Turkish guns above them. After a few desperate attempts at debarking, the thousand or so troops remaining stayed in the ship, protected by her steel sides. Larger Turkish guns fired on the ship. The four large-caliber shells that did strike her did not explode.

Offshore a trio of British battleships opened a furious bombardment of the Turkish positions. With darkness the thousand survivors left the *River Clyde* without additional casualties and established a small beachead.

Ten miles to the west, at the larger ANZAC landing site between Cape Helles and Tekke Burnu, a slightly larger beachead was secured under Turkish fire. This was 'W' Beach. The situation there was potentially as disastrous as at Cape Helles. According to one account: "[General] Sir Ian Hamilton said that 'so strong were the defences that the Turks may well have considered them impregnable'. It was his firm conviction that 'no finer feat of arms had ever been achieved by the British soldier than the storming of these trenches from open boats on the morning of April 25.' The beach was practically in a bay enclosed by hills, and the way out of it led through a narrow gully. The Turks had fully expected a landing at this point, and had prepared for it. They had laid both land-mines and sea-mines, and on the edge of the sea had constructed broad wire-entanglements along the whole length of the beach. Heights overlooking the beach were covered with entrenchments, to which the gully gave sheltered access. Machine-guns were concealed in holes in cliffs and trained on the edge of the barbed wire.

Once the assailants emerged from the cup-like bay, they were instantly exposed to fire from two strong infantry redoubts near Hill 138, protected by wire-entanglements 20 feet broad. The fire swept a bare, open zone which had to be crossed in attacking the Turks. From these redoubts another strong wire-entanglement had been carried to the edge of the cliff, thus making communication between 'W' Beach and the adjacent beach impossible until the redoubts were taken. Add to these defences a host of snipers concealed behind sand-dunes and tufts of grass, and it was not surprising that the Turks firmly believed 'W' Beach able to resist any attack."[5]

The only flaw in the Turkish defenses were groups of rocks at both ends of the bay. These gave the assaulting troops enough cover to enfilade the Turkish lines. By the afternoon troops landed here had captured some of the Turkish trenches that overlooked the beach at Cape Helles, finally bringing some relief to the British troops there. At night the remainder of the ANZAC force was able to come ashore at 'W' Beach without the Turks firing a shot. At about eleven that night, the remaining Turkish positions did open fire, but by then it was too late. The next day the ANZAC troops made frontal attacks against the Turkish positions overlooking the beaches and, with severe losses, drove the Turks out.

Inititial efforts to reinforce the small Gallipoli beachheads were hampered by the shortage of boats, poor planning, and poor British leadership. Finally, the British and ANZAC forces were able to land reinforcements and they were able to stabilize their beachheads. Despite being under enemy fire, the troops were able to retain their toeholds on the Gallipoli beaches throughout December 1915. Neither the Turks nor the British could displace their enemy. By the end of the year a half-million Commonwealth and French troops had been committed. Casualties in the entire campaign would be almost half that number 1,609 British and Commonwealth officers and 23,670 men dead; another 88,000 wounded. While Turkish casualties were also high (Turkish sources list more than 86,000 killed), the Turks had prevented the British from moving toward Constantinople and had in fact tied up a massive Anglo-French naval and ground force.

Finally, the decision was made in December 1915 to withdraw the British and ANZAC forces that remained ashore. In a series of night actions 115,000 troops were safely withdrawn in an operation that would presage the Dunkirk evacuation of the next war, except that the Gallipoli evacuation was undertaken without the knowledge of the Turks through an excellent series of deceptions and camouflage.

The amphibious assault against Gallipoli was very costly in terms of troops and marked the first failure of a major amphibious assault (at least since the defeat of the Mogul force sailing for Japan in the 13th century, although that force was defeated by a "divine wind" and not by the defending force). In England, Gallipoli had led the ingenious First Sea Lord, Admiral Sir John Fisher, to resign in protest over sending more ships to support the campaign; subsequently, the chief architect of the assault, Winston Churchill, was forced out of the government; the failure was to haunt him always. Several senior officers also had their careers destroyed.

Had the campaign succeeded, Russia might have been provided with sufficient arms to permit her armies to fight more effectively–just possibly changing the course of the war and delaying the Russian Revolution.[6] In his bitter summary of the Gallipoli campaign, Winston Churchill wrote in *The World Crisis*: "The end of the Dardanelles campaign closed the second great period of the struggle. There was nothing left now but the war of exhaustion—not only of armies but of nations. No more strategy, very little tactics; only the dull wearing down of the weaker combination by exchanging lives; only the multiplying of machinery on both sides to exchange them quicker."[7]

From the viewpoint of amphibious warfare, many of the military analysts who studied Gallipoli concluded that an amphibious assault against a beach defended by modern weapons would be impossible. This conclusion was widely accepted until, two and a half decades later when Japanese forces and the U.S. Marine Corps demonstrated that a successful amphibious assault could be conducted against any enemy-held objective.

Failure at Zeebrugge

If the Dardanelles campaign demonstrated that major amphibious landings against even partially defended beaches were impossible, the subsequent Zeebrugge operation demonstrated that amphibious *raids* were feasible although not necessarily successful.

In 1918 the German U-boats were still a major threat to Allied victory in Europe, having almost defeated Britain in April 1917, on the eve of American entry into World War I. In an effort to bottle up the U-boats in their German and Belgian ports, a massive minefield was laid across the North Sea by the British and U.S. Navies, and blocking raids were planned against the U-boat bases of Ostend and Zeebrugge in Belgium. Command of this expedition fell to Vice-Admiral Roger Keyes, who as a commodore had been a senior staff officer in the Dardanelles campaign and, after the failure at Gallipoli had proposed another thrust up to the Black Sea.

Keyes planned simultaneous assaults on both Ostend and Zeebrugge to sink concrete-filled block-ships to close the entrances to the channels used by the U-boats. The ports were heavily defended by shore batteries and machine-guns.

Admiral Keyes led his assault force to sea on April 22. The old protected cruiser *Vindictive* had been especially modified for the raid, mounting additional light guns and being fitted with a series of ramps for marines to clamber ashore. In addition, the blockships and an old submarine, laden with explosives, set forth surrounded by escorting warships.

The *Vindictive* entered Zeebrugge just before midnight. Under heavy German fire, the cruiser missed her intended position on the main mole by some 350 yards. This placed her Marines under heavy fire and they were unable to destroy the gun batteries. In the midst of the heavy fighting, the explosives-filled submarine was soon under the viaduct to the mole, her crew set fuzes, and escaped in a small boat. The submarine blew up, wrecking the structure.

Meanwhile, the block-ships reached their assigned positions, under heavy German fire, and were scuttled. Admiral Keyes gave the order to withdraw. Most of the British force was able to make the open sea, but 1,200 British sailors and troops were killed, wounded, or captured.

After only a few hours the Germans were able to dredge a channel around the sunken ships at Zeebrugge, while the block-ships at Ostend were unable to block that harbor at all. Thus, the raid was a failure, and had cost heavily. Britain, however, needed a victory and the raid was hailed as a great triumph. Churchill would write "The famous story of the blocking of Zeebrugge on St. George's Day by Admiral Keyes . . . may well rank as the finest feat of arms in the Great War, and certainly as an episode unsurpassed in the history of the Royal Navy."[8]

Right: The British amphibious raids against the U-boat bases at Ostend and Zeebrugge in Belgium failed in their purpose of denying German submarines access to the open sea. This aerial view of the entrance to the Bruges Canal at Zeebrugge shows the sunken ships *Thetis*, *Intrepid*, and *Iphigenia* following the British assault. Although the raid was a failure, it established the reputation of then Vice-Admiral Roger Keyes as an expert in raiding operations in the mind of Winston Churchill. Keyes had also been a key staff officer in the abortive British-French landings at the Dardanelles. (IWM)

2.
THE AMERICAN EXPERIENCE

THE U.S. Marine Corps would become the master of amphibious warfare in the 20th century. Beginning in 1775, some Colonial soldiers were pressed into service as Marines, and fought on Lake Champlain and other inland waters.

In November 1775, the Second Continental Congress authorized the raising of two battalions of Marines for use in the war against Britain. These battalions — each with 500 privates plus officers — were to provide detachments to sail in the ships of the fledgling Continental navy. The first major operation of the American fleet involving Marines came with the sailing of the small ships *Alfred* (30 guns) and *Columbus* (28 guns) with six lesser vessels from Delaware Bay on January 17, 1776. Embarked in seven of the vessels was a total of twelve officers and 234 enlisted Marines (in addition to the ships' companies of officers and men). Shortly after sailing one of the sloops and a schooner collided, both dropping out of the force; but only one Marine officer had been embarked in those two craft.

The surviving ships sailed into the Atlantic and southward. Their mission was to raid New Providence in the Bahamas to capture gunpowder badly needed by George Washington's troops. On March 3, Captain Samuel Nicholas, the first and most senior Marine officer, led an assault of 230 Marines and 50 seamen. The island's defenses consisted of a provisional militia of some 300 men, but less than half this number was readily available to man the protecting forts and to garrison the town. The two forts mounted a total of 63 guns, but their condition (and that of some of the guns) made them unsuitable for combat.

British intelligence had learned of the approach of the American ships, but the island's governor took no defensive action. The Americans also had good intelligence about the state of the islands from the captains of two captured British sloops. The colonial landing force was transferred to the *Providence* and two sloops.

The American ships were observed approaching the harbor, but the Americans persevered and

Below: Even as the American colonies began their fight for independence from Britain, an amphibious landing was undertaken at New Providence Island in the Bahamas to capture guns and powder for George Washington's army. Both sailors and marines took part in this operation, initially against Fort Montagu (left background). British opposition to this landing was nil. Still, it marked the debut of American amphibious warfare. (U.S. Navy photograph of a painting by V. Zeg)

shortly after noon the 280 Marines and sailors came ashore in the fleet's whaleboats some two miles to the east of New Providence. By two o'clock the Marines and sailors were formed up in marching order and Captain Nicholas led them toward the town and its defending forts.

A party of militia sent out to meet and delay the Americans was badly outnumbered and returned without a shot being fired. Indeed, under a flag of truce the militia was informed by the Americans of their identity and the purpose of the landing!

The governor, cowed by the approaching Americans, abandoned the first fort (spiking the guns) and withdrew toward the town. Both sides settled in for the night and the following day the commander of the American fleet sent ashore a manifesto offering to spare the town and individual property in exchange for non-resistance. At sea, however, the American ships had failed to blockade the fort properly and most of the gunpowder was loaded on board several ships which successfully eluded the Americans.

The second fort and the town were quickly secured. The remaining powder as well as considerable shot were loaded in the American ships. Despite much of the powder having been carried away earlier, the military booty was so great that a merchant ship in harbor was contracted to help the Americans. Although the Americans suffered no battle casualties in the operation, several died and others were hospitalized by small-pox and fever before the small fleet set sail on March 17.

Beyond the capture of badly needed military stores, the New Providence raid expanded the War for Independence beyond the boundaries of the thirteen colonies, forcing the British to undertake naval protective measures over a larger area. And, while the Marines were not involved in fighting, they did demonstrate the feasibility of long-range landing operations and established a tradition of amphibious warfare. During the American Revolution the Marines fought with General Washington at Trenton-Princeton (1776–77); with George Rogers Clark in the West (1778–79); in the ill-fated Penobscot expedition in 1779; and in the defense of Charleston in 1780. At sea, Marines were part of ships' companies in several engagements with British ships.

After independence was won the Marines, like the rest of the Continenal forces, went out of existence. A small Army contingent was retained. The Marines were reconstituted in 1794 when the United States, plagued by Algerian pirates in the Mediterranean, rebuilt its fleet, but when the crisis had passed the enlistment of Marines was cancelled. Marines were recruited during the 1798 quasi-war with France over the issue of American neutrality at sea. While these Marines served mainly as snipers in warship rigging, they did carry out landings on Curaçao and Puerto Plata in Santo Domingo (both in 1800). These were relatively small operations generally accomplished by the ships' seamen and Marines coming ashore in the ships' boats.

In the war with Tripoli, which began in 1801 after attacks on American ships, Marines took part in several naval engagements in the Mediterranean and the blockade of the city of Tripoli. A Marine lieutenant and seven men were with the 400 troops that marched 600 miles from Alexandria, Egypt, to participate in the only land campaign of the war. Joined en route by 700 desert tribesmen, the army captured the coastal town of Derna (Libya) in a joint operation with U.S. warships. Holding Derna for several weeks against counterattacks helped to end the war with Tripoli on terms favorable to the United States.

During the War of 1812 with Britain, the Marines fought in every major naval engagement, including the Battle of Lake Erie. On land the Marines were cited for their defense of Sackett's Harbor, New York, and Norfolk, Virginia, in 1813; and in the battles of Bladensburg in 1814 (after which the British burned the capital of Washington), and New Orleans in 1815.

With the nation technically at peace, the Navy and Marines took on a new role — serving as a quasi-police force in the Caribbean and Gulf of Mexico as lawlessness grew out of the collapse of the Spanish Empire. During the next century U.S. Marines would be landed on more than a score of occasions in that turbulent region to quell local fighting and enforce U.S. policies. During

Below: The first U.S. Marine landings in Korea took place in 1871 to protect U.S. mercantile interests. These Marines, from the USS *Alaska* and *Coronado*, proudly display a headquarters flag captured from one of the Korean forts during the landings of June 10–11, 1871. The private and corporal, with rifles, won Medals of Honor in the battle; at right is Captain McLane Tilton, commander of the Marines in the landing. (U.S. Marine Corps)

the Mexican War of 1847 the Marines were the first American troops to enter Mexico – by a coastal landing – and took part in the capture of Vera Cruz and Mexico City. Marine landings in Mexican-controlled California led to the brief independence of the Republic of California and its subsequent entry into the United States.

On the other side of the world, the plundering of American merchant ships in the East Indies led to a series of U.S. Marine landings in Sumatra during the 1830s. These were followed by Marine landings on Fiji and Samoa, and in the Gilbert Islands, to pacify hostile natives or redress attacks on American seamen. Similar actions led to landings on the West Coast of Africa in the 1840s.

U.S. Marines first entered China in 1844 when they were landed at Canton in response to anti-American rioting. Marines thereafter had considerable service in the Far East, including assaults against the Salee River forts in Korea in 1871. (The Marines saw extensive combat in China during the Boxer revolt of 1900, serving with distinction as did other nations' Marines at the seige of Peking, but these were land-locked operations.)

Marines had a relatively small role in the American Civil War (1861–65). Marines fought in several major land battles, served on board all major vessels of the Northern blockading squadrons, and conducted several armed reconnaissance operations along the Atlantic coast of the Confederate States. Marines took part in the major landing at Hatteras Inlet, North Carolina, as well as several lesser "forcible entries." The Hatteras assault, undertaken in late August 1861, was the first such operation of the war and a classic example of the difficulties of such operations.

The Northern squadron approached and began a bombardment of the forts at Hatteras Inlet. In the late morning of August 28 ships, boats, and barges began unloading troops, beyond the range of the guns of the two Confederate forts. Several

boats were lost, but 260 soldiers and 55 Marines were safely brought ashore with two boat howitzers. The troops were soaked, disorganized, and without provisions, but they marched toward the forts. Finding the first (partially completed) abandoned, they set up their howitzers. Rough seas prevented provisions from being brought ashore for the troops and they spent the night on an open beach and in the unfinished fort. The next morning the Northern warships resumed their bombardment of the major fort which soon surrendered, without being attacked by the troops.

More landings followed during the four-year war, most being reconnaissance missions. But they caused the Confederates problems and posed a threat of larger operations. Confederate Army commander Robert E. Lee, writing to Confederacy President Jefferson Davis, observed: "Wherever his [the Union] fleet can be brought, no opposition to his landing can be made."

At the end of the century the U.S. Navy defeated Spanish squadrons at Manila in the Philippines and off Cuba. Most of the landings that followed were conducted primarily by Army troops, but Marines were present and, in the Philippines, they would have a major role in suppression of the insurrection against American occupation of the islands (1898–1902).

By the beginning of the 20th century the U.S. Marines had more than a century of extensive combat experience at home and abroad, with innumerable landings of various sizes and degrees of complexity. Most were made simply with ships' boats, often with minimal time available for planning. The Marine reputation was thus firmly established for flexibility as well as amphibious expertise.

When the United States entered World War I in May 1917, the Marine Corps had been modernized, with its own air arm as well as large trucks, radios, field artillery, and automatic weapons. With the movement of American troops to Europe two Marine brigades were dispatched to

France. The 4th Marine Brigade served in the U.S. Army's 2nd Division, successfully clearing well-entrenched German troops from the Belleau Wood area. More intensive fighting followed, and the brigade became the only American unit to be awarded the French Croix de Guerre three times. The 5th Marine Brigade served in France mainly as military police and support units as the overall American commander, General John Pershing, refused to permit the Marines to establish a division formation. Marine pilots arrived in France late in the war. They flew 57 bombing missions and shot down four German aircraft with claims of a few more kills.

The campaigns in France established the precedent of large-size Marine units, but there were no landing operations by the Marines. The experience of the Dardanelles in 1915 now suggesting that landings in the face of heavily armed opposition could be impossible.

Between the world wars the Marines continued to be sent into the Caribbean-Central American region as, from a political perspective, Americans sought to withdraw from Old World politics. During the 1920s and 1930s, however, there were many U.S. Marine, as well as Navy, officers who saw the aggressive attitude of Japan as a prelude to future war between the two nations. Of particular concern to the Marines were the reports of fortifications being built on the Japanese-controlled islands of Saipan and Tinian, and in the Marshall and Caroline groups. Any U.S. fleet seeking to sail westward towards American-controlled Guam and the Philippine archipelago could be subjected to intensive attacks by Japanese ships, submarines, and aircraft based in those islands.

One of the leading Marine spokesmen for the need to develop a capability to assault islands in the Pacific to gain bases for the U.S. Fleet and to deny them to the Japanese was Major

Earl H. (Pete) Ellis. Immediately after World War I, Ellis began lecturing on the role of the Marine Corps in seizing bases for the fleet. His 50,000-word plan, submitted to the Commandant of the Marine Corps in July 1921, became the blueprint for a Marine advance across the Pacific. It began: "In order to impose our will upon Japan, it will be necessary for us to protect our fleet and land forces across the Pacific and wage war in Japanese waters." His assault targets in the 1921 plan included the Marshall, Caroline, and Palau Islands. Ellis listed specific atolls to be captured, troop requirements, weapons, reef-crossing vehicles, and tactics to be used. He concluded:

> "To effect such a landing under the sea and shore conditions obtaining and in the face of enemy resistance requires careful training and preparation, to say the least; and this along Marine Corps lines. It is not enough that the troops be skilled infantry men and jungle men or artillery men of high morale; they must be skilled water men and jungle men who know it can be done – Marines with Marine training."[1]

From 1922 the Marine Corps concentrated on the development of amphibious assault doctrine. In 1933 the Fleet Marine Force (FMF) was organized to provide the basis for tactical and support organizations for amphibious operations. The FMF doctrines developed over the next few years would serve the Marines virtually unchanged during the coming Pacific War.

Two technological developments that would be key components of amphibious landings were fostered by the Marines during the 1920s and 1930s. The first was the amphibious tractor or "amtrac." Until this time U.S. Marine landings – like those of Peter the Great and General Abercromby – used primarily ships' boats for

coming ashore. Their use forced the troops to wade through surf, with difficult footing, often under enemy fire. The Marines sought a better method of coming ashore in an opposed landing.

Several small craft with bow ramps were developed. More significantly, in the early 1920s American tank designer J. Walter Christie developed an amphibious vehicle that had a barge-like hull with tank-like tracks and a rudder. Although his craft performed satisfactorily in river tests, it was found unseaworthy in fleet exercises off Culebra in 1924.

The next major efforts in this field were those of Donald Roebling, in the early 1930s, who began development of an amphibious vehicle for rescue work. His design included curved cleats fitted on the tracks for both water and land propulsion. In 1940 the Marines provided funds for two of Roebling's "Alligators." The pilot models of the LVT-1 were built in 1941, the designation LVT indicating Landing Vehicle, Tracked. Because of general inefficiency with its machinery, the craft was planned to be used mainly to move supplies inland from the beach, and not as a ship-to-shore vehicle. But the vast potential of the LVT-1 would be proven in combat.

The second development of the inter-war period was the dive bomber. The precise origin of dive-bombing – where the aircraft dives at an angle of 60 degrees or more to the horizon before releasing its bomb – is not clear. At least one writer has cited a dive-bombing attack in the Mexican Civil War of 1913–15, while several probable dive-bombing attacks were flown by British pilots in World War I.

However, it was in the United States that the doctrine of dive-bombing was perfected. U.S. Army pilots, flying de Havilland DH-4B biplanes, experimented with dive-bombing during 1919–21 patrols along the Mexican border. At about the same time the U.S. Marines began intensive development and training in dive-bombing techniques. The U.S. Marines were unique in having an integral air arm (as a component of U.S. naval aviation).

Marine aircraft were dispatched to both Haiti and the Dominican Republic in 1919 to support Marine ground operations in the typical U.S. police operations of the Caribbean during that period. Flying de Havilland biplanes, the Marines conducted dive-bombing runs in close support of ground troops. Soon the entire Marine air arm as well as the naval air force was practising dive-bombing tactics. For both services this became the principal mode of attack against hostile ships and for providing close air support. In 1931, German World War I aviator Ernst Udet was in the United States watching Navy dive bombers demonstrate their tactics. Two years later, in Germany, Udet was asked to help build the new German air force, the *Luftwaffe*. Udet convinced *Luftwaffe* chief Herman Goering of the potential of dive-bombing and within a few years the notorious Junkers Ju 87 *Stuka* was being produced.

With the establishment of the Fleet Marine Force in 1933, the principal role of Marine air was to support amphibious landings, especially to strike enemy defensive positions in advance of the landings, and then to provide close air support to Marines fighting ashore. (The U.S. Army lost interest in dive-bombing, concentrating instead on level bombing with larger aircraft, the harbinger of the so-called precision daylight bombing strategy; later, in the Pacific War, the Army did effectively develop "skip bombing" techniques to attack shipping, but dive-bombing was never to be a primary tactic.)

The U.S. Marine Corps in the 1920s and 1930s thus concentrated on developing the doctrine and the tactics for an amphibious campaign in the Pacific.

3.
THE JAPANESE EXPERIENCE

THE OCTOPUS

The Japanese armed forces were also looking toward amphibious operations in the Pacific in the 1920s and 1930s. Japanese moves into Manchuria and China were but a prelude to expansionist plans to farther reaches of the Pacific. The Japanese had earlier used standard transports to carry soldiers to Korea in the Russo-Japanese war of 1904–05, unloading troops on the open beaches.

When Japan began operations against China in the early 1930s there was a new requirement for transports and the first specialized amphibious ships were constructed – *by the Japanese Army*. The *Shinshu Maru* was built to Army specifications in 1933, a precursor of the landing ship dock (LSD). The ship was built along the lines of a whale factory ship, with a stern ramp and large, garage-like interior which could accommodate several landing craft. The ramp was closed to the sea by large doors. There were several side ports in the *Shinshu Maru* to permit landing craft to come alongside and load equipment into them. A total of fourteen standard, 16-foot landing boats could be carried, while an upper deck could accommodate a dozen aircraft for catapult launching. The *Shinshu Maru* displaced 8,100 tons and was 479 feet

long; numerous 75-mm and 20-mm anti-aircraft guns were fitted for self-defense. (The *Shinshu Maru* was accidently sunk in 1942 off Java; she was salvaged and continued to operate until early 1945. Two more ships of about this size, the *Akitsu Maru* and *Nigitsu Maru*, were similarly completed as LSD-type ships, but with a flight deck so that each ship could operate as transports, flying off the aircraft in the objective area. The Army converted two more merchant ships under construction to an LSD configuration while several other cargo ships were rebuilt as conventional landing ships.)

With plans being formulated for the Pacific war, the Japanese Navy began a large program to provide adequate ships for amphibious landings in the U.S., British, and Dutch possessions in the Far East. Ten outdated destroyers of World War I design, which had previously been modified to patrol ships, were further refitted in late 1941 to carry 150 troops (250 troops in two ships). These ex-destroyers, like their contemporary American APDs, retained guns and depth charges. Ramps at their sterns permitted them to carry and launch landing craft.

These ships, plus a large number of mercantile

Right: The first specialized landing ship of the World War II era was the Japanese Army's *Shinshu Maru*. Built for the amphibious role, she originally had the additional mission of carrying floatplanes with space forward for two catapults (not installed). The ship participated in several landings in the Sino–Japanese War and in Java in 1942. Accidently torpedoed and sunk in 1942, she was salvaged but later sunk by U.S. forces. The forward funnel shown here was a camouflage dummy. (Courtesy *Ships of the World*)

Right: The 46-foot *Diahatsu* was the standard Japanese Army landing craft (there were also smaller and larger landing craft with this designation). During the Sino-Japanese War some were modified for use as gunboats, others were employed for inshore anti-submarine work in World War II, and some boats were rigged to carry torpedoes. The version shown here was constructed of wood; the larger (55-foot) steel version could carry a medium tank.

transports and passenger ships, were the principal means by which the Japanese carried out amphibious landings during the early stages of the war.

For actually bringing troops and vehicles ashore on hostile beaches, the Japanese Army developed a 46-foot landing craft (*Diahatsu*). A small LCT, the craft became the basis for the standard Navy and Army landing of the war. Several Army units were modified for use as gunboats on Chinese rivers, while the Navy fitted others with guns up to 25-mm plus depth charges and, in some instances, launchers for two 21-inch torpedoes. A smaller Navy variant, 42½ feet long, was developed for the Type 1 destroyer-transports. Several other variants were also produced for amphibious landings.

WORLD WAR II OPERATIONS

When France capitulated to Germany in the summer of 1940 the Japanese occupied bases in French Indochina, adding further demands on the Army and Navy. In the fall of 1941, as preparations were being made for war, the Japanese Army stood at 51 divisions, of which 28 were engaged in operations in China, and thirteen were stationed in Manchuria and Korea for defense against the Soviet Union. Only ten divisions remained in the homeland, of which five were newly formed. The Imperial General Headquarters decided to allocate five divisions from China and six from Japan to the Southern Operations. In addition, the Navy would provide several battalions of Special Naval Landing Force, i.e., Japanese Marines. Only limited amphibious shipping – cargo ships and transports – were available to move these troops southward. The planned Southern Operations were ambitious: to exploit the psychological advantage of the outbreak of war the American and British holdings in the Pacific would be attacked simultaneously.

There would be an air strike against the U.S. fleet at Pearl Harbor to prevent reinforcement of the American-held Philippines. The idea of a landing on Oahu in the Hawaiian Islands was quickly discarded because of the shortage of shipping and the need for the carrier strike force to transit rapidly on the stormy, northern route for maximum secrecy.

Simultaneously with the Pearl Harbor strike, the Japanese would assault the Philippines and Malaya. The Dutch East Indies with its oil resources would be the primary goal, but it would be necessary to deny Britain and America bases from which they could interdict the flow of oil and other resources to the home islands. Thus, the invasion of the Philippines and Malaya would be followed by the seizure of Borneo, the Celebes, Sumatra, and Java. Beyond these principal objectives, it would be necessary to take Burma to help hold Malaya, and some Japanese planners were even looking farther south to the northern coast of Australia. It was an ambitious plan, so ambitious that the assigned troops and ships would have to be used in successive landings.

On the morning of December 7, 1941, some 350 aircraft from six Japanese aircraft carriers successfully attacked the U.S. fleet at Pearl Harbor. Although the three U.S. aircraft carriers in the Pacific were not present, several battleships and destroyers were sunk or heavily damaged, and the fleet was effectively prevented from immediately undertaking operations against the Japanese except for hit-and-run carrier raids.[1] This left only a few Allied cruisers, destroyers, and submarines in Asian waters.

Other naval aircraft struck American bases on Guam, Wake, and the Howland Islands. On the 10th some 500 Japanese Marines from the Special Naval Landing Force came ashore on Guam and occupied the island without serious resistance, giving Japan control of the entire Marianas group.

A DELAY – BUT NO PROBLEM

Wake Island was not quite so simple. Actually an isolated atoll with two main islands having a total land area of three square miles, Wake is 480 miles north of the Marshall Islands and 1,025 miles west of Midway atoll.

On December 7, 1941, Wake was garrisoned by the 1st Marine Defense Battalion of 388 troops with six 5-inch and twelve 3-inch coastal defense guns, and a Marine squadron of 12 F4F Wildcat fighters, plus a naval detachment (without arms), and 1,200 civilian construction workers. The first Japanese air strike (from Kwajalein in the Marshall Islands) destroyed seven of the twelve Marine fighters.

The surviving fighters rose to do battle with the Japanese twin-engine bombers on the 9th and again on the 10th. The bombers were able to inflict considerable damage and before dawn on December 11 the Japanese invasion force assembled offshore.

The Japanese had one new and two old light cruisers, eight old destroyers (two fitted to carry troops), two small transports, and two submarines. On board were 450 Marines of the Special Naval Landing Force. Commenting on the small number of troops, the Chief of Staff of the Japanese force stated:

> "We expected to have a rough time and that we would have difficulty with a landing force of only 450 men. It was at the beginning of the war; we couldn't mass as many men as we considered necessary, and it was planned in an emergency to use the crews of the destroyers to storm the beach."[2]

The Japanese ships were sighted approaching Wake early on December 11. Shortly after 5 a.m. the Japanese cruisers opened fire on the atoll with 6-inch guns until the Japanese ships has approached to approximately 4,500 yards of the atoll. At 6:15 the Marines opened fire. The cruiser-flagship *Yubari* was struck several times and steamed out of range of the Marine guns. Next the destroyer *Hayate* was hit and exploded, breaking in two and sinking within a few minutes. Two other destroyers were also hit as were another cruiser and one of the small transports.

Meanwhile, four Marine F4Fs, which had been aloft since the start of the action, dived on the withdrawing ships. They were armed with small, 100-pound bombs in addition to their .50-caliber machine guns. During the withdrawal they flew a total of ten sorties, coming back to Wake to rearm and refuel and fly another strike. Their attack sunk a second destroyer and damaged other ships.

The same day Japanese Navy bombers returned to strike the hapless atoll, followed by more strikes on successive days, at times the twin-engined "Betty" bombers being supplemented by four-engine Army bombers flying from Majuro. These land-based bombers were joined, without warning to the Americans, by planes from two carriers on the morning of December 21. The carriers *Hiryu* and *Soryu* had been diverted to strike Wake on their way back to Japan from the Pearl Harbor attack. The eighteen Zero fighters and 29 attack planes bombed and strafed the Marine gun positions. (The appearance of these carrier planes led the U.S. admiral at Pearl Harbor to recall the carrier task force that was steaming toward Wake to relieve the Marines.) The Japanese carrier planes returned on the 22nd – six fighters and 33 attack planes. In this attack the last pair of patched-up Marine F4Fs was shot down.

Meanwhile, at Roi in the Marshall Islands, the Japanese conducted rehearsals for another landing on Wake. In addition to the availability of the two carriers and land-based bombers, the next assault would be supported by four older heavy cruisers and six destroyers. Two destroyer-transports, *Patrol Boats No. 32* and *No. 33*, would be run aground to unload their troops while several landing barges, each with some 50 troops, would join in the landing. There would be two Special Naval Landing Forces – 1,000 men – with a reserve of 500 sailors organized from the ships' crews.

The Wake invasion force, under Rear Admiral Sadamichi Kajioka, departed Roi on the morning of December 21. The covering and support forces were already at sea. Before dawn on the morning of December 23 the Japanese destroyer-transports and landing craft approached Wake's beaches where they grounded on the south shore. Minutes later, at 2:45 a.m., the Marines opened fire with machine guns and small arms. The 5-inch guns had been unable to bear on the transports as they approached the shore. The 3-inch guns fired into the transports as they beached. The *Patrol Boat No. 33* was hit and burst into flame. The *No. 32* may also have been hit.

But Japanese Marines were ashore, with mortars and automatic weapons supporting their advance. Wake's land mass consists of some 2,600 acres of sand and coral, much of it covered with dense brush. The U.S. Marines and the now-armed sailors fought tenaciously, but there was no possibility of resisting the assault. Just after 1:30 on the 23rd, the American commander surrendered.

A total of some 1,200 Japanese troops had landed in the assault, about three times the number of surviving U.S. Marines on the atoll when they came ashore. The U.S. losses were 49 Marines, eight sailors, and 70 civilians killed, plus about 40 Americans wounded. The survivors became prisoners of the Japanese. Exact data on the Japanese losses are lacking; U.S. sources estimated 820 killed – 580 in the sinking of the two destroyers and damage to other ships, another 100 in the aircraft shot down, and 137 killed in the assault of December 23.

The first Wake assault was the first Japanese reverse of the war. It was but a temporary and unimportant delay.

SOUTHERN OPERATIONS

Early on December 8 troops of the Japanese Army's 5th and 18th Divisions, supported by naval forces and the 3rd Army Air Group, began landing at Singora and Pattani in northern Thailand, and Kota Bharu in northern Malaya. The Kota Bharu force was attacked by British aircraft, and was forced temporarily to withdraw. The troops came ashore a second time later that same day.

Concurrent with the landing operations, naval aircraft from bases in Indochina bombed military installations in Singapore. The two British capital ships in the Far East, the battleship *Prince of Wales* and the battle cruiser *Repulse*, sortied with four destroyers in an effort to stop these landings. The two warships were easily sunk by naval land-based bombers flying from Indochina.

Having occupied Singora, Pattani, and Kota Bharu, Japanese Army air units immediately began operations to gain control of the air over Malaya. By late January 1942 ground units had reached the Johnore Straits at the southern end of Malaya. Singapore fell on February 15.

To the north, the Imperial Guards Division moved across the Indochina border into Thailand on December 8 while some of its units landed at points along the Kra Isthmus. These operations were accomplished without resistance. Reinforcements followed as the Japanese began their invasion of Burma.

In the Borneo and Celebes area, the Kawaguchi detachment of three battalions plus a Special Naval Landing Force landed at Miri on the east coast of Borneo on December 16 to occupy the oil fields

and airbase. Then, moving by sea, the troops took Kuching and the remainder of the island's ports in subsequent operations.

Strategic points in Dutch Borneo were occupied by elements of the Sakaguchi detachment which, after taking Davao in the southern Philippines, were taken by ship to Jolo Island in the Sulu Archipelago. This force occupied Tarakan on January 11 and Balikpapan on January 24, 1942. Simultaneous with these operations, Navy landing forces invaded the Celebes, taking all of the key positions by the end of January. These landings gave the Japanese control of key oil areas and stepping stones for the coming assault on Java.

In China, joint Army-Navy amphibious operations began against British Hong Kong on December 18. Outnumbered and with no realistic defensive positions, the British forces surrendered on the 25th. At the same time, the foreign areas of Shanghai and Tientsin were taken over by the Japanese.

The major Japanese operation of the period, however, was the assault on the Philippines. The Imperial General Headquarters allocated the assault to the 14th Army under Lieutenant-General Masaharu Homma. Under his command, to take Luzon were two of Japan's best divisions, the 16th and 48th, plus a brigade and numerous supporting units, and almost 400 Army aircraft and some 300 land-based naval aircraft. The naval forces carrying and supporting Homma's troops included the small carrier *Ryujo* with about 35 aircraft, plus several seaplanes would provide reconnaissance. The Navy had provided five heavy cruisers, five light cruisers, three seaplane tenders, 29 destroy-

Right: The Japanese LST *T-149* unloads a Type 98 light tank during an amphibious exercise. Note the ramp behind the tank which leads up to the main deck. The massive Japanese landings of 1941–42 were undertaken without the use of the specialized landing ships. (Courtesy *Ships of the World*)

Above: The Japanese successes in amphibious landings in the Philippines in December 1941 led to more rapid advances than even the most optimistic Japanese leaders had predicted. This resulted in more American and Filipino prisoners than the Japanese troops could handle, leading to the tragic Bataan death march to the Cabana Tuan prison camp. Here American prisoners have a short rest break on the march. (U.S. Marine Corps)

ers, and several lesser ships, plus the transports and landing ships for the Luzon operation.

Early on December 8 (December 7 Hawaiian and Washington time) aircraft from Formosa struck American bases in the Philippines. The carrier *Ryujo*, from a point some 100 miles east of Mindanao, flew a strike against Davao, which would be attacked by the Sakaguchi detachment (not part of Homma's forces).

At dawn on the following day, December 9, a landing was made unopposed on Batan Island and Japanese aircraft were soon using its small airstrip. On December 10 troops landed at dawn at Aparri and Vigan against no opposition from Philippines troops (who were commanded by Douglas MacArthur, who had been lent to the Philippines to establish their army). Their airfields were quickly occupied and put into use.

Under air support from these airfields and from the major Japanese air bases on Formosa, small Japanese landings continued along the coast of Luzon. Early on December 20 a large force of Major-General Shizuo Sakaguchi's troops landed on Mindanao Island, quickly overcoming resistance by some 3,500 American and Filipino troops. Jolo and Davao were taken and more airfields put

into service.

The main Japanese landing force, from the 16th and 48th Divisions, embarked in 76 transports and landing ships, reached Lingayen Gulf on the morning of December 22 without encountering any opposition. Although there was heavy fire from the beaches, the landings were successful, with light casualties on the Japanese side. That morning General Homma came ashore at Bauang and established his command post while his troops, vehicles, and supplies were unloaded. Shortly after midnight on December 23/24, a secondary landing was made on the east coast of Luzon by the 126th Division. Again, resistance was light. According to Japanese accounts of the operation:

"Fourteenth Army operations on all sectors were proceeding with complete success. No large-scale counterattack against the Lingayen landing force had materialized, and the lack of resistance encouraged the Army Commander to drive rapidly to the final objective – Manila, with no change in plans. The morale of officers and men was extremely high. The two divisions, the 48th from Lingayen and the 16th from Lamon Bay, began a race for the honor of entering the capital city first."[3]

The remainder of the Japanese operation in the Philippines is primarily the record of a successful land campaign. General MacArthur was forced to evacuate Corregidor Island, in Manila Bay, by PT-boat on March 11 (being taken to a still-secure airfield to fly to Australia). On May 6 the American commander in the Philippines, Major General Jonathan Wainwright, surrendered all American forces in the islands.

The Japanese octopus continued to reach out with its tentacles unabated. The small American-British-Dutch-Australian (ABDA) naval force in Asian waters was hunted down by superior Japanese naval forces and finally destroyed in the Java Sea in late February. Japanese troops continued to move southward, landing on Timor, Bali, Java; to the east they took Rabaul in New Britain, and moved south into the Solomon Islands, and landed on the northern coast of New Guinea.

Farther east, in the Gilbert Islands, Japanese Marines had easily occupied Makin and Tarawa on December 10 and immediately began construction of an air base on Makin. The capture of these islands and Wake permitted the establishment of an outer defense line against future U.S. incursions.

The six carriers of the Pearl Harbor strike force, two of which had assisted in the Wake operation, now steamed south to support the Southern Operations, strike northern Australia, and make a devasting foray into the Indian Ocean.

The Japanese assault had been a complete triumph. The setbacks were few and minor. Losses in men, ships, and planes had been far below pre-war estimates. Indeed, no Japanese ship larger than light cruiser had been sunk and not one of the vital aircraft carriers had even been damaged by an enemy bomb or torpedo. The U.S. carrier raids into Japanese territory had been a nuisance, but not a concern, at least not until the April raid by Doolittle-Halsey in which sixteen Army B-25 bombers had struck Japan. Even that raid was only an embarrassment but one that could not be tolerated.

At Imperial General Headquarters the issue of what to do next was raised. It was felt that the Americans could not go on the offensive in the Pacific before the end of 1942. The Navy's leaders wished to remain on the offensive; the Army felt that it was over-extended. The Navy proposed an invasion of Australia, at least of the northern coast, to take Australia out of the war, deny its bases to Americans, and add more resources to Japan's booty. The Army estimated that it would require twelve divisions to invade Australia, and there simply were not enough ships available for such a venture.

Finally, by April 28 a compromise had been reached. There would be an occupation of strategic points in New Caledonia, the Fiji and Samoa Islands, after the invasion of Port Moresby at the southern end of New Guinea and the establishment of seaplane and airbases on Tulagi and Guadalcanal in the Solomons. Already, partially because of the Doolittle-Halsey raid, the Japanese Navy was planning to assault Midway atoll to force a battle with the surviving U.S. fleet units and to establish Midway – 1,140 miles north-west of Oahu – as a defensive position to prevent future carrier raids against Japan.

This meant that only two large aircraft carriers and one light carrier were available to support the Port Moresby landing. The Kure 3rd Special Naval Landing Force and Army forces would carry out the landings. It was this invasion force that led to the Battle of the Coral Sea in early May 1942, in which U.S. naval forces were able to stop the Japanese thrust.

Landings were carried out on Guadalcanal and Tulagi, and work began on constructing an airfield on the former. The assault on Port Moresby was postponed until July. Meanwhile, all available naval forces were concentrated for the coming Battle of Midway.

For the Midway Operation, which would be under the direct command of the Commander-in-Chief of the Japanese Combined Fleet, Admiral Isoroku Yamamoto, the Japanese assembled four fleet carriers, two light carriers, eleven battleships, sixteen cruisers, 55 destroyers, and numerous lesser warships. The Midway Invasion Force, with nineteen cargo ships and transports, embarked the Kure and Yokosuka 5th Special Naval Landing Forces, and the Army's Ichiki Detachment, plus construction and other support units – a total of some 5,000 troops.

As related in numerous other accounts, the Battle of Midway was the "turning-point" in the war; never again would U.S. forces be so badly outnumbered by the Japanese. The Japanese carriers flew a major strike against Midway at the outset of the battle on June 4. But except for a submarine bombardment, that was the only attack against Midway as the three U.S. carriers lying in wait for the Japanese sank the four large fleet carriers in a historic carrier-versus-carrier battle.

Even if the U.S. carriers had not been able to surprise and defeat the Japanese carrier force, a Japanese landing might not have been successful unless the Army, Marine, and Navy aircraft on the atoll had been destroyed first. There were on Midway, when the battle began, 121 combat planes, almost 3,000 personnel, of which the principal combat unit was the reinforced 6th Marine Defense Battalion, and ten motor torpedo boats. The defenses included 7-inch and 3-inch gun batteries.

In the event, after the carrier battle on June 4, the Japanese fleet withdrew (see Chapter 5), but a diversion force did land on American territory. To distract the American high command from the Midway Operation, it was preceded by landings in the Aleutians.

Under Vice-Admiral Boshiro Hosogaya, the Northern Area Force consisted of two light aircraft carriers (with 90 aircraft), three heavy and three light cruisers, thirteen destroyers, and lesser ships. The Hokkaido Army Detachment of 1,200 troops was to land on Adak and the Maizuru Special Naval Landing Force of 550 marines plus 700 construction troops were to be put ashore on Kiska. Four transports carried the troops.

On June 3, the Japanese carriers made a small air strike on the American base at Dutch Harbor, to the east of the assault targets in the Aleutian Island chain. Dutch Harbor was a naval and seaplane base. The major U.S. airfield in the area was on the Alaskan peninsula, at Cold Bay, 155 miles to the east. The Japanese carrier planes inflicted considerable damage at Dutch Harbor. A second strike was flown the next day. This time U.S. Army Air Forces B-26 and B-17 bombers from Cold Bay were able to attack the Japanese ships but – as at Midway – without effect.

Discovering that a U.S. fighter strip had been cleared on Umnak Island, Admiral Hosogaya ordered that the landing planned for Adak be shifted to Attu to move the operation farther away from the U.S. base. The Japanese ships landed 1,200 troops at Attu's Holtz Bay on the morning of June 7. The troops marched overland to capture the island's village (inhabited by 39 Aleuts and two "mainlanders"). The troops landing on Kiska, also on June 7, encountered no resistance from the ten U.S. weather observers they found on the island.

The Japanese were entrenched on American territory.[4]

FUTURE PLANS AND SHIPS

In mid-1942 the Imperial Japanese forces had reached the limit of their expansion, but this was not yet known – to either side – and more amphibious operations were being planned. Several options seemed available to the Japanese leaders, who believed that despite the loss of four carriers at Midway, the new construction programs and the American losses would lead to continued Japanese naval supremacy in the Pacific.

The immediate post-Midway options, from the Japanese viewpoint, included building forces for another thrust at Midway or another move to the south to capture Port Moresby (which had been deterred by the Coral Sea battle in May). From Port Moresby the Japanese could bomb Australia on a continuous basis, possibly to be followed by landings at the few points on the northern coast. The denial of that area to the Allies would insure the security of the East Indies for Japanese exploitation.

But what next? With Malaya and Burma in Japanese hands, the next logical target would be India, where there was already a vibrant anti-British movement which the Japanese sought to exploit. Looking farther west was the large island of Madagascar off the coast of Africa. The island was under Vichy control when the war started and although the British invaded it in May 1942, the

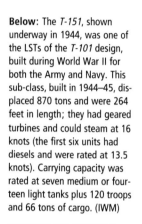

Below: The *T-151*, shown underway in 1944, was one of the LSTs of the *T-101* design, built during World War II for both the Army and Navy. This sub-class, built in 1944–45, displaced 870 tons and were 264 feet in length; they had geared turbines and could steam at 16 knots (the first six units had diesels and were rated at 13.5 knots). Carrying capacity was rated at seven medium or fourteen light tanks plus 120 troops and 66 tons of cargo. (IWM)

Right: The Japanese LST *T-138* was rated as a second-class transport. (First-class transports displaced more than 1,000 tons.) In addition to operating as landing ships, the T-series LSTs were used extensively as coastal cargo ships with the *T-131* and *T-149* modified to serve as communications ships. After World War II the *T-137* was transferred to the USSR and the *T-172* to China. (Courtesy *Ships of the World*)

Below: The Japanese Type 1 landing ships were similar in concept to the U.S. Navy's high-speed transports (APD). The Japanese ships, however, were purpose-built amphibious ships. A stern ramp was fitted for launching four landing craft (*Daihatsu* type) or two *Koryu* midget submarines or four *Kaiten* manned torpedoes. Displacing 1,800 tons with a length of 315 feet and speed of 22 knots, the Type 1 ships could also carry more than 200 Marines plus 400 to 500 tons of cargo. (IWM)

troops in garrison there were mostly second-rate African units.

Further, if, after India was captured, the Japanese made a thrust into the Middle East, there was the potential of linking up with the Germans, who were heading that way, through the Caucasus.

Whichever route was taken, the Japanese would require more amphibious ships. Several programs were put in hand. The Japanese Army began construction of a series of LST-type ships, given the designation ES. These 950-ton, 174¼-foot ships were small by Allied standards; they could carry 170 troops plus four small tanks, unloaded by a bow ramp.

The Japanese Navy took over the ES program, completing 22 ships in 1943–44. These were followed by over 50 T-series ships completed by the Navy in 1944–45. The design of these ships was extremely simple to permit construction in private yards. They used prefabrication and electric welding techniques, making it possible to build a ship in three months. Their hulls, however, were found too light for the rough waters near the home islands and they had to be strengthened.

In this same period, the Japanese Navy took delivery of 22 purpose-built, destroyer-type transports (APD) of the Type 1. These ships, with a speed of 22 knots, could carry almost 500 troops with landing craft unloaded over their ramped stern. A pair of 5-inch and fifteen 20-mm guns were fitted.

Thus, plans were put in hand for the ships needed to continue the Japanese expansion. There were, however, a few problems as the various alternatives were considered: First, troops were a critical factor – the occupation of Korea and Manchuria, the Philippines, and the East Indies, as well as the on-going campaign in China; second, there were some indications that the U.S. Fleet in the Pacific might consider offensive actions, foolhardy as those might seem in the Japanese view.

4.
EUROPEAN INTERLUDE

GERMANY MOVES

World War II officially began in Europe with the German invasion of Poland on September 1, 1939. Immediately Britain and France declared war on Germany, although they were unable to inflict damage on the German forces ravishing Poland. The Germans rapidly overcame Polish resistance and divided the devastated country with the Soviets. This was followed by the so-called "phoney war" in Europe (although the conflict was very real at sea).

The Germans moved again on April 9, 1940, invading Norway and Denmark. The landings in Norway were made at six ports, mostly by troops carried in merchant ships. The first ships to enter port were disguised as innocent freighters and, despite losses of several supporting warships, the German assault was successful. A month later the Germans attacked Belgium and France. A new term was coined from the German victories of 1939–40 *Blitzkrieg* or lightning war. Belgium and France fell and by June the victorious German armies faced an isolated, poorly armed Britain across a channel some twenty miles wide.

The master of Germany, Adolf Hitler, awaited the British surrender delegation. But none would come as the British, under the leadership of the intrepid Winston Churchill, promised an all-out defense of the island nation. With significant assistance from the United States as well as from the Commonwealth countries, Britain would not only defend its own beaches, but would struggle against Germany in the occupied countries and along the periphery of the German empire. Thus, the only options left to Hitler were to defeat Britain by blockade or invasion. Germany had neither the air nor naval strength to effect a blockade in 1940 and, after extensive discussions with his senior military officers, on July 16, 1940, Hitler issued a directive for the future course of the war:

> "As England, in spite of the hopelessness of her military situation, has so far shown herself unwilling to come to any compromise, I have therefore decided to begin to prepare for, and if necessary to carry out, an invasion of England.
>
> This operation is dictated by the necessity of eliminating Great Britain as a basis from which

the war against Germany can be fought, and, if necessary, the island will be occupied."[1]

The distinguished historian and Nuremberg prosecutor Telford Taylor observed: "For the Germans, considerable risk of failure could justifiably be taken. A successful invasion would ensure enormous, and perhaps immediately decisive, benefits. If the invasion were repulsed, the consequences would probably not be fatal to the Germans' fortunes, and the hazards of not making the attempt were almost as great as those of failure."[2]

With the July 16 directive the operation was given the codename *Seelowere* or Sealion. The German Army immediately began organizing and preparing for an assault. The real burden, however, would fall to the German Navy and to the German Air Force, the *Luftwaffe*. The Navy was charged with transporting and protecting the invasion force, including minesweeping and planting defensive minefields; the *Luftwaffe* was to prevent British air attacks and engage naval vessels approaching the invasion force, and to destroy coastal defenses and annihilate reserves behind the beachheads. To accomplish these missions the *Luftwaffe* would have to destroy the Royal Air Force's Fighter Command. Neither the German Navy nor the *Luftwaffe* was capable of such assignments in view of their respective weaknesses and the existing strengths of the Royal Air Force and Royal Navy.

Staff studies for an invasion of England had been undertaken by the German armed forces as early as November 1939 and by the time of Hitler's July 16 directive a considerable amount of work had been accomplished. The German Army looked at the invasion as a "gigantic river crossing." The initial Army planning was for the main landing to be in East Anglia with a diversionary attack north of the Humber. The first assault wave would consist of two motorized and eleven infantry divisions, supported by paratroopers from two *Luftwaffe* airborne divisions. The Army units would number 90,000 combat troops with 650 tanks and several thousand horses. They were to establish beachheads at Yarmouth and Lowestoft.

The second landing wave would have nine divisions, six of them *panzer* (tank) divisions, to advance westward to sever communications between London and the north. The third wave would bring into England nine infantry divisions to capture London. A reserve force would have available another eight infantry divisions for a total commitment of 41 divisions, many with extensive combat experience in Poland and France, with seasoned commanders. This would be about double the number of divisions the British were expected to have available to oppose the invasion, with most of those lacking suitable weapons. By early July an invasion date of mid-August had been established.

Both the *Luftwaffe* and Navy considered the Army's plan too ambitious. The troops and their equipment would be ferried across the English Channel in specialized landing craft, barges towed by tugs and trawlers, and by coastal steamers; it was highly questionable if sufficient craft were available and could be modified in time to transport the invasion force. Naval officers estimated that it would require *ten days* to transport the entire first wave of troops and their equipment across the English Channel.

At a meeting with Hitler on July 31 the Navy described the difficulties of the planned invasion. Earlier, in a memorandum to the Supreme High Command, Admiral Erich Raeder, Commander-in-Chief of the Navy, had declared: "The task allotted to the Navy in Operation 'Sealion' is out of all proportion to the Navy's strength and bears no relation to the tasks that are set [for] the Army and Air Force."[3]

Hitler put off the assault date to September 15 and the size of the invasion was soon scaled down as the military staffs began to understand the complexity of an amphibious landing. The assault force was revised to a first wave of nine divisions, the second wave of eight divisions (only four of them *panzer*), the third wave of six divisions, plus a reserve force of two divisions. The Navy now estimated that it would take a week to ten days to put ashore the first two waves, assuming that the weather and the British "cooperated." (Airborne troops would also participate – three regiments of paratroopers and one of glider troops.)

Preparations went forward at a furious rate at all levels. Along canals and rivers the Germans assembled hundreds of the *prahms* (barges) used extensively on European waterways and modified with bow ramps to be used as landing craft. These would be towed to the invasion beaches by tugs. A variety of self-propelled craft were modified and built for the assault. By the end of August there were 168 coastal steamers, 1,900 *prahms*, 221 tugs, the same number of steam-powered fishing trawlers that could be used as tugs, and more than 1,000 motor launches. The assembly and preparation of these craft for the assault constituted a remarkable achievement by the Navy. At the same time, Army engineers were training to unload the barges as they came ashore while signal troops prepared plans for handling the complex communications inherent in a large amphibious operation.

The key factor was control of the air over the Channel and southern England. Without that control there could be no invasion. The *Luftwaffe* was charged with destroying the RAF's Fighter Command in an operation given the codename "Adlerangriff" (Eagle Attack). For the revised, mid-September invasion date the *Luftwaffe* was to begin the destruction of the RAF on August 5, but was delayed by bad weather until August 13. This was the beginning of the Battle of Britain. The principal targets would be the British airfields and aircraft factories, the destruction of which – coupled with air-to-air kills of British fighters – would alleviate the threat to the invasion forces.

The story of the Battle of Britain has been well told elsewhere. Suffice to say that the *Luftwaffe*, designed to support the Army, was incapable of destroying the RAF in the Battle of Britain. By August 20 the situation was sufficiently clear – at least in London – that Winston Churchill could applaud the RAF Hurricane and Spitfire squadrons and the supporting radar/fighter direction organization by declaring in the House of Commons that, "Never in the field of human conflict was so much owed by so many to so few."

The Battle of Britain was decided, although neither side could be certain at that time. Broadcasting to the British people on September 11, Churchill told of the continuing battle in the skies and warned:

> ". . . we must regard the next week or so as a very important period in our history. It ranks with the days when the Spanish Armada was approaching the Channel, and Drake was finishing his game of bowls; or when Nelson stood between us and Napoleon's Grand Army at Boulogne. We have read all about this in the history books; but what is happening now is on a far greater scale and of far more consequence to the life and future of the world and its civilization than those brave old days."[4]

Significantly, this was the day when the German Navy would have had to begin sweeping British mines and laying its own defensive minefields if there were to be landings on the English coast ten days later. But Hitler did not give the order to initiate these pre-invasion activities and at the working level of the German naval staff there was now uncertainty as to whether an invasion could be carried out before late September, when the Channel weather was expected to become too poor for an invasion.

The *Luftwaffe* continued daylight fighter and bomber attacks against England. In early September the first raids were flown against London, a significant action for it meant that *Luftwaffe* resources were being diverted from attacks against fighter bases and factories and the effort to gain control

Above: During the summer of 1940 the German Army and Navy prepared to invade England, waiting only for the Luftwaffe to defeat the Royal Air Force. This RAF aerial photograph of Dunkirk taken in the summer of 1940 shows scores of barges being prepared for the assault. Buildings around the docks and the adjacent railroad tracks and cranes have been heavily damaged by British bombers. Careful analysis revealed several sunken barges. (IWM)

of the air over the Channel and south-eastern England. (However, the raids on London did bring RAF fighters aloft to engage the bombers, in turn bringing them into combat with escorting German fighters.)

Soon the *Luftwaffe* tactics shifted entirely to night raids against British cities, the air campaign labeled the "Blitz." The RAF still controlled the skies over England and the Channel in daylight and the German invasion was defeated before having left port. At a meeting on September 14, Hitler acknowledged to his senior military officers that the *Luftwaffe* had so far failed to destroy the RAF. Hitler declared that four or five days of clear weather, however, could bring about the needed aerial victory. He then postponed for three more days his decision of whether or not to launch the invasion. But during that period

the *Luftwaffe* suffered heavy losses in comparison with the RAF. And, RAF bombers had been mounting an offensive against the assault shipping clustered in Dutch and French harbors with some ten per cent of the ships and barges being sunk or damaged. On the 17th Hitler postponed "Sealion" indefinitely. Preparations were seen to continue until October 12 in an attempt to maintain political and military pressure on Britain.

The Commander-in-Chief of the German Navy from 1928 to 1943, Grand Admiral Erich Raeder, observed:

"Hitler was never wholeheartedly in favour of Operation 'Sea-lion'. By contrast with the driving force he put behind other operations, he was very sluggish with regard to the planning of the English invasion. It may be that he regarded the prepara-

Above: The Germans developed a variety of landing craft during the war, and carried out small coastal operations with them. These had the designations of transport ferry (MFP), supply lighter – gun (MAL), and, as shown here, transport ferry – gun (AFP). (U.S. Army)

tion as principally the means for bringing heavy moral and psychological pressure on the enemy. This, combined with the air Blitzkrieg on the British capital, he counted on to bring England to negotiate for peace."[5]

With the cancellation of "Sealion", Hitler's attention turned to the east and Russia, and never again was there a threat of German landings in England. Indeed, almost immediately the invasion initiative shifted to England.

In a memorandum remarkable for its scope, naïvety, and the time that it was written (June 4, 1940), Churchill ordered that planning begin for "raiding forces on those coasts where the populations are friendly" within German-occupied Europe.[6]

COMBINED OPERATIONS
The British were already developing specialized landing capabilities. In 1937, the Commander-in-Chief at Plymouth, Admiral Sir Reginald Ernest-Ernle-Plunkett-Drax, proposed that "one or two brigades of Royal Marines should be entered [into service] and specifically trained as an amphibious striking force. It would be of great value if even one division of the British Army could be given special training in combined operations."[7]

Although no specialized landing forces were raised before the German invasion of Poland, less than a year later, in May of 1938, the British Chiefs of Staff established the Inter-Service Training and Development Centre near Portsmouth in response to proposals and arguments being put forth by a number of naval officers. A small Centre staff, comprised of Navy, Marine, Army, and Air Force officers, soon developed a policy for amphibious landings which – like the U.S. Marine doctrine for the Pacific theater – became the basis for many of the Allied landings in Europe during the war. The Centre studied and developed recommendations for specialized landing craft requirements, naval gunfire support, floating piers to alleviate the need for unloading large transports in captured harbors, the concept of headquarters or command ships, and raiding doctrine and tactics.

On June 14, in response to Churchill's order of June 4, 1940, and taking advantage of the previous planning done by the amphibious Centre, the British Chiefs of Staff established the position of Commander of Raiding Operations and Adviser to the Chiefs of Staff on Combined Operations. The position – later changed to Director, Combined Operations – first fell to Lieutenant-General Sir Alan Bourne, the senior Royal Marine officer, who was appointed to the post on June 11. He was directed to "harass the enemy and cause him to disperse his forces, and to create material damage. . . ." Bourne's tenure, however, was brief, just over one month.

On June 23, France capitulated to the Germans. That night, 113 raiders of the 11th Independent Company crossed the English Channel in eight RAF air-sea rescue launches to three points near the port of Boulogne.[8] The damage inflicted by the raiders was nil with two Germans being killed. The raiders escaped back across the English Channel, the only British casualty being the senior officer whose ear was partially severed by a German bullet. A German seaplane was approached by the raiders but took off without its crew becoming aware of the danger.

The next raid, on the night of July 14 against the German-occupied Channel Island of Guernsey, also achieved little. The 11th Independent Company and a Marine commando landed from six launches escorted by two ancient destroyers with the intention of destroying the airfield. Although the German machine-gun positions were not manned, the difficulties of navigation, miscalculation of time and height of tide, and the shortness of the summer night caused the raid to be aborted.

Churchill wanted more aggressive action – he wrote notes about landing "raids" of thousands of men on the French coast. On July 17, 1940, he named Admiral of the Fleet, Roger Keyes, to succeed Bourne as Director of Combined Operations. Aged 65, Keyes had served in the Royal Navy until 1931, after which he entered Parliament. He had commanded the raid on Zeebrugge that had greatly impressed Churchill (despite the raid's failure to accomplish its purpose of closing U-boat access to the North Sea). A few days after the outbreak of war, on September 17, 1939, Keyes had written to Churchill on the subject of amphibious landings "to suggest the possibility of a stroke which might be delivered with great effect by the Navy and RAF within the next 36 hours or so."[9]

Already in hand were the formation of raiding parties – independent companies and commandos of soldiers and Marines for the express purpose of raiding German-held territory. When the war began Royal Marine strength stood at just over 12,000 officers and men. Their principal duty was security of naval facilities ashore and manning the secondary gun batteries in warships. Their ranks were increased by recruiting and the call-up of reserves.

While plans were being drawn up to form a Marine Division, Army commandos and independent companies were also being raised. Some considered that the Marines should operate in Ireland if the Germans tried to establish bases there. Thus, Keyes envisaged the Army units as the principal tool for his raids. It was also proposed that airborne troops would come under Combined Operations and 500 paratroops were being trained. Landing ships were being converted and landing craft constructed (see Chapter 7).

ASSAULTS ON THE FRENCH COLONIES

During this period of growing interest – and confusion – concerning amphibious operations, the first major effort was attempted. Several French colonies in Africa had rallied to General Charles de Gaulle, who was establishing his Free French Forces with headquarters in England. Senegal, with its capital of Dakar on Africa's Atlantic coast, remained loyal to the Vichy government in France. If Dakar were to come under direct German control, aircraft based there could threaten British shipping travelling around Africa, while in British hands it could be invaluable as an aircraft refuelling point and for anti-submarine patrols over the eastern Atlantic. There were several French ships at Dakar, including the battleship *Richelieu*. Dakar could also serve as a headquarters for de Gaulle's forces on French territory. In August 1940, at de Gaulle's urging a directive was issued by Churchill to undertake an expedition to Dakar – Operation "Menace."

Vice-Admiral J. H. D. Cunningham was appointed naval commander of the operation and Major-General Noël M. Irwin as military commander. Although Irwin was a Marine officer, neither Keyes nor the Marines would be involved in this operation, the available Marines having been assigned to the Commander-in-Chief, Home Forces for the defense of Britain against a German invasion. On the last day of August the expedition set sail from British ports to rendezvous with major naval forces coming south from Gibraltar. Cunningham was in the cruiser *Devonshire* and Irwin and General de Gaulle were in the battleship *Barham* with no one in overall command of the operation. Of course, the Free French troops and ships would obey only de Gaulle and not the British officers.

The landing force consisted of 4,200 British soldiers and 2,700 Free French troops embarked in six transports escorted by a British cruiser-destroyer group, plus one Free French destroyer and three sloops. From Gibraltar came Force H with two battleships, the aircraft carrier *Ark Royal*, three cruisers, and ten more destroyers. Thus, Operation "Menace" could boast the largest naval force yet to engage in a landing operation. There were no specialized landing ships available.

While these ships were en route to Dakar word was received that a French force of three cruisers and three large destroyers had departed French Mediterranean ports, passed through the Straits of Gibraltar, and were in the Atlantic – possibly heading toward Dakar. Relations with Vichy France were already spoiled because of British action against French warships in North African ports (undertaken to prevent them from returning to France and possibly coming under German control).

From this point the story of Operation "Menace" is tangled and confused. There was confusion over which naval commander was under whose command, of who held which responsibilities, and of British policy toward the French warships and, indeed, toward the French administration at Dakar.

The warships from Vichy France reached Dakar, which had not been their original destination, further complicating the situation. Emissaries from de Gaulle flown into Dakar in an *Ark Royal* aircraft failed to bring about an agreement and departed under fire. On September 23, the day of the planned landings, mist in the area, the threat of attack from French submarines and surface ships, and fire from shore batteries contributed to the confusion. The British ships finally opened fire in preparation for a landing. Three ships were struck by fire from the shore batteries, with one cruiser being forced to withdraw. No major landing was attempted, although a few Free French troops did attempt a landing east of Dakar that evening but were repulsed.

The following day the situation deteriorated still further. *Ark Royal* aircraft attempted to attack the *Richelieu* in Dakar harbor, but were prevented by the heavy mist. A British destroyer sank a French submarine attempting to make a torpedo attack on the British force, while further British attempts to bombard the harbor were impeded by the mist and a smoke screen. The British ships came off worse in this exchange of fire, with the battleship *Barham* sustaining four hits. The British withdrew.

September 25 was clear, but as the British warships took up their bombarding stations the battleship *Resolution* was seriously damaged by a torpedo from a French submarine. The artillery duel resumed, with the French gunners ashore proving to be more adept at this exchange. Finally, shortly before noon the British commanders decided to withdraw. A short time later Operation "Menace" was cancelled.

British warships were in great demand elsewhere as both Germany and Italy had major naval forces with which to contest British use of the seas, and Operation "Menace" had taken away from other critical areas several important warships, with a battleship and a cruiser suffering major damage. The Dakar fiasco demonstrated the need for more air support in an amphibious operation than could be provided by a single carrier with a maximum capacity of some 60 aircraft, and had the landings begun the shortage of specialized landing ships and craft would have been keenly felt. Finally, the embarking of the force commander in a major warship, as at Dakar, was insufficient for the complexities of an amphibious operation. A specialized headquarters or command ship was required.

ROGER KEYES AND THE RAIDS

The failure at Dakar had only emphasized the inability of the British to undertake major amphibious operations. In 1940–41 the British amphibious efforts in Europe and the Mediterranean were still limited to raids – important and some successful but none the less raids.

Under Keyes's direction, the independent companies and the commandos were being increased in numbers. Keyes was also calling for ships and small craft, and for squadrons of RAF aircraft to support his operations. In all of these efforts he antagonized other British military leaders who were desperately seeking to build up conventional air, ground, and naval forces. Even the Royal Marines were becoming antagonized by Keyes, who wished to deploy them on garrison duty in the Azores.

Plans were being hastily drawn up by various staffs for landings on the Italian island of Pantelleria between Sicily and Tunisia, on the large islands of Sardinia and Sicily, on the Italian-held Aegean islands, including Rhodes off the coast of (neutral) Turkey, and assaults against the French and Dutch coasts, with multi-division landings proposed.

But the Keyes operations carried out during this period were failures. An airborne drop of 36 Royal Engineers was made into southern Italy to destroy the Apulian Aqueduct. One of the aircraft developed engine trouble and sent a signal that should have alerted the Italians to the raid. The admiral at Malta then cancelled the submarine rendezvous with the raiders. Meanwhile, the raiders were unable to destroy the aqueduct – poor intelligence concerning its construction prevented them from doing so – and the raiders blew up a bridge and then fled to the hills, later surrendering to Italian police.

In February 1941 an attempt to land raiders on the island of Kasos in the Aegean failed because of improper charting of the waters. Another operation to land 200 commandos on Castellorizo failed because of German air attacks, poor communications and changes in British plans; the eventual counter-landing by Italian troops led to the capture of the British force.

The only successful British raid during this period came in early March when five destroyers and two landing ships sent to the Lofoten Islands destroyed the fish oil factory and took off several hundred Norwegians and Germans. This was undertaken by some 500 Marines of the 3rd and 4th Commandos, 50 Royal Engineers, and 50 Norwegian troops, and not by the lightly armed raiders that had been employed in the Aegean. The Lofotens raid, Operation "Claymore," was a total success, with several small German ships also destroyed. But the prize was a fishing station, fish factory, and store of fish oil, hardly a significant military objective.

Meanwhile, British commandos were carrying out raids behind German lines in the Libyan desert. The first major coastal raid was planned for the night of April 16–17, 1941, with two Army battalions to come ashore at Bardia from *Glen*-class ships and another battalion landing from a destroyer 90 miles farther west.[10] Scouts were to land first by Folbot from submarines. The ships sailed from Alexandria, but the sea was too heavy for the submarines to launch the canoes, and there was some doubt as to whether the landing craft could operate in the surf. The operation was cancelled.

Another attempt was made on the night of April 19–20, when a battalion was put ashore from the *Glengyle* at Bardia. But the town was empty of the enemy. There were several difficulties, including a British officer being shot by his own men, the submarine in which the scouts were embarked being attacked by a British aircraft, and 60 of the troops becoming separated from the main party and eventually captured. A few buildings were blown up, but that was the only damage inflicted on the Germans.

Most of the commandos were then sent to the ill-fated campaign in Crete where they were captured. The surviving commandos were dispersed to other commands except for a small cadre. In response to reports that the Germans would move into Vichy-held Syria and make use of airfields there, the British high command decided to occupy the desert state. Australian and Free French units were sent north from Palestine and Egypt to occupy Syria.

The Litani River, 20 miles north of the Palestine border – between Tyre and Sidon – was a significant obstacle to the planned invasion. No. 11 Commando (referred to as the Scottish Commando) was to be landed by sea at dawn on June 8 to seize the bridge over the Litani at the start of the Syrian campaign.

In this Keyes-planned operation, heavy swell delayed the landing by a day. Two hours before dawn on June 9 the raiders began landing from the *Glengyle*. The main attack, by 140 commandos, was led by Lieutenant-Colonel Geoffrey Keyes, son of Admiral Roger Keyes. Two more parties – of 140 and 100 raiders – would then come ashore north of the Litani.

This operation was also a fiasco as the group led by the younger Keyes landed *south* of the river and had to be ferried across by the Australians. The bridge that had been the target of the commando raid was already destroyed. In the subsequent fighting the Vichy defenses cost the lives of 123 of the commandos, a heavy toll with little accomplished in return.

The surviving commandos and the other special units in the Mediterranean continued to undertake raids against German and Italian positions. These groups, carried by landing craft, by submarine, by surface warship, and often by local sailing craft, struck at Sardinia, the Aegean islands, and the mainland of Italy as well as behind German lines in North Africa. In many instances the British raiders worked with local guerrillas, at times supplying them with weapons with which to fight the Germans.

Some of these raids, under the direction of local commanders, were successes, other failures. Meanwhile, the fiasco in Syria had only added to the deterioration of Admiral Keyes's reputation, while antagonism with the Chiefs of Staff increased. The Chiefs of Staff attempted to re-define the role of Combined Operations – under their direction. Keyes could not accept the new charter that inhibited his freedom of action. Finally, on October 4, 1941, Churchill sacked Keyes. He wrote:

"My dear Roger, I am sorry that you do not feel able to fall in with the proposal which the COS [Chiefs of Staff] have made to you. I have really done my best to meet your wishes. I have to consider my duty to the State which ranks above personal friendship. In all the circumstances I have no choice but to arrange for your relief."[11]

Admiral Keyes was oblivious to the situation. He asked Churchill to appoint him First Lord of the Admiralty or First Sea Lord; Churchill did not reply to these suggestions.

On October 10, Churchill sent a telegram to Captain Louis Mountbatten who was visiting the United States and awaiting command of an aircraft carrier: "We want you here at once for something which you will find of highest interest." Mountbatten's father had been First Sea Lord at the outbreak of World War I and was forced to resign because of his German ancestry. The younger Mountbatten had seen extensive action in destroyers in the Mediterranean. Now aged 41, Mountbatten was given the rank of Commodore and formally made Director of Combined Operations on October 17. He was soon promoted to acting Vice-Admiral and given equivalent honorary rank in the other services, and made a permanent member of the COS committee, reflecting the importance being given to amphibious landings.

5.
THE FIRST PACIFIC ASSAULTS

OPERATION "WATCHTOWER"

The U.S. amphibious invasion of Guadalcanal in August 1942 – Operation "Watchtower" – was the result of extensive planning and political consideration by the Allies. Having decided in May 1941, and then again in January 1942, to concentrate on defeating Hitler first, the United States and Britain were forced to make major compromises in order to halt the Japanese advance after the surprise attack against U.S. military installations in Hawaii and the Philippines as well as the subsequent defeat of British naval and ground forces in south east Asia. These victories, in these strategically important areas, allowed the Japanese to rampage throughout the Pacific and into the Indian Ocean.

While not destroyed, the U.S. Fleet was severely crippled by the devastating attack on Pearl Harbor on December 7, 1941. For the next few months the American forces in the Pacific could only fight delaying actions against the Japanese.

The Allies at last stopped the Japanese advances in early May 1942 in the Coral Sea, the large body of water south of New Guinea, between the Solomon and New Hebrides Islands to the east and Australia to the west. The Japanese had planned a major assault against the Australian-held base at Port Moresby at the southern end of New Guinea. From Port Moresby, Japanese aircraft could control the Coral Sea and carry out strikes against Australia. In support of the operation – designated Operation "MO" (for Moresby) – the Japanese established a seaplane base at Tulagi, adjacent to Guadalcanal in the Solomons. The Japanese assault force in Operation "MO" was preceded into the Coral Sea by two fleet carriers and a light carrier. The U.S. Pacific Area Command, under Admiral Chester W. Nimitz, who was forewarned by his Intelligence specialists of the Japanese move, was able to send two carriers into the Coral Sea. The ensuing battle was history's first naval battle in which the opposing warships never had sight of their opponents – it was fought entirely by carrier- and land-based aircraft.

The Battle of Coral Sea, on May 7–8, 1942, was the first Japanese defeat of World War II. The Japanese light carrier *Shoho* was sunk and one of the large flattops, the *Shokaku*, damaged, while U.S. Navy lost the large carrier *Lexington* (CV-2) – the first American carrier loss of the war – as

well as an oiler and a destroyer. The U.S. loss, the large carrier "Lex," was far more significant than the light carrier *Shoho*, but the Japanese lost many irreplaceable carrier pilots, the larger *Shokaku* had to enter a shipyard and would not be available for operations for a month (and hence would miss the Battle of Midway), and the Japanese assault force heading toward Port Moresby was turned back.

But Port Moresby was only one target of the Japanese octopus. Another arm of the Japanese war machine sought to capture the atoll outpost of Midway, 1,100 miles north west of Pearl Harbor. For this assault, planned for early June 1942, the Japanese assembled the largest fleet yet seen in the war. The main force consisted of seven battleships, including the *Yamato*, at 70,000 tons the largest dreadnought ever built, while the main carrier force had four fleet carriers. Several smaller carriers were distributed among the Japanese task forces while the amphibious group had five transports and three cargo ships carrying the troops for the actual landing on Midway.

Again warned by intelligence, which made extensive use of deciphered Japanese codes, Admiral Nimitz was able to deploy three carriers to the area, unbeknown to the Japanese. In the carrier-versus-carrier battle that followed on June 4 the Japanese lost all four fleet carriers and most of their pilots as well as aircraft, plus a cruiser. The American losses were one carrier, the *Yorktown* (CV-5), which had been previously damaged at Coral Sea. Midway was an overwhelming American tactical victory in terms of losses, and a strategic victory, as again, the Japanese invasion force was turned away.

With the victory at Midway, the United States suddenly had the Japanese off balance and major naval forces available for operations in the Pacific, including the 1st Marine Division. While the primary Allied effort was to be mounted against the Axis forces in Europe and North Africa, more had to be done to stop the Japanese, especially since their next major objective would almost certainly be another thrust to take Port Moresby and then an assault against the northern coast of Australia.

The Battle of the Coral Sea in May 1942 temporarily postponed the Japanese plans (although several towns on the Australian coast were attacked by Japanese aircraft). But the Japanese were continuing their attention toward the Solomons as a prelude to a renewed assault on Port Moresby. Tulagi, the capital of the British Solomon Islands government, was invaded and the town captured in May 1942. Since most of the defense forces had been evacuated, the Japanese troops of the 3rd Kure Special Navy Landing Force and the accompanying contingent of laborers that came ashore found little opposition. They set to work building a seaplane base. From Tulagi, the Japanese could look across Sealark Channel to Guadalcanal, which offered an advantageous position for airfields to support the renewed thrust toward Port Moresby and Australia. A survey was completed in June and by July work was begun on an airstrip. The effort was observed by Australian coastwatchers, courageous men under Commander Eric Feldt, who led solitary and incredibly dangerous lives as they monitored Japanese activities and radioed the information from behind enemy lines.

One coastwatcher sent back reports about the efforts of the 3,000 Japanese construction workers to build the airfield on Guadalcanal. These reports, together with other intelligence, convinced Allied planners that a major invasion of the area had to be undertaken to permanently deny the Japanese this base. As early as February, Admiral Ernest J. King, Commander-in-Chief U.S. Fleet and Chief of Naval Operations, had told General George C. Marshall, the U.S. Army Chief of Staff, that it would be necessary to invade the Solomons, not only to protect

Australia but to provide bases for offensive bombing attacks against the major Japanese naval base at Rabaul in northern New Britain.

General Douglas MacArthur, displaced hero of the Philippines, also wanted to attack Rabaul. It was a bold wish. The small force of U.S. and Australian army units available to MacArthur could not undertake so ambitious an operation, in part because of their lack of amphibious training and the shortage of amphibious ships and landing craft.

Only the U.S. 1st Marine Division had a realistic landing capability and the Marines were under the control of Admiral Nimitz, the Pacific Area commander. Also, the Navy, with only three carriers available – the *Saratoga* (CV-3), *Enterprise* (CV-6), and *Wasp* (CV-7) – and a correspondingly small number of aircraft, was not anxious to place its limited resources, including the 1st Marine Division, under the control of an Army general. So King directed Nimitz to begin planning his own invasion. MacArthur's plan to attack Rabaul was stillborn nearly from the start.

To further confuse matters, the Santa Cruz Islands, part of the overall objective of Operation "Watchtower," lay in the Pacific Area, under Admiral Nimitz, while another objective, Tulagi, was in the South west Pacific Area, under General MacArthur. And, the overall invasion force would have to come together from several geographic points and operate in both areas.

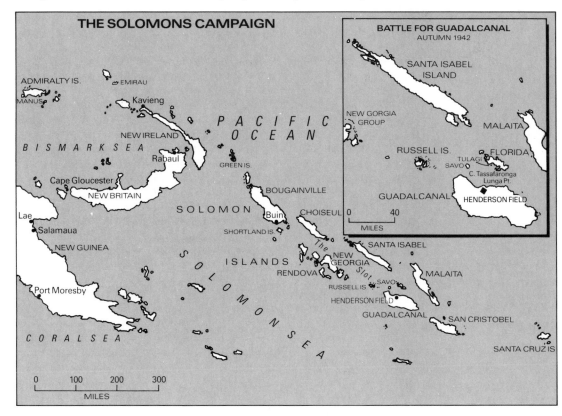

Arguments ran heavy until King and Marshall resolved their differences, giving control of the Tulagi operation to Nimitz, shifting the jurisdictional boundary to place both objectives under one commander. Australia-based bombers under General MacArthur's command would provide the necessary air support – reconnaissance and bombing. A tacit agreement was that after the initial, primary invasion was satisfactorily completed by the Navy-Marine team, the Army would be free, under MacArthur, to begin its drive northward toward the Philippines.

BUILDING AN ASSAULT FORCE

The assault force in "Watchtower" would be the 1st Marine Division. Although the United States had long had Marine regiments and brigades, no division structure had existed before World War II. When the war began in Europe in September 1939, the U.S. Marine Corps numbered 19,700 officers and enlisted men. Within a week of German troops marching into Poland, President Roosevelt proclaimed a state of limited emergency and began increasing the size of the armed forces.

Marine recruiting increased and, in October 1940, 5,245 Marine reservists were called to active duty. On February 1, 1941, the 1st and 2nd Marine Divisions were established. The divisions would each have three rifle regiments and one artillery regiment, plus supporting battalions and companies.[1] By the end of 1941, when the United States entered the war, there were 70,425 Marines – only 4,000 "leathernecks" short of the peak World War I strength. In addition to the Marine divisions and their regiments, the Marines were organizing Parachute and Raider battalions, with Defense battalions being formed to protect advanced bases (e.g., the Marines on Wake when the Japanese attacked were the 1st Defense Battalion).

The Raider battalions were the most controversial of the special Marine units. In January 1942 the 1st Battalion of the 5th Marine Regiment was transferred to the Amphibious Force of the Atlantic Fleet and redesignated as the 1st Separate Battalion. The battalion was to serve as a commando unit, to carry out small raids or operate as part of a larger assault force. Some wanted the term "commando" in the unit's designation, but the Commandant of the Marine Corps declared that "Marine" was alone "sufficient to indicate a man ready for duty at any time and that the injection of a special name, such as Commando, would be undesirable and superfluous."

But there was political pressure for such specialized units and it was proposed that William O. Donovan, a colonel in the Army reserve, who was known for his interest in special operations, be commissioned as a brigadier general in the Marines and placed in command of Marine raiding forces.[2] The 2nd Separate Battalion was quickly established, but that same month, February 1942, these units were changed to Raider battalions. Their mission was to: (1) spearhead amphibious landings by larger forces onto difficult beaches; (2) conduct raids; and (3) carry out guerrilla operations behind enemy lines.

Opposition to the formation of Raider units and Parachute battalions continued. In addition to disrupting regular personnel assignment and training, these units generated considerable demands for new and exotic equipment.[3]

For the assault on Guadalcanal – Operation "Watchtower" – General A. A. Vandegrift would command the landing force, centered on the 1st Marine Division. The division had problems in reaching operational readiness, and the order on May 1, 1942, to move his men from the United States to New Zealand did little to help Vandegrift's confidence. The men needed additional training and equipment. They were a mix of career-hardened professionals – the "Old China Hands" of the 1920s and early 1930s – and the green recruits barely out of boot camp. Moreover, combat had not been anticipated before January 1943.

The first echelon of the 1st Marine Division landed in Wellington on June 14, with Operation "Watchtower" set for August 1, little more than six weeks away. The division's specific responsibilities were the capture of Tulagi (codename "Ringbolt"), the airfield on Guadalcanal ("Cactus"), and Ndeni in the Santa Cruz Islands. The 2nd Marines, a regiment from the 2nd Marine Division, the 1st Raider Battalion, 1st Parachute Battalion, and the 3rd Defense Battalion were added to the 1st Division's strength.

While U.S. reconnaissance aircraft overflew the Solomons to gather as much intelligence as possible, a rehearsal was held in the Fiji Islands during the third week of July. Rough weather and landing-craft engine problems prevented adequate practise of landing operations. A disgusted General Vandegrift declared the rehearsals "a complete bust." The rehearsals did, however, allow the first large-scale use of bow-ramp landing craft and of close air support by carrier-based aircraft, soon to become prime ingredients in amphibious operations.

PREPARING THE INVASION

When Admiral King ordered the creation of one amphibious force each for the Atlantic and Pacific Fleets in February 1942, most of the new amphibious ships and landing craft were either being designed or under construction. Only a few types of small landing craft were available for Operation "Watchtower." The ship-to-shore movement of men and material would take time and expose the landing force to enemy fire.

It soon became clear – at least to the ordinary sailor and soldier – that this first important U.S. offensive of the war, the first major U.S. amphibious landings since the Spanish-American War of 1898, would not receive much benefit from America's great industrial and shipbuilding capability. The U.S.-British decision to win in Europe first still overshadowed support for Pacific operations, even the upcoming assault of the Solomons. Thus, the irreverent, unofficial title of Operation "Shoestring" was bestowed on the Guadalcanal invasion.

The invasion fleet of more than 100 ships, including the three protective carrier groups, was none the less one of the largest such gatherings in history for the purpose of landing troops on a hostile beach. This invasion was also to be the first wartime test of amphibious doctrine developed in the 1930s. Vice Admiral Robert L. Ghormley was in overall charge of Operation "Watchtower" as Commander, South Pacific Force (reporting to Nimitz), with headquarters in Auckland, New Zealand.

The problems in the training exercises, as well as operational and logistic considerations, led to the rescheduling of the invasion, first to August 4, then to August 7. On the last day of July, the invasion fleet set course from Fiji for Guadalcanal, a week's trip. The amphibious attack force cruised in a circular formation, with five columns of transports and cargo ships (23 in all) in the center, and their cruiser/destroyer escort force surrounding them. There were misgivings and uncertainties in the highest levels of command, beginning with Vandegrift, himself, but the first American invasion was under way.

THE ASSAULT

To coastwatcher Martin Clemens in his jungle hideout on Guadalcanal it was "a fleet majestical"; to the 19,000 troops and crews of the Allied ships and aircraft, it was the first chance to repay the Japanese for Pearl Harbor. But for the Japanese on Tulagi and Guadalcanal the landings in the early dawn hours of August 7, 1942, were a total surprise. Bad weather had kept Japanese scouting aircraft grounded and the bombing raids by U.S. Army B-17s from July 31 had apparently given the Japanese little cause for concern.

Rear Admiral Richmond Kelley Turner's South Pacific Amphibious Force sent its transport ships toward the shore, while the carriers *Saratoga, Enterprise,* and *Wasp* and their screening ships positioned themselves 100 miles south of Guadalcanal. The combined U.S.-Australian surface escort – five cruisers and nine destroyers – took station north-west of Savo Island to guard against Japanese warships approaching.

At 6:41 a.m., the order to "Land the landing force!" sounded in all the transports. The electrifying call would be heard many more times in the three years of war to come. As thousands of Marines descended the cargo nets to their landing craft – 30-odd men to a boat – there was still no indication that the enemy knew of their approach.

The first landings, by a company from the 2nd Marine Regiment, hit Florida Island, just beyond Tulagi to the north of Guadalcanal, at 7:40 on the morning of August 7, but met no opposition. At 8 a.m. the 1st Raider Battalion stormed onto Tulagi, again meeting no defenses, a fortunate development since their landing craft hung up on an uncharted reef and the troops waded ashore from distances of 30 to 100 yards out.

The Japanese force on Tulagi, earlier estimated to be about 8,000, was, in reality, closer to 500; they re-grouped at their headquarters on Tulagi and defended themselves almost to the last man. The spirit and resourcefulness of the Japanese defenders dashed hopes that Tulagi could be secured by nightfall and the Raiders and reinforcing 2nd Battalion, 5th Marines, fought through the night against Japanese counterattacks, a frightening foretaste of things to come during the Guadalcanal campaign. But by the afternoon of the 8th, Tulagi was declared secured by U.S. troops.

The accompanying, though not simultaneous, assault on nearby Tanambogo and Gavutu Islands at noon on August 7 met more determined fire, and the call for help sent to aircraft and support ships to bombard enemy positions. After a quick strike by aircraft from the *Wasp,* six landing craft approached Tanambogo at 6 p.m. With darkness approaching, one landing craft hung up on a reef, and the remaining five headed toward a small pier. However, a shell fired from a U.S. supporting ship offshore struck a fuel depot, and the resulting fire illuminated the hapless landing craft. They soon became the target of concentrated fire from the Japanese, who inflicted heavy casualties on the men in the boats.

While initial action to the north was heavy, the Marines who landed on Guadalcanal at 9:10 a.m. had walked ashore. There had been a bombardment by American cruisers and destroyers offshore beginning at 6 a.m. The Japanese were taken by complete surprise. The two battalions of the 5th Marines waded through the surf unopposed.

Although Guadalcanal marked the first use of amphibious tractors – LVT "alligators" – by the Marines, the craft were not considered reliable enough to land the assault troops. All the initial landings at Guadalcanal and the adjacent islands were made from landing craft, mostly LCVPs with bow ramps, the LVTs being used to bring ashore the follow-up supplies. Troops of the 1st Marine Division landed at 9:30, followed by their heavy weapons – 75-mm and 155-mm howitzers. Even after the Marines left the beach to push inland toward the steaming jungle, there were no Japanese. Finding no one to fight, attention turned to bringing supplies ashore through the night.

The LVTs were invaluable for bringing supplies ashore, but the Marines were reluctant to help the struggling sailors unload them. Mountains of cases rapidly accumulated on the beach. Tempers were short and the limited number of landing craft avail-

Above: Marines unload supplies on the beach at Guadalcanal following the landings of August 5, 1942. The campaign demonstrated the massive amounts of supplies needed to sustain a landing. The few amphibious tractors (LVT) available were also used in the supply role as their reliability was questionable. The craft beached at left is an LCVP based on the designs of Andrew Higgins. Several cargo ships are visible offshore. (U.S. Marine Corps)

able did not help. The lesson of working together in this phase of the assault had not yet been learned.

FIRST ENEMY CONTACT

The Japanese on Guadalcanal finally woke up to the fact that there was a full-scale invasion underway. During the first 24 hours of the assault 11,145 Marines landed on Guadalcanal while 6,805 more had landed on adjacent Tulagi and Gavutu-Tanambogo. The Japanese on Tulagi radioed frantically and Japanese area headquarters at Rabaul mounted an immediate air strike against the invasion force. Rabaul is some 600 miles north-west of Guadalcanal. Twenty-seven Betty bombers – Mitsubishi G4M twin-engine aircraft – with an escort of eighteen Zero fighters flew over coastwatcher Paul Mason's position at 11 on the

morning of August 8.[4] Mason radioed his sighting and Rear Admiral Turner ordered the landing craft away from the beach and got his fleet underway. The Bettys had been armed for a strike against New Guinea, and were unable to change their bombs for the more appropriate torpedoes with which to attack ships. Since the Allied ships were moving, the bombers found their targets difficult to hit with bombs and no damage was inflicted on the ships. Two of the Bettys were shot down. A later strike by Japanese dive-bombing D3A Vals also had no success. Three Vals were shot down and six more came down at sea en route back to Rabaul.

By now, the Marines were headed inland toward their main objective, the airfield, where the Japanese had retreated when they realized the strength of the U.S. landing. The period of relative

Right: The prize: Henderson field – named after a Marine aviator – was the prize in the Guadalcanal campaign. The Japanese had planned to use the dirt airstrip and a floatplane base on an adjacent island to help capture Port Moresby at the southern end of New Guinea, paving the way for air strikes and possibly landings in Australia. These planes are SBD Dauntless dive bombers, an outstanding aircraft flown by U.S. Navy and Marine pilots. (U.S. Marine Corps)

Right: Five smashed Japanese tanks stand on a sand spit across the mouth of the Matanikau River on Guadalcanal. These tanks, attempting to outflank U.S. Marine positions, were destroyed by Marine artillery. Savo Island is in the right background. At Guadalcanal and elsewhere in the Pacific the Marines continued to fight the land campaigns after the beachhead had been gained. (U.S. Marine Corps)

easy-going on Guadalcanal was about to end. The nighttime naval battle called The Battle of Savo Island on August 8–9 ended in a tactical victory for the Japanese as their cruisers and destroyers made a successful attack against an Allied cruiser-destroyer force, sinking three U.S. cruisers and one Australian cruiser. Other U.S. ships were damaged or disabled, and Vice Admiral Fletcher withdrew his carrier groups for fear of further Japanese attacks, leaving the men ashore on their own. (Fletcher had told Turner he could not keep his carriers at Guadalcanal for more than 48 hours. He was worried about exposing aircraft carriers to the massive Japanese air strength that was reported at Rabaul.)

Eventually, the Guadalcanal campaign developed into a land battle supported by offshore ships and aircraft. By mid-October, 23,000 U.S. Marines and soldiers faced 20,000 Japanese ashore. The amphibious phase of the battle had done what it was supposed to do: get the men and their weapons ashore.

LESSONS OF OPERATION "WATCHTOWER"

The haste with which the invasion of Guadalcanal was planned and executed should not overshadow the lessons of this first U.S. amphibious operation of World War II. The pressure to deny the Japanese their airfield base for further forays also gave the Allies their first major land victory against the seemingly unbeatable Japanese. For their part, the Japanese were stunned by their defeat and never recovered their earlier momentum. It was as though the myth of their invincibility, to which they themselves had fallen victim, had been shattered.

There were several trade-offs as well. The poor showing of the U.S. landing force during the Fiji exercises, although it brought together all the elements of a large, modern amphibious naval force, could not have prepared the participants for the vigorous campaign at Guadalcanal. The landing craft, with their bow ramps, and the LVT amphibian tractors, efficient as they proved to be, caused major headaches on the night of August 7, piling up supplies on the beach until they could be dispersed. Better organization immediately *after* the landings was an obvious necessity. Then, too, the logistical chain needed much work, as the lonely Marines left on Guadalcanal could certify as they watched the ships that had deposited them on the island disappear over the horizon.

The Japanese certainly did not give up without a fight, their initial reaction – or lack of it – not withstanding. They even mounted their own limited amphibious landings behind Marine lines to counterattack the U.S. invaders. The Japanese conducted their own supply operation with night runs down "The Slot," the passage between the main islands of the Solomons. The troops and supplies sent down The Slot by the "Tokyo Express" at one point seriously threatened the Allied hold on Guadalcanal.

Once they understood that Guadalcanal had been lost the Emperor gave his permission to evacuate on December 31, 1942. The Japanese conducted a massive, largely successful, effort to get their troops off the island, beginning on the night of February 1–2 and concluding on February 7–8. Under the cover of ably handled destroyers, the Japanese made amphibious landings in reverse, evacuating the 12,000 remaining men, most of them suffering from dysentery and malnutrition.

But perhaps the most important lesson was in the area of Navy-Marines command relationships. Dogged by the Navy's demands to exercise control over the Marine landing force, Major General Vandegrift appealed to the Marine Commandant to intercede. The Navy agreed to a major change in the Fleet Training Publication (FTP) 167, namely that the landing force commander would be under the amphibious task force commander *only* during the movement to the beachhead and the initial landing. During the planning stages, they would be equal. And, the I Marine Amphibious Corps was established in the South Pacific to coordinate such planning and perhaps to help protect Marine commanders from Navy interference.

Below: These battle-weary Marines are leaving Guadalcanal in January 1943. The lengthy battle for the island was an intolerable drain on Japanese resources, preventing action in other areas while the United States could built up its forces for the Pacific War. These "Marines" waiting to board transports include Navy chaplains and medical personnel who wear Marine uniform while assigned to the Fleet Marine Force. (U.S. Marine Corps)

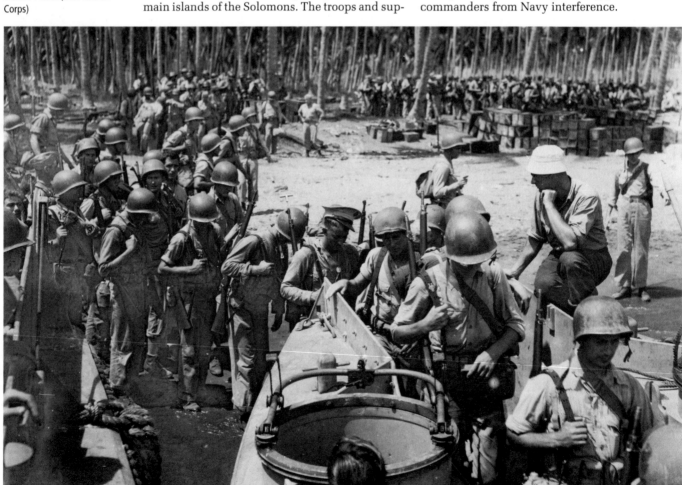

6.
THE FIRST ATLANTIC ASSAULTS

THE DIEPPE EXPERIENCE

The war in Europe was two years old and, except for occasional delaying actions and the aerial Battle of Britain in 1940, the British had not won a contest against the Germans. The loss of Denmark, Norway, the Low Countries, and, especially, France, had left Britain standing almost alone. Although in 1941 the Soviet Union and then the United States had entered the war against Nazi Germany, their direct contribution to the efforts against Germany would not be felt for several months.

In early 1942 the German Army was still on the march in Russia, having occupied France, the Low Countries, Czechoslovakia, Austria, Denmark, and Norway, with troops in the Balkans and fighting in North Africa. Germany had approximately 50 divisions which, with interior lines of communications, could conceivably retain their holdings for the foreseeable future. Although blockade and bombing, mainly from bases in Britain, could take their toll, it was unlikely that such action would seriously hurt the Nazi empire, especially if U-boats continued to take their toll of merchant ships carrying fuel, munitions, supplies, and food to the British Isles.[1]

Britain's leaders felt that something had to be done in Europe to counter the German success. An assault, even a small one somewhere along the French coast, could demonstrate to the people of the occupied countries that they were not forgotten and that help — and eventually liberation — would come. Also, there was a build-up of Canadian troops in Britain who were impatient for action. The leadership decided that a hit-and-run assault would provide needed experience in modern landing techniques for both British and Canadian troops.

The coastal town of Dieppe on the English Channel was chosen as the most suitable target for a massive hit-and-run amphibious raid. The wide beaches adjacent to the town provided good prospects for landing troops. The German defenses, however, were formidable: coastal defense guns, an offshore minefield, and nearby airfields and troops to reinforce the town's garrison would not permit an easy landing. But Dieppe was within range of the limited British amphibious assault capability and could be reached by fighter aircraft based in the south of England, a vital consideration for an amphibious operation.

British planners felt that the best weapon for a successful assault would be surprise, and great caution was exercised as the participants were brought together for Operation "Jubilee," the code-name given to the Dieppe landings. Initial planning called for parachute drops to support three amphibious landings on the flanks of the town and two frontal assaults on Dieppe. (The planned airborne landing was deleted prior to the actual assault.)

A total force of more than 6,000 troops was to be used. There would be some 5,000 Canadian soldiers, just over 1,000 men of Nos. 3 and 4 Royal Marine Commandos and a token force of 60 U.S. Army Rangers — the "shock troops" of the new American army. To carry these troops to the beachheads, and then evacuate them, would be nine large infantry landings ships, 24 tank landing craft embarking, and more than 100 smaller landing craft as well as scores of coastal launches and gunboats. Close support for the landing and defense against German attacks en route to and from the objective would be provided by eight destroyers with one, HMS *Calpe*, serving as headquarters ship for the "Jubilee" commanders — Captain J. Hughes-Hallett, RN, for naval forces, and Major-General J. H. Roberts, commander of the 2nd Canadian Division, for military forces.

Air support would be available from 67 squadrons based in England. Their aircraft would include the North American fighter-reconnaissance Mustang I which would score its first kills in the forthcoming assault.[2]

The original Dieppe target date of July 4, 1942, brought rain and poor weather. The assault was postponed until July 8, and, as the bad weather continued, it was put off until mid-August. The sailing date of August 18, 1942, again brought rain and poor visibility, but the ships and craft of the invasion fleet sailed from the English ports that night. Minesweepers led the way, followed by infantry landing ships, the destroyers and a varied collection of other support ships and landing craft. They arrived eight miles off Dieppe at 3 a.m. on the 19th, having covered the 70-mile crossing in strict radio silence.

The fleet positioned itself, the headquarters ship *Calpe* and another destroyer at the center. The other six destroyers formed a screen while other combatants, including a strike force of seven Free French destroyers, made ready to dash toward Dieppe Harbor to seize the German invasion barges intended for the long postponed invasion of England.

The rest of the force was to land the 2nd Canadian Division, the British Marines, and the U.S. Rangers who would occupy Dieppe for a short time, destroy whatever German installations they could, and then re-embark.

The landing sites were: Berneval (Beach Yellow 1), Belleville-sur-Mer (Yellow 2), Puys (Blue), Dieppe (Red and White), Pourville (Green), Varengeville (Orange 1) and Quiverville (Orange 2). The assault teams for Blue and Green Beaches left their ships at 3 a.m. and soon the 6,000 men were making their way toward their targets in a host of landing craft.

Vice-Admiral Louis Mountbatten, the British Chief of Combined Operations, and Canadian Lieutenant-General H. D. G. Crerar, waited with Air Marshal Leigh-Mallory at No. 11 Group, Fighter Command, in England. Major-General J. H. Roberts of the military forces and Captain J. Hughes-Hallett, commanding the naval force, waited in their ships for word of the landing.

Operation "Jubilee" hit its first snag at 3:47 a.m. when five armed German trawlers discovered the approaching assault boats and opened fire. Surprise was lost. In the confusion, one British landing craft of the group of twenty cleared the battle and brought its twenty men to Belleville-sur-Mer, Yellow 2. These men went for a gun battery, preventing it from firing accurately. Six other landing craft managed to come ashore at Yellow 1, but were caught in heavy crossfire, with only a few Canadians reaching the beach. The Marines of No. 4 Commando hit the beach and destroyed a coastal defense battery on Orange 2, and rapidly withdrew to return to their ships.

However, the attack met bitter defensive fire from the other German batteries. The efforts of the British fire-support ships and aircraft failed to disable the German defenses. At Pourville (Green), the South Saskatchewan Regiment, followed by the Queen's Own Camerons, ran into heavy fire. The Royal Regiment of Canada hit Blue Beach to the north and was nearly wiped out.

The Germans established a deadly crossfire in the pre-dawn darkness. The Essex Scottish on Red Beach and the Royal Hamiltons on White Beach — Dieppe proper — never had a chance. All their courage and stamina in returning the enemy's fire could not turn the tide of battle.

The 24 tank landing craft trying to reach the shore were pulverized. Seventeen tanks succeeded in reaching land, but of those only five made a contribution to the battle. Eventually, 28 tanks were landed.

As the landing foundered, the skies over Dieppe came alive with formations of British Bostons and Blenheims — twin-engine, light attack bombers — that were desperately trying to support the troops below. Spitfires and Hurricanes broke up German bomber strikes against the ships offshore and intercepted German fighters attacking the English bombers. The Royal Air Force aircraft flew 2,617 sorties, losing 106 aircraft including 88 Spitfires. The Germans lost 48 aircraft in what was the largest air battle in Europe since the Battle of Britain.

The landings had begun at 3:47 a.m. By nine, after the carnage on the beaches brought the realization of failure, the British commanders decided to withdraw the surviving troops as soon as possible. By 10:22 a.m. the destroyers formed a line to escort the rescue boats in. The evacuation took three hours under murderous German fire.

By early afternoon, the battered remnants of the Dieppe raiders were headed back to England, leaving 24 officers and 3,164 men behind — killed or prisoners. Of the 5,000 troops from the 2nd Canadian Division, some 900 were dead and almost 2,000 had been captured. All the vehicles they had dragged with them in the assault also remained behind. The débâcle at Dieppe did not auger well for future amphibious efforts. Though severely tested, the Germans could not have taken the raid too seriously and must have breathed a sigh of relief for having beaten back what many in the German high command initially considered to be the beginning of the invasion of Europe.

Dieppe — which Churchill later termed a "reconnaissance in force" — is rationalized by some historians as providing invaluable experience for future assaults. This premise is highly questionable. It is debatable as to whether the lessons of Dieppe had a direct impact on the subsequent North African and later Allied landings. In particular, the distances from Allied ports (and airfields), the specialized amphibious ships that were being built, and numerous other factors greatly changed the nature of the Allied landings only three months later along the North African coast.

There was one major benefit to the Allies from Dieppe. As astutely observed by British naval historian S. W. Roskill: "The Germans decided that the Dieppe raid indicated that, when the time came for the Allies to invade the European continent in earnest, their initial thrust would be aimed at capturing a large port. It is likely that this false deduction contributed greatly to the successful landing on the Normandy beaches in June 1944."[3]

In 1942, President Roosevelt, General George C. Marshall, the U.S. Army Chief of Staff, and the British Chiefs of Staff were pressing for an invasion of continental Europe as soon as possible. It

Above: President Roosevelt and Prime Minister Churchill were the final decision-makers with respect to amphibious operations in World War II. Both had naval experience – Roosevelt had been Assistant Secretary of the Navy in World War I, with Churchill having served as First Lord of the Admiralty at the beginning of both World Wars. Immediately behind the leaders in this 1941 photograph aboard the battleship *Prince of Wales* are Admiral E. J. King, General George C. Marshall, and General Sir John Dill. (U.S. Navy)

was generally realized that a 1942 assault across the Channel would seek to seize only the port of Brest or Cherbourg (Operation "Sledgehammer"); if delayed until 1943, the proposed cross-Channel assault was to be a full-scale landing into France (Operation "Round-Up").

Churchill, however, was now fully aware of the difficulties of an amphibious assault into Europe and while determined to defeat Hitler's legions and liberate Europe, he sought primarily to undertake actions that were possible with the available resources. Such operations on Europe's flanks, he reasoned, would dissipate German strength and provide battle and amphibious experience for Anglo-American commanders. British historian Ronald Lewin has written:

"This is a matter which justifies hindsight. In view of what is now known about D-Day and the Normandy campaign it can hardly be denied that Churchill was correct in resisting the enormous pressures from Russia and America for a premature Second Front. It was fortunate that by securing an invasion of North Africa in 1942 he made an invasion of Northern France – though he sought one for 1943 – impossible until 1944. A cross-Channel offensive in 1942 would have been a guaranteed, and in 1943 an almost certain, failure."[4]

ANOTHER FRENCH COLONY

In the first half of 1942 the British also assaulted a French Colony in the Indian Ocean. The island of Madagascar off the eastern coast of Africa is larger than France. When the French government capitulated to the Germans in June 1940 the officials in Madagascar threw in with the Vichy government. In early 1942 the British feared that if

Japanese forces entered the Indian Ocean they would seize Madagascar, as they had Indochina, and employ it as a base for cutting off India and Australia from Europe and the Middle East.

In view of the failure at Dakar, the British took more pains in planning the Madagascar operation – given the codename "Bonus" and then "Ironclad" – including undertaking the assault with all British troops; the Free French would not be involved. Still, a plan to carry out a practice landing at Loch Fyne in early February had to be cancelled because the ships and troops were needed elsewhere.

The shortage of troops in Britain and the need for secrecy, to prevent the possibility of the Vichy government sending reinforcements from Dakar to Madagascar, led the British to employ troops that were being sent to India. The principal British formations were the Army's 13th, 17th, and 29th Brigades. It was originally proposed that Marines be used in the assault, as the British were in the process of forming the Marine Division.

However, with the manpower problems being encountered in forming new Army units, the British Chiefs of Staff generally opposed the formation of such a large Marine unit, which would require certain Army support components. Although established on paper, the division was never formally raised and soldiers en route to India were to make the assault, plus a small Marine contingent from the flagship *Ramillies*.

The battleship *Ramillies* carried both the naval commander, Rear-Admiral E. N. Syfret, and the ground commander, Major-General Robert Sturges, the designated commander of the non-existent Marine Division. Two British aircraft carriers were made available to support the operation by withdrawing Force H from Gibraltar. This was compensated, in part, by the United States sending a battleship to British home waters.

In April the various forces steamed southward for the 9,000-mile voyage from Britain to Madagascar. At a stopover in Freetown, Syfret and Sturges met for the first time and attempted to meld their plans. Both men were true professionals and there was no friction as they began to work together.

The assault force consisted of the flagship *Ramillies*, the fleet carriers *Illustrious* and *Indomitable*, two cruisers, nine destroyers, six corvettes, and six minesweepers. An assortment of transports, some modified for the amphibious role, carried the troops and their material. Among the ships was the *Bachaquero*, one of Britain's first LSTs. There were some 30 LCMs carried on board ships of the force, but none of the more capable LCTs could be embarked. Out in the Indian Ocean the small British Far Eastern Fleet would provide distant defense against a Japanese thrust into the area.

By May 4 the force was approaching Diego Suarez at the northern end of the island and making preparations for the landing. The key to Madagascar was the naval base at Diego Suarez, The bay on which Diego Suarez sits cuts deeply into the eastern side of the island with the defended port of Antsirane controlling the entrance.

The British force covertly assembled offshore. On the morning of May 5 the first troops were landed without opposition at five points on the western side of the island, touching ashore at 4:30 a.m. The reefs, which the French believed would deny passage to an assault force, were successfully navigated and the mines in the anchorage area were successfully swept. Within hours several thousand British troops were on shore.

A cruiser carried out a feint on the eastern side of the island, at the approach to Diego Suarez, and as the sun climbed into the eastern sky the two British carriers launched aircraft to bomb and strafe the French airfields and naval ships in the harbor.

The French resisted the assault, but it was too late. By the afternoon of the 5th the entire 29th Brigade and most of its equipment, including tanks and artillery, were ashore, an outstanding feat in view of the limited numbers of landing craft and the exposed position of the transports and cargo ships. The 17th Brigade followed.

Still, French resistance ashore stiffened. General Sturges asked Admiral Syfret to land a party of Marines directly into the port of Antsirane as a diversion. Fifty Marines from the *Ramillies* were transferred to the destroyer *Anthony*. With great skill, the destroyer ran the entrance of the harbor at nightfall and successfully came alongside a quay in the town to land her Marines. In the darkness the ship escaped under heavy fire from shore batteries while Captain Martin Price and his men created the diversion, contributing to the surrender of Antsirane on the morning of the 7th. The taking of the approaches to Diego Suarez was complete when, after being fired upon by the *Ramillies*, the defending forts also capitulated.

All fighting ceased by 11 a.m. and that afternoon the British fleet steamed into the harbor. Total British casualties were 105 killed and almost 300 wounded. The French lost some 150 killed and 500 wounded, plus a submarine sunk. The only French attempt to attack the invasion force was an ambush attempt by a submarine, which was spotted and sunk by carrier-based Swordfish aircraft.

The remainder of Madagascar was still controlled by Vichy forces and a low-level of conflict followed until early November. That "mopping up" was done mostly with African troops, as most of the British soldiers were withdrawn from the island and sent eastward.

While the Japanese sent no assault forces into the

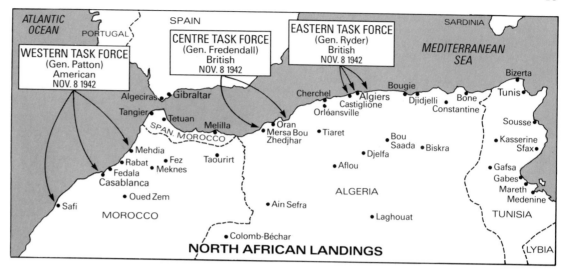

NORTH AFRICAN LANDINGS

Indian Ocean, a Japanese carrier strike force had already hit Ceylon, and Japanese troops moving south from Burma did take over islands in the eastern Indian Ocean. And, Japanese submarines and armed merchant cruisers did operate in the Indian Ocean. Two of these submarines launched midget undersea craft off Diego Suarez on the morning of May 31. The midgets entered the harbor and torpedoed the battleship *Ramillies* and sank a tanker. Neither of the two-man subs returned to their mother ships. (Two other submarines in this five-submarine group carried floatplanes, which had earlier reconnoitered Diego Suarez as well as other British ports in the area.)

The French had prepared Diego Suarez against an assault by the British for two years. Good planning, good cooperation, and good leadership plus adequate forces had triumphed for Britain's first major amphibious success of the war.

OPERATION "TORCH"

As with Madagascar, the fall of France in June 1940 left the French territories in North Africa as "wild cards" in the wartime lineup. The British wished to prevent German control over French North Africa and its military installations, including a sizeable fleet. The Germans and their Italian allies were already in Africa and could bring reinforcements down through Italy. It was a complex situation watched intently by the British and their newly involved American allies.

Animosity between Britain and France after the British attacks on French warships in 1940 (to prevent their falling under German control) would not allow a solo operation by the British against French territory in North Africa. "Torch" had thus evolved from the Atlantic Conference in August 1941 at Argentia, Newfoundland, between President Roosevelt and Prime Minister Churchill. Among the topics discussed at the meeting was the use of American forces in landings in French North Africa. The subject was brought forth again

immediately after the Pearl Harbor attack in December 1941, with Churchill proposing a U.S. landing in Morocco. An early landing in Europe was desired by some U.S. military leaders, but the British said that they were not ready for such an incursion, an odd consensus when viewed in the hindsight of the disastrous Dieppe raid of August 1942.

Arguments for landings in Europe and North Africa reached a head when unexpected German gains in Libya in June 1942 destroyed much of the British power in the region and left the British Eighth Army in battered disarray. Churchill flew to Washington on June 17 to meet Roosevelt again, and the two leaders agreed that a landing in North Africa was a better considered option that a premature landing in Europe. The initial codename of the North Africa invasion was "Super Gymnast," but was later changed, at Churchill's insistence, to "Torch" – a more dynamic title. After limited resistance by the U.S. Chiefs of Staff, who favored a larger landing operation in Europe, planning for the "Torch" landings began in earnest. (During this period, however, Churchill was actively planning and working out the details for the cross-Channel assault; Appendix B is one of his more comprehensive memos on this subject written at that time.)

Planning for "Torch" began in the summer of 1942. This first Anglo-American assault of the war would be under the overall command of Lieutenant General Dwight D. Eisenhower. "Ike," a relatively unknown West Pointer from Kansas, had made his mark as an aide to General MacArthur in the Philippines in the 1930s and as plans officer for General Marshall in Washington during the early stages of the war.

"Torch" would be fully an Anglo-American operation, but with overall military command vested in the hands of an American general. The naval forces of this complex operation would be under the command of Admiral Sir Andrew Brown Cunningham, RN, while Air Chief Marshal Arthur

W. Tedder, RAF, would have overall direction of air operations.

In general, cooperation between the Allies was excellent. However, Eisenhower would remark about the problems he had in dealing with the U.S. Navy – problems similar to those that the Marines in the Pacific were having with the Navy. After the war, in his public history, *Crusade in Europe*, Eisenhower would write:

> "We had to co-ordinate our plans not only with the British but also with the United States Navy. This was by no means simple, and it required a great many conferences. Two of the Navy's capable officers had been assigned by Admiral King to assist in planning, and they were welcomed ... with the statement that there were a thousand questions the Navy could help answer. 'We are here only to listen,' was their answer. I knew that if I could talk personally to Admiral King there would be no difficulty, but under the circumstances these snarls had to be worked out with care and patience."[5]

In his diaries Eisenhower apparently was not as charitable toward King and the Navy: "One thing that might help win this war is to get someone to shoot King. . . He's the antithesis of cooperation, a deliberately rude person, which means he's a mental bully." For Admiral King – and most senior naval officers – the principal theater was the Pacific, and every warship or escort or landing craft diverted to the European war, let alone to North Africa, was diversion away from the main theater of operations.

Shortly before the "Torch" landings began, Eisenhower and his staff flew in five B-17 Flying Fortress bombers from England to Gibraltar, the British bastion in the western Mediterranean which would serve as his forward headquarters. In the meantime, one of Eisenhower's deputies, U.S. Army Major General Mark Clark, sailed from Gibraltar in the British submarine *Seraph* (P-219) for a secret meeting with the U.S. Consul-General in North Africa, Robert Murphy, and representatives of the Vichy French forces in North Africa. The purpose of the meeting was to secure promises from the French not to resist – and perhaps to help – Allied landings. The anti-British fervor in North Africa made it highly probable that the French troops would oppose any landings by the British. The French were worried that any German perception of French collaboration would bring retaliation against German-occupied France.

General Clark's clandestine meeting in a beach house, from the morning of October 21 late into the night of the 22nd, brought an agreement for tacit cooperation. Unknown to the French, who were promised a month's warning prior to any landing, the ships for Operation "Torch", had already left the United States and were due to arrive off the North Africa coast only two weeks

later. After the meeting, Clark returned to the *Seraph*, was taken to sea for a rendezvous with a Catalina flyingboat, and flown to Gibraltar to advise Eisenhower of his meeting (see Chapter 10 for details of the *Seraph*'s role in Mediterranean amphibious operations).

"Torch" would be comprised of three landings with all ground forces under U.S. Army generals: Casablanca (Western), under the flamboyant but highly capable Major General George S. Patton; Oran (Center) under Major General Lloyd Fredenhall; and Algiers (Eastern), under Major General Charles Ryder. Casablanca would be an all-American landing, with Anglo-American troops going ashore at Oran and Algiers, but with Americans in the first waves of the two latter landings in an attempt to reduce French resistance.

The North African invasion was set for November 8, 1942. "Torch" saw the largest concentration of Allied naval forces yet assembled in the war. The Allies were able to muster twelve aircraft carriers of varying sizes – most of them small, American-built escort carriers, generally referred to as "jeep" or "Woolworth" carriers. They carried 78 U.S. Army P-40F Warhawk fighters and three spotter aircraft to be flown into North African airfields when they were captured. There were some 350 naval fighters and bombers on the decks of the four large carriers (one U.S. and three British), five other escort carriers, and the ancient flattop, *Argus*, ready to provide air support for the landings.[6] Longer-range aircraft from Gibraltar would also provide support.

An armada of U.S. and British battleships, cruisers, and destroyers screened the carriers and the scores of transports. And, for the first time, three tank landing ships, the harbingers of more than a thousand such LSTs, were en route to the invasion beaches.

Despite these many ships at sea, none was intercepted by German reconnaissance aircraft or U-boats, and the German high command would be taken by surprise. The Germans believed that the Allied air and naval activities they had detected were related to forthcoming operations to assist Malta, in the central Mediterranean, or possibly to land troops in southern France. The Italian government properly predicted the Allied objectives would be in North Africa.

"Torch" would be the major combat debut for the U.S. Army. The American troops under Patton were assigned to the most important area, Casablanca, which included the French naval anchorage with the large, although immobile, battleship *Jean Bart*. The use of U.S. troops to capture such an important objective would, it was hoped, defuse French resistance. Roosevelt strongly stated his belief that the initial landings should be by U.S. forces alone to reduce French hostility toward the invasion. Even a simultaneous landing by U.S. and British troops, he said, "would result in full resistance by all French in Africa." (There were few Germans in the French territories; they were mostly functionaries – the kind fictionalized as SS Major Heinrich Strasser in the movie "Casablanca.")

Patton's troops were embarked in 23 troop transports with eight supply ships and five tankers – no specialized landing ships were available to this task force. Screening this Western Task Force, and to provide support to the landing, were the battleships *Massachusetts* (BB-59), in service only six months, and *Texas* (BB-35), completed before World War I. With them were one large and four of the escort or "jeep" carriers, seven cruisers, 38 destroyers, and several lesser naval ships, the largest assembly of U.S. naval ships in the Atlantic since the war began.

Patton's troops consisted of the 2nd Armored Division, the 3rd Infantry Division, and most of the 9th Infantry Division. They totalled 34,300 troops.

The Center Task Force, under General Fredenhall, comprised 39,000 U.S. troops escorted by a British task force. With two British escort carriers, two light cruisers, thirteen destroyers, and other escort ships, the troops were embarked in nineteen landing ships and 28 cargo ships. The assault would be carried out by the U.S. 1st Infantry Division and half of the 1st Armored Division.

The Eastern Task Force, whose objective was Algiers, consisted of 23,000 British and 10,000 American troops under American command. The escort and covering ships were one older British carrier (*Argus*), an escort carrier, three light cruisers, a monitor, three anti-aircraft ships, thirteen destroyers, and lesser ships. The troops were carried in seventeen landing ships and sixteen cargo ships and transports. Those troops were the U.S. 3rd Infantry Division, part of the U.S. 9th Infantry Division, half of the U.S. 1st Armored Division, and the British 78th Infantry Division.

Operations in the Mediterranean would be additionally covered by the British Force H from Gibraltar with three battleships, one battlecruiser, three aircraft carriers, three light cruisers, and seventeen destroyers to guard against interference by the Italian fleet.

A somewhat hidden tenet of this composition of assault forces was that once the initial landings were accomplished, presumably by November 9, overall command of the continued offensive would revert to the British, with Lieutenant-General Kenneth Anderson, commander of the British First Army, taking charge.

The Center and Eastern Task Forces sailed from Britain, in two convoys, one on October 22, and another on the 26th. The reason for the split sailing was to allow the first and slower group to arrive with the second group at Gibraltar on November 5, and enter the Mediterranean with an escort of the British Mediterranean Fleet under Admiral Cunningham, overall commander of "Torch" naval forces.

THE WESTERN TASK FORCE LANDS

General Patton's Western Task Force landed at Fedala on the morning of November 8 at three locations: 15 miles north of Casablanca; at Mehdia, 55 miles to the east; and at Safi, 140 miles to the south west. Fedala had the best beaches and harbor, while Mehdia's importance lay in a nearby airfield, Pt. Lyautey.

The Fedala landings, scheduled for 4 a.m., did not begin until 5 a.m., and eighteen of 25 landing boats in the first wave were wrecked in the approach to the beach. Inexperienced crews and resulting confusion hampered the Americans as they tried to get their overloaded assault craft ashore. Heavy ocean swells did not help.

Two old U.S. four-stack destroyers, the *Bernadou* (DD-153) and *Cole* (DD-155), raced

Below: Jeeps and other equipment are lowered into landing craft from transports off Fedala, Morocco, during the Anglo-American invasion of North Africa in November 1942. The British were able to employ the first LSTs – converted from tankers – in the North Africa landings, but the U.S. Navy had no specialized landing ships available. Fortunately, opposition to the landings by the Vichy French was relatively light and scattered. (U.S. Navy)

for the harbor mouth at Safi, each ship carrying 200 Army Rangers. As the *Bernadou* approached the entrance, she was fired upon by the French batteries protecting the harbor. All pre-invasion hopes of French acceptance of an "accommodation" were dashed. The destroyers returned the French fire and were intentionally run aground to quickly offload their troops. The landing craft from the transports followed and by 5:30 the first light tanks came ashore as the French retreated from their half-hearted defense.

Many of the leaders of the French forces were divided between helping the Americans and their own sense of duty to defend their positions. The Vichy batteries continued firing at the half-hidden invaders in the dark. Perhaps if the French had fully realized the scope and size of the landings, they might not have resisted.

U.S. warships – including cruisers and the battleships *Massachusetts* and *Texas* – fired into the harbor at Casablanca, disabling the *Jean Bart*, whose 15-inch guns were a major threat to incoming assault craft. Seven French destroyers and eight submarines that tried to leave the harbor were immediately attacked by U.S. surface ships and carrier-based aircraft. The French ships

were driven back, losing two destroyers and three submarines. One of the great successes of the Casablanca operation was the naval gunfire support, which quickly suppressed many of the Fedala batteries and other Vichy defenses.

The main landings at Fedala experienced delays and losses, mainly through inexperience, but by 6 a.m., 3,500 U.S. soldiers had come ashore. The problems with French resistance continued due to confusion and Vichy loyalties to their German masters. Messages broadcast by President Roosevelt to the French territories did not have the desired effect and clashes between elements of the invasion forces and French army, navy and air units continued.

The naval and air battles were the most intense, the aerial action occasionally pitting American planes against one another flown by crews who, historically, were allies. Grumman Wildcats and Douglas Dauntlesses from U.S. Navy aircraft carriers bombed and straged French airfields and ships, and fought with French fighters, among them Curtiss P-36s supplied in the hectic days before France's collapse in 1940. Several of the colorfully marked French P-36s, which sported red and yellow engine cowlings and tails, also carried

Below: The French battleship *Jean Bart* at Casablanca opposed the U.S. landings with 15-inch gunfire. The French warship was silenced by return fire from a U.S. battleship and cruiser (and later by U.S. aircraft), while U.S. carrier aircraft stopped French destroyers and submarines from attacking the Anglo-American task forces.

the uniquely American insignia of a screaming Indian, emblem of the famous Lafayette Escadrille of World War I.

The battle was not completely one-sided; the French coastal guns hit several ships, including the battleship *Massachusetts* and the heavy cruiser *Augusta* (CA-31), which carried General Patton and his staff. Patton was getting ready to disembark into a landing craft when a French shell destroyed his boat, leaving the frustrated general stranded but unharmed.

By November 9, General Patton and his troops had established a beachhead at Fedala, although they were still open to French attack. By November 10, the *Jean Bart's* guns had been repaired and the big ship again opened fire, but Dauntlesses from the carrier *Ranger* (CV-4) dropped 1,000-pound bombs on her, again putting the French battleship out of action.

The escort carrier *Chenango* (CVE-28) flew off her load of Curtiss P-40 Tomahawk fighters on the 10th, giving the U.S. forces air cover based ashore.

French resistance ended when Admiral Jean Darlan radioed the French general in Morocco to stop fighting until an armistice could be arranged. By noon on the 10th, Casablanca had surrendered.

THE CENTER TASK FORCE AT ORAN

The Center Task Force, whose objective was Oran, within the Mediterranean, hit the beach at 1:30 a.m. on November 8. Like the Western Task Force, it, too, split into groups to attack important secondary targets along the flank of the main attack. Submarines with directional beacons were in position and made preliminary weather and surf reports.

The U.S. Army's 1st Infantry Division, under Major General Terry Allen, landed on "Z" Beach on the Gulf of Arzeau, and Brigadier General Theodore Roosevelt, son of the American president, led the men of the 26th Combat Team of the 1st Division ashore on "Y" Beach, west of Oran. The early morning operations met no opposition. This allowed the uncontested arrival of necessary armored vehicles brought in by landing craft, including three pioneer LSTs known as "Maracaibos." These British LSTs could beach themselves, permitting the rapid unloading of tanks and other heavy vehicles without need of piers and cranes.

However, one of the three Maracaibo landing ships, HMS *Bachaquero*, carrying twenty light tanks and other vehicles, ran aground 360 feet offshore, with water only seven feet deep. U.S.

Below: The North Africa landings marked the debut of the LST in the Royal Navy. Three so-called Maracaibo shallow-draft tankers were converted to the LST role. As shown in this view of one of the trio, the ships retained their tanker lines with a new, flat bow being provided. In addition to tanks, the ships were invaluable for carrying the trucks and other vehicles needed to sustain a modern army once ashore. (IWM)

Army engineers rapidly erected a pontoon bridge to shore and had the tanks off the grounded LST by 8:15 a.m.

As the morning light revealed the invaders, the French guns opened fire against those British ships still offloading troops. The ruse of displaying U.S. flags did not work and two British ships were damaged, with many in their crews killed or wounded. Meanwhile, those units already ashore pushed inland toward the city. The U.S. Army Rangers captured several coastal defense batteries, with the fighting continuing through the afternoon.

U.S. and British aircraft contributed close air support for the landings. British carrier-based aircraft attacked La Senia airfield, six miles south-east of Oran. The planes bombed hangars and strafed French aircraft on the ground. Skirmishes and pitched battles on the land and at sea continued. The battered remnants of the French Navy tried to sortie, but a concerted thrust by Allied troops on the 10th entered Oran by 10:15 a.m., and by 12:15 a ceasefire had been arranged. Word of the cessation of hostilities did not immediately reach outlying areas, and French and American units continued firing at one another for several hours more. Despite occasionally heavy fighting, U.S. Army losses were only 85 dead and 221 wounded. The French losses were put at 165 dead.

THE EASTERN TASK FORCE AT ALGIERS

As the capital city of French North Africa, Algiers was one of the primary objectives of the invasion. An estimated 15,000 Vichy French troops were within a 20- to 30-mile radius of the city, supported by nearly 100 aircraft on two airfields. The nearby beaches were protected by coastal batteries. The invasion of Algiers looked as if it would be the most difficult of the three main landings of Operation "Torch."

The first British troops, 7,230 men of the British 11th Infantry Brigade Group, landed near Castiglione at 1 a.m. on November 8. Six miles to the east, the first U.S. troops, combined with a British Commando contingent, took the surrender of the French forces at Fort Duperre. These French seemed to welcome the arrival of American and British troops.

By afternoon, troops of the 11th Brigade Group were on the outskirts of the city, although problems arose at Blida airfield, where the French air commander allowed Allied aircraft to land but not take off again. Eventually, additional British troops arrived to keep the field operating.

The phase involving seizure of the harbor, however, met with considerable resistance. The British destroyers *Malcolm* and *Broke* sustained heavy casualties and damage as they led the thrust into the harbor. The *Malcolm* was forced to retire, but the *Broke* sent her raiding parties ashore at 5:30 a.m. and they took several important facilities.

Pro-Vichy forces in the French command began to mount a stout defense of the city, firing into *Broke* until the battered destroyer withdrew under heavy covering fire from sister ships of the task force. (The *Broke* was taken in tow for Gibraltar but sank the following day.)

Landings around Algiers continued under supporting fire from the assembled British ships, and from aircraft from the British carriers. Spitfires and Hurricanes were sent off from Gibraltar to the airfield at Maison Blanche, which was taken by American troops. However, British aviation support personnel trying to come ashore found it rough going in the heavy swells and were not in position to service the incoming fighters. Several aircraft were able to take off in the afternoon for patrols over the city.

American Consul-General Murphy received word from the French that they had orders to resist the Allied landings, and that they were angered by not receiving the promised one-month notification of an impending invasion. Murphy was placed under house arrest at one point. The German general in Algiers, previously arrested, was released.

Although word to continue fighting came from Marshal Philippe Pétain, head of the Vichy government in France, the message was also interpreted as giving complete authority to Admiral Darlan at Algiers to act as he saw fit, as on-scene commander of French forces. Accordingly, the French sought a ceasefire and surrendered Algiers to the Americans at 10 p.m. on November 8. More formal arrangements were worked out during the next two days, bringing the assault phases of Operation "Torch" to a successful conclusion. Ahead lay the long desert campaigns, as well as more immediate German air attacks on the American and British forces arriving in North Africa. This first large-scale amphibious operation had attained most of its major objectives and gave the Allies confidence and a much-needed boost as they began planning the invasions of Europe.

Opposition to the North Africa landings was half-hearted; the Vichy French were poorly armed and not prepared for an invasion. To come ashore against veteran German troops, in a heavily defended *Festung Europa*, would be a different matter. But the landings had been a success – their military and political goals being achieved, with relatively light losses. Much more than Dieppe, the "Torch" landings in North Africa provided needed experience in landing techniques, naval gunfire and air support, communications, and other essential elements of amphibious warfare. And, a command team was forged – Eisenhower, A.B. Cunningham, and Tedder, and a phalanx of their lieutenants and captains who would lead future landings in the European-Mediterranean theater.

7.
LANDING SHIPS AND CRAFT

SPECIALIZED vessels for landing operations date from antiquity, when soldiers and horses were transported along coasts in specially configured small craft. Subsequent practitioners of amphibious warfare developed improved craft, mainly to permit the rapid unloading of horses and cannon onto beaches.

In this century the first truly specialized landing ship of significance was the ill-fated *River Clyde*, converted for the Gallipoli landings on April 25, 1915 (see Chapter 1). Most of the Commonwealth and French troops landed in that amphibious operation were carried to the beach in barges towed by tugs and steam launches. This represented the height of specialized landing craft development in World War I.

During the inter-war years, two nations led in the development of amphibious warfare techniques – the United States and Japan (see Chapter 3). The U.S. Navy–Marine Corps began conducting practical landing exercises in the winter of 1922 when a battalion of Marines was landed at Culebra, Panama, in conjunction with a fleet exercise. More annual exercises followed, usually at Culebra or at San Celemente Island, off the southern California coast.

For the Marines, the exercises generally consisted of daily debarking from warships or a trans-port (going down the gangway) into ships' boats, transiting to the beach, and jumping into the surf to wade ashore. Small howitzers were manhandled from the boats to shore. (There were also some efforts to provide naval gunfire against shore targets in preparation for the landings.)

The exercises tended to reveal a lack of suitable amphibious doctrine, tactics, and landing craft. For a decade it was obvious to the more astute observers of these exercises that standard ships' boats were not suitable for landing troops and, especially, their weapons and equipment.

The relatively large Culebra landing of 1924, although having many shortcomings, was notable for the debut of two types of specialized landing craft. First, the so-called Troop Barge A was a 50-foot, twin-motor landing barge with a bow ramp for discharging wheeled equipment.

The Marines evaluated a variety of landing barges over the next decade and a half. Because there were no specialized transports, it was planned to carry the landing barges in boat davits of battleships and cruisers. This requirement dictated a maximum length of about 30 feet and a weight of five tons.

Second was an amphibious tractor, designed by J. Walter Christie, featuring tracks and rudders for water navigation. It performed satisfactorily in

Below: The U.S. Navy–Marine Corps "team" experimented with a variety of landing craft in the late 1930s. This is a 38-foot tank lighter unloading a "mini-tank" during a 1939 evaluation. The coxswain of the landing craft appears to be a Marine (with campaign hat). In U.S. forces all Marine landings used landing ships and craft manned by Navy Coast Guard personnel. (U.S. Marine Corps)

Below right: A prototype LVT-1 amphibious tractor undergoes tests at Culebra Island off the eastern coast of Puerto Rico, a long-time site for amphibious exercises. The "amtrac" could carry troops and supplies through the surf and up onto the beach, providing a new degree of flexibility in amphibious operations. The LVT-1 had an open cargo compartment and rear ramp. (U.S. Marine Corps)

Right: The World War I-built destroyer *Manley* became the first U.S. high-speed transport (APD-1) when she was modified to carry Marine raiders. Originally a four-stack ship, this 1940 photograph shows her with two stacks after the forward half of her propulsion plant had been removed to provide troop berthing. Four LCVPs are carried in davits. The *Manley* was followed by 35 more destroyers of 1,020 to 1,190 tons being converted to transports. (U.S. Navy)

river tests, but was found unseaworthy in the fleet exercises off Culebra in 1924. Still, it marked the start of Marine support for the "amtrac" that would achieve fame on Pacific atolls two decades later.

During subsequent fleet exercises of the 1920s and 1930s there were Marine landings, still mostly with ships' boats although a variety of specialized craft were tested. But the learning and development processes were slow. Addressing the 1935 fleet landing exercise, two Marine historians noted:

> "The results merely confirmed the obvious — that heavy slow-fuzed armor-piercing shells buried themselves in the ground before detonating and did relatively little damage to exposed targets. Some 1,500 Marines learned, if they did not already know, what it was to ride the sea in open boats and get wet up to their waists in a surf. . . . A converted naval motor launch was found to be useless to ferry vehicles. . . . A clumsy tank lighter was tested with dubious results."[1]

Development continued. The ships carrying the Marines, their equipment, and howitzers, were conventional warships or transports. The Marines would run down gangways or climb down cargo nets, while their equipment would be lifted over the side by cargo booms and lowered to the boats bobbing alongside. There were also exercises in night landings, which, of course, were even more difficult.

In 1936 the USS *Manley* (DD-74), originally a flush-deck, four-stack destroyer completed in 1917, was converted to a "fast transport."[2] In that role her torpedo tubes and half her propulsion plant were removed (reducing speed to 23 knots); berthing for 120 troops was provided and davits were installed for carrying four LCP-type landing craft.

The ability to cram up to 200 troops on board, the relatively high speed, small size of the ship, and retention of guns and depth-charges soon demonstrated the value of this configuration. This was the progenitor of 36 destroyer-APD conversions and 96 destroyer escort-APD conversions. The *Manley* was the U.S. Navy's first truly specialized amphibious ship.

THE LANDING CRAFT

By 1938 there was definite progress in the Navy-Marine development of landing craft. That year a self-propelled tank lighter, which would carry a single light tank, was successfully employed in a landing exercise. Its tank had been off-loaded *nineteen seconds* after the craft beached. Several converted fishing boats were also employed with success in moving troops ashore.

The following year the first landing craft produced by Andrew J. Higgins was evaluated by the Marine Corps. In 1926 Higgins, a New Orleans boatbuilder, had built a shallow-draft boat called

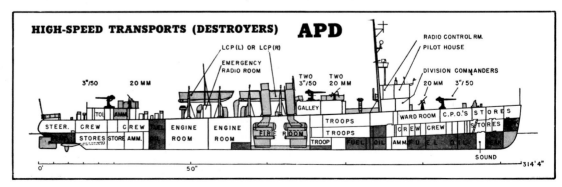

HIGH-SPEED TRANSPORTS (DESTROYERS) **APD**

Right: After the 36 APD conversions from four-stack destroyers, 96 destroyer escorts (DE) were similarly converted to high-speed transports. The *Lloyd* (APD-63, formerly DE-209) could carry 160 troops and four LCVPs in the transport role. Note that the *Lloyd* retained the 5-inch gun forward as well as lighter anti-aircraft weapons plus depth charges aft, permitting the ship to still serve in a limited escort role. (U.S. Navy)

the *Eureka* for use on the lower Mississippi River and along the Gulf coast. In the summer of 1936 the Marines tested Higgins boats, which immediately proved superior to all previously tested craft. It had a shallow draft and could easily run onto the beach and pull off again. After a 1939 exercise a Marine participant wrote, "The Higgins boat gave the best performance under all conditions. It has more speed, more maneuverability, handles easier, and lands troops higher on the beach than the other craft evaluated."[3] The Marines – especially Brigadier General Holland M. Smith – enthusiastically supported Higgins but the Navy's Bureau of Ships opposed a design by an "outsider" and sought to procure for the Marines its own, less capable craft.

The Higgins design won, but barely. In 1942 the U.S. Senate War Investigating Committee, chaired by the indomitable Harry S Truman, observed:

"It is clear that the Bureau of Ships, for reasons known only to itself, stubbornly persisted for over five years in clinging to an unseaworthy tank lighter design of its own. . . . The Bureau's action has caused not only a waste of time but has caused the needless expenditure of over $7,000,000 for a total of 225 Bureau lighters which do not meet the needs of the Armed Forces."[4]

Many hundreds of Higgins LCP(L)s – Landing Craft Personnel (Large) – would become the standard U.S. and British landing craft in World War II. Sometimes called the "Eureka" for the name of Higgins' prototype landing craft, the standard LCP(L) was a spoon-bowed craft, just under 37 feet in length, powered by a gasoline engine which could drive it at 8 to 11 knots fully loaded, and could carry 36 troops or four tons of cargo. When Higgins was shown a photograph of a Japanese landing craft with bow ramp in April 1941, he quickly evolved the modified LCP(R) (ramp) which could land small vehicles on the beach.

These craft could easily be carried in davits of landing ships and transports. The LCP series led to the improved Landing Craft Vehicle and Personnel (LCVP), of which thousands would be

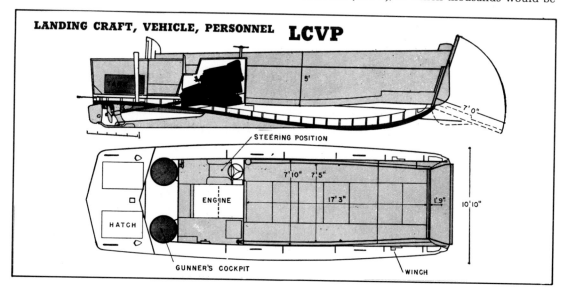

LANDING CRAFT, VEHICLE, PERSONNEL **LCVP**

built. General Smith would opine that this craft "... did more to win the war in the Pacific than any other single piece of equipment."

The British LCA – for Landing Craft Assault – was similar, also carried in shipboard davits, and could transport 35 troops or light vehicles. The wooden-hulled LCA design was also adapted for several fire support configurations.

Simultaneously, the U.S. Marines sponsored the continued development of amphibious tractors which would eventually succeed conventional landing craft in wartime assaults – the Landing Vehicle Tracked (LVT). The Marines persisted in this interest after the failure of the Christie designs.

In the 1930s Donald Roebling developed a tracked amphibious vehicle for rescue work in the Everglades, the swamps of central Florida. A photograph of the Roebling craft in *Life* magazine caught the eye of an admiral, who passed it on to the Marine general commanding the Atlantic Fleet Marine Force. After examining the swamp vehicle, the Marines took steps to evaluate pilot models

of a military version. (There was some immediate opposition as an amphibious tractor program would divert funds from the landing craft effort.) In 1940 the Marines obtained funds to produce the first "Alligators," which became the LVT-1. The first vehicle came off the assembly line in July 1941.

Production of the LVT-1 was underway and continued development efforts produced the improved LVT-2 in October 1941. These vehicles had cleated tracks which could move them on land at 25 m.p.h. (as against 15 m.p.h. for the LVT-1) and in water at 4 knots (as against 5.4 knots for the LVT-1). They could carry 20 to 24 fully equipped troops, or up to 3 tons of cargo. Their ability to cross coral reefs and other obstructions and to move supplies and troops out of the surf and up onto the beach would prove vital in future landings.

In 1940 the Marines initiated development of an LVT with a gun turret fitted in place of the cargo compartment. This would prove useful as

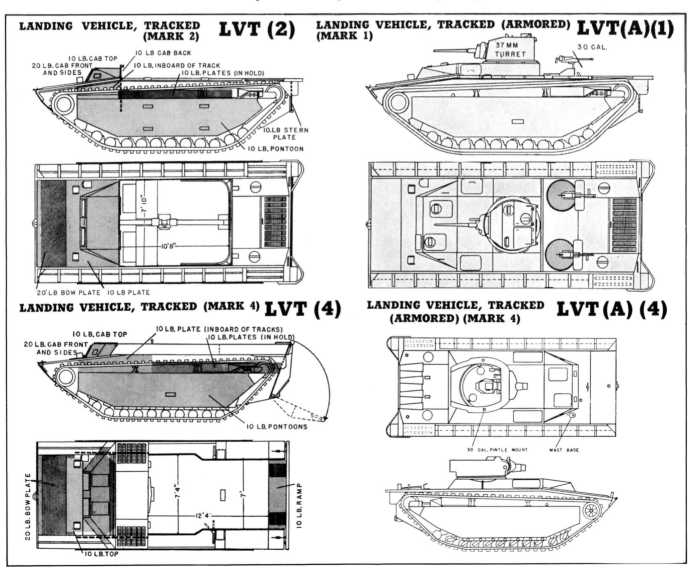

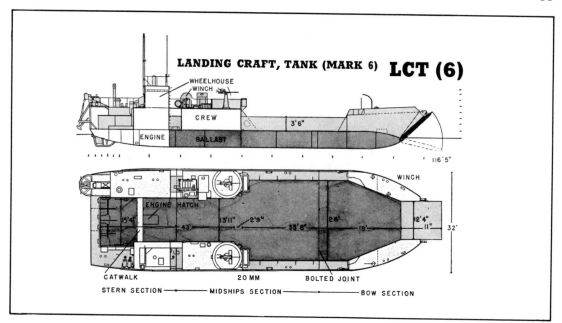

an amphibious tank that could accompany the personnel carriers onto the beach, providing fire support after naval bombardments were lifted. The LVT(A) – A for armored – models initially carried a 37-mm gun, with the definitive LVT(A)-4 having a 75-mm howitzer. (Most models also had one or more machine-guns fitted.) The Marine Corps would procure 18,620 LVTs of various models during World War II.

When, in the traumatic days of June 1940, Winston Churchill proposed that planning be undertaken for actions against enemy-held coasts, he directed that suitable craft be developed for landing tanks on beaches. In 1917, Churchill had suggested bullet-proof lighters and tank-landing lighters for amphibious operations.

There was already recognition within the British military leadership that such craft were needed, with the Inter-Service Training and Development Centre experimenting with assault boats in 1938–39. The naval programs of 1937–38 provided funds for landing craft and these were available to participate in the landing of British troops in 1940 (not opposed landings) and for the evacuation of Dunkirk that same year.

Under Churchill's direction, the Admiralty ordered twenty of a new, larger landing craft in July 1940 – the Landing Craft Tank (LCT). These initial LCTs displaced 226 tons light, were 152 feet long, and had a maximum speed of 10 knots. Their cargo capacity was three 40-ton tanks or six 16-ton tanks, or 250 tons of general cargo.

The first twenty LCTs plus another ten ordered in October were delivered in 1941 and were employed for raids on the Continent as well as for coastal operations at Tobruk in Libya. Improved, larger LCTs followed. Even the later LCTs were small enough to be built by engineering firms not engaged in shipbuilding, and thus the labor and

facilities needed for warships and merchant ships were not interrupted by the large LCT program.

The LCTs were considered critical for operations in European waters, and their shortage contributed to Churchill and Britain's military leaders opposing American urgings to open a Second Front in 1942 and again in 1943. While the LCTs – which were also constructed in the United States – were invaluable, they lacked the ability to travel long distances at sea. Rather, they had to be shipped into the assault area or to forward bases as deck cargo. Still needed was a more seaworthy vessel, one that could transport tanks and other vehicles on ocean voyages – what was initially called an "Atlantic LCT" or "Atlantic Tank Lighter."

THE LARGE SLOW TARGET

The LST – officially Landing Ship Tank – was in some respects the most significant ship of World War II. Of this ship, Churchill would record:

> "In this period of the war [1943] all the great strategic combinations of the Western Powers were restricted and distorted by the shortage of tank landing-craft [sic] for the transport, not so much of tanks, but of vehicles of all kinds. The letters 'L.S.T.' (Landing Ship, Tank) are burnt in upon the minds of all those who dealt with military affairs in this period."[5]

The Admiralty set to work designing the "Atlantic LCT," also known in its early development as the "Atlantic Tank Landing craft" (ATL). But the British could not wait for new ships to be designed and built. Three Maracaibo-class tankers were taken in hand and converted to the first tank-carrying ships, which were soon being called LSTs. These were shallow-draft tankers which had been designed to pass over the bars of Lake Maracaibo, Venezuela. Two were 382½ feet long

Right: The pioneer LST *Bachaquero* of the Maracaibo class is shown loading Bren gun carriers through her bow doors while preparing for Mediterranean operations. Note the broad beam of the former tanker with 20-mm anti-aircraft guns visible just above the bow. These ships were an interesting experiment, but were inferior in most respects to the series-produced LST(2) design. (IWM)

Below: The *Boxer* was lead ship for the first LST design built by the Royal Navy. Only three LST(1) ships were constructed before the more-familiar, Anglo-American LST(2) design was mass produced. The *Boxer's* single funnel is offset to starboard to provide a clear tank deck. The ship's 20-mm anti-aircraft guns can be clearly seen forward (a total of ten were carried, the others being on the bridge wings and aft); later LSTs also carried 40-mm guns. (IWM)

with a gross tonnage of approximately 4,900 after conversion, the third ship being slightly smaller. The conversion provided bow doors and a double ramp, to permit bridging of 100 feet from the ship to shallow waters.

The first LST conversion was ready in July 1941, being followed by two sister ships. The British LST requirement was to lift 500 tons. Each Maracaibo could carry eighteen 30-ton tanks or twenty-two 25-ton tanks, or 33 heavy trucks. There was berthing for 217 troops in addition to the ship's company of 98.

The Maracaibos were not considered a success, but they were available while the first purpose-built LSTs were under construction. These were the *Boxer* class, initially called "Winettes" for Churchill. These were officially designated LST(1). They were 400 feet long, displaced 5,410 tons fully loaded, and could carry thirteen 30-ton tanks or 27 trucks plus 193 troops.

The *Boxers* were relatively fast – 17 knots compared to 10 knots for the ex-tankers – but they were long on the building ways. The first ship was not completed until early 1943. In the event, only three of the LST(1)s were built. British

shipyards were giving priority to anti-submarine escort ships and merchant ships; facilities simply were not available for the LSTs, which, unlike the LCTs, were full-sized ships. The British took their plans to the United States.

Those who participated in designing the next-generation landing ship, the LST(2) series, differ as to how the design evolved. Churchill: "... the Admiralty had prepared a new design of the landing ship tank (L.S.T.), and this was taken to the United States, where the details were jointly worked out."[6] An official U.S. Navy history of the LSTs: "In November 1941, a small delegation from the Admiralty arrived in the United States to pool ideas with the Navy's Bureau of Ships. ... Within a few days, John Niedermair of the Bureau of Ships sketched out ... the basic design for the more than 1,000 LSTs which would be built during World War II."[7] According to the designer John Niedermair, on November 4, 1941, a dispatch from the Admiralty was brought to him outlining "in a very brief manner the need for larger landing craft that could be seagoing. . . I drew the original sketch that afternoon in a matter of a couple of hours on a scale of 50 feet to the inch."[8]

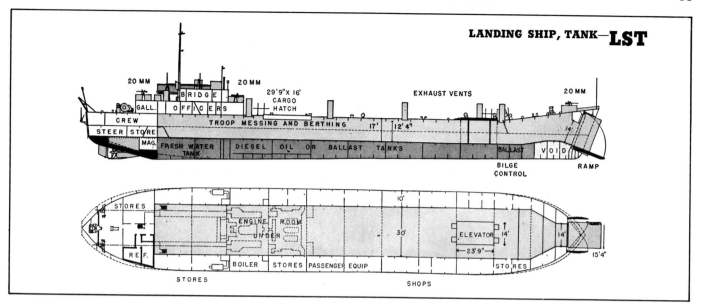

Regardless of its origins, Niedermair produced the basic LST(2) design, which was completed and approved in record time.

Because the major U.S. shipyards were also engaged in building warships and merchant ships, a smaller yard, the Dravo Corporation in Pittsburgh, Pennsylvania, was selected as the lead LST yard and the USS *LST-1* was laid down on June 10, 1942. She was completed six months later – on December 14, 1942. The ship was 328 feet long, and had a beam of 50 feet; displacement was 4,080 tons full load with 2,100 tons of cargo, although for beaching, 500 tons was a more feasible load (i.e., eighteen 30-ton tanks or an equivalent in other vehicles and cargo). Vehicles could be parked on the upper (main) deck or lower (tank) deck, which were connected by ramp in the early ships and by an elevator in the later units. There were two to six davits for landing craft, and an LCT could be carried on the main deck. In addition to a crew of some 210, the LSTs could accommodate 160 troops. Self-defense was provided by up to seven 40-mm guns and six 20-mm guns in the U.S. ships, while those that served with the British had a 12-pounder and six 20-mm guns. Diesel engines

drove the ships at a maximum speed of 11.6 knots.

The pioneer *LST-1* would participate in the invasions of Sicily and Salerno in 1943, and Anzio and Normandy in 1944. Many more ships followed – by 1943 there were 1,152 LSTs under contract in U.S. shipyards (with 101 being cancelled because of shifting priorities). Of the 1,052 ships actually completed, 113 were transferred to Britain and four more were turned over to the Greek Navy. The definitive LST(2) design first saw combat in the Solomons and in Sicily in 1943.

There were many LSTs – but never enough. There were constant problems over the allocation of LSTs. The U.S. Navy – which controlled their construction – wanted them for the Pacific campaigns; General Marshall, the U.S. Army Chief of Staff, wanted them for an assault on the French coast; Churchill wanted them for peripheral operations, in the Mediterranean, Aegean, and Norway, to help keep the pressure on Germany until the French coast could be assaulted.

British leaders felt that the Americans were using their control of the LST program to dictate Allied policy. To quote Churchill again, in a telegram to Marshall on April 16, 1944, discus-

Below: The *LST-229* at sea carrying an LCT on her main deck; a pair of LCVPs are on davits alongside the low stern superstructure. The LSTs were invaluable for Anglo-American landings in Europe and the Pacific. Only these ships could effectively carry large numbers of tanks and other vehicles to the beachhead early in a landing operation. (U.S. Navy)

sing the strategy for the Italian campaign and the forthcoming landings in Normandy and southern France:

> "The whole of this difficult [strategy] question only arises out of the absurd shortage of the L.S.T.s. How it is that the plans of two great empires like Britain and the United States should be so much hamstrung and limited by a hundred or two of the particular vessels will never be understood by history. I am deeply concerned at the strong disinclination of the American Government even to keep the manufacture of L.S.T.s at its full height so as to give to us to help you in the war against Japan. The absence of these special vessels may limit our whole war effort on your left flank, and I fear we shall be accused unjustly of not doing our best, as we are resolved to do."[9]

Page after page of Churchill's six-volume history of World War II carries references to LSTs, as do his personal papers. Again commenting on American control of LSTs, Churchill wrote:

> "Had we known they intended to do this, we would have built our portion of L.S.T.s rather than concentrate upon other things for the common interest, such as anti-U-boat craft of all kinds and later the materials for synthetic harbours [at Normandy]. Of these they have had the benefit, and they ought not to use their monopoly resulting from a proper parcelling out of [shipyard] production against us in an extraneous manner."[10]

Reluctantly, in response to the problems of LST allocation, the British initiated their own, small LST production with the LST(3) design. No diesel engines were available in Britain or from the United States, and there was a shortage of ship welding facilities in British and Canadian shipyards. As a result, the LST(3) had standard steam reciprocating engines (as were being installed in corvettes and frigates), and were largely riveted, resulting in larger, deeper draft, and slower landing ships without any increase in payload. Only 64 LST(3)s

were built in British and Canadian yards for naval service, those being completed in 1944–45.

During the war the LSTs demonstrated a remarkable capacity to absorb damage and survive. Despite the sobriquet "Large Slow Target," which was bestowed by irreverent crew members, the LSTs suffered few losses in proportion to their numbers. Their structural arrangement provided unusual strength and buoyancy. Of the 1,052 American-built LSTs, most of which were in combat, only 26 were lost to enemy action and another thirteen were victims of weather, groundings, or accidents. None of the British LSTs was lost.

The LSTs also proved to be highly versatile. In the basic configuration, they were used as hospital ships (on D-Day at Normandy, LSTs brought 41,035 wounded men back across the English Channel), for providing ammunition to battleships, for carrying railroad rolling stock (on rails fitted in the tank deck), and to launch light observation aircraft (fitted with flight decks or the Brodie aircraft launch/recovery system). Other LSTs became repair ships for battle damage (ARB), landing craft (ARL), aircraft (ARV-A), and aircraft engines (ARV-E). The unofficial designation LST(M) was used for LSTs modified into "mother ships" to support small landing craft during landings. These had Quonset huts erected on their main deck to house 40 officers, and bunks fitted in the tank deck for 200 enlisted men to operate and support landing craft. A bakery, sixteen refrigeration boxes for provisions, extra distilling units, and other facilities were fitted in these ships.

Two of the British LSTs were converted to headquarters ships (designated LSH – see below).

Although the LCT and LST became the critical landing craft of the Allied forces in World War II, several intermediate size landing craft were developed and had an important place in the history of amphibious warfare.

The designation LCI was used for Landing Craft Infantry. The British built the small LCI(S), a wooden-hull raiding boat, 105 feet long, displacing 100 tons loaded. The LCI(S) carried 102 troops, who came ashore over four bow ramps.

Unrelated in concept and design was the U.S. LCI(L) – for large. A larger craft, 158½ feet long, displacing 380 tons, it carried 200 troops or 75 tons of cargo, and had an ocean-going capability. More than a thousand of these craft were ordered. Of these, 164 were modified to provide close-in fire support for landings. The LCI(G) gunboats had one or two 40-mm guns, several 20-mm guns, and small rocket-launchers fitted; the LCI(M) mortar craft had 40-mm and 20-mm guns plus three 4.2-inch (105-mm) mortars, the largest in U.S. service; and the LCI(R) rocket craft, six 5-inch rocket-launchers plus the guns.

Another 130 LCI(L)s were more extensively converted to support craft and redesignated LCS(L). These units had a 3-inch or twin 40-mm gun mount fitted forward, a second twin 40 forward of the bridge, and a third twin 40 aft, plus 20-mm guns and small rocket-launchers. Small and relatively maneuverable, the LCI/LCS craft could steam up to the beaches with the troop-carrying craft, providing truly close-in support.

The British developed their own style of landing craft gunboats with various LCG designations. The LCG(M) were the medium craft, 154½ feet long, carrying a pair of Army 17- or 25-pounder guns plus machine-guns. The LCG(L) was larger, 192 feet, displacing 500 tons loaded, with an armament of two 4.7-inch naval quick-firing guns. The latter were converted LCT(3)s. Another LCT(3) conversion was the LCF or "flak" boat armed with four or eight 2-pounder single pom-poms plus several 20-mm guns.

The LCTs continued to increase in size with successive series until the U.S.-built LCT(7) became a "ship." This 203½-foot, 1,095-ton ship could carry five medium tanks or six LVTs in an open tank deck. Several hundred of these diminutive LSTs were built with the designation LSM for Landing Ship Medium. The flexibility of landing craft designs was demonstrated when twelve LSMs were converted to LSM(R) rocket ships, with a 5-inch gun installed aft and up to 85 automatic rocket-launchers fitted on the covered-over well deck. Subsequently, an improved LSM(R) was built with the hull and propulsion of the LSM, but with the superstructure aft and 20 continuous-

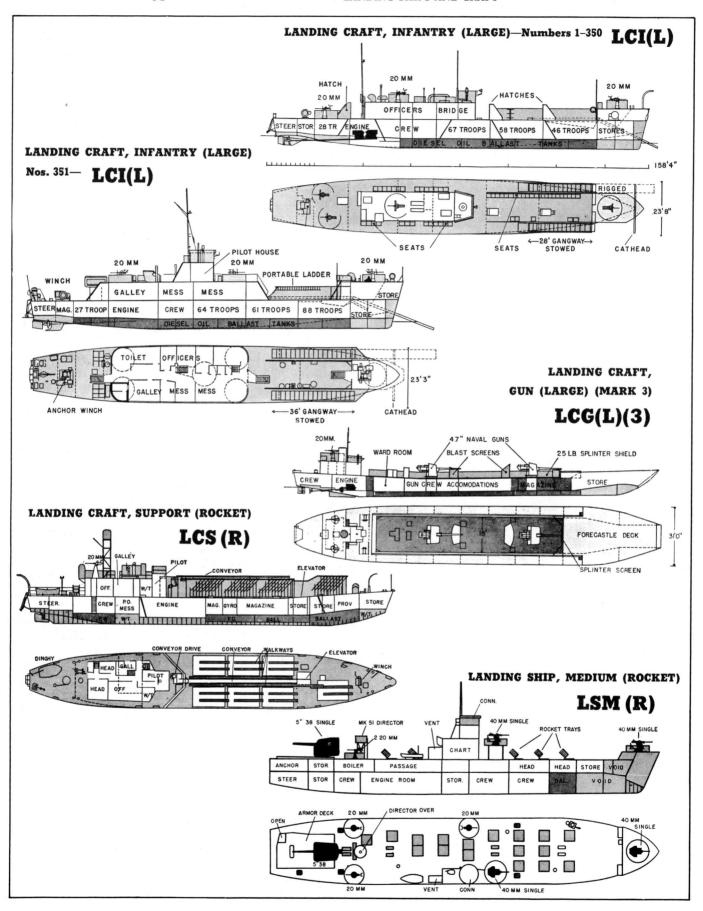

LANDING CRAFT, INFANTRY (LARGE)—Numbers 1-350 LCI(L)

LANDING CRAFT, INFANTRY (LARGE)
Nos. 351— LCI(L)

LANDING CRAFT,
GUN (LARGE) (MARK 3)
LCG(L)(3)

LANDING CRAFT, SUPPORT (ROCKET)
LCS (R)

LANDING SHIP, MEDIUM (ROCKET)
LSM (R)

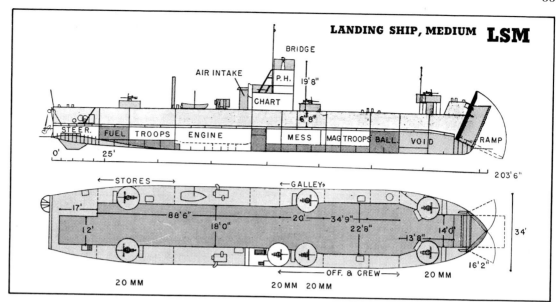

LANDING SHIP, MEDIUM **LSM**

Right: The LCT(7) design was redesignated landing ship medium (LSM) during construction. The *LSM-44* shown here off Iwo Jima carrying Marine casualties to a hospital ship, was one of 558 units built to this design. The LSMs had a displacement of 885 tons with a length of 203½ feet. Several were armed with rockets to support landing operations and were designated LSM(R). (U.S. Navy)

Right: The British *LCG(L)-939*, converted from an LCT(4), was typical of the large number of landing ships and craft converted by the British and U.S. navies to provide close-in fire support for amphibious landings. This craft, fitted with a ship's bow, had two 4.7-inch guns and seven 20-mm single mounts, the latter subsequently replaced by twin mountings. The 4.7-inch weapons were taken from destroyers. (IWM)

Opposite page, top: A stern view of a landing ship dock with the stern ramp lowered shows the docking well, with a pair of LCMs about to back out. (Another LCM is alongside.) Note the trucks parked on the removable superdeck. The United States built LSDs as well as LSTs for the Royal Navy to free British shipyards for the construction of anti-submarine/escort ships. (U.S. Navy)

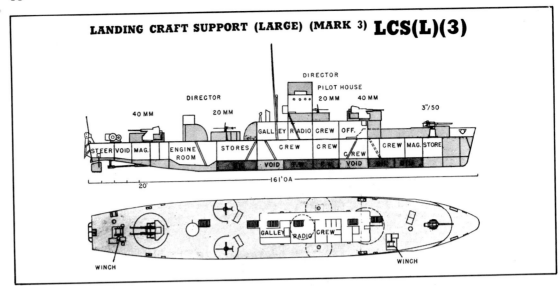

LANDING CRAFT SUPPORT (LARGE) (MARK 3) **LCS(L)(3)**

Right: The U.S. Navy AKA and APA amphibious ships carried numerous LCMs and LCVPs for landing troops and material. This view of the bow of the USS *Matthews* (AKA-96) shows LCVPs "nested" in LCMs stowed atop the ship's forward cargo holds. Booms lift the landing craft over the side and load them with cargo. The *Matthews* and her sister ships displaced 12,800 tons and were 459¼ feet long, with steam turbines driving them at 16 knots. (U.S. Navy)

Below: Of major importance in amphibious operations were the large troop and cargo carriers. This is the Royal Navy's LSI(L) *Glengyle* entering Malta's Grand Harbor. She could carry 700 troops; two sister ships could each lift 1,090. The U.S. Navy's equivalent ships were the attack transports (APA) and attack cargo ships (AKA), of which hundreds were built. The typical Victory-design APA could carry 1,560 troops. (IWM)

loading 5-inch rocket-launchers fitted forward, supplemented by a 5-inch gun mount and four 4.2-inch mortars.

The British converted several smaller classes of landing ships to the specialized rocket-firing role as this means of beach bombardment would prove highly effective. Although rockets lacked the accuracy and bunker-smashing capability of naval guns in direct fire, rockets could saturate a beach area to force defending troops to keep under cover until the assaulting troops were ashore. (War-built LSM(R)s served in the U.S. Navy during the Vietnam conflict.)

THE "BIG BOYS"

The largest of the amphibious ships, which carried the bulk of the troops and cargoes for amphibious assaults, were converted liners and merchant ships. In the Royal Navy these were designated landing ship infantry (LSI), with suffixes indicating the size. In the U.S. Navy these were the attack transports (APA) and attack cargo ships (AKA).

The largest of the British LSIs could carry a thousand or more troops plus several davit-mounted LCAs. The most capable ships were the so-called "Glen" conversions, the sister ships *Glenearn, Glengyle, Glenroy,* and *Breconshire,* all requisitioned from mercantile service in 1939. Each of the ships, 507 feet long with a gross of 9,800 tons, could load three LCMs and 24 LCAs, making a significant contribution to an assault force.

In addition to the large number of merchant ships taken in hand for permanent or temporary conversion to LSIs, the British obtained thirteen cargo hulls built in the United States and completed them as transports.

The U.S. Navy similarly acquired a variety of merchant ships for the APA and AKA roles, followed by large numbers of ships built specifically for these roles. More than three hundred ships were built specifically for the APA and AKA roles and would carry the bulk of the troops and cargoes for the Pacific assaults.

LANDING CRAFT CARRYING SHIPS

As noted above, the British LSIs and the American AKAs and APAs differed from "straight" cargo ships and troop transports because they were not pier-to-pier carriers, but could unload their troops and cargoes into landing craft in the assault area. Both types had davits for LCVPs and LCPs, and booms to unload the larger medium landing craft (LCM). But they could not accommodate enough

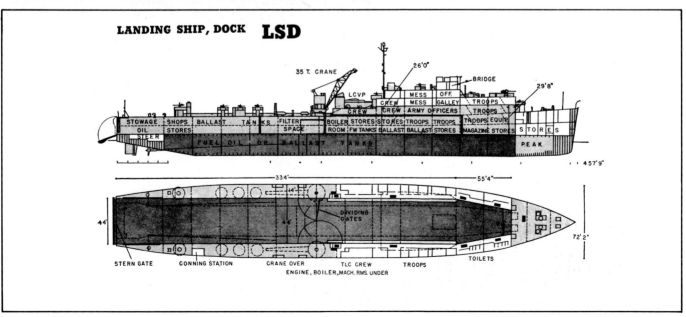

landing craft and amphibious tractors for the numbers of troops and amount of cargo needed in large-scale invasions.

The answer was the docking-well ship. These ships used the floating dry dock concept, whereby a floating dock could flood ballast tanks, be lowered into the water, and have ships float in or out. The new Landing Ship Dock (LSD) design was a large, non-beaching amphibious ship (457¾ feet long, displacing 8,700 tons full load), with a docking well 252 feet long and 44 feet wide. The ships could each transport two or three loaded LCTs (depending upon series) or 36 loaded LCM(3)s in the docking well, plus cargo and troops internally, and vehicles could be carried on a removable super deck fitted above the docking well. With the additional deck, instead of landing craft an LSD could carry the impressive total of 90

LVTs or about 110 wheeled DUKW vehicles. (The DUKW was an Army-developed amphibious truck – see Chapter 8.)

Once in the amphibious area, previously loaded landing craft could be floated out from the stern of the LSD, or empty craft carried by the ship could come alongside an AKA or APA and take on cargo or troops.

All war-built LSDs were constructed in the United States, with the preliminary design being done by the Bureau of Ships, with British input, in November 1941. Seven of the 27 ships ordered were built for the Royal Navy (with the British designation APM being used for mechanized artillery transport). The first of these ships to enter service was the USS *Ashland* (LSD-1), commissioned in June 1943. Starting that September, she participated in the landings on Baker Island, Tarawa,

Right: Among the most flexible of the amphibious ships built for the British and U.S. Navies during World War II was the landing ship dock (LSD). The *Comstock* (LSD-19), shown here after World War II, could accommodate a variety of landing craft or vehicles in the long docking well; the funnels and cranes are outboard of the well, which has a superdeck for vehicles installed. The *LCU-1481* shown alongside is a post-war version of the LCT. (U.S. Navy)

Kwajalein, Eniwetok, Saipan, Tinian, Leyte, and Iwo Jima.

In those operations she and her sister ships transported landing craft and LVTs, and once in the assault area served as tender and repairs ships for the small craft.

The British did produce four similar though smaller ships – two Landing Ships Carrier (LSC) and two Landing Ships Stern-chute (LSS). They were converted to carry nine or 21 LCM(3)s. Four other merchant ships converted while under construction to Landing Ship Gantry (LSG). These were larger landing craft carriers (483 feet, 16,750 tons loaded) which could stow fifteen loaded LCM(1)s and off-load them by overhead gantry cranes.

While the above-described amphibious ships carried landing craft and, in the case of the LSDs, amphibious tractors, the U.S. Navy also built six large "amphibs" with the designation Landing Ship Vehicle (LSV). These ships, just over 450 feet long, displacing some 8,100 to 9,000 tons full load, had an internal ramp system for carrying LVTs and DUKWs, which were unloaded over a stern ramp. The ships were also among the fastest amphibious ships in service, being rated at 19.5 knots.

Each LSV could accommodate some 50 vehicles and had accommodations for 800 troops. Although a successful design, these ships lacked the flexibility of the docking-well ships. (After the war five LSVs were redesignated as mine warfare command and support ships (MCS), but only two were actually converted to support small minesweepers and helicopters, and they were not successful in that role.)

The development of these landing craft carrying ships introduced a new element of versatility to amphibious operations, which made them valuable in landings, for their small craft were needed even when LSTs and LSMs as well as large numbers of amphibious vehicles were available.

AMPHIBIOUS FLAGSHIPS

The ill-fated British expedition to assault Dakar in 1940 and the Anglo-American landings in North Africa in November 1942 demonstrated the need for specialized flagships to accommodate the amphibious force commander, the landing force commander, and their staffs.

For example, in the North Africa operation, Rear Admiral H. K. Hewitt, commander of the Western Task Force, which landed troops on Morocco's Atlantic coast, flew his flag in the heavy cruiser *Augusta*. The warship, which carried two rear admirals and an Army major general and their staffs, was fitted with additional radios and extra bunks. But there were still far too few radio circuits for so large an operation, and the *Augusta* was so crowded that the staffs could hardly carry out their tasks. Most important, the embarked staffs were often required at one location just as the ship's

8-inch guns were needed elsewhere for fire support. As Admiral Hewitt stated in his after-action report:

"No ship of the Western Naval Task Force was suited to be a headquarters ship due to the small space alloted to communications equipment and personnel. The Torch Operation clearly demonstrates that a headquarters ship with adequate communications facilities is essential to amphibious operations."

The British and U.S. Navies were already working to solve this problem. In the Dakar operation the naval and ground commanders were in different ships, which had other responsibilities as well as serving as flagships (see Chapter 4). Also, the staff of the British ground force commander, General Irwin, had one typewriter in his flagship with which to make 200 copies of the 140-page operational order!

In March 1942 – eight months before "Torch" – the Admiralty had ordered the conversion of a 9,100-ton armed merchant cruiser, HMS *Bolulo*, to the first specially configured amphibious flagship. For her new role the British established the designation Landing Ship Headquarters (LSH).

The *Bolulo*'s new communications suite featured separate radio networks for air, ground, and naval units, with joint channels provided for the overall coordination of an amphibious operation. To minimize electromagnetic interference, the ship's many transmitters were located aft and her even more numerous receivers were well forward. The *Bolulo* had separate operations rooms for the different service staffs, and one for interservice operations. The ship also carried several landing craft to take the ground force commander and his staff ashore.

As an LSH the *Bolulo* had a complement of 300 plus about 200 officers and men of the embarked staffs. The ship's ability to handle high volumes of information led to her being assigned to support Prime Minister Churchill at Casablanca during his January 1943 meeting with President Roosevelt.

In addition to the *Bolulo*, the Royal Navy converted three other merchant ships to the LSH role, with several destroyers, frigates, and gunboats being temporarily pressed into service as LSHs. Because the British command ships were smaller than their American counterparts, the Royal Navy used separate ships for controlling aircraft in the amphibious area. With the designation Landing Ship Fighter Direction (LSF), several LST(2)s and auxiliary anti-aircraft ships were converted to this role.

The U.S. Navy worked out plans for amphibious command ships in 1942, the first ships being approved early the following year, with the designation AGC for amphibious force flagship.[11] A

Far left: HMS *Daffodil* (shown here) and her sister ship *Princess Iris* were train ferries converted to landing ship stern chute (LSS) to carry small landing craft for amphibious assaults. Built in 1917, the ships were 2,680 tons *gross* with a length of 363½ feet. In the LSS role the landing craft were carried in a long well deck and unloaded through a stern chute. (IWM)

Left: HMS *Bulolo* was the first British landing ship headquarters (LSH). Converted in 1942 from an armed merchant cruiser, the *Bulolo* could accommodate 260 command and staff personnel. Her role as a headquarters ship is readily evident from the large number of radio aerials; six LCP(L)s were carried in davits. The ship's first amphibious operation was with the Eastern Task Force of the North Africa landings in November 1942. King George VI was on board when this photograph was taken. (IWM)

Right: Radio operators from the Royal Navy, Royal Air Force, and Army work side by side in a British headquarters ship. Elsewhere in the ship combined planning, intelligence, logistics, and operational staffs could plan and execute amphibious landings – the most complex of all military operations. In addition to the large LSH conversions the Royal Navy also operated several modified escort destroyers and frigates in the LSH(S) role. (IWM)

Opposite page, top: The LST(1) *Boxer* was converted in 1944 to a landing ship fighter direction (LSF), one of six LSTs as well as four merchant ships reconfigured to this role. The fighter direction ships were used to detect approaching hostile aircraft and vector defending fighters to intercept them. While various warships had similar capabilities, they could not be spared for this role in the amphibious assault area. (IWM)

Opposite page, centre: The USS *Ancon* (AGC-4) was the first U.S. amphibious force flagship to enter service. Built in 1938 and used as an Army and then Navy troop transport (AP-66), she displaced 13,144 tons in naval service with a length of 493 feet. She was used in the 1942 North Africa landings and then converted to an AGC in early 1943. Serving in the Mediterranean, at Normandy, and in the Pacific, the *Ancon* was Press ship for the Japanese surrender in Tokyo Bay in September 1945. (U.S. Navy)

Opposite page, bottom: The U.S. Navy built and converted 23 ships to amphibious force flagships (AGC). The *Adirondack* (AGC-15) was one of fifteen C2-series cargo ships completed to an AGC configuration with extensive flag accommodation and communications gear. These ships displaced 12,800 to some 15,000 tons and were 459½ feet long. Like most large U.S. amphibious ships, they generally carried a 5-inch gun forward and aft plus 40-mm and 20-mm anti-aircraft weapons. (U.S. Navy)

total of fifteen single-screw, C-2 merchant ships being built under contract to the Maritime Commission were tagged for the AGC role during the war. But to meet the flagship need while the ex-merchant ships were being completed, the large, 14,150-ton Army-operated passenger ship *Ancon* was taken in hand for conversion (to be the AGC-4). The 453-foot ship was converted during the winter of 1942 (having participated in "Torch" as a Navy transport).

The *Ancon*'s combat debut came in July 1943 off Sicily, where she was the flagship of Rear Admiral A. G. Kirk, commander Task Force 85, and Major General Omar O. Bradley, commander of the Army's II Corps. The *Ancon* then served at the Salerno landings in September 1943 as flagship of newly promoted Vice Admiral Hewitt, whose earlier report had helped to accelerate the AGC program. Also on board at Salerno was Lieutenant General Mark Clark, commanding the U.S. Fifth Army.

It was the Salerno landing that brought the amphibious flagship concept to the attention of historian Samuel Eliot Morison, who mistakenly reported that the new ship type had been "improvised for Admiral Hewitt in the Salerno operation." Despite this misunderstanding of the *Ancon*'s origins, Morison was correct in his conclusion that the new ship type had come about because,

> ". . . the network of communications in modern amphibious warfare had become so vast and complicated, and the officers and men necessary to staff amphibious force headquarters so numerous, that no ordinary combatant or auxiliary ship could hold them."[12]

The fifteen C-2 merchant hulls completed as U.S. Navy amphibious force flagships were of two similar sub-types. All were 459 feet long and displaced about 12,800 tons full load. The exact number of officers and men on board varied with the operation and the role of the embarked admirals and generals. Most of the C-2 AGCs had staff accommodations for approximately 55 officers and 580 enlisted men, but could embark more when necessary. Each ship carried a few LCVPs or similar-size craft to carry commanders ashore, and had a defensive armament of two 5-inch guns plus several 40-mm and 20-mm anti-aircraft guns. But their main battery was the various operations rooms and various communications spaces. In 1944 the "comm gear" in a typical AGC consisted of 30 general-purpose transmitters (high to low frequency), four very-high-frequency receiver-transmitters, 70 general-purpose receivers (high to low frequency), and 44 radio-telegraph positions.

The first of the C-2 design AGCs to join the fleet was the *Rocky Mount* (AGC-3), commissioned in October 1943. Together with her sister ship *Appalachian* (AGC-1), the *Rocky Mount* went into action for the first time in the January 1944 assault on Kwajalein atoll in the Marshall Islands, where she served as flagship for Rear Admiral Richmond Kelly Turner, commander of the amphibious force.

As additional AGCs joined the fleet it was commonplace for several ships to participate in the same operation, and for the AGCs to take on special duties. In the February 1945 assault on Iwo Jima, for example, the *Estes* (AGC-12) was assigned to control the underwater demolition operations and pre-assault bombardment in addition to other functions, while the *Eldorado* (AGC-11) served as then Vice Admiral Turner's flagship for the assault and headquarters for U.S. war correspondents, providing long-range communications for news broadcasts back to the United States. Also at Iwo Jima was the command ship *Biscayne* (AGC-18), a converted seaplane tender,

tasked with coordinating the destroyer screen protecting the entire invasion force. In the next major assault, the Okinawa operation, a total of five AGCs participated.

The AGC facilities also made them useful for certain non-combat activities. In January 1945 the *Catoctin* (AGC-5) steamed from the Mediterranean through the Dardanelles into the Black Sea, and up to the Soviet port of Sevastopol to serve as an advanced headquarters for the Yalta conference. During the meeting the AGC provided communication support for President Roosevelt, and her crew provided transportation, canteen, hospital, and dental services for the U.S. delegation ashore.

There was one other *Navy* AGC in the war, the *Biscayne*. She was one of 35 *Barnegat*-class seaplane tenders (AVP) built during the war. These were $310\frac{2}{3}$-foot, 1,695-ton ships. The *Biscayne* was completed in 1941 as the AVP-11 and serviced seaplanes in Atlantic and North African waters. In May 1943, while at Mers-el-Kebir, Algeria, she was converted to a command ship (although not redesignated as the AGC-18 until October 1944). The *Biscayne* served in the flagship role for the invasions of Sicily, Salerno, Anzio, Southern France, Iwo Jima, and Okinawa.

In addition to the above seventeen Navy amphibious flagships, six U.S. Coast Guard amphibious command ships served in World War II. These were large, 327-foot Secretary-class cutters built between 1935 and 1937. During the war the Coast Guard became a part of the Navy and these ships were employed as anti-submarine escorts early in the war, but were converted to an AGC configuation to meet the Navy's growing demand for amphibious flagships.

One of the cutters, the *Duane*, was given a Navy designation (AGC-6) in anticipation of being taken over by the Navy. But neither the *Duane* nor five sister ships, which retained their Coast Guard gunboat designations, were ever transferred to the Navy. The six cutters had Coast Guard captains and crews throughout the war who jealously guarded the separate status of their ships. The *Duane* receiving an AGC designation touched a sore spot and led to the following memorandum from the Chief of Naval Operations to the Commander Amphibious Force Training Command of the U.S. Atlantic Fleet:

"Attention is invited to the status of the *Duane*. It is a Coast Guard vessel, owned and manned by the Coast Guard. However, it operates under the Navy. In order to avoid any misunderstanding, it should be called the CGC *Duane*."[13]

These amphibious force flagships served as the command ships for the massive armadas of amphibious and landing ships and craft assembling for the assaults being planned in the Atlantic and Pacific theaters.

8.
THE MEDITERRANEAN

ASSAULT ON SICILY

One of the objectives of Operation "Torch" was to relieve German pressure on the Soviet Union. The British had promised Stalin that they would try to keep the Germans occupied in the hope that the North African landings would force the Germans to delay sending more divisions to the Russian front. A secondary purpose of the "Torch" landings was to continue draining German resources while planning the major invasion of Europe. From the British viewpoint the success of "Torch" and subsequent ousting of the Germans from North Africa would lead to the invasion of Sicily as a prelude to landings in Italy. This would, in turn, lead to a drive up the "boot" and the liberation of the Italians.

The British plan was not well received by the Americans, who did not want to devote more effort to the Mediterranean, which they considered the secondary front. The Americans wanted to go after the Germans directly and not waste time fighting Italy, their second-rate ally.

A meeting in Casablanca in January 1943 of President Roosevelt and Prime Minister Churchill with their military staffs brought U.S. agreement, however, that the momentum gained by such success as "Torch" should not be allowed to dissipate. Therefore, if the Allies were not ready for a main landing in France in 1943, another invasion elsewhere on the European mainland – perhaps Italy – would be in order.

The Allied leaders also agreed that the Italians were nearly ready to overthrow their dictator, Benito Mussolini, and would welcome a combined U.S.-British invasion. American agreement to the joint operation was also contingent on a limited commitment of men and supplies that would not affect the planned cross-Channel invasion, now delayed from 1943 to 1944.

For the August 1943 invasion of Sicily, General Eisenhower, who had commanded the North African invasion, was given the position of Supreme Allied Commander. He had three British sub-commanders: Admiral Cunningham, again his naval commander; General Harold Alexander, head of ground forces; and Air Chief Marshal Tedder, again his air commander. Three task forces would cover the British and American landing forces, provide landing forces – with British and Canadian troops – for operations on the south eastern tip of Sicily, and an American task force, with troops under the redoubtable Lieutenant General George Patton, to strike the southern shore. The invasion of Sicily was given the codename "Husky." It was an appropriate name for the biggest amphibious operation of the war in terms of area covered and the number of vehicles used.

Axis troops in Sicily numbered some 405,000 men – 315,000 Italians and 90,000 Germans. The Allied force counted only 180,000 U.S. and British troops together with contingents from Canada, Poland, France, Belgium, Norway, Greece, the Netherlands, and Brazil. The principal Allied units were the U.S. 1st, 3rd, and 45th Infantry Divisions, with portions of the 9th Infantry Division, and the 2nd Armored Division; the British 5th, 50th, and 51st Infantry Divisions, the 231st Infantry Brigade, 4th and 23rd Armoured Brigades, and 3rd, 40th, and 41st Royal Marine Commandos; and the Canadian 1st Infantry Division and 1st Armored Brigade – the largest Allied force yet assembled in the conflict. Indeed, the equivalent of approximately seven combat divisions would be afloat at one time.

They sailed for Sicily in some 2,500 ships and landing craft. The landing ships carried 600 tanks, 14,000 other vehicles, and 1,800 guns, over which flew a vast aerial cover of 4,000 aircraft from British carriers and from airfields in North Africa.

Several new types of amphibious ships made their appearance during "Husky," including purpose-built LSTs, the smaller LCTs, and LCIs, and a peculiar landing vehicle called the DUKW – or "duck" – which could not only operate in the water (through the use of a single screw mounted below its rear hull), but also wade ashore on six wheels, carrying troops or 2½ tons of material.

By mid-summer 1943, American production of the all-important LSTs had reached its stride in time for the invasion of Sicily. The LST, with a flat bottom and large bow doors, would greatly facilitate sea-to-shore movement of heavy vehicles and supplies. The number of these valuable LSTs was, however, limited. Hundreds of conventional transports and cargo ships were also employed, with their troops unloading into conventional launching craft and "ducks." Pontoon

2½-TON, 6 × 6, AMPHIBIAN TRUCK   DUKW

CARGO SPACE 6'9 3/4"
12'5"
8'0"
31'0" OA
21'3 3/4" LIFT SPACING
COLLAPSIBLE HOOD   CANVAS COVER
5'09/16"   7'1 3/16"   5'9 3/4"
18 1/2" LOADED   RUDDER PROPELLER
13'8" WB

bridges were included in the assault force to help unload ships onto the shallow beaches that could keep the LSTs from reaching a proper grounding distance from the shore.

THE INVASION

A storm on July 9, the day before the planned invasion, made the approach of the main assault force hazardous. The Italians, who had nervously waited for the approaching fleet, decided the landings would not take place and retired from their primary defensive positions, but the storm abated sufficiently for the landings to commence nearly on schedule.

The first landings by General Patton's Seventh Army in the Gulf of Gela and the British Eighth Army, under Lieutenant-General Montgomery, south of Syracuse, met with little opposition. While the Italian soldiers remained quiet, their German allies began to move toward the beaches in company with air support from the *Luftwaffe* and a few units of the Italian *Regia Aeronautica*. (The total Axis aircraft available was about 1,600, against the 4,000 planes available to the Allies.)

Supported by aircraft from U.S. bases in North Africa and British carriers offshore, the landing forces secured their respective beaches with little opposition and moved inland. By sunrise on the 10th, all the troops and vehicles of the assault force were ashore. Daylight brought attacks by German dive bombers, resulting in intensive aerial combat.

One of the main successes of "Husky" was the new amphibious ships and craft, especially the LSTs and DUKWs, which greatly reduced time and problems in bringing troops and heavy vehicles to shore. The men and weapons arrived so quickly that the beach teams could not arrange proper supply depots fast enough.

"Husky" also provided a chance for naval gunfire to prove its worth in support of landing operations. Patton was himself given a first-hand demonstration on July 12 while observing the action in Gela. The General watched a U.S. Navy ensign assigned to him call down gunfire from cruisers offshore against German tanks bearing down on units of Patton's infantry. Patton became an instant advocate as he cheered the big guns. (On the previous day the U.S. destroyer *Cowie* (DD-632) was standing offshore providing fire support when German tanks attacked the 180th Regimental Combat Team near the beachhead. The *Cowie* turned her 5-inch guns on the Tiger tanks and won history's first destroyer-versus-tank engagement.)

While the energetic Patton pushed his troops toward their assigned objective of Palermo on the northern Sicilian coast, Montgomery's Eighth Army secured Syracuse, but bogged down at Catania on the way to Messina, which guards the strait between Sicily and mainland Italy. Rugged terrain inhibited British movement while providing the Germans with defensive positions. Patton

Above: American soldiers at a Sicily beachhhead unload supplies from LCTs into DUKWs for movement inland. The Army used the DUKW extensively; it was not popular with the U.S. Marine Corps, which preferred the LVT-series amphibious tractors or "Alligators" and "Buffalos." Soldiers liked the land mobility of the DUKW; the Marines preferred the light protection of the LVT which was more suitable for assault landings although it had limited shore mobility. (U.S. Army)

reached his objective of Palermo on July 22, but the British did not arrive at Messina until August 17.

The delay of the British in reaching Palermo and intelligent decisions by the Axis commanders permitted a successful withdrawal of German and Italian troops across the two-mile-wide Strait of Messina. Although the distance was shorter than the English Channel at Dunkirk, American naval historian Samuel Eliot Morison believed that the evacuation from Sicily was "in a class with Dunkirk, Guadalcanal, and Kiska" – the two latter being Japanese operations. According to Morison, "the main reasons for success [of the Messina evacuation] were long practice in the reverse direction and the Allies' failure to make any serious attempts to stop it."[1] Despite intensive U.S. and British air attacks – the Allied air forces had been trying to bomb out the Messina train ferries for months – the Germans were able to evacuate 39,569 troops (including 4,444 wounded), 47 tanks, 94 heavy guns, 9,605 vehicles, more than 2,000 tons of ammunition, and much other gear – all in six days and seven nights. The

subsequent fighting in Italy would cost the Allies more because of this remarkable German success. The Italians were able to bring 62,000 troops, 41 artillery pieces, 227 vehicles, and twelve mules across the Strait before the Allies could belatedly halt the evacuation.

The Sicily landings demonstrated that massive amphibious landings were practicable and that using *tactical* surprise coupled with massive air and naval support could successfully assault defended beaches.

The conquest of Sicily paved the way for the invasion of the Italian mainland. From a strategic viewpoint the capture of Sicily marked the close of the struggle to expel Axis forces from North Africa and gain control of the Mediterranean for Allied naval operations. The decision to invade the Italian mainland initiated a new phase of the grand strategy, of which the invasion of France would be a later step. The decision to invade Europe initially through the Italian peninsula rather than across the English Channel was taken by Churchill and Roosevelt only after extensive debate.

Because of the light losses of landing craft

Top: The Salerno landings were heavily opposed by the Germans. This Spitfire VC, flown by the U.S. Army Air Forces, crashed on the beachhead at Paestum, near Salerno. The *LST-359* is in the background. At the Normandy landings U.S. gunfire spotters for warships offshore also flew land-based Spitfires. (U.S. Navy)

Above: Unique to the Royal Navy during the Anglo-American invasions of World War II were four monitors. These were shallow-draft bombardment ships, each armed with two 15-inch guns and eight 4-inch guns, plus lighter weapons. This is the *Roberts* firing; she supported the Salerno landings and subsequently the Normandy assault. (IWM)

during the Sicily assault and the poor showing made by Italian forces, the Allies immediately began preparations for a mainland landing in early September. The jump to the Italian mainland would be a two-pronged affair, with one Allied army crossing the Strait of Messina onto the "toe" of the Italian "boot," followed a day later by a major amphibious assault by another Allied army up the coast at Salerno.

"AVALANCHE": LANDING AT SALERNO

Having conquered Sicily and arrived at Messina across the Strait of Messina, the Allied leaders knew they must continue the push toward Rome. The ease of the victory in Sicily and rising discontent among the Italian populace foretold the end of Mussolini's regime. All that was needed was another push, this time toward the capital city. As before, the Americans were afraid that continued fighting in the south would detract from the main invasion, that of France in the coming year. The U.S. commanders also wanted better cooperation between air and ground forces in any future invasion in Italy.

Thus, agreement on the size of the invasion force – 30,000 British and 25,000 American troops in 600 ships – as well as a revamping of control of air support, again brought an Allied force, under the same commanders as in "Husky," to the shores of southern Italy in Operation "Avalanche."

The initial landing site was the Bay of Salerno, twenty miles south of Naples, primarily because it represented the northern limit for aircraft based in Sicily. Following quick rehearsals, the invasion fleet sailed from North Africa and landed on September 9, approximately two months after the invasion of Sicily. While the American Fifth Army, under Lieutenant General Mark Clark, landed at Salerno, the British Eighth Army struck Taranto. (This was the scene of a famous air raid by British carrier-based bombers in 1940 which, some hold, gave the Japanese the idea for their attack on Pearl Harbor.)

Although Mussolini's days as Italian dictator were almost at an end and many of his troops had joined the Allies – Italy had, in fact, withdrawn from the war on September 8 – the Germans fought hard against the invaders, trying to shore-up the sagging defense of the Axis alliance. Naval gunfire support was mainly responsible for beating the determined German defense which threatened the Allied bridgehead to Italy.

American aircraft of the Northwest African Strategic Air Force, under Lieutenant General Jimmy Doolittle of "Tokyo Raiders" fame, attacked Italian airfields, while the Northwest African Coastal Air Force, under Air Marshal Hugh P. Lloyd, shielded fleet convoys from lurking submarines. Air Marshal Arthur Coningham's Northwest African Tactical Air Force provided close air support in conjunction with American planes from Sicily. Five British aircraft carriers also provided air support for the Sicily operation.

The relative ease with which Sicily had been taken was not repeated as the Allies struggled to maintain their hold on the mainland. German attacks against the Anglo-American amphibious shipping and their mining of the Bay of Salerno indicated that the Germans intended to fight hard. They reinforced their beach defenses and forced many of the Italian troops still under their command to remain at their posts to meet the oncoming invasion.

Proceeded by minesweepers, U.S. assault teams headed for the beaches at Salerno on September 9. The main landings met little direct opposition, but by noon the German defense had mounted a counterattack with machine guns and tanks. A German gun battery struck *LST-357*, causing heavy casualties. Destroyers returned fire on the battery.

Another innovation in amphibious assault was introduced at Salerno – the "hedgerow" rocket support ship. The British had been experimenting with spigot mortars to fire bombardment rockets into an assault area. While limited in accuracy,

Above: U.S. soldiers, jeeps, and ambulances crowd the main deck of an LST en route to Anzio. Six LCVPs are hung in davits – two forward and four aft, alongside the ship's bridge. The six-davit LSTs carried 145 troops, with berthing for the troops in the sidewalls of the ships; ship and passenger officers were berthed in the superstructure; the two-davit LSTs carried 160 troops. (U.S. Navy)

the rockets could cause extensive casualties to unprotected personnel. When the commanders in the Mediterranean heard of the "hedgerow" experiments (there had been *one* test firing from a landing craft), they ordered five specially modified, rocket-equipped LCAs to North Africa to be included in the Salerno landing.

When the landing craft arrived at the staging port of Algiers no one knew of their significance and the launching gear was removed and the craft assigned to other duties. When their significance was discovered only two sets of "hedgerows" could be found. They were quickly installed in the *LCA 403* and *LCA 446*, neither of which had been strengthened to withstand launching the salvo of 60-pound rockets.

On August 29 a test firing was conducted. The blast of the rockets opened the sides of the *LCA 446* and she sank almost immediately; also damaged, the *LCA 403* struggled back to port. At 3:30 a.m. on the morning of September 9 the *LCA 403* fired her rockets from 40 yards off Red Beach in Salerno Bay. Twenty-three rockets hit the beach, some exploding a minefield. But the spigots were damaged and the crew, under enemy fire, attempted to make repairs. A second salvo was unsuccessful and the craft withdrew. Rockets, however, had proved their worth in amphibious assaults and would now be a part of future Allied assaults.

The following day brought intensified German air attacks, even though British fighters from the carriers did their best to turn them back, destroying twenty German aircraft.

The fighting at Salerno continued to intensify, and units of British X Corps, part of the main landing force with Clark's Fifth Army, found the going

especially rough on September 11, the Germans taking 1,500 prisoners, mostly British. The Germans gathered themselves for a massive counterattack to drive the invaders back into the sea. They nearly succeeded on September 13, having discovered a gap between the two Allied forces. British ships stood offshore to evacuate the Allied beachhead should Clark give that order.

The Americans and British gathered all the resources available to them, but in the end, it did not appear to be enough to contain the Germans. Clark ordered Major General Matthew Ridgeway to ready his 82nd Airborne Division for a night parachute drop on the night of September 13–14. Ridgeway sent in two battalions – 1,300 men jumping into the battle. On the 14th, another 2,100 men of the 82nd jumped to further bolster the Allied lines. The U.S. 509th Parachute Infantry Battalion contributed another 600 men to help the British X Corps. Also joining the effort were men whose normal assignments were supply, transport, and cooking, and this, coupled with air raids by U.S. land-based bombers, and gunfire from the ships offshore eventually dulled the German offensive to the point where the Salerno beachhead was officially declared secure by September 17. Although the Germans were satisfied they had not allowed the Allies another romp, as they had in Sicily, Operation "Avalanche" was generally a success for the British and American forces who eventually took the main objective, Naples, adding to Italian disenchantment with the war and with the Germans. At Taranto on September 9, British airborne troops sailed into the harbor aboard light cruisers and minelayers to be welcomed by the Italian people.

From September 9 until October 10, the Allies landed 200,000 men and 35,000 vehicles. Ahead was the next goal of the invasion – Rome.

ANZIO AND THE LIBERATION OF ROME

With the Allies firmly in southern Italy, the next objective was clear, the taking of the ancient city of Rome and a drive up the Italian "boot". The determined German defense throughout Operation "Avalanche" made progress up the Italian peninsula slow. But growing German indecision at the top levels – including Hitler – as how best to defend Italy and the Balkans eroded much of the battlefield advantage won by the German forces under the astute Field Marshal Albert Kesselring.

Hitler wanted to risk his troops in Italy without reinforcement or resupply. He was advised by the now legendary Rommel of North Africa fame to bring his remaining troops northward in an orderly retreat and stand fast to defend northern Italy under Rommel's unified command. But Kesselring's success at impeding the Allied advance made Hitler finally give complete control to Kesselring. He appointed him Commander-in-Chief, South-West (Army Group C) on November

21, 1943. Hitler's faith in Kesselring seemed initially justified, for by December, bad weather and adroit German tactics had all but stopped the Allies just north of Naples at the so-called Gustav Line. Spurred on by Churchill, the Allied command ordered a two-division assault behind German lines, to cut their communications with the troops facing the Allied armies. The Germans would then have to withdraw forces from the Gustav Line to counter the landing.

An immediate concern for the Anzio landing was the availability of landing craft – the perpetual problem of Anglo-American operations until after the Normandy landings. The Anzio landing would delay the dispatch of landing craft to England for preparation of the Normandy landings by about three weeks. At this time Normandy – Operation "Overlord" – was scheduled for May 5. The next date on which the phase of the moon and other factors would be satisfactory for the Normandy landings would be early June. At Churchill's urgings, the "Overlord" date would be postponed until early June, reducing the debate over Anzio.

The coastal town of Anzio on the Tyrrhenian Sea was the target of a landing by British and American troops on January 22, 1944. Thirty-three miles south of Rome, the Anzio landing was a back-door surprise to the German command. Significantly, the initial landing on January 22 – dubbed Operation "Shingle" – was at once a triumph and a disaster. Led by American Rangers, the British 1st Division and the American 3rd Infantry Division began the landings *at night*. A few minutes after 2 a.m. on the 22nd, the Rangers landed on the undefended beach just outside the Anzio harbor. A group of German engineers sent to Anzio to destroy a mole in the harbor were easily captured and the important port was secured. Minefields on each side of the city delayed troops from moving inland, but there was no active opposition to the landings.

The American general commanding the invasion troops, Major General J. P. Lucas, was conservative and overly pessimistic despite the unhampered landing of more than 36,000 troops and 3,000 vehicles, without casualty, in less than

Right: The British *LCT(R)-125* fires a salvo of 5-inch rockets. These converted LCT(2) and (3) landing craft could carry 792 or, 1,064 5-inch rockets, respectively. They were fired from stands of six launchers at a fixed 45° angle; their range was 3,500 yards. Fitted with a 79-pound warhead, the rockets were most effective in forcing defending troops to take cover. (IWM)

Below: A German shell explodes on the beachhead at Anzio, narrowly missing DUKW amphibious trucks carrying supplies and munitions ashore to Anglo-American troops. The landing of almost 69,000 Allied troops within a week was successful, with minimal opposition. However, timidity on the part of the American General commanding the landing gave the Germans time to marshal their defenses, a delay which cost many British and American lives. (U.S. Navy)

Above: U.S. LSTs unload supplies at Anzio to support the Anglo-American landings. Up to 1,900 tons of cargo could be carried (less for beaching operations). Up to six LCVPs could be accommodated in davits and an LCT(5) or (6) could be embarked while pontoon causeways (Rhinos) could be lashed to the sides of the ship. The tank deck of the LST(2) was 288 feet long and 30 feet wide, and was without obstructions. (U.S. Navy)

24 hours. And, with the port captured without damage, LSTs and others ships were rapidly unloading the sinews of war.

The troops slowly began moving inland. There were virtually no German troops between Anzio and the objective of Rome. The day following the landings the Germans began intensive air attacks while gales inflicted damage on landing craft and pontoon causeways. Still, the buildup continued against very light ground opposition.

After a week there were almost 69,000 U.S. and British troops ashore, the beachheads had been consolidated, and supplies were pouring ashore against minimal German interference except for the continuous and heavy *Luftwaffe* attacks. Still, General Lucas was cautious – far too cautious in the opinion of most historians and military analysts. As Lucas delayed, the Germans moved rapidly to bring major ground forces to block the invaders and to force them back into the sea. In the ensuing battles there was terrible carnage on both sides, but the Germans failed to dislodge the Allies.

The landings at Anzio were a classic use of amphibious forces to turn an enemy's flank. Churchill would telegraph Stalin, "Although the landing was a brilliant piece of work and achieved complete surprise, the advantage was lost and now it is a question of hard slogging."

After breaking out of the beachhead, the Allied armies faced the Germans at the ancient monastery of Monte Cassino. The Battle of Monte Cassino lasted from January to March 1944 and resulted in 52,000 Allied casualties. Finally, however, Kesselring had to pull his forces back when Cassino fell in May. As the Allied forces broke from Anzio and Cassino, the road to Rome lay open and on June 3, General Patton's tanks and troops entered the Eternal City.

The North African and Italian landings taught the Allies much, preparing them for the ultimate test: landing in France. The Americans felt comfortable with their doctrine of giving command of the operation to the naval task force leader until the troops were firmly established ashore. Then the ground forces commander would take over and the Navy would become a support force. The high degree of cooperation between British and U.S. participants also contributed to the overall success of the extensive landings in the Mediterranean. Knowledge of tactics and equipment was shared freely, as was the equipment itself. This spirit of cooperation toward a common goal was largely responsible for the ultimate success of the next large amphibious operation in Europe, Operation "Overlord."

While Churchill fully backed the cross-Channel assault, he also continued to see opportunities to assault the Germans on the flanks of Europe. With the fall of the Italian fascist government in September 1943, Churchill believed that two or three brigades of troops and sufficient LSTs to carry them would permit easy capture of the Italian-held island of Rhodes off the Turkish coast, and the opening of a route to the Dardanelles and into the Black Sea, establishing a southern water route to the Soviet Union. Disappointed, Churchill explained to a meeting of Dominion prime ministers that:

> "It was said that [the LSTs] were all required for the battle in Italy. In the event, many of the LST had been used for the build-up of the Strategic Air Force, which, though it was now doing excellent work, might well have been delayed three months in order to allow us to secure the rich prizes that were offered in the Aegean."[2]

But now "Overlord" had priority over all.

9.
"OVERLORD": THE GREATEST ASSAULT

AFTER their success in North Africa and Italy, the Allied leaders began the final planning and rehearsals for the invasion of France and the liberation of Europe. Initially, two invasions were considered, the main landings in north western France in Normandy and simultaneously a smaller landing in the southern part of the country, on the Mediterranean coast. A total of 36 Allied divisions would be available in the United States and England by mid-1944 for employment in the coming campaign, with another ten available after withdrawal from the Italian campaign.

The impetus to mount the cross-Channel invasion in Normandy with all possible forces would cause a delay in the southern operation. Plans for the main assault forged ahead as men and supplies poured into the limited area and ports of southern England. This geographical overloading soon created problems in maintaining any degree of secrecy, thereby providing more momentum to the projected landings. But geography would impose yet another, more important constraint on the coming cross-Channel invasion – the positioning of forces upon landing (see below).

Formal planning for the cross-Channel landing began in March 1943, with the appointment of Lieutenant-General F. E. Morgan as "Chief of Staff to the Supreme Allied Commander." While no Allied commander had yet been designated, Morgan, a veteran British tank commander, soon organized his COSSAC headquarters and with a small staff began drafting the necessary tons of paperwork to undertake what would be history's largest amphibious assault.

By January 1944, as Allied operations in Italy reached their peak, all the force commanders for the Normandy invasion were in Britain to begin final arrangements. Earlier, Churchill and Roosevelt had agreed that the nation providing the majority of the forces for the invasion would name the overall commander. Significantly, Churchill had already told Field Marshal Sir Alan Brooke that he would be commander of the cross-Channel invasion.

Most Americans assumed that General George C. Marshall, the U.S. Army Chief of Staff, would command but Marshall was surrounded by controversy because he was being mentioned for the Republican presidential nomination (as was General MacArthur) to run against Roosevelt in November 1944; if he were sent to Europe it could be seen as a political move by Roosevelt to destroy his possible candidacy.

Roosevelt told an obviously disappointed Marshall that he would remain as Chief of Staff of the Army. Marshall quoted Roosevelt as closing the discussion with: ". . . I didn't feel I could sleep at ease if you were out of Washington."[1]

The obvious choice to command the Anglo-American invasion would be Eisenhower. "Ike" had feared that if Marshall came to Europe he ("Ike") would be sent back to Washington; he let it be known that he would rather command an army under Marshall in the coming assault than return to the capital. Eisenhower would write that Roosevelt had told him that he had originally planned to give the invasion command to Marshall and that the senior officers should rotate to share the burdens and honors of staff and command duty.[2]

Having been chosen to head the overall operation, General Eisenhower requested RAF Air Chief Marshal Tedder as his principal deputy,

Below: American soldiers board an LCI(L) at an English port for the assault on Normandy. The Normandy landings, despite the short distances from the embarkation ports to the assault beaches, stand as the largest amphibious assault in modern history. The LCI(L)s here are from the No. 351–1139 series with a rounded conning tower/bridge and 20-mm gun mount forward of the tower; No. 1–350 had a square tower with 20-mm gun amidships. (U.S. Army)

with British General Bernard Montgomery to lead the British Army and General Omar Bradley to head American ground forces. Admiral Bertram Ramsay, RN, would direct all naval forces and RAF Air Chief Marshal Trafford Leigh-Mallory would command the Allied air forces supporting the invasion. (Admiral Cunningham was not available for Eisenhower's team, having become First Sea Lord, the senior officer of the Royal Navy.) U.S. Lieutenant General Walter Bedell Smith became Eisenhower's Chief of Staff with General Morgan – COSSAC – staying on as his deputy. These men and their staffs were referred to as SHAEF for Supreme Headquarters Allied Expeditionary Force (which absorbed the COSSAC headquarters).

The "Overlord" command team had a good relationship. One major issue, however, was the role of the U.S. and British heavy (strategic) bombers in supporting the landings. At the Churchill-Roosevelt conference in Quebec during August 1943, Leigh-Mallory had been named to command the *tactical* air support for "Overlord" (at the time he was Commander-in-Chief, RAF Fighter Command). The commanders of the U.S. and British bomber forces objected to being placed under Eisenhower's control, for their bombers could strike at targets beyond those related to the Normandy landings, such as U-boat bases, aircraft and submarine factories, and the V-1 and V-2 missile facilities that were just being revealed. Finally, it was agreed by Churchill and the Allied strategic bomber commanders that Tedder, both Eisenhower's deputy and an RAF officer, would develop the strategic air plan in consultation with

Left: British LCTs and other landing craft in a British port awaiting D-Day. It took the British and Americans years to build up the invasion force in Britain, all the time being called upon to support large-scale operations in the Mediterranean, the Central Pacific, and the South-west Pacific. The production of landing ships and craft in this period was remarkable in view of the simultaneous demands for merchant ships, aircraft carriers, anti-submarine ships, and other naval units. (IWM)

Right: One of the most unusual – and most important – craft in the Normandy assault was the landing barge kitchen or LB(K) which provided hot meals for the crews of the smaller landing craft. This is the *LB(K).1* with LCVPs and LCMs alongside. In the Pacific the U.S. Navy used larger landing ships for this role, informally referred to as LST(M), the "M" indicating "mother." During its first day on station the *LB(K).1* served more than 1,000 hot meals. (IWM)

Left: The availability of LSTs was a key factor in the scheduling of the Normandy landings. This view shows the *LST-4* loaded with trucks and tanks. The cargo nets hanging from her sides were used for troops to climb into the LCVPs after they were lowered. Her bow doors are open and the ramp is lowered as she approaches the beach. The *LST-4* participated in the landings at Sicily, Anzio, Salerno, and Southern France, earning four battle stars. The LCVP in the foreground is from the *Samuel Chase* (APA-26). (U.S. Navy)

the bomber commanders, while Leigh-Mallory would handle the actual employment of aircraft, under Tedder's supervision. It was a workable plan and it would prove a successful one.

British and American bombers began pounding the transportation targets in France. From February to June 1944, aircraft of the U.S. 8th and 9th Air Forces and Britain's 2nd Tactical Air Force dropped 76,200 tons of bombs on 80 rail and road targets. Meanwhile, the massive invasion fleet assembled, becoming the mightiest armada ever to have sailed. There would be more than 4,400 ships and landing craft to carry 154,000 troops – 50,000 of which were the actual assault troops from five divisions – plus 1,500 tanks. The accompanying table lists the ships allocated to the assault – mostly from the British and U.S. Navies, but also flying the flags of France, Greece, Holland, Norway, and Poland.

A number of exercises were held off the British coast and beaches as the Anglo-American-Canadian landing force trained for the forthcoming assault. These exercises were marred by tragedy in April 1944, when early on the morning of the 28th a large group of German E-boats from Cherbourg fell on the landing ships of Operation "Tiger," a mock assault on the coast of Devon, on the English Channel. The torpedo boats struck savagely at the landing ships, which were carrying some 30,000 U.S. soldiers, sinking the U.S. *LST-507* and *LST-531*. In the attack and confusion that followed, 749 soldiers, most from the 4th Infantry Division, were killed. Many died instantly in the explosions, but hundreds more drowned, many bodies being washed ashore on the English coast. While all the troops apparently wore life belts, they were worn improperly, causing many of the heavily laden soldiers to tip upside down in the water and drown.

Those bodies that were recovered were buried in secret and the disaster was hushed-up to avoid the psychological impact on the Allied troops preparing for the invasion. Despite these losses, the army, air forces, and fleets were being readied for an early June invasion, the opening of the long-awaited "second front."

Above the invasion fleet, a vast aerial armada of 11,000 fighters, bombers, transports, and gliders would provide protection and supply, including a massive parachute-glider assault behind German lines as the opening act of the landings. Codenamed "Neptune-Overlord" (Neptune would be the naval aspect of the operation), the Normandy invasion promised to be the most ambitious operation of the entire war. In total, nearly 2,000,000 men would eventually be landed in France, supported by 140 major warships and almost 300 minesweepers plus hundreds of lesser craft as well as the 4,000 landing ships and craft.

In addition, the invasion force included ten LB(K)s or landing barges (kitchen). These were small craft fitted with stoves and ovens to provide hot meals and bread to the thousands of British and American sailors in the small craft that were carrying troops and supplies between English ports and the French beaches. When the landing began these floating galleys would each provide hot meals for 500 to 700 men per day and bake up to 1,000 pounds of bread per day. A typical dinner menu would consist of roast pork, cabbage, and baked potatoes, with fruit and custard for desert, sent aboard the landing craft in insulated canisters together with soup, coffee, and tea. Each LB(K) could carry about a week's supply of food for 800 men.

Finally, the assault force had two British midget submarines, the *X-20* and *X-23*, the only Allied undersea craft participating directly in Operation "Neptune".[3] These submarines sailed from

Portsmouth to serve as beacons for the invasion armada. After spending a day resting offshore on the bottom when D-day was postponed 24 hours, the two craft surfaced off the invasion beaches just before 5 a.m. on June 6. Special, telescoping masts with lights flashing seaward were erected on both submarines to guide in the first landing ships. (Once the landings began they weighed anchor and sailed back to England.)

THE MULBERRY AND GOOSEBERRY PROJECTS

The size of the invasion force, and the need for vehicles, munitions, and provisions for this army in sustained conflict were considerable. Massive amounts of material would have to be brought over the beach, as it would be weeks before a major port could be expected to be captured. Proposals for simple causeways and pontoon-type piers were impracticable because of the exceptional spring tides – as high as 24 feet – and expected storms for that time of year.

In addition, any scheme for piers and breakwaters had to be mobile, so that the components could be towed from England to the beachheads, easily assembled in a short time, and able to withstand heavy weather. Further, in view of the size of the assault, each of two planned harbors would be about the size of Gibraltar.

After considering and evaluating a variety of concepts, the Royal Navy developed the Mulberry harbor concept, with credit for the design going to Commodore John Hughes-Hallett, who had been involved in earlier amphibious operations. (Churchill had expressed specific thoughts on this problem during World War I and early in World War II.)

Each Mulberry harbor would have breakwaters consisting of sunken merchant ships and huge concrete caissons, dubbed Phoenix units. After being towed to their proper position the ships and concrete caissons would be flooded and sunk.

Floating piers several hundred yards long – called Whales – could then be installed for ships to come alongside to unload, with trucks carrying their cargo ashore. These floating Whales were on "legs," to permit them to rise and fall with the tides. Only the Mulberry harbors could permit the massive invasion to be successful without the capture of major ports on the French coast; Mulberry "A" would support the American beachhead at St-Laurent with Mulberry "B" at Arromanches for the British landings.

In addition, another 60 ships would be sunk to provide shallow-water shelters to protect the smaller landing craft from rough seas while they were unloading larger ships, and when they were at rest. The old British battleship *Centurion*, the French battleship *Courbet*, the British cruiser *Durban*, the Dutch cruiser *Sumatra*, and a number of merchant ships would be sunk as the blockships for these so-called Gooseberry harbors.

Some of the components of the Mulberry and Gooseberry projects began their tow from British ports six days before the invasion.

THE ASSAULT PLAN

The Normandy beaches were divided into five areas. The western Utah and Omaha Beaches were given to the Americans, while to the east, the Gold, Juno, and Sword Beaches would be assaulted by British troops. While General Montgomery would be overall commander of the ground forces during the assault, General Bradley would command the American First Army in the landings and General Dempsey would command the British Second Army. It was planned that after the landings General George Patton would arrive with his Third Army to form the U.S. 12th Army Group.[4] When fully ashore the British 21st Army Group would be commanded by General Montgomery.

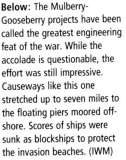

Below: The Mulberry-Gooseberry projects have been called the greatest engineering feat of the war. While the accolade is questionable, the effort was still impressive. Causeways like this one stretched up to seven miles to the floating piers moored offshore. Scores of ships were sunk as blockships to protect the invasion beaches. (IWM)

Right: The Germans had expected the Allies to seize French ports as soon as they landed. To avoid this restriction on their plans, the British developed the Mulberry and Gooseberry artificial harbors. In this photo taken after D-Day a hospital ship takes aboard casualties at one of the floating piers. Note the pier design allows for the 20-foot tidal change off Normandy. (IWM)

The major components of the U.S. assault force were the 1st and 4th Infantry Divisions, which would land on Utah and Omaha, respectively, and the 2nd Ranger Battalion, which would come ashore between them, at Pointe de la Percée. Under Dempsey, the assaulting units would be the British 3rd and 50th Infantry Divisions, 8th and 27th Armoured Brigades, the Canadian 3rd Infantry Division and 2nd Armored Brigade, and the British 4th, 41st, and 48th Royal Marine Commandos. (No U.S. Marines participated in the assault.)

Arrayed against the oncoming invasion was an impressive force of German troops and machines with many ingenious inventions to stop the invasion in the water and on the beaches. Subsurface traps to tear the bottoms from landing craft, massive coastal batteries, and extensive fortifications would form Hitler's defenses, all commanded by Field Marshal Irwin Rommel who believed, with Hitler, that the Allies would land in Normandy, and not elsewhere on the French coast, most likely, it was thought, at a major port. Some members of the German high command disagreed with this view, and there was also disagreement concerning the stage at which reserve formations should be released to the local commanders for defense of the beaches. Would the Allies first feint a landing, or make a raid to distract the German high command and force them to commit the reserves too early? These were critical questions for the German high command, attesting to the potential flexibility of amphibious warfare.

The Germans — using engineer troops and French labor — continued to strengthen the Atlantic Wall, as some called it. Concrete bunkers, barbed wire, mines, underwater obstacles, and coastal artillery were emplaced to hinder if not stop an assault from the sea.

The date of the invasion was also debated, some of Hitler's generals believing it would come in May. When no attack came in May, the Germans relaxed, and as the weather worsened in the Channel, they believed that the invasion would not come for several weeks. Eisenhower postponed the invasion once, from June 5 to the following day, because of poor weather in the Channel area, but by the evening of June 5 the huge fleet was approaching the French coast, preceded by U.S. and British paratroops who would drop from the skies that night. Any further delay would force the landing ships and craft to return to port, imposing a delay of at least several weeks.

LANDINGS IN NORMANDY

The scope of the massive Normandy landings precludes in-depth discussion in an overview such as this. Shortly after 1:30 on the morning of June 6, 1944, two divisions of U.S. Army paratroops took-off from England. From nine airfields, 822 C-47 Dakotas carried 13,000 men of the U.S. 101st and 82nd Airborne Divisions and dropped them in scattered sections over sleeping French towns behind the American beaches; the British 6th Airborne Division was parachuted behind Sword

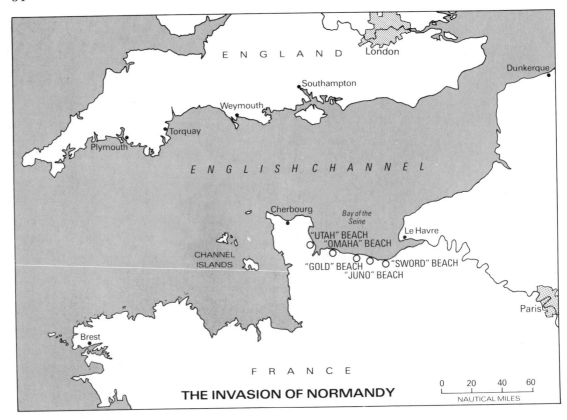

THE INVASION OF NORMANDY

Beach. It was the beginning of D-Day, the long-awaited invasion of France. The paratroopers' objective was to secure bridges and roads, to hold them for advancing Allied armies and to deny them to the Germans.

In the ships of the invasion fleet, the men clambered down the nets to their landing craft bobbing crazily in the rough, choppy seas. Forming up presented several problems, not the least of which, was simply coming together. Escort vessels assigned as control boats tried to locate their positions while the assault boats endeavoured to form up and get underway. In the dark, heavy seas the task was extremely difficult.

The American sector of the invasion – the landings on the western Utah and Omaha Beaches – immediately had trouble with poor visibility and the fact that two of the control craft for the Utah landing were sunk by mines. German defenses, especially the formidable network of coastal batteries with 110 guns of 75-mm to 280-mm in size also caused concern.

Over the beaches, the aircraft of the spotting pools gave directions to the cruisers and battle-

Right: Viewed from the amphibious force flagship *Ancon*, a flotilla of U.S. LCI(L)s and other amphibious ships steam toward Omaha Beach at the start of the Normandy invasion. The overhead barrage balloons are to deter low-flying bombers. At Normandy the *Ancon* carried Major General L. T. Gerow, commanding general of the U.S. V Corps, and Rear-Admiral J. L. Hall, commander of the Omaha Beach landing force. (U.S. Navy)

Right: U.S. soldiers en route to the Normandy assault in an LCT. The initial landings were carried out by British, U.S. and Canadian soldiers and Royal Marines. No U.S. Marines were present except as ships' companies in U.S. battleships and cruisers which stood offshore on June 6 and provided bombardment for the assault. (U.S. Army)

Right: This was the view of the Normandy beach as the first assault waves arrived on June 6, 1944. These U.S. soldiers were brought ashore in an LCVP manned by U.S. Coast Guardsmen. Casualties were heavy at Omaha.

ships. British and American aviators flew constantly from Britain during the initial assault, including an unusual U.S. Navy squadron flying land-based British Spitfire Mk Vb fighters on gunfire spotting missions. From the aerial spotting reports, American and British warships pounded German shore positions as the first groups of landing craft approached their respective beaches. In one experiment, eight LCT(A)s carried amphibious tanks ashore with the first troops instead of waiting for a follow-on wave.

Despite initial concern, the Utah landings, beginning at 6:30, were relatively successful, thanks to heavy bombardment by ships and aircraft. However, on Omaha – "Bloody Omaha" – the story was very different. The Germans had implanted extensive underwater beach obstructions which ripped open the fragile bottoms of the assault craft, leaving the heavily weighted troops to struggle in the water, desperately trying to find their footing before they drowned. Many did not make it.

The German defenders also took full advantage of Omaha's terrain and fired down at the beach from behind their concrete walls or rows of wooden pilings. The amphibious tanks brought with the first wave foundered and offered no protection. The ten-mile stretch of Omaha became a killing-ground for the American infantrymen who struggled in the pounding surf and dark, wet sand.

Some tanks did manage eventually to come ashore and as they left their LCTs they fired into the German positions, but the initial phases of the American assault were difficult at best. For two hours the men who did get ashore were pinned down by German fire. Even destroyers that ran in as close as 1,000 yards to shore could not offer effective fire support.

Throughout the assault phase U.S. battleships, cruisers, and destroyers standing offshore fired thousands of rounds at German defenses. In a contest between the battleships *Arkansas* (BB-33) and *Texas*, armed with 12- and 14-inch guns, respectively, and "Battery Hamburg" with 11-inch guns, the U.S. dreadnoughts fired 264 main battery rounds while U.S. destroyers fired 552 5-inch rounds at the German battery. Only a single "lucky hit" from the *Texas*, which knocked out one of four 11-inch guns, had any effect on the steel shields and concrete casemates of the battery, but the naval gunfire did destroy scores of lesser guns and observation positions.

Finally, toward late morning, as wave after wave of Americans were landed, the tide seemed to turn

as those who made it onto the beach worked their way inland to destroy the German positions, eventually taking the gunners prisoner. As the naval gunfire and sheer tenacity of the U.S. troops began to take effect, the situation on Omaha stabilized; the U.S. 5th Corps sustained 2,000 casualties in contrast to 210 on Utah.

THE BRITISH BEACHES

To the east of Utah and Omaha, the Gold, Juno and Sword Beaches were the targets for the British Second Army. As with the American sector, paratroops preceded their comrades in the boats with a drop by the British 6th Airborne Division to

Right: The chaos of an amphibious assault is evident in this view of Omaha Beach following the landing. The banner at right is for beach identification. This photograph, taken on or shortly after June 6, shows dead soldiers awaiting burial (left and center), supplies, and stranded landing craft. These include an LCVP from the USS *Thurston* (AP-77), the U.S. *LCT-199*, *LCT-555*, and *LCT-638*, and the British *LCT(A)(5)-2421*. The soldiers at right rest on a DUKW. (U.S. Army)

capture the important bridges over the Caen Canal and the Orne River, thereby protecting the assault forces from German reinforcement.

The first wave for Sword Beach, the easternmost beach, hit at 7:30 a.m., one hour after the Americans, which gave additional time for pre-landing bombardment by ships and aircraft. The first assault waves – men of the British I Corps – struggled ashore and headed straight for the German guns.

The landing on Gold Beach was more bloody than on Sword, but the armor accompanying the assault forces quickly cleared safe paths up the beach, firing into the fortified houses and pillboxes from which German gunners threatened the landing. On Juno Beach, between Gold and Sword, the troops – nearly all Canadian – stormed the beach behind their tanks and gained a solid foothold.

By the end of the day, the Allies were firmly entrenched on French soil. The only major threat on D-Day from the German forces poised to throw the Allies back into the sea came when a *Panzer* tank battalion drove a spearhead to the sea between the British 3rd and the Canadian 3rd Divisions. Allied air attacks made it impossible for the Germans to use roads to bring up infantry to exploit the armored thrust, and the Germans were thrown back. Ahead lay several weeks of moving into the French countryside, but it was clear that the Germans had failed to throw the invaders back in the decisive first 24 hours and were now completely on the defensive.

Meanwhile, massive quantities of vehicles, equipment, munitions, and provisions were being carried across the Channel to exploit the Anglo-American landings. The needs of the growing armies were insatiable. After only 24 hours there were 66,000 troops on just the two American beaches; at the end of a week there were almost 250,000 Americans ashore. The British buildup was similar. The Allies could not count on the capture of a port in the first weeks of the invasion, and hence they brought ports with them –

the Mulberries. By June 18, less than two weeks after the assault, the combined daily cargo moving across Omaha-Utah was averaging about 14,500 tons.

The beachhead was struck by a major storm which lasted from the night of June 18 until June 22. The winds and high seas destroyed Mulberry "A" off Omaha Beach and damaged the British Mulberry. Scores of ships and hundreds of landing craft were sunk or damaged, and an American division, forced to wait out the storm aboard ship, eventually came ashore sick and exhausted. Loss of the Mulberry harbors, the British one soon being repaired with components from Mulberry "A," temporarily disrupted the flow of supplies, but these were soon coming across the beaches at increasing rates.

Indeed, weather was the major threat to the invasion force. German naval and air forces achieved few successes. The *only* naval contact in the invasion area during D-Day came when four German torpedo-boats attacked the eastern task force launching 18 torpedoes. They sank a Norwegian destroyer, and then left without inflicting other damage. Two U.S. destroyers, the *Corry* (DD-463) and *Meredith* (DD-726), struck mines and sank, as did several landing craft and the 173-foot patrol craft *PC-2161*. The mass of German shore batteries inflicted only one ship loss on the Allies, sinking a British LCI. Similarly, the *Luftwaffe* was ineffective. The first significant damage by air attack was on June 7 when a bomb hit the headquarters ship *Bulolo*, and the following night the British frigate *Lawford* was sunk by bombs.

During the coming days German submarines and torpedo boats did sink several LSTs and escorts, but without affecting the invasion. In return, British anti-submarine forces sank two U-boats during the week after D-Day.

Twenty days after D-Day U.S. troops reached the outskirts of Cherbourg and on the night of June 23–24 the Germans evacuated the port. Although

Below: U.S. LSTs and a variety of other amphibious and cargo ships pour troops and material into the Normandy beachhead. Barrage balloons float overhead; some have been hauled down onto the deck of LSTs. Several landing craft have been stranded by the receding tide. Note the vast numbers of vehicles required by a modern army; most of those in this view are half-tracks. (U.S. Coast Guard)

Below right: The 15-inch guns of HMS *Warspite* bombard German coastal positions during the Normandy invasion on June 6. Battleships of both the United States and Britain were invaluable in this role. Although supplemented by rockets, guns, and mortars on smaller fire support ships and landing craft, only the dreadnoughts could provide the "heavy punch" to destroy major coastal fortifications. (IWM)

the Germans wrecked the harbor, it was soon made partially usable. Ships carrying cargo were soon unloading, with some LSTs arriving with rails fitted on their tank deck and carrying rolling stock which could be used to move supplies along the rebuilt French railway lines.

History's largest and most complex amphibious assault was, in every sense of the word, a success.[5] While the subsequent operations ashore are beyond the scope of this book, a key aspect of the landings was to be a major detriment to the battle for France and the drive toward Germany. Historian Russell Weigley has noted:

"... from the beginning of the American reinforcement [of Britain], when plans to invade Europe had barely begun to be formulated, the Americans entered Britain from the west and erected their cantonments mainly in western Britain. Lines of supply and reinforcement would most conveniently run to the western flank in Normandy. Furthermore, as the first OVERLORD plan stated: 'Lines of communication will be simplified if the British-Canadian forces are based on ports nearest the United Kingdom. In consequence, United States forces should normally be on the right of the line, British-Canadian forces on the left.'"[6]

By the time the situation was recognized, it was far too late to change over. Thus, as the battle for France developed, the American forces, with more resources, especially armor, and more aggressive commanders (in particular Bradley and

Patton), would be on the right side of the Allied drive, where the Bocage country with its intricate pattern of hedgerows would severely restrict U.S. movement. To the left, the British forces (under Montgomery) lacked the resources and the aggressiveness to exploit the more open country before them.

Ships and Craft Participating in Operation "Neptune," June 6, 1944

Type	British	U.S.	Other	Total
WARSHIPS				
Battleships	4	3	–	7
Monitors	2	–	–	2
Cruisers	17	3	2 French 1 Polish	23
Fleet Destroyers	46	34	2 Norwegian 4 Polish	80
Hunt-class Destroyers	21	–	1 French 1 Norwegian 2 Polish	25
Midget Submarines	2	–	–	2
Sloops	14	–	–	14
Frigates and Destroyer Escorts	53	6	4 French	63
Corvettes	63	–	3 French 2 Greek 3 Norwegian	71
Patrol Craft	–	18	–	18
ASW Trawlers	60	–	–	60
Minelayers	4	–	–	4
Minesweepers	262	25	–	287
Coastal Craft (including Motor Torpedo-Boats)	360	111	13 Dutch 8 French 3 Norwegian	495
Seaplane Carriers	1	–	–	1
LANDING SHIPS AND CRAFT				
Command/ Headquarters Ships	10	2	–	12
Attack Transports	–	10	–	10
Landing Ships Infantry	55	–	–	55
Landing Ships Dock	12	–	–	12
Landing Ships Tank	130	143	–	236
Landing Craft Assault	448	54	–	502
Landing Craft Control and Headquarters	11	15	–	26
Landing Craft Infantry	130	118	–	248
Landing Craft Tank	607	230	–	837
Landing Craft Flak	18	11	–	29
Landing Craft Gun	9	16	–	25
Landing Craft Support	85	36	-	121
LCT (Rocket)	36	–	–	36
LCP (Smoke)	106	48	–	154
Miscellaneous small landing craft, barges, trawlers	*	*	–	1,850

*Not identified according to nationality.
(Table derived from Captain S. W. Roskill, RN, *The War at Sea*, Vol. III, Pt. II (London: HMSO, 1961), pp. 18–19.)

Below: Four years after Hitler planned to invade England in Operation "Sealion", thousands of German soldiers landed on British shores – as prisoners of war. These Germans debark from a British LCT at a British port shortly after being captured during the Normandy assault. (U.S. Coast Guard)

THE INVASION OF SOUTHERN FRANCE

While the main invasion of Normandy established the growing Allied armies in western Europe, the invasion of southern France, originally meant to keep German attention divided between operations in the north and in the south, also became a point of contention among the Allies. The American commanders wanted the southern France landings to proceed while the British leaders feared that the ongoing Italian campaign would be jeopardized. At first, the invasion of the French Riviera was intended to coincide with "Overlord", but the southern operation was postponed in order to give full attention to Normandy. By the time Operation "Anvil-Dragoon" was finally launched on August 15, 1944, it was too late to distract the Germans from the main, northern invasion.

At American insistence, the southern invasion was mounted complete with a carrier task force – seven British and two American flattops – under British Rear-Admiral T. H. Troubridge, who had gained amphibious support experience in the "Torch" operation two years before.

The "Anvil" assault force comprised 880 ships and 1,370 landing craft which staged out of Corsica, arriving off the southern French coast by 10 p.m. on August 14. A commando group of French, Canadian, British, and American troops made a preliminary landing and set up roadblocks on coastal and inland arteries. Following the parachute drops – 5,000 men from 396 transport planes – and a sweep by 125 minesweepers, 1,500 land-based bombers hit the beach areas for 90 minutes. This was the first time in the Mediterranean theater, that so much emphasis had been given to pre-landing bombardment and preparation.

H-Hour was at 8 a.m. on August 15, and the first of seven waves drove onto the beaches behind the DUKWs and LSTs. By 9:10 all of the initial waves were safely ashore. The desultory German defense occasionally tried to score a hit. A Dornier 217 bomber with a glider bomb sank the *LST-282* causing 40 casualties, but these attempts were few and of no import.

The main "Dragoon" landings near Toulon were made by two divisions from the Free French First Army and the U.S. Seventh Army. Within three days, the invaders had secured 40 miles of beach, and within eight days, with relatively light casualties, the important port of Marseilles. The southern ports were important because they eventually allowed the massive influx of men and matériel that kept the Allied drives going through France and ultimately Germany itself.

By August 17 about 30,000 troops and 5,000 vehicles had come ashore, and 2,800 Germans had been taken prisoner. The one-two punch of "Overlord" followed by "Anvil-Dragoon" rendered the German position in France untenable and signalled the beginning of the end for the Nazis.

In two years the Allies had learned much about amphibious operations in the European-Mediterranean theaters. From the chaos and poor planning at Dieppe, and the unwieldy, yet successful landings of "Torch" in 1942 and southern Italy in 1943, to the meticulously arranged, massively supported invasions of Normandy and southern France in 1944, amphibious operations at last emerged as effective, carefully orchestrated weapons. Cooperation between Allies, the availability of sufficient amphibious shipping and landing craft, and pre-invasion bombardment by naval gunfire and aircraft nearly always ensured a successful landing. However, on the other side of the world in the Pacific, these and other lessons had to be learned.

Below: American soldiers wade ashore from the *LCI(L)-522* while an LCM prepares to land jeeps on the beach during the landings in Southern France. German resistance was minimal. The eight-foot concrete and steel wall along the beachhead has been blasted open by engineers to permit the troops to move inland. (U.S. Army)

Bottom: U.S. LSTs unload men and supplies at Yellow Beach at Pamalonne Bay during the August 1944 invasion of southern France. Originally intended as a simultaneous assault with the Normandy landings, they were delayed because of the call on amphibious assets for the continued Mediterranean operations. The LSTs shown here are all the six-davit type. (U.S. Navy)

MEDITERRANEAN AFTERMATH

Following "Overlord" the Allies sought to continue operations in Italy because of the large German forces engaged there. Accordingly, under General Alexander's direction, it was decided to employ an amphibious force or five divisions to take Trieste, followed by the capture of the Ljubljana area. While the landing ships and craft could be made available, with the continuing Italian campaign and the massive campaign ongoing in France, no troops could be spared for such flanking operations.

Rather, the amphibious forces that had served so well in the Mediterranean and in the cross-Channel assaults would be shifted to the Pacific war.

Top left: U.S. LSTs unloading at St-Michel in southern France were trapped by the tidal flows. This photograph shows clearly the flat-bottom configuration of the LST. The *LST-983*'s small superstructure is lost in the clutter of LCVP davits, 20-mm and 40-mm gun tubs, railings, and life rafts. The ships have twin propeller shafts and rudders. (U.S. Navy)

Below: For the invasion of Southern France U.S. LSTs were fitted with flight decks to fly off Piper Cub observation aircraft for use by artillery spotters. (In other operations in the Mediterranean and Pacific the light aircraft were carried in larger aircraft carriers.) The take-off deck was 200-feet long and 16-feet wide. The small superstructure is evident here, with the *LST-16*'s LCVP davits empty.

Left: Ten Piper Cubs could be carried on these LST aircraft carriers. As shown here, prior to launching the aircraft were parked on the after end of the take-off deck and alongside the deck. In the Pacific theater LSTs were fitted with a cable launching/recovery system for these aircraft.

10.
SUBMARINE OPERATIONS

THE MAKIN RAID

During the late 1930s the U.S. Navy conducted experimental exercises with submarines landing raiders by rubber craft. Submarines could approach an enemy's shore clandestinely and put raiders ashore for raids or to garner Intelligence.

With the outbreak of World War II such plans were put aside as available submarines of all nations were sent to seek out and destroy enemy warships and merchant shipping. But as the war progressed, U.S. and British submarines were employed in amphibious operations.

The two largest submarine landings of World War II were conducted by the U.S. Navy. The first was a Marine raider operation against the Japanese-held Makin atoll in the Gilberts. The August 1942 raid was intended primarily as a diversion, to distract the Japanese from sending reinforcements to Guadalcanal and Tulagi, where Marines had landed earlier in the month. The raid

on Makin, more than a thousand miles north-east of the Solomons, would also gather intelligence and destroy enemy positions on the lightly fortified atoll.

Roughly triangular in shape, the atoll's principal island, Butaritari, is approximately eight miles long and less than half a mile wide. The island is covered by a thick growth of coconut palms which extend to the waterline.

The raiders would be carried to the island in two large submarines, the *Argonaut* (SM-1) and the *Nautilus* (SS-168). The former, 381 feet long, was the U.S. Navy's largest undersea craft; originally built as a submarine minelayer, she was converted to a transport submarine during the first half of 1942.[1] The *Nautilus* was slightly smaller, 371 feet long. Both ships had two 6-inch deck guns.[2] Reload torpedoes and some other gear were removed to accommodate the raiders, their weapons and equipment.

The landing force consisted of two companies of the 2nd Marine Raider Battalion under Lieutenant Colonel Evans F. Carlson.[3] His executive officer was Major James Roosevelt, son of the president. "Carlson's raiders" totalled 13 officers and 208 enlisted men for the Makin operation.

The two submarines left Pearl Harbor on the morning of August 8. At sea they separated and proceeded independently because the *Nautilus* was required to arrive off Makin early to make a last-minute periscope reconnaissance before the landing. The crowded submarines travelled mainly on the surface, for speed. No enemy ships or aircraft were sighted during their transit.

The *Nautilus* arrived off Makin at 3 o'clock on the morning of August 16 and conducted a reconnaissance of the planned beach areas. The *Argonaut* rendezvoused with the *Nautilus* late on the 16th. At 3 o'clock on the following morning the two submarines surfaced and began loading the raiders into inflated rubber landing craft. This evolution was difficult because of the 1½-knot current which pulled the submarines in toward the reef, heavy swells, and the roar of the surf made voice communications difficult. Fifteen of the boats, fitted with outboard motors, headed toward the primary beach, with two other boats inadvertently travelling about a mile to the north.

The initial landing was unopposed. The Japanese had no knowledge that U.S. Marines were on Makin until one of the raiders accidently fired his rifle. Although they had now alarmed the enemy, one company of Marines managed to occupy the former British Government House without opposition. But that company soon found their route to rendezvous with the other company blocked by Japanese armed with machine-guns, grenade-launchers, and flame-throwers. Aided by a platoon from the other company, the Marines broke through the road-block.

Meanwhile, a small Japanese freighter and a patrol boat were sighted in the lagoon. The U.S. submarines opened fire with their deck guns and sank both ships. The submarines also provided some fire support for the Marines ashore.

The Marines continued to engage the few Japanese troops and periodically Japanese aircraft overflew the island. The submarines submerged safely, but the troops ashore were bombed on several occasions. At one point Colonel Carlson was able to withdraw from a position moments before the planes made a bombing run, causing some casualties on the advancing Japanese troops.

Although no prisoners had been taken and no significant facilities were destroyed, the decision was made to withdraw on schedule that evening. But Carlson and his raiders had difficulty launching their rubber boats in the heavy surf. Some Marines were in the surf for an hour before getting away. Boats were overturned and most of their weapons and equipment were lost. Several Marines were drowned. Only seven boats, with less than 100 raiders, made it out to the submarines that night.

Carlson was forced to keep most of his Marines on Makin for another day, with the submarines submerged offshore. Patrols sent out to forage for food and weapons found very few Japanese. Two were shot and the Marines were not attacked. On this day the Marines found a store of 1,000 barrels of aviation gas, which was blown up, and captured a number of Japanese documents.

That evening, with rubber rafts lashed to a native outrigger, *most* of the surviving Marines returned to the submarines. Thirty of the raiders failed to return. Of those, fourteen had been killed, seven had been drowned, and nine had been left behind under circumstances not fully clear. These nine were captured by the Japanese and executed. Japanese records indicate that about 70 troops were on Makin when the Marines struck. Probably 46 were killed.

The *Argonaut* and *Nautilus* returned to Pearl Harbor while the raiders and, subsequently, U.S. Navy and Marine leaders evaluated the raid. Marine casualties were higher than had been expected and only marginally less than those of the surprised and small defending force. General Holland M. Smith, commenting on the raid some years later, wrote that the raid served no

Below: Marine raiders exercise on the deck of the submarine *Nautilus* en route to the landings on Makin Island. Both the N-boats and the *Argonaut* mounted a pair of these 6-inch deck guns, the largest ever mounted in U.S. submarines. Evaluations of the Makin raid varied; in some respects it was a failure and may have caused the Japanese to fortify the Pacific atolls more heavily. (U.S. Navy)

Bottom: The *Nautilus* exercises with U.S. Army scouts at Dutch Harbor, Alaska, prior to the landings at Attu. Here the submarine landings made a significant but by no means critical complement to the main U.S. landings. During the war these submarines made a more important contribution in supplying the vast anti-Japanese guerrilla network in the Philippines. (U.S. Navy)

useful military purpose and had in fact alerted the Japanese to U.S. intentions in the Gilberts, resulting in the heavy fortifications of Tarawa and Makin. It was, he contended, "a piece of folly."[4] Still, the raid demonstrated that such submarine-launched operations were feasible.

LESSER U.S. OPERATIONS

The next major U.S. submarine landing was also a two-boat operation, in May 1943, involving the *Nautilus* and her sister submarine *Narwhal* (SS-167).[5] The target was Attu, one of two islands in the Aleutians which the Japanese had occupied in June 1942 as part of the diversion for the attack on Midway.

The two submarines unloaded their spare torpedoes and other equipment to make space for the Army's 7th Scouts. They conducted a rehearsal at Dutch Harbor on April 30, and then took aboard 200 scouts on May 1 and set off for Attu as part of Operation "Landcrab."

The submarines arrived off Attu on May 11 and successfully landed their troops five hours before the main assault. Also, the submarines served as navigation beacons for the main landing force (see Chapter 11). The submarine landings were a useful complement to the main landings, but were not a critical factor in the recapture of Attu.

After the Attu operation, the *Nautilus* spent several months in overhaul. She then slipped out of Pearl Harbor and on September 16, 1943, again arrived in the Gilberts where she conducted clandestine photo-reconnaissance of Makin, Tarawa, Kuma, Butaritari, and Abemama in preparation for the forthcoming U.S. amphibious assaults. The submarine returned safely to Pearl Harbor on October 17.

The *Nautilus* returned to Tarawa on November 18 to obtain last-minute information on surf and weather conditions, and to land Marine scouts. On the night of November 19–20 a U.S. destroyer sighted her on the surface and opened fire, putting a 5-inch round through her conning tower. The *Nautilus* dived as soon as she had sufficient water under her keel. The damage was repaired and the following day she surfaced off Kenna to unload her passengers into rubber-boats – 77 scouts from the 5th Marine Reconnaissance Company and an Australian.

The scouts landed safely, and the next day the *Nautilus* used her 6-inch guns to pound the 25-man Japanese garrison on the island. The troops of the small garrison were either killed by the gunfire or committed suicide, and the small island soon became the site of an American airfield.

For the September 1943 photographic mission into the Giberts, an enlisted photographer was assigned to the *Nautilus* and a space was modified for use as a darkroom with a photographic laboratory provided. This would permit development of the film on board so that, to some extent, photographs could be retaken if the original shots were not suitable.

Eleven more dedicated photographic missions were undertaken by U.S. submarines, mostly in support of specific amphibious operations. One more was planned, by the *Swordfish* (SS-193) in anticipation of the Okinawa landings, but that submarine was lost in January 1945, apparently to Japanese surface ships.

(The principal camera used in these operations was the Primarflex with a single-lens reflex viewfinder and a focal-plane shutter. The camera, however, was of German manufacture and could not be procured in the United States during the war. The Navy advertised for the camera in various photographic journals and ten second-hand cameras were obtained, to be issued to submarines embarking on these reconnaissance missions.)

Both the *Nautilus* and *Narwhal*, joined by several other submarines, also kept up a steady flow of supplies to the American-Filipino guerrillas in the Philippines. These two large submarines could each carry some 90 tons of munitions plus special personnel on each voyage to the Philippines; the smaller, fleet-type, submarines carried about 35 tons of arms and supplies on each mission to the Philippines. (Early in 1942 U.S. submarines had taken off the gold reserves of the Philippines as well as military nurses, code experts, and other high-priority passengers.) The submarines carrying supplies to the Philippines also conducted offshore reconnaissance of potential beaches for the 1944 landings.

The guerrilla supply operations, which required a two-week round trip from Australia, were expensive in terms of submarine requirements. Still, the guerrilla force in the Philippines, estimated to range from 15,000 at their low point to 100,000 when the Americans landed, was largely kept armed by the submarine missions, and in turn tied down large numbers of Japanese troops.

THE MEDITERRANEAN EXPERIENCE

U.S. submarines did not operate in the Atlantic-European theaters, that region being assigned by the Allied leadership to British submarines.

The major use of submarines in landing operations were conducted in the Mediterranean region. After the failures of the commando landings in Libya and Syria, and the loss of several hundred commandos in the attempt to reinforce Crete in 1941, the various British special forces in the Mediterranean carried out no major operations until November 1941. The principal British commando units in Egypt at the time were the Special Air Service Regiment (which evolved into the Army's Special Air Service or SAS), the Special Boat Section (which became the Special Boat Squadron),[6] the Long Range Desert Group, and No. 11 (Scottish) Commando.

In conjunction with the planned British des-

ert offensive to recapture Cyrenaica and relieve German-surrounded Tobruk, an attempt would be made to assassinate Rommel, the brilliant German commander in North Africa. It was planned that on the eve of Operation "Crusader" two British submarines would land troops of No. 11 Commando at four points behind the German-Italian lines to strike the communications center near Cyrene, the Italian headquarters at that town, the Italian Intelligence center at Apollonia, and Rommel's quarters and headquarters at Beda Littoria.

The landing would take place on the night of November 14–15, two nights before Operation "Crusader" was to start. A small party of the British Long Range Desert Group would meet the raiders on the beaches.

All went well until the submarines, the *Torbay* and *Talisman*, began launching their folbots (canoes) and rubber rafts. The submarines carried six officers and 49 enlisted men for the raids, all under the nominal command of 24-year-old, Lieutenant-Colonel Geoffrey Keyes. Rough seas began swamping the folbots and only 38 of the raiders were able to get ashore.

The centerpiece of the operation, the raid on Rommel's quarters was now allocated to Keyes and eighteen others. They were to trek some 125 miles from their landing site. When they reached the house it was dark. Keyes, a captain, and a sergeant burst in and began firing with automatic weapons. Rommel was not there. He was in Italy for conferences; further, he and his senior officers had ceased using the house some time before and a supply unit was using it.

In the firefight in the darkened house Keyes was fatally wounded and the captain who had entered with him was also hit. Several Germans were killed.

Other aspects of the raid went awry and when the survivors reached the beach the submarine *Torbay* was offshore, but unable to send in boats because of the rough seas. With Germans arriving, the survivors set off in small parties in an effort to escape. One officer and a sergeant had a remarkable 41-day ordeal in the desert before they reached British lines. Most of the raiders were captured by the Germans.

Less ambitious but more successful clandestine operations from submarines were undertaken throughout the Mediterranean during the war. On a regular basis, using folbots and rubber rafts, commandos would go ashore from submarines off Sardinia, Italy, Greece, and various Aegean islands as well as along the German-held coast of Libya. These commandos blew train tracks and bridges, airfields, and other installations; conducted coastal and shore reconnaissance; and carried munitions and other supplies to guerrillas. Greek submarines also carried British raiders in these operations.

Submarines also made a few supply trips to the besieged British island base of Malta, but this was a much smaller effort than the transport of supplies to the Philippines by U.S. submarines.

IN PREPARATION FOR "TORCH"

As the Allies made preparations for the landings in North Africa, submarines were called upon to support Operation "Torch," in both conventional and unusual ways. In the original plans for the North African landings it was envisioned that the beaches of Algiers and Oran would be carried by reconnaissance teams working from submarines.

However, through misunderstandings the scope of these operations was reduced until only HM submarine *Seraph* (also P.219) carried out a periscope reconnaissance of the Algerian coast during the last two weeks in September 1942. This was the *Seraph*'s first combat mission, having commissioned earlier in the year, with Lieutenant N. L. A. (Bill) Jewell as commanding officer.

The *Seraph* returned to Gibraltar where, instead of being given orders to operate against the German and Italian forces in the Mediterranean, she was assigned to Operation "Flagpole." Loaded with folbots, "tommy guns," walkie-talkie radios, and other supplies, the submarine embarked Lieutenant General Mark Clark, who was General Eisenhower's deputy, two other Army generals, U.S. Navy Captain Jerauld Wright, a couple of colonels, and three commandos.

With this party embarked, the *Seraph* sailed to the Algerian coast. There the collapsible canoes were launched to carry General Clark and his party ashore for discussions with Vichy officials concerning the pending North Africa invasion. These meetings helped to reduce French opposition to the landings, although the French were not told that the troop ships were already at sea and that the landings would commence in a few days.

There were delays and some problems, but the *Seraph* finally came to within 300 yards of the beach on the morning of October 23 to embark her VIP passengers. Because of the importance of returning them to Eisenhower's headquarters at Gibraltar as soon as possible, the Americans were transferred at sea to a PBY Catalina flyingboat.

As General Clark left the *Seraph*'s bridge to be transferred by boat to the PBY, he remarked to Lieutenant Jewell, "Thanks for everything, Bill. Don't go away from Gibraltar too soon. I shall have another job for you in a few days."

The job, Jewell soon learned, was also related to the North Africa landings. The *Seraph* was to sail to France and secretly take aboard General Henri Honoré Giraud. The General, a hero in France, had escaped from Germany after two years as a prisoner and was in Vichy France while the Vichy French leadership decided whether or not to return him to the Nazis. Meanwhile, he was obviously the right man to take into North Africa in the wake of the Ango-American invasion to gain support for the Allies from the French colonies.

But Giraud would not travel in a British submarine, so strong were the anti-British feelings among Frenchmen at the time. Captain Jerault Wright, who had been in the Clark party, embarked in the *Seraph* as nominal commanding officers of the submarine, which was temporarily transferred to the U.S. Navy. Lieutenant Jewell remained on board to actually direct operations (Wright not being a submariner).

The *Seraph* was joined by the submarine *Sybil* in this operation. The Giraud party, being picked up from the town of Le Lavendou, was to be taken out in two groups. Giraud, his son, and some associates were taken off on the night of November 5–6, and at sea transferred to a PBY for the flight to Gibraltar. The *Sybil* followed a few days later.

The *Seraph* finally sailed on her first combat patrol – her fourth mission since completion – on November 24, but she was soon called upon to join sister submarines in carrying U.S. and British commandos for reconnaissance operations ashore.

In early 1943 the *Seraph* sailed for England and a needed refit. In April she set out again for the Mediterranean, still under command of Bill Jewell. In addition to her normal crew, packed in dry ice was the unidentified body of a dead man dressed as a Royal Marine officer, with a briefcase containing several secret documents handcuffed to his wrist. On the night of April 19–20 the *Seraph* surfaced off the coast of Spain and, wearing a life jacket, the body was lowered over the side.

Operation "Mincemeat" was a success – the body was washed ashore, the Spanish gave the briefcase to German diplomats, and the German high command provided evidence that the next Allied assault would be in the eastern Mediterranean, and not against Sicily.

The *Seraph*'s association with the Sicily landing – Operation "Husky" – did not end with the fictitious Major Martin. In late June the *Seraph* loaded special beacon equipment and, with HM submarines *Safari* and *Shakespeare*, moved to within a few hundred yards of the invasion beaches. On the night of July 9 the submarines planted special buoys offshore to guide the first waves of assault craft.

British submarines also carried out beach reconnaissance in preparation for "Husky," and served in the reconnaissance and beacon roles for the subsequent Anglo-American landings on the Italian mainland. In the Normandy landings in June 1944, the Royal Navy employed two midget submarines, the *X-20* and *X-23*, as beacons to lead in the first assault waves.

Following the invasion of Normandy, the Royal Navy shifted many ships to the Pacific, to join U.S. forces in the final operations against Japan. British and Dutch submarines carried commandos for several raids against Japanese-held islands in South-east Asia. British and Dutch submarines were employed in attempts to infiltrate agents and supplies into Malaya. But unfavorable coastal conditions made it more effective to use long-range aircraft based in India to parachute men and supplies.

U.S. and British submarines made significant though limited contributions to amphibious operations in World War II. The Japanese Navy also employed submarines extensively in the resupply role, but apparently not in direct support of amphibious operations. This U.S. experience during the war would lead to submarines being specially configured as transports after the war.

The Soviet Union also made extensive use of submarines for raids during the war. Northern (Arctic) Fleet submarines carried small raiding parties on numerous missions behind German lines along the Arctic coasts of Finland and Norway.

Below: The Jolly Roger battle flag of the *Seraph* shows the submarine's accomplishments under Lieutenant Norman (Bill) Jewell. The six daggers at the bottom of the flag indicate special operations, including the landing of Lieutenant General Mark Clark, deputy to General Eisenhower, in North Africa prior to the November 1942 Anglo-American amphibious assaults. (IWM)

11.
ON THE OFFENSIVE IN THE PACIFIC

ALEUTIANS SIDESHOW

In 1942 the Americans won the great carrier battles of Coral Sea and Midway against superior Japanese naval forces. While these victories turned back the Japanese assaults against Port Moresby and Midway atoll, the Japanese had landed on two of the remote islands of the Aleutians chain, Attu and Kiska. The Japanese troops were at the end of a lengthy supply chain; the islands were unimportant to the Japanese high command and hence they were virtually forgotten.

The Americans began small air raids on the Japanese-held islands beginning in June 1942, using PBY Catalina flyingboats and B-17 Flying Fortresses flying from Atka and Cold Bay, respectively. They inflicted minimal damage on the Japanese. The Japanese did, however, reinforce Kiska early in July 1942 when a large carrier force screened a transport and seaplane tender delivering another 1,200 troops, supplies, and six midget submarines to Kiska. While no U.S. surface ships challenged the Japanese, two U.S. submarines each sank one destroyer and another two were damaged. (One U.S. submarine was sunk probably by Japanese forces during this period.)

There were now 2,400 Japanese on Kiska and about one-half that number on Attu. In August 1942, Rear Admiral Robert A. Theobold, Commander North Pacific Force, was directed to expel the Japanese from Kiska. With his headquarters ashore, Theobold began the American operations with a shore bombardment against Kiska with five cruisers and five destroyers on August 7 (virtually simultaneous with the Guadalcanal landings). Kiska-based Zero floatplanes chased off the cruisers' spotting planes and the ships' bombardment was only moderately successful.

As U.S. preparations were being made to assault the islands, Admiral Theobold sought an airfield closer to the Japanese positions. Accordingly, on August 30, troops were landed on Adak and rapidly constructed an airfield which, by mid-September, was used to launch fighter and bomber strikes against Kiska and Attu. At the same time, the Japanese high command realized the vulnerability of Attu and, from August 27 until September 16, used destroyers and transports to evacuate the entire garrison. U.S. forces remained unaware of the withdrawal.

The American activity on Adak alarmed the Japanese, who felt that this could be a prelude to long-range attacks against the Japanese homeland. Accordingly, Attu was reoccupied and another 1,100 troops were sent into Kiska. The Americans were on the move in this rigid war, and the large island of Amchitka – 140 miles west of Adak and 60 miles east of Kiska – was occupied by Army troops in December 1942. However, problems between the Army and Navy commanders led to Admiral Theobold's being relieved by Rear Admiral Thomas C. Kinkaid as commander of U.S. forces in the region.

The increased U.S. and Japanese activity led to a cruiser-destroyer battle on March 26, 1943, the Battle of the Komandorski Islands. The U.S. ships were outgunned, but the battle was a standoff, both sides suffering major damage but no losses. By May the Americans were ready to retake the captured islands. Attu was first, the landing being dubbed Operation "Landcrab." The American assault force consisted of no less than three older battleships, an escort carrier, seven cruisers and a score of destroyers to provide shore bombardment and screen the transports. The assault troops were 3,000 men of the Army's reinforced 17th Infantry Regiment. (Several days earlier, in preparation for the main landing, two U.S. submarines had sent ashore 100 troops see Chapter 10).

Two U.S. battleships opened fire on Attu and planes from the escort carrier *Nassau* (CVE-16) dropped surrender leaflets. There was, however, no sign of the Japanese.

When the Americans landed on May 11 there were 2,630 Japanese troops on the island. They were prepared to fight to the last man and had selected their defensive positions well. Supported by aircraft and naval gunfire, the Americans fought for a week before resistance ended. Twenty-eight Japanese surrendered; the remainder died in the fighting or simply disappeared. About 600 Americans were killed in the fighting and double that number were wounded.

Attu was soon the site of another American airfield, as was the island of Shemya, 25 miles to the east. Kiska was next. The assault began with a battleship bombardment on July 22, 1943, but the actual landings would not commence until August 15. The Japanese high command correctly assumed that the battleship bombardment was a prelude to invasion, and, using cruisers and destroyers, the Japanese evacuated the entire garrison – 5,183 Army troops and civilians – safely and without the Americans being aware of what was happening.

U.S. air and naval strikes against Kiska continued intermittently until August 15, when the landing began. An armada of almost 100 ships arrived off Kiska carrying 29,000 U.S. soldiers and 5,300 Canadian troops. The landing was preceded by a violent bombardment from battleships, cruisers, and destroyers. Then an array of LSTs, LCTs, and LSIs headed for the beach and unloaded thousands of assault troops.

Two days later the troops discovered why the landing had been unopposed. Still, trigger-happy soldiers on patrol killed 25 friendly troops and wounded more, and one of the U.S. destroyers struck a Japanese mine killing 70 men and injuring another 47. The second and final amphibious landing of the Aleutians campaign was over.

THE SOLOMONS CAMPAIGN CONTINUES

Although the British – citing several Anglo-American agreements – wished no diversion of U.S. troops and landing craft to the Pacific campaigns, it soon became obvious that the Allied success at Guadalcanal meant that the Solomons campaign would continue. Burying their internal disputes for the moment, the U.S. Joint Chiefs of Staff presented a united front, and developed a five-phase plan for the South Pacific. Under the overall name of Operation "Elkton," the plan included capturing New Georgia, Bougainville, New Britain, Kavieng and New Ireland, and, ultimately a mass assault on Rabaul by no less than 23 Allied ground divisions and 45 air groups. The Japanese could defend Rabaul with aircraft on five airfields, and a formidable harbor defense fleet of cruisers and destroyers.

By February 1943, as the last living Japanese soldiers departed from Guadalcanal, the Allies were ready to begin Operation "Cleanslate," the seizure of the Russell Islands, 50 miles north-west of Guadalcanal. On February 21, U.S. Army and Marine assault teams landed unopposed on Baruka and Pavuvu.

Stung by the easy American victory, the Japanese sent a huge troop convoy, with the crack LI Division, toward the Huon Gulf on March 1. The convoy was attacked by U.S. Army Air Forces B-17s, which sank the LI Division's command ship. But the enemy pressed on, and was again attacked, loosing nine troop transports and four destroyers to Allied dive bombers.

Japanese air strikes on Guadalcanal in early April were unsuccessful in halting the Allied buildup, and by mid-June the Allies were ready to launch a series of landings in the Solomons. The landings on New Georgia consisted of six separate operations. On June 21, two companies of Lieutenant Colonel Mike Currin's 4th Raiders landed on the southeastern tip of the island. Another landing by Army and Marine forces took Vangunu Island. Eventually, Marine and Army operations gave the United States control over the entire island of New Georgia.

The main landings began on June 30, with the 9th Marine Defense Battalion landing on Rendova together with the Army's 45th Division's 103rd Infantry Regiment. On July 5, the 43rd Infantry Division hit New Georgia, with little reaction from the enemy, but by the night of July 6, the Japanese attacked troops of the Army's 169th Infantry Regiment, which had paused to rest on the Bariki River. The Americans were pummelled badly and called for support from the offshore naval task force. Four destroyers delivered a barrage while eighteen SBD Dauntless dive bombers struck enemy positions.

Marine air squadrons based on Guadalcanal, had been getting a workout for the last several weeks, flying standing patrols to protect U.S. troops and ships from Japanese bombers. In addition to interceptor duties, Marine aviation exercised its new role of close air support. An important develop-

Below: Under the direction of General MacArthur, American, Australian, and New Zealand troops moved steadily toward Japan through a series of highly successful amphibious landings. Here U.S. Marines are aided by Coast Guardsmen as they push a jeep ashore during landings at Cape Gloucester on New Britain. This was a very different environment from the coral atolls of the Central Pacific campaign. (U.S. Coast Guard)

ment during the New Georgia campaign was the use of air/ground liaison officers – later called Forward Air Controllers (FAC) – whose job was to coordinate air strikes with the immediate needs of the ground troop commanders.

During the New Georgia campaign, Marine pilots took turns serving as FACs with Army and Marine ground units, and although the use of aircraft in close support of ground troops was still in its infancy, results could be considered promising, even though confusion sometimes resulted in friendly troops suffering casualties from wrongly placed bombs. Official displeasure at such incidents did, however, overshadow the overall success on New Georgia. The report issued by the commander of Marine aviation on New Georgia, Brigadier General Francis P. Mulcahy (an early Marine aviator who had one of the few confirmed kills by Marines in World War I), said, in part:

> "The use of aircraft in close support of ground troops proved to be impractical. . . . The dense jungle encountered made the location of enemy positions suitable for air attack impossible until friendly troops were too close to the prospective target for safety. . . . The targets selected were always well clear of friendly troops. . . ."[1]

In all, 1,833 aircraft sorties were flown in support of the New Georgia operations, 1,649 by Marine-piloted SBDs and TBF Avengers.

The Japanese on New Georgia put up a spirited defense, but on July 13, after several days of fierce combat, the Americans pushed through to beaches on the opposite coast, forcing the enemy to fall back to Munda on the extreme south-west corner of New Georgia. Eventually, Marine and Army operations gained control of the entire island.

BOUGAINVILLE

The various sub-operations of Operation "Elkton" continued throughout the summer of 1943. By late October, the island of Choiseul and several smaller islands had been taken, leaving only the largest of the Solomons, Bougainville, 200 miles east of Rabaul. The landing was given the fancy name

Below: Although the European theater had first call on available amphibious shipping – such as the U.S. *LST-263* and her numerous sister ships – the American naval leaders and General Douglas MacArthur constantly sought more resources for the campaigns against Japan. Only the massive, unscathed U.S. industrial capacity could provide sufficient ships as well as aircraft, tanks, and other weapons, for simultaneous Allied movement on multiple fronts. (U.S. Navy)

of "Cherryblossom" and was set for November 1. In conjunction with "Cherryblossom," Operation "Goodtime" would land troops on the nearby Treasury Islands on October 27 to establish a base for long-range radars for the burgeoning night-fighter effort to be provided by Marine fighter squadrons.

The I Marine Amphibious Corps under Lieutenant General A. A. Vandegrift, veteran of the Guadalcanal campaign, would provide the assault teams for Bougainville, together with the U.S. Army's 37th Division. The Treasuries would be taken by the 7,000-man 8th New Zealand Brigade Group, under Brigadier R. A. Row. It was hoped that the operations in the Treasuries and surrounding islands would draw Japanese attention away from the main U.S. landings at Bougainville. The landings by the New Zealanders were successful and by October 31 they were firmly established, finishing off the last Japanese defenders the next day.

With the Japanese looking elsewhere, the first elements of the U.S. forces landed at Torokina, on Bougainville's western coast. Five minutes before the landings, at 7:15 a.m., Marine TBFs and SBDs covered by Marine and Navy F4U Corsair fighters attacked the beach defenses in conjunction with naval gunfire.

At 7:22 a.m., the landings commenced in heavy surf. Many LCVPs and LCMs broached and were left stranded. But the Japanese were unprepared, and by nightfall 14,000 Marines of the 3rd and 9th Regiments, along with 6,200 tons of supplies were ashore. Although largely unopposed, the Marines did run into some problems from Japanese gun emplacements and from sparse bombing raids from Rabaul.

After the landings, the role of naval gunfire came under discussion since it had been adjudged less than effective. Accuracy was the main concern, and many Marine planners bemoaned the inefficiency of the bombardment at Torokina. The efforts of the various air units were more appreciated, however, since besides the pre-landing strafing and bombing, the Marine, Navy, and New Zealand squadrons kept Japanese bombers and strafing Zeros occupied while the men and material came ashore. Total Allied claims were 24 to 26 enemy aircraft shot down.

While the initial landings on Bougainville were highly successful, further operations met determined Japanese resistance, reminiscent of the bloodiest Guadalcanal encounters. The Japanese sent four destroyers to the landing beaches on the night of November 6. Embarked in the destroyers was a composite battalion – about 475 men – which was to land at Torokina and throw the enemy off the beach. The counter-assault was to begin at dawn.

The Japanese were sighted, but in the morning mist and fog, the Americans were not completely sure of the approaching force's identity and withheld their fire. Struggling through the same heavy surf that the Americans had encountered, the Japanese troops landed in a dispersed manner, but regrouped and quickly engaged the Americans. The outcome was rarely in doubt and by November 8, the entire Japanese invasion force had been wiped out or captured. The Marines continued to move inland, supported by their TBF Avengers. Although torpedo bombers, the Avengers were being loaded with bombs and used to attack enemy positions directly ahead of advancing Marine columns.

On November 9, the 3rd Marine Division called for TBF support during an attack on a Japanese-held village the following day. Accordingly, twelve Avengers dropped their bombs within 120 yards of their appreciative audience. Three days later, on November 13, Navy Avengers did the honors. Close air support for amphibious landings was quickly evolving.

By late December, Bougainville was in American hands after a series of battles against remaining Japanese defenders.

MACARTHUR TAKES NEW GUINEA

While the Marines, with the help of the Army and New Zealanders, took the Solomons, MacArthur's forces began the campaign to regain New Guinea, thereby catching Rabaul in a pincer. New Guinea was never totally occupied by the Japanese due to the stubborn resistance of Australian troops at Port Moresby on the south eastern tip of the large island. By mid-1942, the Japanese had to admit that they could not win total control, and instead kept the northern sector for themselves, operating a major base at Lae which became an important staging area for the Zero fighters flying escort for bombing raids. (The so-called Lae Wing included many famous Japanese aces, among them Sakai, Sasai and Nishizawa.) In late August, when a Japanese convoy from Rabaul attempted to land troops at Miline Bay, at the southernmost point of New Guinea, MacArthur set a trap with the 7th Australian Division, veterans of Middle East fighting. The Aussies, with assistance from land-based aircraft, fought off the end-run landing attempt, inflicting heavy losses on the Japanese.

Determined to hold up his end of the south west Pacific campaign, MacArthur turned his attention to Buna, an important Japanese stronghold at the southernmost point of the Japanese-held territory. Although Australian troops had fought against the Japanese around Buna throughout December 1942, they were unable to completely win their objective, particularly the important Kokoda Trail. Over 7,000 Japanese stood off the combined Australian and American forces around Buna. The Allied troops seemed to be the victim of what Robert E. Sherwood called "a hopelessly defensive state of mind."

From his headquarters at Port Moresby, MacArthur on November 30, 1942, summoned Lieutenant General Robert L. Eichelberger from Australia. Eichelberger was ordered to take command in the field, relieve the commanding general of the U.S. 32nd Infantry Division, a former National Guard unit which had received no jungle training before being sent to New Guinea. MacArthur, after promising Eichelberger honors and publicity, concluded with the words: "Bob, take Buna or don't come back alive."

Eichelberger took command, wearing his general's stars as he toured the front lines to obtain a first-hand picture of the situation. He relieved several officers, had the men rest for two days, and then initiated an attack which, in 32 days, would destroy the Japanese garrison at Buna. (Eichelberger then spent most of 1943 training MacArthur's troops in Australia for coming campaigns. He was to become MacArthur's leading field commander and an outstanding practitioner of amphibious warfare.)

Having won Buna, the Allies could now turn their attention to the main target on New Guinea — Lae. MacArthur's plan was to launch two assaults, by sea and by air. On September 4, after a pre-landing bombardment by U.S. destroyers, Australian troops of the 9th Division came ashore in rubber boats, followed by large numbers of landing craft. Assembling on the beaches, the Australians headed toward Lae. The following day, American paratroopers jumped into Nadzab twenty miles north west of Lae.

No Japanese opposition was encountered until September 10, but by September 14, the Australians had come to within seven miles of Lae. The Japanese base was taken on September 16, as the Japanese, convinced that all was lost, fled into the jungles, where many died of hunger and disease.

The third objective, after Lae, was an old German fort at Finschhafen, occupied by several thousand Japanese. Finschhafen controlled the Huon Peninsula, and the important sea approaches to New Britain, the next target. MacArthur ordered another seaborne assault. The Australian 20th Brigade left their American amphibious ships and landed six miles north of the fort on September 22. By October 2, they had taken the town. Fighting on the Huon Peninsula continued sporadically throughout December, but by Christmas the entire area was firmly in Allied hands, thanks to the efforts of the Australian contingent, supported by American naval and air forces.

The U.S. Fifth Air Force put up a tremendous effort, flying continuous raids against Japanese positions, patrolling the skies against enemy bombers, and, most particularly, maintaining a massive supply chain without which the entire Allied effort would have been impossible. The airlift from the main Allied base at Port Moresby over the Owen Stanley mountain range and forbidding jungle by Fifth Air Force C-47 Dakotas kept MacArthur's New Guinea campaign going. The C-47s also served for the paratroop drops.

NEW BRITAIN

As the Australians settled into their positions on the Huon Gulf, the U.S. 1st Marine Division struck out for the western tip of New Britain across the Vitiaz Strait on Christmas Day 1943. Seventy thousand Japanese were estimated to be on the island, primarily in the north. Ten thousand were in the western part of the island.

Next day the Marines landed from destroyer transports (APDs), because there were no large transports available, and from the now-familiar LCIs and LSTs. The 1st and 7th Marine Regiments went in, with the 5th Marines in reserve. The actual landing site was Cape Gloucester, near an enemy airfield.

The landings began at 7:45 a.m., meeting little initial opposition. By the afternoon, however, the Japanese had appeared in strength on the ground and in the air. U.S. Army P-38 Lightnings intercepted 88 bombers and escorts, destroying many of the Japanese aircraft, which did manage to sink

Above: At Cape Gloucester, Coast Guardsmen who manned the landing ships and Marines build a temporary causeway to facilitate the unloading of landing ships. The U.S. Coast Guard manned numerous naval transports, landing ships, and small craft as well as their own fleet of cutters, patrol craft, and six amphibious flagships. (U.S. Coast Guard)

one U.S. destroyer. The Japanese put up a stiff resistance, complicated by monsoon rains, but the Marines were able to advance, taking the airstrip by December 31. The 5th Marine Regiment went ashore on the 28th and were able to help capture the airfield. Western New Britain was declared secured by April 28, 1944. Rabaul was surrounded.

Although the Marines had accomplished their tasks by January, MacArthur held them to help his Sixth Army tighten its grip on the entire island. This sense of exploitation did not go down particularly well with the Marines, but there was little they could do, considering MacArthur's position. It had taken MacArthur nearly a year to get to Rabaul, a fact not lost on the Navy and Marines who, respectively, had suffered more than 10,000 and 8,400 combat casualties in the South Pacific.

Marine aviation at Cape Gloucester, and during much of the New Britain operation, did little in the way of close air support. Indeed, this was the period of Marine fighter ace, Major Gregory "Pappy" Boyington and his Black Sheep squadron, VMF-214. They used their big F4U Corsairs as escorts and bomber interceptors, rather than in direct support of the troops in combat on the ground.

The Marines did introduce a new development during the Cape Gloucester operation: flying Piper Cub spotter planes obtained from the Army. Captain T. A. Peters, aide to Major General W. H. Rupertus, Commanding General of the 1st Marine Division, formed an unlikely group of officers and enlisted men with light plane experience and flew 1,000 hours in spotting, reconnaissance and transport duties over Cape Gloucester.

The Marines and Army were continuing to learn about amphibious operations. The most important areas of development and education concerned ship-to-shore movement – an on-going point of consideration – protection of the landing forces, and the selection of poorly defended beaches that would allow the landings to be made with a minimum of casualties.

Rabaul was blasted by raids from every available source: bombers, fighters, carrier- and land-based. Although the Japanese never completely evacuated their harbor base, hanging on until the end of the war, it was eventually bypassed as the main Allied thrust surged toward Japan. Thus, the planned major assault on Rabaul, the main reason for the year-long Operation "Elkton," never took place.

12.
ACROSS THE PACIFIC, 1943

A S the final battles of the Solomons Campaign were fought, the U.S. Navy and Marines embarked on the sequence of amphibious landings in the Gilbert and Marshall Islands, north east of the Solomons. Much had been learned during the amphibious landings in New Guinea and Bougainville, but the landings of Operation "Galvanic" were totally without equal in the ferocity of opposition encountered.

The Gilberts, seized by the Japanese from the British on December 10, 1941, were some 2,4000 miles west of Pearl Harbor, and would be retaken less than two years later by American amphibious assaults. There would be two landings: one by troops from the Army's 27th Infantry Division on Makin Atoll, and the main landing by the 2nd Marine Division on Tarawa Atoll. Makin had already been invaded by U.S. Marines – in August 1942 submarines had landed men of the 2nd Marine Raider Battalion on a hit-and-run reconnaissance raid (see Chapter 10).

For two weeks prior to the 1943 Gilbert landings, U.S. carrier aircraft had struck repeatedly at Rabaul and other Japanese airfields in the region. By D-Day on November 20 the Japanese were thought to have no more than 50 operational aircraft in the entire Gilbert-Marshalls area.

On board the approaching U.S. transports and landing ships all three major assault commands were headed by a "Smith": The V Amphibious Corps was under Marine Major General H. M. (Howling Mad) Smith; its Army contingent, the 27th Division, was under Major General R. C. Smith, and the 2nd Marine Division was commanded by Major General J. C. Smith.

Army troops landed on Makin on November 20. A 6,472-man regimental landing team took the atoll from the 848 Japanese defenders in four days. Casualties were light. Three days after landing, Army General Smith was able to radio the Navy task force, "Makin taken." The Navy suffered the most casualties at Makin. The light carrier *Independence* (CVL-22) suffered a hit from a Japanese torpedo bomber on the night of the 20th. She limped away for repairs. On the morning of November 24, the escort carrier *Liscome Bay* (CVE-56) was torpedoed by the Japanese submarine *I-175*. The carrier's bomb magazine blew up, breaking the ship apart; she sank in 23 minutes taking 644 of her crew and pilots with her. But these were the only losses to the massive U.S. invasion force from the several Japanese sub-

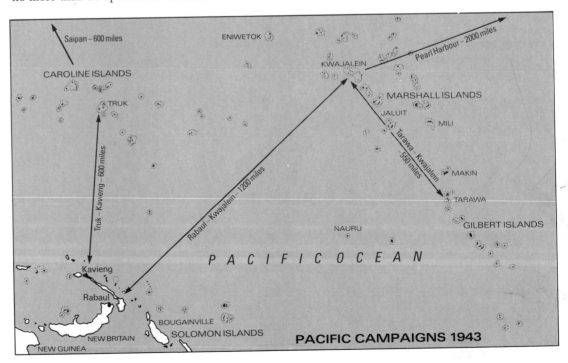

PACIFIC CAMPAIGNS 1943

Allied aircraft to control the remainder of the area. But the Japanese could also see the value of the atoll and fortified their defenses accordingly. Betio, especially, was heavily reinforced. Besides an influx of troops, the Japanese took advantage of Betio's natural reef and constructed beach obstructions and concrete and barbed wire fences to defend against amphibious vehicles and their assault troops. There was also a formidable array of heavy-caliber harbor defense guns to confront invaders. The possibility of considerable losses was obvious and unsettling for the Marine leaders.

An initial problem for the landing forces was poor communications, so vital in controlling the huge assault. Special command ships would not be available and the transport ships carried only limited equipment.

The staff of Rear Admiral Harry W. Hill, whose ships would carry the 2nd Marine Division, arranged special communication centers on the bridge of the admiral's flagship, the battleship *Maryland* (BB-46). However, this arrangement ran the risk of being damaged by the blasts from the ship's main guns when they fired in support of the landings.

A second problem was getting over the obstructions, including the reef at Betio. The landing was scheduled during low tide, and the reef would be exposed. The vehicle which the Marines hoped would provide the answer was the "Amtrac," or Landing Vehicle, Tracked (LVT), which had made its debut at Guadalcanal with less than satisfactory results. Unarmored, they were vulnerable to small-arms fire. The 2nd Division had improvised armor plating for some LVTs during their stay in New Zealand. General Smith also obtained 50 LVT-2s, which had more powerful engines and light armor protection, as well as a company of Sherman tanks which were re-equipped with heavier, 75-mm guns.

In addition to the major requests for new equipment, General Smith also asked permission to land artillery on adjacent islands but was turned down by his senior, Holland Smith, the V Corps commander, because of the time needed to make the additional landings. Various last-minute details had to be worked out, even as the invasion force neared its target area. Many Marines did not know their destination because of tight security. Lieutenant Colonel David Shoup, who would become Commandant of the Marine Corps in 1960, was elevated to full colonel and placed in charge of Combat Team 2, the assault force headed for Betio.

As usual, prior to the landings, Navy ships and aircraft blasted enemy positions. Three escort carriers, including the ill-fated *Liscome Bay*, furnished close air support for the Makin landings; five more escort carriers supported the Tarawa assault. The eight ships carried aircraft and flew 2,278 support sorties during the landings.

Above: Rear Admiral Harry W. Hill, one of the U.S. Navy's leading amphibious commanders, and his staff watch the bombardment of Tarawa atoll from the flag bridge of the battleship *Maryland* (BB-46) on November 20, 1943. The *Maryland* and other battleship survivors of the Pearl Harbor attack were invaluable in the shore bombardment role. (U.S. Navy)

marines seeking to break up the assault force. Their loss caused absolutely no delay to the U.S. timetable.

BLOODY TARAWA

The relatively easy victory at Makin would not be duplicated on Tarawa, 100 miles to the south. The Marines also hit their target on November 20, beginning a bloody nine-day campaign. The 2nd Marine Division had rested in New Zealand after leaving Guadalcanal in early 1943. Marine Major General J. C. Smith and his staff had little time to plan their phase of "Glavanic," the seizure of 290-acre Betio, one of the two small islands making up the Tarawa Atoll.

The Navy had won a victory against MacArthur by obtaining permission to launch its Central Pacific drive which the Navy claimed would shorten the war by going directly for Japan instead of liberating the Philippines, MacArthur's primary goal.

Tarawa was a likely target due to its position between Pearl Harbor and the Japanese bastion at Truk, sometimes referred to as the Gibraltar of the Pacific. The airfield on Tarawa would permit

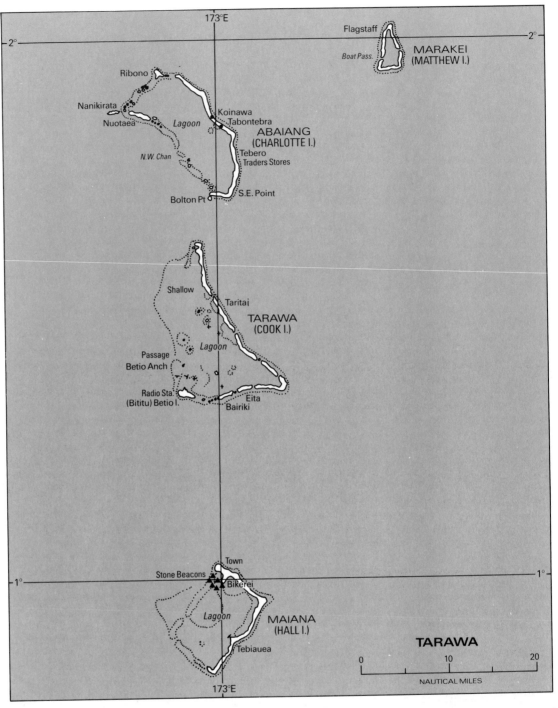

The Japanese actually began the battle for Tarawa by firing at the transports assembled offshore. The U.S. support force of three battleships, six cruisers, and nine destroyers responded with a fearsome deluge of shells. As the U.S. ships approached Betio, the enemy guns fell silent under their heavy fire and aerial bombs.

Marines of the 2nd Division clambered into their LVTs, LCVPs, and LCMs in preparation for the assault. It was 3½ miles to the beach and the sea was choppy. With a covey of minesweepers leading the way, the landing craft headed toward the beach as the enemy shore guns opened fire once more. Destroyers gave counterfire.

As feared, the concussion from *Maryland*'s main armament knocked out the makeshift communications center on her bridge, leaving the assault commander with no direct link to the slow-moving landing craft. The amtracs wallowed in the heavy seas and were not going to reach the beaches by the scheduled 8:30 a.m. The smoke and coral dust raised by the heavy bombardment obscured the view, and Admiral Hill decided to halt the fire for 30 minutes to allow the smoke to clear. This respite, however, allowed the Japanese to regroup and prepare to receive the assault troops.

The extremely low tide inhibited the movement of the landing craft. Even the tracked vehicles had trouble. The problem was so bad that the LCVPs deposited their troops half a mile from the shore. The Marines waded ashore in a hale of gunfire. It was here that the phrase "Bloody Tarawa" was born.

The first Marines to reach the objectives used flame-throwers to clear out the enemy. Other troops poured onto the beaches; some were trapped in the barbed wire or were cut down in the water by the murderous defensive fire. Men left the questionable protection of their lightly armored LCVPs, stranded on the reef, to confront the storm of fire ahead of them. Colonel Shoup managed to get ashore after he was forced to leave his amphibious tractor under heavy fire. On the beach he established a command post near an apparently abandoned bunker, but the original owners were still inside and re-opened fire. They were quickly dispatched by Marine grenades. Although wounded, Shoup remained where he was for more than two days, trying to get the chaos organized. He received one of the four Medals of Honor awarded at Tarawa.

The night of November 20–21 passed with no further confrontation, although the Americans fully expected a furious *banzai* charge at any moment. Instead, Japanese bombers flew a minor raid which actually hit their own men. The Americans got their supplies ashore, as well as reinforcements. The flow of supplies was still causing problems.

At 6:15 next morning, more Marines came ashore, wading into the same treacherous fire from Japanese positions. As their comrades watched, the newcomers floundered in the surf, weighted down with ammunition and equipment. The Japanese had taken a position in the hulk of an old, grounded freighter and poured fire into the Marines struggling to wade ashore. General Smith sent in more Marines. There were now eight battalions on Tarawa.

The Americans were able to form up, aided by tanks and howitzers, and begin to sweep the atoll. By the end of the second day, Shoup declared, "We are winning." The Japanese had weighted their defenses on the beach and thus their interior defenses were light. By early afternoon on the fourth day, the 23rd, Tarawa was fully in American hands.

The cost for taking Makin and Tarawa had been high. The Marines suffered nearly 3,000 casualties, including 984 dead; total American casualties in the assault were 1,027 dead and some 3,300

Below: Tarawa, bloody Tarawa, was one of the most difficult assaults in amphibious history. Despite tactical mistakes, the Marines were better trained, equipped, and led than their predecessors at Gallipoli and the issue of their success was never in doubt. Here Marines move out of the beachhead area of Betio toward the atoll's airstrip. These Marines are armed with M1 Garand rifles and M1 carbines; all have entrenching tools on their packs and two water canteens on their belts. (U.S. Marine Corps)

better coordination between the armor and infantry units.

American public revulsion at the flood of articles by war correspondents about Tarawa prompted a Congressional investigation that was only stopped by General Vandegrift's personal attention and request. Operation "Galvanic" had not been a disaster as the news stories seemed to suggest. Many valuable lessons were learned and the initial invasion of the Central Pacific had been successfully accomplished. A larger invasion was to come next – the Marshalls.

The American success in the Gilberts gave the overworked Fast Carrier Task Forces a much-needed rest, since the airfields on Tarawa were well within striking range of the Marshalls. The Marshalls were heavily defended, however, and Operation "Flintlock" – the invasion of the Marshalls – would be difficult. Planning for "Flintlock" had begun in May 1943 and concentrated on seizing major islands, rather than the entire Marshalls chain.

Initial plans called for invading the eastern atolls of Wotje, Maloelap, and Mili since they were closest to Allied bases. But, Admiral Nimitz, at a December 7 meeting of his principal commanders, proposed striking at the heart of the Marshalls, Kwajalein Atoll. His subordinates raised several objections to this, especially Marine General Smith, who complained that he was going to lose a major proportion of his Marines to support operations elsewhere, and could not promise to maintain control of recently captured territory with such a diminished force.

Admiral Nimitz overruled all the objections, but agreed to invade Majuro Atoll in the eastern Marshalls to give Smith a logistics base. As Commander-in-Chief, Pacific Area, Nimitz knew through intercepted Japanese radio traffic that the enemy had decided to pull back to the Marianas and more or less leave the 30,000 troops in the Marshalls on their own, to repel the invasion or die.

A lengthy pre-invasion bombardment of the Marshalls began in January 1944 with the invasion set for the 31st. The Gilberts had demonstrated the need for lengthy periods of shelling enemy installations by surface warships. The two-island Kwajalein Atoll was defended by 5,000 Japanese, with another 5,000 garrisoned on Kwajalein Island, 40 miles to the south. The 300 ships and 53,000-man assault force would have little trouble taking the lightly defended atoll. The Marshalls invasion would emphasize fire support, and included the debut of the LCI(G) gunboat armed with rockets and 40-mm guns. These new gunboats would escort the LVTs to the beaches.

The Army's 7th Division would land on Kwajalein Island, while the newly established 4th

wounded. Almost the entire 4,836-man garrison of defenders was wiped out. Only 17 wounded Japanese and 129 Korean laborers survived.

While the Gilberts were being finally taken from the Japanese, several hard lessons were learned concerning amphibious operations in the Pacific. The two main points were: efficient, well-protected communications, and better organization and delivery of naval support gunfire. The question of communications affected both sides, for the Japanese commander, Rear-Admiral K. Shibasaki, had lost his communications in the naval bombardment and was left with little effective means of coordinating the atoll's defense. This U.S. loss of communications could also be linked to the poor performance of the naval bombardment, heavy though it was. The ships fired into the interior of Betio rather than responding to requirements to hit specific targets on the beach, where Japanese defensive fire was the worst. There was also a need for heavier tanks, the refining of logistics – always a problem – as well as generally

Far left: Marines capture a Japanese pillbox by frontal assault on Betio during the Tarawa landings. This is believed to be a particularly heavily fortified Japanese position which held out for four days after the initial Marine landings. Some of these fortifications withstood aerial and naval bombardments and could only be taken by frontal attacks by infantrymen. (U.S. Marine Corps)

Far left: This was Betio Island on about November 20, 1943, immediately after the cessation of the naval bombardment. The circular coral atolls generally had a few islands as large as this and many sand spits. Unlike the volcanic islands that were later assaulted, there were no hills or other significant heights on these atolls. Note the stranded landing craft on the beach. (U.S. Navy)

Marine Division would assault Roi and Namur, the two islands in the north east corner of the atoll. While Navy carrier planes swept the sky of the remaining Japanese aircraft, the Japanese defenders prepared themselves for the invasion. They knew there was little hope of surviving the powerful American force.

Fire support ships bombarded Roi-Namur for two days at close range until the 25th Marines with two artillery battalions landed on the tiny islands on January 31. Kwajalein got the same treatment. Rear Admiral Richard L. Conolly, commanding the Northern Attack Force, and a veteran of the recent Sicilian campaign, told his ships to "move really close-in . . ." and was thus given the nickname "Close-in Conolly."

The next day, February 1, the 23rd and 24th Marines made the main landings on Roi and Namur respectively, finding little enemy resistance except for individual pockets of Japanese defenders. A problem getting the Marines ashore developed due to a shortage of LVTs. The amtracs assigned to lift the 24th Marine Regiment had also carried the 25th Marines the previous day, and a fuel shortage and what one writer has called "uncooperative Navy officers," caused a delay in getting transport for the assault teams.[1]

The new LCI(G)s had a field day, pumping 40-mm cannon shells into the beach ahead of the assault forces. Roi was quickly taken, but Namur was somewhat more involved, with densely wooded areas that hid Japanese bunkers and pillboxes.

The 24th Marine Regiment fought its way inland, but without the support of their gun-armed LVT(A)s, which had been foiled by anti-tank traps. The Japanese even tried to mount a *banzai* charge but failed. On February 2, the tanks came ashore, however, and behind armor the Marines secured Namur by the mid-afternoon.

To the south, the U.S. Army found Kwajalein Island's defenders more of a problem. The 7th Infantry Division took four days to secure the island. The Japanese counter-attacked at night in small groups. But under constant artillery barrages, the Japanese were finally defeated, with many committing suicide. The Japanese lost nearly 8,400 men in defending Kwajalein, while the Americans had suffered a total of nearly 500 men killed in action. The Americans were learning their trade well, for in comparison to the Gilberts, the Marshalls yielded twice as many enemy losses, while exacting only one-half the casualties on the American side.

ENIWETOK

The assault of Kwajalein had barely been completed when Operation "Catchpole" hit Eniwetok Atoll, 325 miles north west of Roi. Rear Admiral Harry Hill again commanded the Navy ships, while Marine Brigadier General Thomas Wilson led the newly established Tactical Group 1, the

landing force. The landings were set for February 17. The 22nd Marine Regiment and the Army's 106th Infantry Regiment would form the bulk of the assault force, with a composite battalion of LVT(A)s and LVTs from the 7th Infantry Division. The 4th Marine Division would provide additional support.

The Japanese had reinforced Eniwetok, so that approximately 3,500 troops were on the atoll. The airfield on Engebi was to be the focus of carrier attacks. Truk was also hit by Task Force 58 carriers in attacks preliminary to the Eniwetok landing, with the anchorage recently captured at Majuro providing a convenient staging area. U.S. aircraft losses were light, although the carrier *Intrepid* (CV-11) – one of five fleet carriers supporting the operation – took a single torpedo launched by a Kate torpedo bomber during a night raid. The damaged carrier retired safely for repairs.

Operation "Catchpole" began on schedule, with dawn landings on Engebi. Preceded by naval bombardment and air strikes, and with close cover by LCI(G)s, the initial waves of Marines were landed. Their DUKWs brought ashore howitzers and by nightfall, their artillery was in position.

At 8:42 a.m. on the 18th, the 22nd Marine Regiment landed and moved inland behind carefully orchestrated naval gunfire, aircraft strikes, and artillery barrages. The following day brought additional landings. Battleships came to within 1,500 yards of the beach to blast Japanese positions. The defenders fought hard, but by February 23, Eniwetok was secured. Most of the 3,500-man Japanese garrison was killed. The Americans suffered 348 soldiers and Marines killed.

Eniwetok continued to prove the value of heavy pre-invasion bombardment. It also highlighted the growing family of amphibious tractors and vehicles, especially the DUKW, which, though perhaps unsuitable for the direct assault, could be used to transport supplies and artillery ashore immediately after the main landings.

There was considerable friction between the Army and Marines, who viewed their specific modes of operation differently. The Army tended to be more cautious while the Marines pressed forward at every opportunity. Some Marines thought the Army exhibited less courage and aggressiveness than themselves, confusing the caution and less ambitious leadership for lack of moral fibre. The Marines were angered when the commander of the Army's 27th Infantry Division received the Navy Cross for heroism at Eniwetok.

The Marshalls soon became the hub of Marine night-fighter activity, with squadrons based on Roi, Kwajalein, and Engebi to control the skies over the area at night as well as in daylight. Marine aircraft also mounted a tedious but important bombing campaign against Japanese outposts on Wotje, Maoelap, Mille, and Jaluit atolls. Landings would not be needed if the bombing sealed these

Above: Marines halt during the assault on Eniwetok while, at center, two Navy hospital corpsmen attend a wounded Marine. The sailors and Navy medical officers as well as a few chaplains served alongside the Marines in every landing operation. Again, the Marines (and sailors) have entrenching tools on their packs. (U.S. Marine Corps)

outlying islands from the mainstream of the war.

In the meantime, the planning for the invasion of the Marianas pointed to the use of Marine aircraft on carriers to support this major amhibious operation. The Navy had been reluctant to put Marine aircraft on carriers, believing that while the Marines could perform pre-assault strikes and close air support, they lacked training and experience to fly from carriers for fleet operations against Japanese warships and aircraft. With the widening war in the Pacific, however, it was obvious that the Marine air squadrons would be needed to support the men on the beaches in future amphibious operations. The Navy could not do it all, and Marine squadrons in the Gilberts and Marshalls could not reach the Marianas. Thus, the issue of Marines on carriers finally demanded definitive attention. With 10,000 pilots, 126 squdrons, and 100,000 aviation support troops, Marine aviation was impressive. And, in mid-1944, the Navy could not completely man all its aircraft carriers, especially the growing fleet of small, escort carriers (CVE).

The decision was made to put the Marines aboard the CVEs, after establishing a major training program to qualify them for carrier operations. However, Navy reluctance and the time needed for proper training dictated that the first Marine carrier squadrons could not be available until early 1945, too late for the capture of the Marianas. In October 1944, General Vandegrift, now Commandant of the Marine Corps, agreed to allow Marine squadrons to join selected fleet carriers, and to generally consolidate support organizations. The Navy then promised to let Marine air return to its primary role of close air support. Refinements, especially in the area of controlling aircraft during amphibious operations, were begun during this time, and were to bear fruit during the final amphibious operations in 1945, such as the Philippines and Okinawa. But first, came the Marianas.

INDIAN OCEAN INTERLUDE

In 1943, as the Anglo-American amphibious forces undertook the landings in Sicily and Italy, and planned for the cross-Channel landings, and U.S. Army and Marine forces carried out landings in the Pacific, consideration was given to amphibious operations in still another theater, the Southeast Asia area.

Admiral Louis Mountbatten, after serving as Chief of Combined Operations, took command of the Southeast Asia theater.[2] Mountbatten immediately proposed an amphibious landing to push the Japanese out of the Andaman Islands in the Bay of Bengal, given the codename "Buccaneer."

Late in the year Roosevelt and Churchill met in Cairo as a prelude to their meeting with Stalin at Teheran. The Americans came to Cairo seeking an operation in Southeast Asia that would support Chiang Kai-shek in China. An operation such as "Buccaneer" fitted in perfectly with American proposals. But Churchill was aghast at Mountbatten's proposal – more than 50,000 British and Commonwealth troops to assault the islands held by an estimated 5,000 Japanese troops. Even the explanation that, of that total, only 18,000 men would be in the assault and immediate follow-up forces, was unacceptable to the Anglo-American leadership. Roosevelt himself expressed the thought that 14,000 troops "would be ample" for the assault.

Churchill and most senior British officers were against "Buccaneer," knowing that the operation would divert troops and landing craft from the Mediterranean, and possibly delay their availability for the cross-Channel ("Overlord") landings in 1944. Finally, the American commanders began to concur with the British view, and by the afternoon of December 5 the Combined Chiefs of Staff, meeting in Cairo, decided to signal Mountbatten that European operations had priority and that "Buccaneer" must be postponed. That evening Churchill received a terse message from Roosevelt: "Buccaneer" is off."

Churchill, however, still held hopes for another amphibious operation in the area, an assault to capture Sumatra (Operation "Culverin"). This assault could, he believed, give the Allies command of the Malacca Straits and open the approach to Malaya and Singapore. Although his proposal to capture the entire island was soon changed to a raid in force, the requirements of troops and landing craft soon led to the abandoning of this proposal.

Rather, amphibious landings in 1944–45 would be limited almost exclusively to the on-going European and Western Pacific campaigns.

13.
ACROSS THE PACIFIC, 1944

ASSAULT ON THE MARIANAS

Successful as the operations in the Gilberts and Marshalls were, they were only preparatory to the final twelve months of the Pacific war that would see amphibious landings raised to new levels of size and complexity, and the violence of the conflict increase. The U.S. Marine Corps and Army had learned much during the quick, bloody, thrusts in the Central Pacific. These lessons would be invaluable in the coming campaigns. The first assault of the last year of the war would be against the Marianas.

The Marianas were important for several reasons: strategically, the large islands of Saipan, Tinian, and Guam, offered attractive staging sites for U.S. forces. Saipan and Tinian, especially, would make ideal airfields for Army Air Forces' B-29s from which to mount attacks against the Japanese home islands. The Marianas also lay across the Japanese lines of communication and supply between Japan and conquered territories in Malaya and the Dutch East Indies. To cut these strategic shipping lines would obviously inflict heavy damage on the Japanese economy and military capabilities.

Psychologically, the capture of the Marianas would return Guam, conquered by the Japanese in the dark days after Pearl Harbor, to the American

flag and would signify the growing might and momentum of the impending Allied victory. The first moves against the Marianas came from carriers of the U.S. Fifth Fleet under Admiral Raymond Spruance, one of America's most capable admirals of the war, who had commanded the Navy's victorious fleet at Midway in 1942. Task Force 58 planes struck the Japanese in the Marianas in February 1944 to destroy enemy installations and take photographs for the subsequent invasion. Set for June 15, the assault was codenamed Operation "Forager."

The 2nd and 4th Marine Divisions, veterans of earlier campaigns, and the equally experienced Army 27th Infantry Division, would carry the main brunt of the landings. Newly promoted Lieutenant General Holland Smith again commanded the Marines. Saipan was selected as the first target, mainly because it offered the closest base to Japan from which to stage the B-29 raids. Its capture would also effectively block the Japanese forces on Guam from direct support from Japan.

Task force 58 sortied from Majuro on June 6, 1944, as word of the D-Day Invasion of Normandy cheered the Americans and seemed to fill them with a flood of renewed patriotic fervor. But the size of the Marianas amphibious operation, which was underway at the very moment of the "Overlord" landings half a world away, demonstrated graphically the unprecedented military capabilities of the United States. And, the fact that in both ocean areas the major American thrust was an amphibious operation also spoke for the importance of this form of warfare.

In all, the U.S. Fifth Fleet, steaming toward the Marianas, consisted of more than 800 ships, including fifteen fast carriers and eleven escort carriers, as well as a phalanx of 28 submarines driving ahead of the main fleet, seeking enemy contacts. Indeed, one of the secondary hopes of the huge "Forager" strikes was that the remaining Japanese fleet would be drawn into one final destructive battle with a superior American force, to be taken out of the war for good.

In fact, the Japanese *were* coming out for battle. Aware of the importance of the coming battle in the Marianas, the Japanese quickly gathered a large fleet, built around their remaining aircraft carriers, for one massive strike at the American fleet.

Below: U.S. amphibious assaults in the Central Pacific were spearheaded by the fast carrier task forces. The Third/Fifth Fleet carrier forces (Task Forces 38/58) had up to sixteen fleet (CV) and light (CVL) carriers available for supporting the American drive westward. Seen here in column are *Essex* (CV-9)-class fleet carriers, *Independence* (CVL-22)-class light carriers, and fast battleships en route to the next assault. Each CV carried approximately 100 aircraft, the CVLs about 40. (U.S. Navy)

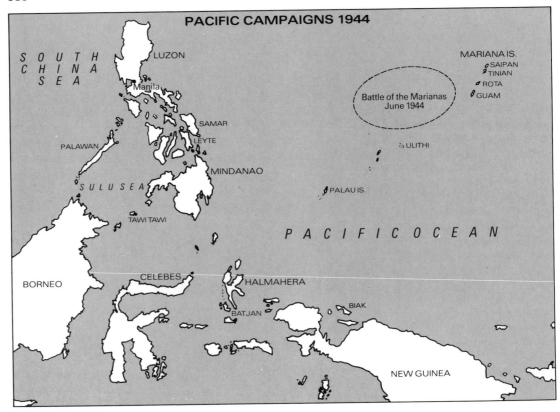

PACIFIC CAMPAIGNS 1944

The first aerial contact came on the morning of June 11, when Grumman F6F Hellcats on combat air patrol engaged aerial snoopers from the Marianas and shot them down. That afternoon, 200 miles east of the Marianas, the American carriers launched fighter sweeps and bombing raids against Japanese installations on Saipan and Tinian. For the next three days, the opposing fleets played cat and mouse with each other, neither sure of the other's positions and strength. The Japanese First Mobile Fleet had left the anchorage at Tawi Tawi on June 13, observed by a U.S. submarine. More than 400 planes in five fleet carriers and four light carriers were available to strike the Americans. However, as the Japanese warships proceeded eastward they were harassed by American submarines, which extracted a toll in destroyers and carriers.

Eventually, the two fleets' aircraft met in battle on June 19, in what is considered the last major carrier-versus-carrier battle of the Pacific war. The resulting débâcle – as far as the Japanese were concerned – was immediately christened the "Marianas Turkey Shoot" when it was realized that the Japanese had lost – 400 aircraft. In a running, two-day series of strikes and counter-strikes, the Japanese lost nearly all their aircraft, including 100 land-based aircraft, and three carriers. The Americans lost 100 aircraft, many during the night landing of June 20–21, when, after a long-range final raid against the fleeing Japanese ships, the returning aircraft came down into the sea as their fuel was exhausted.

The Battle of the Philippine Sea, as the carri-er battle was called, broke the back of Japanese naval air power, although it did not deliver the final crushing blow the Americans had sought. The Japanese fleet was still a dangerous surface opponent and it would take a final engagement in the Philippines to destroy the Imperial Fleet. However, the Turkey Shoot and carrier losses ended any chance of Japanese naval or air interference with the U.S. landings.

While the U.S. and Japanese fleets jockeyed for position, trying to find each other in the vast ocean, the amphibious force under Vice Admiral Richmond Kelly Turner, approached Saipan. D-Day was June 15. The landing force of 71,000, under General Holland Smith, waited as the Navy went to work on the 13th, pounding enemy positions with aircraft and heavy shells. Spruance's battleships bombarded the west coasts of Saipan and Tinian for seven hours from only two miles offshore.

Clandestine preliminary scouting by Underwater Demolition Teams (UDTs) brought back important information on water depth, channels, tides and currents. Turner decided to come in through the "back door," avoiding the more obvious and more heavily defended beaches of Magicienne Bay on the island's south eastern coast. Instead, he made a feint toward the capital, Garapan, and then landed the assault elements of the 2nd and 4th Marine Divisions on the southern coast near Aslito airfield.

As the first wave of LVTs approached the beaches, aircraft from the carriers began strafing Japanese positions. Battleships and cruisers pos-

itioned themselves close in, between the line of departure for the LVTs and the beach. Covered by 24 LCI(G)s, amphibian tanks with 75-mm howitzers came in first, taking the brunt of surviving Japanese defensive fire. This allowed the troop-carrying vehicles behind them to land with few losses. Within 20 minutes, 700 LVTs and 8,000 Marines were on the beach. The 30,000 defenders fought viciously. A problem developed when the LVTs could not move inland and were stuck on the beach, and before the end of the day, 2,000 Marines had been killed or wounded. But 20,000 were on the island.

The Marines needed reinforcements, and Holland Smith ordered the Army's 27th Infantry to come ashore. The soldiers took a position on the 4th Marine Division's right flank, and helped take the Aslito airfield. As Marine and Army troops fought side by side toward a common objective, their respective generals fought their own struggle. Holland Smith, whose nickname "Howling Mad" was well-earned, was not a tolerant man, especially during inter-service conflicts.

Dissatisfied with the 27th Infantry's performance, and its general's apparent inability to press the attack, the Marine Smith relieved his subordinate, Major General Ralph Smith, and assumed direct command of the Army operation, much to the disgust and frustration of the Army.

By June 20, the Americans had cleared most of the southern end of Saipan, although the extreme southern tip was a warren of concealed caves and bunkers occupied by Japanese survivors. On July 7, 3,000 of the remaining Japanese charged the 27th Infantry Division in a vicious attack. Staggered by the *banzai* charge, the Americans fell back, but the charge spent itself and two days later Holland Smith declared Saipan secured.

The loss of Saipan, coming with the débâcle of the carrier battle in the Philippine Sea, brought down the government of the Japanese premier, Hideki Tojo, who resigned on July 18. All but approximately 1,000 of the 30,000 Japanese on Saipan died on the island, some having committed suicide at the last by jumping from cliffs, together with their civilian counterparts who had listened to horrible tales of American barbarism told by the Japanese. American casualties numbered 16,525 killed and wounded.

The American carrier component was much preoccupied with the Marianas Turkey Shoot during the invasion of Saipan, but as the battle raged to the west of the island, Navy FM Wildcat fighters from escort carriers kept the skies clear of Japanese planes while TBM Avengers and the fighters provided close air support to the Marines and soldiers on the beaches. Little Marine "grasshoppers," two-seat, light aircraft, more at home on a sunny Sunday touring flight than a bloody battlefield, flew off the carriers on June 17 to provide artillery spotter services. On the morning of June

Above: Logistics were always a key factor and limitation in amphibious operations in World War II. Landing craft from the U.S. attack transport *Harris* (APA-2), a Coast Guard manned ship, unload an LCVP on the beach at Saipan. Just offshore are an LCM and a DUKW. (U.S. Navy)

22, the CVEs also flew off Army P-47 Thunderbolt fighters, which they had transported to the battle for basing ashore. Within two days, 73 P-47 Thunderbolts had made the flight to the newly captured airstrips on Saipan.

Lessons of the Saipan landings included the much improved coordination between artillery and infantry and considerably more accurate and timely close air support. However, working relations between the Marines and Army had deteriorated at all levels, fanned by Marine contempt for what they considered lack of Army aggressiveness in the field. The relief of Ralph Smith by the Marines' Holland Smith made the matter worse. The conflict rose to the Olympian heights of Navy and Army commands, involving Admirals Spruance, Turner, and Nimitz, and, eventually the Joint Chiefs of Staff in Washington. The senior military leaders had to come up with some sort of patchwork arrangement to mend the rift. An Army investigation organized by Lieutenant General R. C. Richardson, the senior Army commander in the Pacific, declared that although Holland Smith could legally relieve the Army's Smith, the action was unjustified. To smooth things over, Holland Smith was moved out of the command of the Expeditionary Forces to administrative command of Marines in the Pacific – Fleet Marines Force Pacific. He would never again lead Army troops.

TINIAN

The smaller island of Tinian in the Marianas was the next target. It would offer more airfields for B-29 raids against Japan. The narrow beaches on the northwestern edge, flanked by coral cliffs and low bluffs, were selected because landings there would be a surprise to the Japanese looking toward more favorable beaches for the assault. Long-range artillery on Saipan could also provide pre-landing bombardment.

Aerial reconnaissance was flown for a month to gain accurate topographical information. Detailed maps were made in foam rubber, a new process

developed by a special Navy unit and first used for operations in the Aleutians in mid-1943. The bombardment intensified on July 23, including the first use of the jellied gasoline called napalm. Intended to burn away vegetation, the napalm was dropped by the Army P-47s flying from Saipan. After preliminary beach reconnaissance by UDTs, assault elements of the 2nd and 4th Marine Divisions rode their LVTs in on July 24. Intense Japanese fire greeted them on the beaches. The pattern of earlier landings was repeated. A vast umbrella of protective fire covered the landing force. Then LVTs and DUKWs ran forward to the beaches. At Tinian, however, the amtracs left their passengers on the beach and turned back to the ships for more; they would not follow the Marines inland. Too many of the awkward amphibs had been lost struggling up from the beaches on Betio and Saipan against enemy fire. As it was, underwater mines, undiscovered by the UDTs, sank three loaded LVTs, and land mines destroyed many others.

The Japanese organized fierce banzai charges at the Marines who stood fast and dug in. By dawn on the 25th, the 4th Division counted 1,241 enemy dead. The Americans kept coming. By the 25th, more than 40,000 had come ashore. By August 12, the last pockets of Japanese had been eliminated, and Tinian was secured.

GUAM REGAINED

Originally planned for July 18, three days after the landings of Saipan, the assault on Guam was postponed because of the possible intervention of the Japanese carrier force rushing toward the Marianas, and the need to include the Army's 27th Infantry Division in the Saipan assault. Of course, the decisive U.S. victory in the Battle of the Philippine Sea denied the Japanese Navy any influence on the fighting in the Marianas, but the savage fighting on Saipan dictated the need for a further reserve force for the Guam assault.

The delay was put to good use by Rear Admiral Richard Conolly's fire support ships, mostly older

battleships and cruisers, several being veterans of the Pearl Harbor attack. They bombarded Guam's western coast where most of the island's principal facilities, including the major airfield, were concentrated. The Japanese thought the Americans would land in this area.

With coral reefs ringing the island, and steep cliffs along the northern coast, only a 15-mile stretch of beach on the west coast would permit an amphibious landing. Recognizing this fact, the Japanese concentrated their main defense there, with eight of eleven available infantry battalions and most of their armor and artillery moved into that area.

While the Japanese prepared themselves, the Americans also gathered their units for the landings, now set for July 21. Major General Roy Geiger, one of the Marine Corps' first aviators, and first leader of the "Cactus" Air Force on Guadalcanal, would command the landing force, from III Amphibious Force – the 3rd Marine Division, under Major General Allen Turnage and the 1st Provisional Marine Brigade, led by Brigadier General Lemuel Shepherd (who became Marine Commandant in 1952), with

the Army's 77th Division in reserve.

With the battle on Saipan already three days old, the 3rd Division and 1st Brigade Marines came ashore at Guam at 8:29 on the morning of the 21st. Admiral Conolly's fire support ships had lifted their massive barrage only minutes before. The 3rd Division landed north of Apra Harbor, at Asan, while the 1st Brigade struck to the south of Agat. Protected by LCIs with their guns, mortars, and rockets, the 3rd Division ran into intense Japanese artillery and mortar fire, as well as machine guns, situated on the cliffs above the beaches.

General Shepherd's brigade had even rougher going. Its two regiments, the 22nd and 4th Marine Regiments, lost many of their amtracs to Japanese 75-mm guns strategically situated in the cliffs overlooking the beach. The Marines struggled up from the beach all day. After midnight, the Japanese charged the Marines.

The next two days saw the Americans fighting inland against savage opposition. On the night of July 25–26 the Japanese again charged the invaders. Another future Marine commandant, Captain Louis H. Wilson, distinguished himself during

Above: A Marine takes a break after the fighting on Saipan. He is sitting on an unexploded 16-inch shell from a U.S. battleship. While the older U.S. battleships were readily available to support amphibious landings, the allocation of the ten newer battleships was highly controversial. The fleet commanders wanted them primarily to steam with carriers where their massive anti-aircraft batteries – up to 148 20-mm, 40-mm, and 5-inch guns – could help deter Japanese air attacks; the Marines and amphibious force commanders wanted them for shore bombardment. (U.S. Marine Corps)

the night attacks. Five thousand Japanese, many drunk with saki, stormed across the Marine lines, engaging the Marines in fierce hand-to-hand combat. In the event, the charge was not enough to stop the American advance, and the Japanese fell back, leaving half their original number dead and dying.

One innovation during the Guam landings was the night unloading of supply ships. Twenty-five cranes were set up offshore of each beach to shift supplies from landing craft into LVTs and DUKWs, which would ferry them to shore. Since many of the LVTs and DUKWs had been destroyed during the first assault waves, causing a shortage of amphibious vehicles, rubber boats were strung in line along the reefs, making causeways to allow conventional landing craft to lower their ramps for their cargo to be rolled ashore.

The fierce fighting around the Orote Peninsula and Apra Harbor lasted four days, with the Japanese and Marines locked in deadly combat. Eventually, the U.S. flag was raised at the old Marine barracks, witnessed by Admiral Spruance, General Holland Smith, and General Geiger.

Meanwhile, the Marines and Army troops swept northward, and by August 10, supported by naval gunfire, air, and artillery, the Marines declared Guam secure. Sporadic Japanese resistance continued until the end of the war as survivors of the Japanese battalions, who had escaped into the jungles and caves, sniped at the Americans. Incredibly, a few Japanese continued their own private campaign well after the war, the last finally surrendering in the early *1970s*!

The Seabees improved Apra Harbor, constructing a new breakwater and dredging the harbor to allow new docks and accommodation of supply ships simultaneously. Guam became a major naval base in the Pacific, much larger than it had been before the Japanese conquest.

The amphibious campaign in the Marianas had proven the worth of UDT reconnaissance prior to the assault, providing information and clearance of obstructions in the assault area. The use of napalm, first dropped at Tinian, added another weapon to the growing arsenal of assault arms. Despite the distasteful "Smith-versus-Smith" episode, there was a renewed feeling of teamwork among the various factions. Operation "Forager" showed the refinement which continued to develop in the American amphibious operation, and also demonstrated how ultimately hopeless the Japanese situation had become. Human waves and drunken banzai charges could not defend against a smoothly coordinated attack, presaged by a deluge of shells and bombs.

NEW GUINEA AND THE PALAUS

General MacArthur could not forget his promise to return to the Philippines. While General Eisenhower prepared to invade Normandy and Admiral Nimitz gathered his forces for the Marianas assault, MacArthur at long last launched his own campaigns in April 1944 to expel the Japanese from New Guinea.

After his success in taking Buna, Lieutenant General Eichelberger had spent most of 1943 and early 1944 in Australia, training troops assigned to MacArthur's command. By the time of the Hollandia operation in the spring of 1944, MacArthur had nearly 750,000 men of all services under his command, including Australians. The U.S. Seventh Fleet was under his command to provide appropriate naval forces (with a few Australian, Dutch, and Free French ships). But the U.S. Navy high command would provide no fleet carriers to the Seventh Fleet, only escort carriers, land-based aircraft, and seaplanes. (The Third/Fifth Fleet carriers, under Admiral Nimitz's Pacific Area Command, periodically provided temporary support to the Seventh Fleet.)

While MacArthur's transports and cargo ships were Navy, several Army special engineer brigades provided MacArthur with hundreds of landing craft, mostly LCVPs, LCMs, and DUKWs to complement the few Navy- and Coast Guard-manned landing craft. Highly innovative, the Army engineers mounted 20-mm and .50-caliber guns on their landing craft to provide limited anti-aircraft defense for the beachheads, and 4.5-inch rockets for fire support.

Using amphibious tactics to bypass the main Japanese lines of resistance along the coast of New Guinea, U.S. troops under Eichelberger's direct command landed at Hollandia on April 22, 1944.

Under the Seventh Fleet, the VII Amphibious Force coordinated the landing activities. For Operation "Reckless," the codename of the Hollandia landing, the VII Amphibious Force under Rear Admiral Daniel E. Barbey, assembled almost 30 cargo ships and transports of various types, 43 LSTs, two LSDs, and nineteen LCIs with a screen of almost 40 destroyers and destroyer escorts, plus submarine chasers and frigates. The total ship count was 215.

Providing cover the Seventh Fleet had seven escort carriers, two Australian heavy cruisers, three U.S. light cruisers, and two dozen destroyers from the two navies. Long-range reconnaissance and anti-submarine patrol was provided by PBY Catalinas and land-based PB4Y Liberators. MacArthur's V Army Air Force provided bombers to strike at Japanese bases in the area.

Under General Eichelberger, the April 22 landings were made simultaneously at three points along the New Guinea coast, with combat teams drawn from the Army's 24th and 41st Infantry Divisions. The bold amphibious strike was highly successful, with little Japanese resistance. Indeed, the most serious losses were the result of an Army air strike on a Japanese supply dump at Beach White 1 before the landings. During the assault little was done to extinguish the fire and a Japanese aircraft used the flames as an aiming-point on the night of April 23–24, adding to the conflagration. The flames detonated a Japanese ammunition dump, spreading fires along the beach. Twenty-four men were killed and 100 wounded, with twelve LST loads of rations and ammunition being destroyed. Fires and explosions continued until April 27.

In the successful amphibious assault the total U.S. casualties were small, as were those of the Japanese who fled to the mountains. The airstrips and control of the area were firmly in Allied hands.

Next, General MacArthur sent Eichelberger's troops and the VII Amphibious Force against the coastal islands of Noemfor and Biak. While Noemfor was relatively easy to subdue, Biak's defenders let the American soldiers land and then hit them from their sequestered hiding-places, but both islands fell and in September 1944,

MacArthur's forces struck out for Morotai and Peleliu, halfway between New Guinea and the Philippines.

On September 15, the Army hit Morotai, and the 1st Marine Division struck Peleliu, the latter supported by the Army's 81st Division. Admiral William F. (Bull) Halsey, commander of the Third Fleet, had ordered a carrier strike against the southern Philippines. His aircraft sank many Japanese ships and destroyed 200 aircraft. Reconnaissance and Filipino guerrilla reports made it obvious that the Philippines were not well defended, and Halsey strongly urged cancellation of the Palau operation. Although MacArthur agreed to move his Philippines invasion time-table up a month, he went ahead with the Morotai and Peleliu landings, called Operation "Stalemate."

Halsey was overruled by Admiral Nimitz because it was believed Peleliu was lightly defended. There was nearly total ignorance of the Palaus. The last detailed information on the island had come from Marine Major E. H. Ellis, who died in May 1923 under questionable circumstances while in the Palaus. Perhaps he had stumbled upon evidence of Japanese strength in the islands. But even twenty years later, little was known about the islands. In fact, the Palaus were heavily fortified, with protective jungle concealing coral ridges and hundreds of caves, perfect for hiding troops and weapons. In addition, the Japanese commanders had told their field commanders to wait until the invaders were established on the beach and moving inland. The defenders would then establish a defense line in the jungles and run less risk from the massive bombardments as in the earlier American landings.

Pre-invasion bombardment began on September 12, but results were later adjudged disappointing, due, in part, to inadequate targeting information, as well as to the burrowing instincts of the Japanese hiding in the dense jungle. The 1st Division troops pushed off from their transports at 8:30 a.m. on the 15th, meeting little initial resistance, which was, of course, part of the Japanese plan. Then the concealed mortars and machine-guns opened fire, initially knocking out 26 of the Marines' LVTs.

Below: LCS(L) fire support ships bombard the Palau group prior to the Marine assault of September 1944. These craft generally had ten rocket-launchers plus 40-mm and 20-mm guns (some units had a 3-inch gun forward). The Navy converted 130 units from LCI(L) hulls for this role. The LCS(L)s could move up to the beach with the landing craft. (U.S. Navy)

In the late afternoon the Japanese sent tanks and troops against the 1st and 5th Marine Regiments. The night brought the traditional *banzai* charges as the Japanese poured from the concealed caves. The Marines were not prepared for the strength of the enemy resistance, especially since intelligence had led them to believe the overall defenses were light.

In the first week of fierce combat on Peleliu, the Marines suffered 4,000 casualties, with the 1st Marine Regiment nearly wiped out. Marine survivors joined with the Army's 81st in fighting along the coral ridge, gradually overpowering the weakening Japanese. The Marine-piloted F4U Corsair fighters, newly arrived on the captured airstrip at the southern end of the island, dropped bombs and napalm, and strafed the Japanese. The fighting was so close to the airstrip that the Corsair pilots didn't bother to raise their landing gear when they took off for a bombing run, simply dumping their ordnance on the Japanese positions and then banking to come around to land and re-arm.

The arrival of Marine aviation in the western Pacific again raised the question of who controlled Marine air, especially when the senior area commander was General Douglas MacArthur of the Army. Obviously, the Marine aircraft would be useful during the upcoming invasion of the Philippines. The 1st Marine Aircraft Wing was soon tied to MacArthur's Sixth Army in the dedicated close air support role.

The carnage on Peleliu was finally ended amidst bombs and flame-throwers in the caves and burnt-out jungle areas. The 1st Division suffered 6,786 casualties of whom 1,300 were killed in action.

The three assault regiments took heavy casualties. Each regiment had had slightly more than 3,200 men on D-Day. The 1st Marines suffered casualties amounting to 53.7 percent of their strength, the 5th 42.7 percent, and the 7th 46.2 percent. Approximately 12,000 Japanese had been killed when Peleliu – six miles long and two miles wide – finally fell to the Americans.

Although U.S. Marine generals were reluctant to recommend major awards, eight of the nineteen Medals of Honor won by the 1st Division in the Pacific were given at Peleliu. Brigadier General Oliver Smith stated later: "The first five days on Peleliu were just as tough as Iwo Jima, but then tapered off and Iwo Jima kept going."

And the bitter truth was that MacArthur was already headed for the Philippines. The invasion of Peleliu *was not necessary*![1]

THE PHILIPPINES

General MacArthur's long-planned grand return to the Philippines was basically an Army show – although the soldiers were carried in Navy transports and amphibious ships, escorted by Navy destroyers and escorts, with Navy battleships and cruisers for gunfire support, and Navy air support from aircraft carriers. Marine participation, important though it was, was limited to close air support by units of the 1st Marine Aircraft Wing. As the Army prepared for the invasion, the Marine aviators trained with the Sixth Army. The Army Air Forces' Southwest Pacific Air Force was also part of MacArthur's command.

The Philippines operation was on-again, off-again, as the Navy and Army wrangled with each

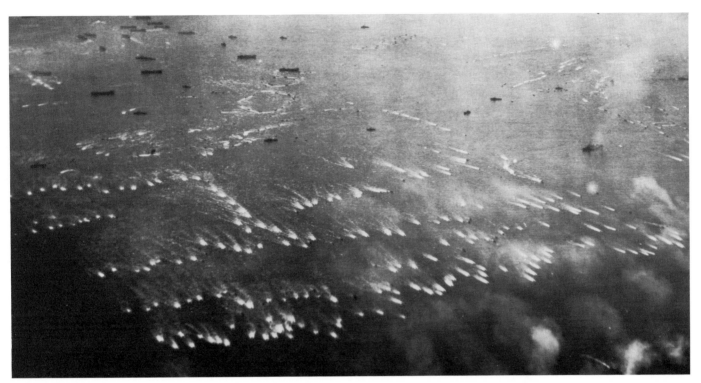

Above: The assault on Leyte as seen from the air revealed hundreds of landing craft moving toward the beach. General MacArthur advocated the return to the Philippines for both political and military reasons. Personally committed to the liberation of the Philippines, he argued against Navy proposals to attack Formosa (Taiwan) for use as a base for further operations against the Japanese home islands or China. (U.S. Navy)

other. MacArthur did not have many friends and supporters, and the Navy was driving steadfastly toward Japan. To create what many considered a sideshow for MacArthur's triumphant return to Manila would put undue stress on the supply chain and commit troops and ships needed elsewhere. However, MacArthur prevailed, the final decision being made by President Roosevelt.

An early battle and resulting benefit of the Philippines operation was the Battle of Leyte Gulf, which finally destroyed the remnants of the once-powerful Japanese fleet. Two American fleets, Halsey's Third and Kinkaid's Seventh, fought the Japanese for four days, October 23–26, in the climatic naval engagements of the war. The desperate Japanese tried to stop, or at least delay, the first landings on the island of Leyte in the southern Philippines, committing their remaining carriers and large surface combatants, including the giant battleships *Yamato* and *Musashi*, and the first organized *kamikaze* suicide air units. But the combat was a decisive American victory, the Japanese losing three battleships, including the *Musashi*, and four aircraft carriers; American losses were two escort carriers and three smaller warships.

The Battle of Leyte Gulf, beyond the final destruction of the Imperial fleet, left the Japanese garrisons in the Philippines without air support or protection for their supply and communication lines to Japan. They had to meet the Americans with what they had to hand.

The Philippines are an archipelago of 7,000 islands of which only four were of primary importance in the upcoming invasion: Luzon in the north, Mindanao, in the south, and Mindoro and Leyte in the central portion. Luzon, with its capital, Manila, and important harbors, was where most of the Japanese troops were located. Besides the 250,000 Japanese troops on Luzon, another 43,000 were on Mindanao. Mindoro had an important airfield, and Leyte offered a geographically strategic link to the other three main islands. Given this strategic position, Leyte was selected as the first target.

MacArthur used two assault forces to get his 202,500 troops to Leyte: the Northern Attack Force and Southern Attack Force, commanded by Rear Admiral D. E. Barbey and Vice Admiral T. S. Wilkinson, respectively. The two forces deployed a total of 500 ships. The Navy minesweepers came in first and the Ranger units landed on October 17 to place navigation beacons and to clear entrance corridors in the Surigao Strait, connecting the Mindanao Sea with the Philippine Sea.

Several hours before dawn on the 20th, the transports arrived at their appointed areas; H-Hour was set for 10 o'clock. The pre-invasion bombardment began at 7 a.m. and lasted until H-Hour. The bombardment was lifted only to allow aircraft to sweep the beaches in strafing runs. The first waves of the Northern Attack Force landed under support fire from LCIs. Troops of the Army's X and XXIV Corps, including 1,528 Marines "on loan" from the V Amphibious Corps, got ashore with little opposition, although there was some Japanese mortar and machine gun fire.

The LVTs and DUKWs took the second waves ashore on the southern beaches, with LSTs moving in close enough to disembark their troops and tanks into the surf. As the tremendous operation successfully brought masses of men and matériel ashore, concern mounted for after-dark attempts by the Japanese to attack these caches of supplies.

A new type of amphibious ship, the Landing Ship, Medium (LSM) assisted in the frantic, but orderly movement. These were similar to LSTs, but smaller and could land vehicles in more shallow areas. Pontoon barges were used to construct causeways to allow wheeled vehicles to come directly ashore from transports. More than 107,000 tons of supplies and equipment were unloaded on the first day, and on the following days the unloading pace was even faster.

However, concern for the threat posed by the huge Japanese fleet entering the area in an effort to oppose the Leyte landings was high. Even after the decisive Japanese naval defeat, MacArthur and his staff knew there were still not enough aircraft available to cover further landings and give protection against enemy air raids, especially at night. Additional problems arose when the Army realized that the Japanese airfields were not ready

for the massive support operation envisioned for the U.S. squadrons scheduled to come into the Philippines. Mud was everywhere, and it would take the Navy's Seabees many weeks to prepare the strips. Every day an inch of rain fell and at times the Tacloban landing strip was only eighteen inches above water. It took two months to put Leyte's airfields into working condition, a second field being constructed near the main strip at Tacloban.

The Army requested the services of Marine night-fighter units stationed on Peleliu. As the Army consolidated its positions on Leyte, the Marines sent in F6F-3N Hellcats, which flew the 600 miles to Tacloban, the first arriving on December 3. A total of five squadrons (four operating F4U Corsairs) were provided by the Marines. These squadrons operated from the strips at Tacloban, and covered landings on Leyte's west coast, at Ormoc on December 7. The Japanese bitterly opposed the Ormoc landings, their troops hidden in well-defended pillboxes and caves.

In addition, the Japanese were supplied directly from Manila, and the famed "Tokyo Express" type

Below: Always LSTs: Coast Guard-manned LSTs unload supplies and equipment onto the beach at Leyte. The soldiers in the foreground are filling sand bags for anti-aircraft gun emplacements.

of supply convoys of Guadalcanal days were alive and well for a time. U.S. planes constantly attacked the Japanese ships and positions for three weeks, sinking 22 ships and shooting down 40 Japanese planes at a cost of 34 Marine aircraft lost and nine pilots killed. The enemy on Leyte dug in, and sent *kamikazes* against the Navy ships supporting the invasion. Several carriers were struck by the suicides with heavy casualties and damage. It was a foretaste of things to come in the late Pacific War.

Action on Leyte continued throughout December 1944, although by Christmas the Japanese had virtually ceased organized resistance and MacArthur declared Leyte secured.

The island of Mindoro to the northwest was the next target. More than 16,000 Army troops landed on December 15, together with another 15,000 construction and Army Air Forces personnel coming ashore to build and operate air facilities. Good weather and little opposition from the Japanese allowed the landing to take place on schedule.

A *kamikaze* struck the cruiser *Nashville* (CL-43), flagship of Rear Admiral Struble, the overall force commander, and he transferred his flag to a destroyer. Enemy resistance on Mindoro was limited because of the small garrison of only 500 soldiers.

LUZON

The main landing of the Philippines campaign on the island of Luzon evolved into one of the greatest land battles of the Pacific war. With the defeat of the Japanese fleet in the Leyte Gulf battles, and the relative ease with which the first phases of the Philippines operation had been prosecuted, the initial decision to bypass Luzon was changed to include a full-scale invasion. The original date of October 1944 was changed because of stiffening enemy resistance on Leyte. The second assault date was January 9, 1945.

The landing operation was to include the 200,000 troops of the Sixth Army under General Walter Krueger, supported and transported by the 850 ships of Vice Admiral Thomas Kinkaid's Seventh Fleet, with carrier cover by Halsey's Third Fleet. The Japanese could field more than 250,000 men on Luzon, although they were largely disorganized and poorly supplied. And, of course, they could no longer depend on support from the once powerful Japanese fleet.

The Japanese knew that the Americans would land at Lingayen; it was where they, themselves, had landed in December 1941. The only hope the Japanese had was to fight a costly delaying action that would halt the drive to Japan. The U.S. Navy daily fought off *kamikaze* attacks as the huge fleets drew nearer to Luzon. Although the suicide raids badly damaged several U.S. ships, pre-invasion bombardment began on schedule on January 6. The shelling took place in concert with attacks by several Marine dive-bomber squadrons now situated in the central Philippines.

Correspondent Robert Sherrod later wrote, "In Marine aviation annals the Luzon campaign provides one of the notable milestones. Here, for the first time, Marine planes furnished true close air support for Army troops. Here the Marines set out to perform a distinct mission and they trained for just that speciality – the assistance of ground troops in advancing against the enemy."[2] The Japanese moved most of their remaining aircraft out from the Philippines, leaving their troops completely without air cover.

At 9:30 a.m. on January 9, assault elements of the Army's XIV Corps landed at Lingayen. The only problems encountered came not from Japanese defenders, but from natural obstacles, including fish ponds and flooded rice fields. By nightfall, 68,000 troops had come ashore, and the usual huge supply chain was well into operation. The Japanese had yet to appear in any strength, and American commanders were uneasy. Where was the enemy? The new Japanese tactic of allowing the landings to take place uncontested, thereby avoiding the punishing bombardment had left the Army troops unmolested.

The Japanese had not completely withdrawn, however. They had devised a new *kamikaze* weapon, the suicide boat. Basically, a 20-foot skiff crammed with depth-charges and mines, these little boats dashed out in night attacks against the much larger American ships, where their crews would heave the explosives by hand toward the U.S. ships and retreat. The Japanese accounted for several LSTs, transports and various other U.S. ships sunk or damaged. However, quick counteraction by the Americans resulted in the destruction of most of the 60 to 70 suicide boats in the area.

Relief at the lack of enemy opposition soon turned to expectant caution as the Army troops

Below: Soldiers storm Fort Drum in Manila Bay from LSMs during the retaking of the forts and islands in Manila Bay. Nearby Corrigedor was assaulted from the air by the Army's 503rd Parachute Combat Team in one of the few parachute drops of the Pacific War. Dropping onto the small island was difficult. The air drop on February 16, 1945, was immediately followed by an amphibious landing. Almost 6,000 Japanese defenders were on the island, with 4,500 being killed in the recapture operation.

moved inland to find an intricate defense system of caves, tunnels, and pillboxes constructed in the now-familiar Japanese manner. It was the beginning of six months of fighting on Luzon, and especially around the capital of Manila.

Eventually, the American Army also landed near Bataan, site of the infamous death march after the fall of the Philippines in early 1942. On January 29, the XI Corps came ashore and took the airfield and Olongapo naval base. Two more weeks were needed to reach Manila, through heavy fighting against the remaining Japanese resistance.

On January 31, yet another U.S. amphibious landing south of Manila Bay, by the 11th Airborne Division, began the drive toward Manila itself. Aided by tanks and troops of the 1st Cavalry Division, the U.S. force drove into the capital, releasing long-held prisoners taken by the Japanese three years before. Heavy fighting continued in what some called the first urban battle of the Pacific war. Not until March 3, when Japanese resistance ended amid the bombed-out shells of Manila's buildings, following house-to-house and brutal hand-to-hand combat, was the capital declared free by a jubilant General MacArthur. On June 30, 1945, MacArthur declared most of Luzon secured and the Philippines liberated.

Significantly, the Japanese used short-range amphibious operations in this campaign to support troops under attack by guerrillas when they could not break through by land routes. For example, Malitbog on Leyte was invested so successfully by guerrillas that the Japanese had to depend totally on seaborne resupply. When possible, the Japanese troops were unloaded in ports, but several amphibious landings were undertaken. For example, in the Agusan River Valley, a small shock unit was sent ashore in landing craft to seize the Butuan town dock to allow the landing of the main force.

But the Philippines campaign was primarily a series of highly successful U.S. amphibious operations. As noted above, one of the major successes of the campaign was the emergence of U.S. Marine close air support as a mature, integral part of amphibious landings and subsequent operations ashore. However, as the Luzon campaign moved inland, the Marine squadrons returned to their own specialized mission. They developed better ground to air communication procedures, bypassing the Army's cumbersome and time-consuming method of relaying requests for close air support to rear areas. By the time these requests had been acted upon, the friendly troops requesting the support had moved and were sometimes in the line of fire, finding themselves caught by the bombs dropped by their own aircraft.

The Marine solution was two-fold: provide radio-equipped jeeps with the ground forces to communicate directly with the aircraft, and have trained ground commanders fly with the Marines so that targets might be quickly and accurately identified.

The Philippines set the pattern for Marine close air support for the remainder of the war, which while short in duration, would be long in effort and expensive in blood and material. Iwo Jima and Okinawa lay ahead.

ON THE ROAD TO MANDALAY, 1944

While the fighting in the main theaters of war captured the headlines — and most of the Allied resources — an intense, isolated war was being fought in the jungles of India and Burma. The Japanese had succeeded in throwing the British out of most of Burma by May 1942, establishing their so-called "Co-prosperity Sphere" in Southeast Asia.

The British fought a guerrilla war against the Japanese, desperately trying to hold on despite lack of supplies and support. Thanks to groups of trained jungle fighters, commanded by Brigadier Orde Wingate and known as "Chindits" (an anglicization of the name of the mythical Burmese griffin, Chinthe, which guarded pagodas), the Japanese did not have an easy time holding their conquered territory.

As Japanese control of the area began to ebb, with the Japanese turning to other areas in the Pacific where they were suffering important defeats, the British decided it was time to mount a major attempt to recapture the whole of Burma. Throughout January and February of 1944, the British and their native allies fought the Japanese for control of the central border of India and Burma around the towns of Imphal (in India) and Tiddim (in Burma). The Chindits harassed their enemy at every opportunity, cutting Japanese communication lines and disrupting supply efforts.

The Japanese, who had crossed the Chindwin River in Burma, were forced to retreat to the river by October. Fighting in the northern areas continued, with an uneasy alliance of British, and American, and Nationalist Chinese troops against the hard-pressed, but tenacious Japanese.

In August 1944, with Imphal in British hands and the Japanese retreating toward the Chindwin, the Allies found themselves literally tire-deep in mud and monsoon rain. Aided by Royal Air Force supply drops, the British hunted their enemy, who were reduced to unsuccessful foraging, and were struck down by disease and malnutrition.

The time was obviously right to recapture Burma, and a September 1944 directive from the Supreme Allied Commander Southeast Asia, Admiral Louis Mountbatten, initiated two operations. Operation "Capital" was to secure land communications along the tortuous Burma Road, and Operation "Dracula" was to capture the capital city of Rangoon with an amphibious and airborne assault. The timing of the assault was important because of the approaching monsoon season. Indeed, if "Dracula" could not be launched and completed by March 1945, it would have to be postponed until November. The opening stages of "Capital," however, were successfully completed by early December 1944.

The stage was now set for the confrontation between a large Japanese army dug in from Mandalay in the east, to Seikpyu in the west. The area around Mandalay featured important rice fields and oil fields. Capture would ensure the final expulsion of the Japanese from Burmna. The Japanese, originally thought to be committed to remaining north of the wide Irrawaddy River, had actually crossed to the southern banks. The British were thus forced to consider crossing the river before engaging the enemy. Lieutenant-General William Slim, commanding the Fourteenth Army, and a veteran of the Burma fighting, took the bold step of following a cattle trail south along the river's bank. Renaming his operation "Extended Capital," Slim notified his superiors of changes in the operation, and established an elaborate sequence of dummy bases, messages, and fake river crossings to fool the Japanese.

The ruse worked, and although the enemy put up a furious fight against the fake crossings, they were unprepared for the actual assault on February 14. At 4 a.m., in the widest amphibious assault of the war — the British were strung out for nearly 200 miles along the river — the Fourteenth Army crossed the Irrawaddy, preceded by a fierce artillery barrage. A regiment of tanks and squadrons of U.S. and RAF aircraft bombed the Japanese on the opposite bank. The defenders were overwhelmed in the massive thrust, and by nightfall the British assault brigade was well established.

From the second day the pace never faltered, as the troops and armored units drove north to Taungtha. Unlike their better-equipped American comrades in the Pacific, the assault forces made do with outboard-powered boats and *mules* to ford the Irrawaddy — no LCTs and LCIs for them. General Slim's bold stroke had thoroughly confused the enemy, allowing his troops to cross over the remaining boundary, and engage the enemy in running battles all the way to Mandalay.

Although both sides suffered heavy casualties during the three weeks of fighting after the crossing, the Japanese were pushed farther back. By the first week in March, the Japanese were surrounded. Rangoon was next, and the planned amphibious and airborne assaults of Operation "Dracula" — aided once again by airlifts of supplies and material — secured the Burmese capital by May 3, the Japanese having evacuated the city by April 29.

14.
ACROSS THE PACIFIC, 1945

WITH the southern Pacific in American hands, and the Philippines partially secured, attention was turned to what became the penultimate amphibious landing in the Pacific. Iwo Jima has been described as a foul-smelling, pork chop-shaped little island, barely 7½ square miles in area. The terrain was dominated by a volcano, Mount Suribachi. Iwo Jima's strategic importance made an amphibious assault imperative.

One of the few Pacific islands belonging to Japan before the war (since 1891), Iwo Jima is only 660 miles from Tokyo, a three-hour flight. The capture of an island so close to the homeland would deal a psychological blow to Japanese morale. Moreover, the island boasted two completed airfields, which would be ideal for emergency landings by B-29s making the 2,800-mile round trip to bomb Japan from the bases in the Marianas. And, since that distance to and from the U.S. bases in the Marianas was greater than the range of escort fighters, the island would also serve as an advanced base for P-51 Mustangs and P-47 Thunderbolts to escort the B-29 heavy bombers over Japan. Iwo Jima was simply too important to bypass.

Planning for the invasion of Iwo Jima actually began in September 1943, and after the Marianas had been taken, Admiral Nimitz told Lieutenant General Smith his next task would be to land on Iwo. As commander of the Marines in the Pacific, Smith had the V Amphibious Corps available, consisting primarily of the 3rd, 4th, and 5th Marine Divisions.

In addition to General Smith, the leaders of other components were the same team that led the Central Pacific campaigns: Admiral Spruance, commanding the Fifth Fleet; Vice Admiral Turner, commander, Amphibious Forces Pacific; and Vice Admiral Marc Mitscher, leading the fast carriers of Task Force 58.

Although planning and preliminary aerial reconnaissance of Iwo Jima had already begun, the unexpected heavy Japanese resistance in the Philippines, which tied up carrier assets, forced postponement of Operation "Detachment" – the name for the Iwo Jima landing – from January 20 until February 19, 1945.

The Navy also began shelling the Japanese in November. The U.S. Army Air Forces began a lengthy bombardment on December 8, 1944, with Army Air Forces B-24s and B-25s bombing the island for an incredible 74 consecutive days. It was the longest pre-invasion bombardment of the

Right: The volcanic island of Iwo Jima, with Mount Suribachi at the near end, was critical for the U.S. strategic bombing effort against Japan. Located 660 miles from Tokyo, the island would serve as a base for fighter aircraft to protect the B-29s and as an emergency landing strip for damaged bombers. The volcanic composition of the island made it difficult for LVTs and other tracked vehicles to gain a footing. (U.S. Navy)

war. And it was justified. Reconnaissance photos revealed a massive Japanese defensive network, including more than 600 blockhouses and gun positions, and the usual labyrinth of caves. By February 1, 1945, there were 21,000 Japanese troops waiting on the island, with 120 guns of 75-mm or larger, 20,000 smaller guns, and a vast assortment of mortars, rockets, and anti-aircraft weapons. The Marines who landed on the beaches would immediately come under devastating fire. General Holland Smith demanded at least ten days of sustained bombardment immediately prior to the landings. According to one historical study, "It was plain that Iwo Jima had fortifications the like of which we had never encountered . . . an island five times the size of Tarawa, with many more times the number of defenses, most of them deep underground."[1]

As the invasion date drew nearer, however, the Navy was reluctant to commit itself to anything but a three-day sustained bombardment. The drawn-out action in the Philippines had shortened Admiral Spruance's timetable to support the projected landings on Okinawa in April. General Smith denounced the lack of Navy support, but the positions of both sides were relatively justified. The Marine general, who always fought for his troops, had his attention centered on the Iwo Jima operation. His Navy counterparts, while wanting to give the Marines more support, had to think of the overall requirements of the continuing prosecution of the war, which was drawing nearer to the ultimate goal: the invasion of Japan. Thus, the Marines had to be satisfied with the intense Army Air Forces' bombing schedule, and an abbreviated bombardment by the Navy prior to the landings.

The first amphibious contingent arrived off Iwo Jima on February 16, and the UDTs went to work.

Supported by twelve escort carriers, six battleships, four heavy cruisers, sixteen destroyers and twelve LCIs, the frogmen surveying and clearing the offshore area were mistaken for the actual landing force by the Japanese. The guns on Iwo Jima opened up, hitting all twelve LCIs, sinking one. The UDTs suffered 170 casualties, but all but one survivor were recovered. In firing on the scouting teams, the Japanese had disclosed many of their hidden gun positions, which was to pay dividends for the Americans two days later.

The morning of the landing brought good weather, a calm sea and a light breeze from the north. The landings would be made on the south-east shore of Iwo. Secretary of the Navy James V. Forrestal and an entourage of journalists prepared to watch the assault from the amphibious command ship *Eldorado*. The pre-assault bombardment began at 6:40 a.m. and lasted until 9 a.m. Besides the array of new and old battleships, twelve of the 203½-foot LSM(R)s with batteries of 4.5-inch rockets and 40-mm guns contributed to the fire. Other specialized landing craft that provided close-in fire support included LCI(G)s, LCI(M)s, and LCI(R)s.

From 8:05 until 8:25 the close-support ships moved into positions, while aircraft from Admiral Mitscher's carriers flew a final strike against the island. LVT(A)s – amphibian tractors with 75-mm howitzers, the now ubiquitous "Buffalos" – escorted the first assault wave toward the beach. At 9:02 the landing elements of the 4th and 5th Marine Divisions scrambled onto the beaches.

Almost mystically, there was only scattered Japanese fire. As the Marines continued to come ashore, the supporting LVT(A)s kept up their support fire, although many were swamped or stalled at the water's edge. The accumulating wreckage

Below: Assault waves of landing craft approach Iwo Jima on D-Day, February 19, 1945. Mount Suribachi gave the Japanese excellent observation and gun positions. Iwo Jima was the largest marine operation of World War II with three divisions participating in the assault. Anglo-American landings in the European-Mediterranean theater were larger but rarely as disputed. (U.S. Navy)

Left: Marines hug the volcanic sands of Iwo Jima. These troops of the 4th Marine Division were making their fourth amphibious assault in just over a year. A beached LSM is in the background with beached LCVPs immediately behind these Marines. Tanks and trucks are already ashore. (U.S. Marine Corps)

Left: This photograph of D-Day on Iwo Jima shows how Mount Suribachi dominates the island. The survival of Marine platoon leaders on Iwo Jima was measured in tens of minutes as they sought to lead their troops inland against the intensive Japanese gunfire. (U.S. Marine Corps)

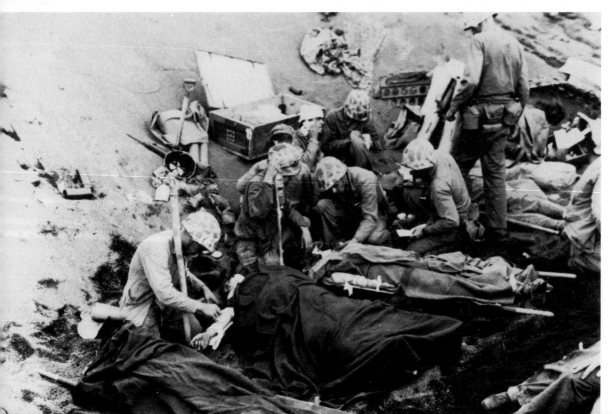

Left: A Navy chaplain (center) kneels beside a wounded Marine on Iwo Jima while Navy medical personnel treat casualties on the second day of the assault. A dead Marine lies on the stretcher at left. The Navy "corpsmen" and doctors as well as chaplains worked in the open on Iwo Jima, continually exposed to Japanese gunfire. The chaplain, Lieutenant (junior grade) John H. Galbreath, was assigned to the 13th Marine Regiment of the 5th Marine Division. (U.S. Marine Corps)

caused problems for incoming elements, whose own vehicles ran into the hulks of the damaged amtracs. But the landing pushed ahead.

The original plan called for the immediate capture of Mount Suribachi, the main bastion at the extreme southern tip of the island, and Airfield Number 1, directly inland from the beaches. But the relative "free ride" ended dramatically at 9:45, shortly after all seven leading battalions had come ashore. The tremendous enemy defenses rained fire down on the exposed Marines, now hugging the soft, sooty beaches. Tanks and wheeled vehicles alike found it difficult to move in the volcanic ash, especially against the intense Japanese 47-mm anti-tank gunfire. By nightfall, the Marines had suffered more than 2,400 casualties — 566 dead, 1,854 wounded — in establishing a beachhead 3,000 yards long and 700 to 1,500 yards deep. Approximately 30,000 troops had come ashore that first day.

On the morning of February 20, the first attempts at taking Suribachi gained only 200 yards. For three days the 28th Marines battled their slow way up the volcano. By 10 a.m. on the 23rd they reached the top and raised a small American flag on a piece of Japanese pipe. Later, a larger flag was sent ashore from an LST, and Associated Press photographer Joe Rosenthal took the famed picture that came to stand for "Marines."

The 23rd, 25th and 27th Marine Regiments also had their hands full trying to take Airfield No. 1. The 21st Marines were called in from

Above: Marines and a Navy corpsman raise the second American flag over Mount Suribachi (the first was a smaller one). This photograph by Joe Rosenthal of Associated Press became the most famous view of the Pacific war.

Right: Mount Suribachi taken. A Marine rifleman looks down at landing ships on the beach at Iwo Jima on February 23. Iwo Jima was the largest Marine landing of the war and earned the most Medals of Honor for Marine participants. (U.S. Marine Corps)

the reserves. Soon the other regiments joined the intense fighting, attacking behind intense naval bombardments. Tanks and halftracks, trying to support the Marine riflemen, fired, then stalled, or fell victim to mines and the heavy Japanese anti-tank artillery firing from holes in the cliffs. It was not until March 9 that the Marines were able to break through the enemy's main defenses. The network of Japanese caves and underground bunkers tested Marine skill and resolve.

The last pockets of Japanese resistance were not overrun until March 16, when Iwo Jima was declared secured. Nearly all the 21,000 Japanese died, but not before inflicting more than 23,000 casualties on the invading Marines and 2,800 on the sailors who had brought them there. Of the 6,821 U.S. dead, nearly all were Marines.

The group of war correspondents witnessing the incredible battles on Iwo made sure the American public got a good taste of the bloody fighting. Repelled by what appeared to be senseless loss of huge numbers of American lives, opinion ran against the men who had planned and led the assault and month-long battle. The Marines blamed the Navy for lack of sufficient fire support; they felt that a longer bombardment could have saved American lives.

Admiral Nimitz, in trying to project the best qualities of the men involved in the fighting, said "Uncommon valor was a common virtue." It was true. Twenty-seven Medals of Honor were won by Navy and Marine personnel at Iwo Jima, the most for any single operation of the war. After observing the Iwo Jima assault first hand, Secretary Forrestal declared that the Marines had earned their future for the next 500 years.

Even before the island had been secured by U.S. troops, on March 4 the first B-29 made an emergency landing on Iwo Jima. Within three months of Iwo Jima's capture, more than 85 B-29s had made emergency landings on the island. By early April, P-51s were staging from Iwo Jima to escort B-29s on their raids to Japan.

When the war ended in August the number of emergency landings by B-29s on Iwo Jima totalled 2,400 with crews aggregating 24,000 men.[3] If Iwo Jima had not been captured, possibly hundreds of the "Superforts" and thousands of aircrew might have been lost.

OKINAWA

The massive, bloody, hotly contested landings on minuscule outcroppings of volcanic rock in the warm Pacific waters indicated the likelihood of equally bloody fighting on Japan's doorstep. Contemporary planners and force commanders knew that Okinawa was only the opening curtain on the ultimate invasion of Japan, itself.

Situated only 350 miles from Kyushu, the southernmost main island of Japan, Okinawa is part of the Ryukyu chain. The island offered several fleet anchorages and airfields. It would be invaluable as an advanced staging base for the coming amphibious assaults against Japan. The more than 100,000 Japanese troops on Okinawa hoped to sell themselves dearly in a series of costly delaying actions, involving the use of the last remaining units of the Imperial Fleet, massive aerial *kamikaze* raids, and suicidal troop actions on land. It was the only way. "One plane for one warship. One boat for one ship. One man for ten enemy. One man for one tank." It was the creed of the XXXII Japanese Army on Okinawa.

The Allied lineup for the Okinawa landings – Operation "Iceberg" – included Admiral Spruance as Central Pacific Task Force Commander, Vice Admiral Turner as amphibious force commander, and Vice Admiral Mitscher leading the fast carriers. Army Lieutenant General Simon B. Buckner, veteran of the Aleutians campaign, would command the land forces, collectively called the U.S. Tenth Army, composed of the Army XXIV Corps and the III Marine Amphibious Corps. Lieutenant General Roy Geiger was the deputy landing force commander. Close air support would be provided by the AAF-Marine Tactical Air Force under Marine Major General F. P. Mulcahy.

The invasion fleet consisted of the largest number of ships involved in a single operation during the entire Pacific war, nearly 1,500 combatant and auxiliary vessels. In addition, the British sent a fast carrier task force of 22 ships, with 244 aircraft in four carriers to supplement the American total of almost 1,000 carrier aircraft. All told, some half a million men – Army, Navy, Marines, and Royal Navy – would participate in Operation "Iceberg."

Initially, the invasion was scheduled for March 1, 1945, but the delays in the Philippines and Iwo Jima set the operation back to April 1, Easter Sunday. Two weeks prior to the invasion, Admiral Spruance's carriers struck the home island of Kyushu. Pre-invasion bombardment of Okinawa began a week before the landings, and on March 26, five small islands of the Kerama Retto group just west of Okinawa, were seized to cut off a force of enemy suicide boats and establish a preliminary anchorage for the U.S. Fleet.

The Okinawa invasion began at 4:06 on Sunday morning, starting with a feint toward the southeastern shore. The real landing would go in along a five-mile stretch of beach on the southwestern coast, near the village of Hagushi. The site was chosen because of the proximity of the two important airfields at Yontan and Kadena. Capturing these airfields as quickly as possible would help relieve the pressure on the covering carrier task forces to provide close air support.

The battleship *Tennessee* (BB-43) steamed to within 1,900 yards of the beach to permit her 14-inch guns to cover the landing force of LVTs and DUKWs, with several other battleships further offshore firing salvo after salvo of 14-inch and 16-

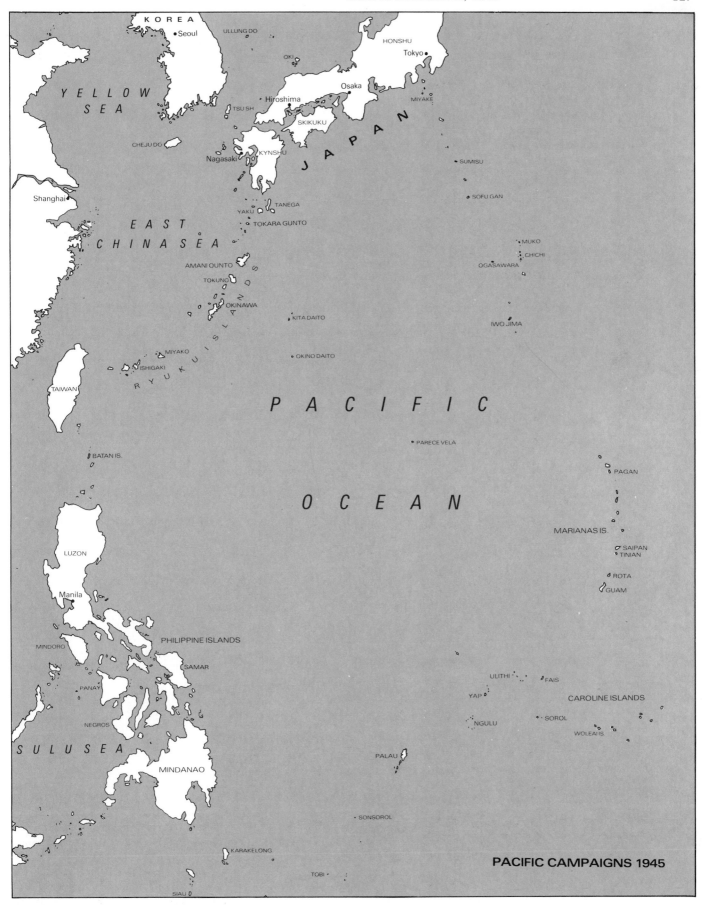

PACIFIC CAMPAIGNS 1945

Right: A battleship of the *New Mexico* (BB-40)-class fires into Okinawa while Marine-laden LVTs pass en route to the beachhead on April 1. The LVTs were carried into the assault area in LSD, LSV and LST landing ships. These are LVT(A) models with a 75-mm howitzer mounted in an open turret. (U.S. Navy)

inch rounds at the Japanese defenses. But except for occasional mortars and machine guns, there was no enemy fire. The Marines and Army troops came ashore, and within four days had attained most of their objectives with limited opposition.

The initial enemy response to the landings came in the form of intense *kamikaze* air raids on the naval task force. The Japanese had forgone the heretofore meaningless suicide charges, allowing the Americans to establish their beachhead unmolested, but were merely biding their time.

The Japanese had established a defense line that became known as the Shuri line, from the ancient nearby castle. The two airfields were allowed to be taken without too much effort. In fact, the Seabees and engineers did so well that the Marines later used Yontan and Kadena as their own defensive positions.

The Shuri line, running east-west, north of Naha on the southern tip of Okinawa, had its first test on April 4, when the Army's XXIV Corps ran up against massive defenses on Kakaza ridge. Eight days of heavy fighting were needed to take the ridge. The Japanese were cleared from these positions cave by cave.

At one point, a second landing to bypass the Shuri line had been considered. The assault could strike either coast and use reserve forces, the 77th Infantry Division and the 2nd Marine Division. General Buckner, however, decided against it because of the supply and logistic problems. The Navy supported Buckner's position, which greatly annoyed the Marines, who questioned the wisdom of having the Army command an amphibious operation of this magnitude. Internal disagreements again emphasized the rift between the Army and Marines, and the Marines and the Navy.

General Buckner ordered a major offensive against Shuri on May 11, which again failed to break the line. Finally, the 1st Marine Division took Shuri Castle on May 29. By that time Japanese strength was failing. More than 62,500 Japanese and Okinawans had been killed around Shuri, and a further 5,000 had died on Ie Shima, a small island off Okinawa's west coast. American journalist Ernie Pyle also died on Ie Shima, victim of a Japanese sniper's bullet.

Below: The battleship *Tennessee* (BB-43) fires into Okinawa while Marine-laden LVTs pass en route to the beachhead on April 1. The Marines sitting on the LVT at left will crouch down as the craft approaches the beach. Light machine-guns were mounted on the LVTs. The LVTs were carried into the assault areas in LSD, LSV, and LST landing ships. (U.S. Navy)

The enemy thus evacuated Shuri, moving south to establish yet another defensive line at Yaeju Dake and Yazu Dake. The situation on Okinawa was determined by early June. The deaths of both the U.S. and Japanese force commanders within five days of each other had no effect on the final outcome. General Buckner died from shrapnel wounds on June 18 while visiting an observation post that came under Japanese shelling. His counterpart, Lieutenant General Mitsuru Ushijima, committed suicide on the 23rd.

Fighting on Okinawa continued until the last week of June. On June 21, General Geiger, who succeeded General Buckner as Commander of the Tenth Army – the only instance of a U.S. Marine leading a field army – declared Okinawa secured. The campaign was officially completed on July 2.

The landings on Okinawa were textbook operations, especially since the intense fighting did not come until after the actual assault. The initial confrontations came offshore, between the Allied Fleet and the swarms of *kamikaze* aircraft. More than 1,900 *kamikaze* sorties were flown during the three-month period of Operation "Iceberg." The suicide planes caused much damage and injury, including 263 ships of all types sunk or damaged. The amphibious force lost 31 ships.

Marine aviation's participation in the Okinawa assault involved Marine squadrons based on fleet as well as escort carriers. Since the Okinawa airfields were taken so quickly, the first Marine aircraft operations began in the early afternoon of April 1, with the two-plane "grasshopper" artillery spotters setting up shop within hours of the landings. Air control units, as well as aircraft squadrons, were soon operating from Okinawa in direct support of the ground operation. The control units directed intense air strikes against the seemingly impregnable Shuri line, monitoring

Above: Smoke rises moments after a Japanese suicide plane crashed into a U.S. cargo ship off Ie Shima on May 11, 1945, during the assault on Okinawa. The Army-Marine assault on Okinawa was unusual because the Japanese defenders did not try to stop the Americans when they came ashore. The campaign, however, was long and bloody. The island was needed as an advanced base for the planned invasion of the Japanese home islands. (U.S. Navy)

650 sorties directed solely against Shuri on April 19. Okinawa provided a final test for the evolving close air support doctrine pioneered by the Marine Corps since the 1920s.

Both sides suffered horrendous casualties on Okinawa and in the U.S. Navy fleet offshore. More than 107,000 Japanese and Okinawian military and civilian personnel died. The Tenth Army losses were 31,807 Marines and soldiers wounded plus 7,163 killed or missing in action, while the Navy sustained 9,731 casualties in ships.

The Okinawa campaign brought the Allies to Japan's doorstep. The only task left was to invade the home islands.

THE FINAL INVASIONS: OPERATIONS "OLYMPIC" AND "CORONET"

The principle behind the Allied drives in the Pacific was frustratingly simple: to destroy the Japanese ability to make war. The two-pronged attack on that capability, through the Central Pacific and through the Solomons, New Guinea, and up to the Philippines, would come together in the planned invasion of the Japanese homeland.

The initial planning for the invasion, eventually codenamed "Olympic," began in June 1944. The U.S. Joint Chiefs optimistically set a date of October 1, 1945 for the landings on Kyushu to be followed by assaults on Honshu, the main Japanese island. The second operation – codename "Coronet" would begin on December 31, and would deliver the final blow to the enemy heartland, ending, it was anticipated, with the taking of Tokyo.

As always, there was considerable wrangling among the Allied planners, at all levels. British concern over the campaign in Malaya caused them to wonder if they could provide adequate participation in "Olympic." Japanese resistance in the Philippines continued to occupy the Army, and General MacArthur's forces could not promise that bases there would be ready for the landings in Japan by the planned invasion date. Traditional

Army-Navy rivalries concerning area responsibilities and command surfaced again.

There was also concern over the remaining defense forces left to the Japanese. Although Japan's naval, air, and ground forces were being destroyed at every encounter, the Empire still had a sizeable reserve in the home islands. Like their German allies, the Japanese counted on patriotism and loyalty to the country – plus devotion to the Emperor – to motivate those who would stand as the last defense against the invading Americans. The carnage on both sides of the assault would be terrible.

A further complication came from Japan's traditional enemy – Soviet Russia. While embroiled in the war against Nazi Germany, the Soviet Union kept an uneasy peace with the Japanese. The defeat of Germany in May 1945 released Soviet troops and resources, and Stalin wanted to get into the Pacific conflict, to garner geographic spoils, before the fighting ended. Soviet entry into the war would tie down valuable Japanese troops in Manchuria, as well as provide more bases for raids against the Japanese home islands. But Anglo-American fears about Soviet post-war policies became a major concern as the final phases of the war were being planned.

Thus, it was not until April 3, 1945, that the Joint Chiefs issued a directive designating General MacArthur as overall commander of ground forces in the Pacific, and Admiral Nimitz as commander of the naval forces. The Joint Chiefs would act as the unified command, assigning missions and fixing strategy. Preoccupied as he was with the Philippines, MacArthur's attention focused away from "Olympic."

Nevertheless, the redeployment of units in Europe began in June, with final relocation by December 1 and April 1, 1946, for use in "Olympic" and "Coronet," respectively. The earlier November 1 date for "Olympic" still held with the Army and Marine units already in the Pacific. (By this time U.S. Marine Corps strength was 485,800 men and women.[2])

A final disposition of responsibilities in late May charged MacArthur with plans and preparations for the grand campaign, while Nimitz took the naval and amphibious sectors of the operation. On July 10, 1945, General Carl Spaatz was put in charge of the U.S. Army Strategic Air Force for the Pacific, which would conduct the final phases of the strategic bombing campaign. The death of President Roosevelt on April 12 further complicated planning because the new President, Harry S Truman, ordered a re-evaluation of the whole invasion strategy. President Truman finally approved the plans and presented them to the British and Soviet leaders at the Potsdam Conference in July 1945. Approval for "Olympic" hinged on agreement for the need of a continued naval blockade and bombardment after the landings in southern

Above: One of history's most unusual "aircraft carriers" and an unusual LST configuration was the Brodie system for launching and recovering Piper Cub-type spotter aircraft. Here the *LST-776* off Okinawa has its two yards outboard to port; a Piper Cub will be hoisted and attached to a cable between the yards, and will then accelerate as it moves between them, breaking away with flying speed. The process could be reversed for "landing." (U.S. Navy)

Japan. However, the invasion of Honshu – Operation "Coronet" – was not given the go-ahead at that time.

Planning for "Olympic" included predictions as high as one million Allied casualties. More realistic estimates put the number at 30,000 to 50,000. Close to five million Allied servicemen would be involved in the campaign against the home islands, mostly American. British and Commonwealth participation would take the form of air support and a limited number of ships for fire support. The reduced Commonwealth involvement was MacArthur's choice due to his forces' limited ability to support British units.

The "Olympic" landings would be conducted by twenty infantry divisions (Army and Marine) and one airborne division, with 53 air groups providing support. More divisions were coming from Europe, but their arrival could not be depended upon in time for the landings on Kyushu.

The Sixth Army, under General Walter Kreuger, would stage the initial assault with half a million men. They would be transported to the landing area by Admiral Spruance's Fifth Fleet, while Admiral Halsey's Third Fleet would provide close air support and conduct bombing strikes against enemy installations.

The Japanese defense relied heavily on suicide units, both air- and waterborne with more than 5,300 aircraft being horded in Japan, together with an estimated 3,300 explosives-laden boats. Ashore in the Japanese home islands were 2,300,000 regular troops to counter the assault. Thousands of civilians would be armed with explosives on sticks, to push under tank tracks or to carry when charging American lines.

Several task forces would come together during the assault, including Task Force 40 which combined, for the first time, all three Pacific amphibious forces – TF-43, TF-45, and TF-47. And, prior to the assault, the Army Air Forces would conduct a strategic bombing campaign with B-29 Superfortresses and B-32 Dominators, the latter newly arrived in the Pacific.

The actual landings would be made in sequence, not the simultaneous assault which had characterized other amphibious operations. This change in tactics was due to the large landing area, and the probable difficulty in coordinating so large an attack. One interesting aspect of the landings involved the maps that each beachmaster would carry. For three years, a group of Navy artisans had developed a method for making rubber maps with incredible detail of the various target islands. The terrain model unit eventually set up shop near Pearl Harbor and by the summer of 1945 was turning out the foldable maps, complete with details drawn from continuous high-altitude photo-reconnaissance efforts of 20th Air Force B-29s.

Plans for "Coronet" were eventually approved with March 1, 1946, the target landing date for the U.S. First and Eighth Armies. The Americans would land on the Kanto Plain, 50 miles east of Tokyo. The area offered large, level beaches and was close to the industrial, political, and communications center of Japan.

Some U.S. military leaders believed that Japan would capitulate before an invasion – that the close blockade by aerial-laid mines planted by B-29s, and area blockade by submarines, and continual battering of Japanese cities and factories by Marianas-based B-29s and carrier-based aircraft would force Japan out of the war. The initial B-29 strategic bombing effort, which began in June 1944 (from bases in China) had been ineffective until Lieutenant General Curtis LeMay, commander of the XXI Bomber Command, had stripped all guns but the tail turret from the B-29s, loaded them with incendiaries, and instead of the prescribed Army Air Forces' high-level, daylight "precision bombing" tactics, had flown the B-29s over Japan at night, at an altitude of only 5,000 feet, fire-bombing Japanese cities.

The steadfast resistance of Japanese troops from Guadalcanal to Okinawa, and the street-by-street fighting in Berlin before the fall of the Third Reich, convinced many American and British leaders that an invasion would in fact be necessary. When it became evident that a small number of atomic bombs could become available by late summer 1945, the initial plans included options to detonate them over the beachheads in advance of the troops, to devastate the Japanese defenses.

The decision was made by President Truman to bomb Japanese cities in an effort to force the Japanese government to capitulate. A single B-29 destroyed Hiroshima with an atomic bomb on August 6, and another was dropped by a B-29 on Nagasaki on August 9. Another atomic bomb was en route to the Marianas when the Japanese government capitulated.

The largest amphibious assaults yet planned were stillborn.

15.
VERTICAL ASSAULT

WITH the end of the World War II the U.S. Marine Corps stood as the world's premier amphibious assault force. Although the U.S. Army had conducted more and larger assault landings in the war, it was the Marine assaults against almost barren atolls and islands – Kwajalein, Tarawa, Iwo Jima – that had earned the Corps the reputation of pre-eminence. Watching the raising of the American flag over Iwo Jima in February 1945, Secretary of the Navy James Forrestal, who was embarked in the command ship *Eldorado*, declared to General Holland Smith: "The raising of that flag on Suribachi means a Marine Corps for the next 500 years."

But within a year the future of the Marine Corps and, indeed, the viability of amphibious assault was being challenged. There were three reasons: first, there were no more beaches to assault. The vanquished Japan had been stripped of its island empire. Certainly the Soviet Union, the new, cold-war enemy, had beaches, but those were either remote and far from strategic centers or, as the Baltic or Black Sea coasts, would require massive, "Olympic"-size assault. Thus, there was the basic question of what role the Marines would have in the future.

Second, the U.S. Army Air Forces had waged a campaign to demonstrate that "control of the air" and "strategic bombing" were now the final arbiters of warfare; the need for navies and armies in the future – let alone a Marine Corps – was at best questionable. In one of the few analyses of AAF planning for the post-war period, Major Perry McCoy Smith observed that during the war AAF planners:

"... were convinced that American airpower was winning World War II. The enormous role that the Russians, the British, and the Chinese, as well as the United States Navy, Marines, and Army were playing in the victory was not recognized by the Air Force planners. Conflict and war, they felt, would always occur, but wars would be brought quickly to an end through American airpower ..."[1]

Many Americans – including several members of Congress – attributed the Allied victories over Germany and Japan primarily to the AAF and British heavy bombers. Now, with the atomic bomb, what could be the role of the other services, especially the Marines?

Third, and in some respects more immediate, was the issue of the atomic bomb. The bombs

exploded over Japan demonstrated that a single atomic bomb was equivalent to some 20,000 tons of high explosives – delivered by a single aircraft. In a future assault the traditional concentration of amphibious ships off an enemy's coast would be a highly inviting target for an atomic bomb.

SEEKING ALTERNATIVES

Amid the massive post-war demobilization, the United States conducted a series of atomic bomb tests at Bikini atoll in the Marshall Islands to determine the effects of nuclear weapons on warships and other military equipment (mostly placed on the decks of the target ships). In July 1946 two atomic bombs were detonated, the first being released over the array of target ships in Bikini lagoon by a B-29, and the second detonated while suspended under a landing ship, the *LSM-60*, which disintegrated instantly.[2]

Many of the target ships were devastated, some sinking immediately and others, because no damage-control crews were on board, slowly settling into the lagoon. The head of the Manhattan Project that developed the atomic bomb, Major General Leslie Groves, concisely described the lessons of Bikini: "The tests clearly established that atomic weapons could easily rout any major beach [amphibious] attack and that a capital ship could not operate in an atomic war."[3]

One of the Marine Corps observers at Bikini was Lieutenant General Roy Geiger. His reaction to the tests was similar to that of General Groves. Writing to the Marine Commandant, General A. A. Vandegrift, Geiger observed:

> "Under the assumption that atomic bombs can be provided in large quantities, that they can be used in mass attacks against an enemy objective, and that our probable future enemy will be in possession of this weapon, it is my opinion that a complete review and study of our concept of amphibious operations will have to be made. It is quite evident that a small number of atomic bombs could destroy an expeditionary force as now organized, embarked, and landed. . . . I cannot visualize another landing such as was executed at Normandy or Okinawa."[4]

Vandegrift was highly receptive to Geiger's concern and directed that a special board of generals examine the issues raised by Geiger. The board looked into various methods of dispersing the amphibious shipping to protect it from destruction by a few nuclear weapons, while still being able to concentrate transport aircraft, gliders, parachutes and transport and cargo-carrying submarines. Of these alternatives, the submarines seemed to offer the most promise.

The Marine board was especially interested in the potential of rotary-wing aircraft or helicopters. In 1931 the Marines and Navy had experimented with the Pitcairn OP-1 autogiro, with the Marines evaluating the aircraft in counter-guerrilla operations in Nicaragua. The Marines also looked at the Kellett autogiro, a wingless craft designated OP-2. Those evaluations came to naught.

But during World War II several Germans and Americans made significant strides in helicopter development. The Marine board looked at available machines, and were assured by helicopter inventors Igor Sikorsky and Frank Piasecki that there would be no difficulty in producing a helicopter that could lift 5,000 pounds – about twenty equipped troops. In particular, Piasecki was developing the 10-passenger HRP-1 and the giant, 40-passenger XH-16.

Below: The Baker underwater atomic test at Bikini on July 25, 1946, demonstrated the effects of nuclear weapons against ships. A number of the U.S., Japanese, and German target ships are visible near the detonation. The potential enemy use of nuclear weapons meant that new assault tactics would have to be developed. (U.S. Army Air Forces)

In December 1946 the special board recommended to the Commandant that "two parallel programs be initiated which would provide for the development of both the seaplane transport and a transport helicopter" as potential means of solving the problems of amphibious assault in the atomic age.

The Convair aircraft firm, which built various transport aircraft, developed a "flying LST," the R3Y Tradewind. Powered by four turboprop engines, the R3Y would fly for the first time on February 25, 1954. With a take-off weight of some 175,000 pounds, the R3Y could carry 100 troops. The R3Y-2 version could taxi up to the beach and unload troops and light vehicles through an upward-lifting bow door directly onto the beach.

In the event, the Navy procured only eleven R3Ys and they were plagued by mechanical problems. Marine interest shifted to the alternative pro-

posal set forth by the special board – the helicopter.

VERTICAL ASSAULT

The Marine Commandant proposed a comprehensive helicopter program with series procurement of the Piasecki HRP-1 planned for 1948. The first Marine helicopter was delivered on February 9, 1948, an HO3S-1 (naval version of the Sikorsky H-5).

The HO3S-1 was a utility helicopter, not a troop carrier, but it marked a start and would permit the development of assault tactics while the larger, HRP-1 "flying banana" was being procured. Meanwhile, studies were being conducted by the Marine Corps to determine the optimum helicopter for the amphibious assault role. A troop capacity of a minimum of fifteen and a maximum of twenty was proposed – fifteen would permit a squad plus two individuals from the platoon or company

Above: A Navy HO3S-type helicopter hovers above a cruiser while lowering a passenger. This was the first type of helicopter flown by the U.S. Marine Corps and was, obviously, suitable only for demonstration purposes in the amphibious role. (U.S. Navy)

Right: The HRP-1 was the first troop-carrying helicopter provided for the U.S. Marine Corps and was soon engaged in the development of vertical assault tactics. During this demonstration at Quantico, Virginia, a squad of Marines deploy from an HRP-1 while other "flying bananas" approach the landing area. The United States pioneered helicopter assault techniques, but the British were the first to use them in combat. (U.S. Marine Corps)

troops at a time, the movement required 35 flights, but the basic concept clearly proved the helicopter's capabilities in amphibious or, in this case, vertical assault.

Further exercises in 1948 and 1949, in some instances with the helicopters overflying choppy seas which swamped several landing craft, continued to prove the possibilities for vertical assault. The first HRP-1 "flying banana" arrived at HMX-1 in August 1948, but these helicopters were only being delivered at the rate of about one per month.

More exercises and studies followed as the Marines developed detailed doctrine and helicopter and ship requirements for vertical assault operations.[7] The Marines took delivery of the first Sikorsky HRS troop carrier in 1951. This was the first helicopter acquired by the Marines in large numbers (151 would go to the Marine Corps). The HRS was the Marine version of the Navy HO4S/Army H-19; the single-engine helicopter could accommodate ten troops or carry over a ton of cargo inside the cabin. The larger, Sikorsky HR2S was a twin-engine helicopter with a cargo compartment featuring front-loading doors to permit jeeps and cargo to be easily carried. Designated H-37 in Army service, the HR2S could carry 23 troops. These Sikorsky helicopters formed the backbone of Marine vertical assault in the 1950s and into the 1960s.

After observing exercises in 1951, Lieutenant General Graves B. Erskine, commanding the FMF Atlantic, who had been chief of staff for the V Amphibious Corps in the early years of World War II, convened a board under Major General Field Harris to look into the operational aspects of helicopter assault. The Harris board began meeting in January 1952, ultimately deciding to hold a series of exercises – HelEx I and II – from January 20 until February 28.

Escort carriers were being used to transport the helicopters. However, the Harris board decided

headquarters to be carried; twenty would be a squad plus a 60-mm mortar or machine gun crew. The report noted: "A capacity in excess of 20 men is not desirable in an assault helicopter since the craft will undoubtedly be extremely vulnerable."[5]

The report cited an "ideal" payload of 5,000 pounds and an acceptable minimum payload of 3,500 pounds. Also, the dimensions of the helicopter had to be compatible with the flight-deck elevators and hangars of an escort (CVE) or light (CVL) aircraft carrier.

With the creation of the first Marine helicopter squadron, HMX-1, in January 1948, exercises were undertaken to prove the validity of the vertical assault concept.[6] Taking off from the escort carrier *Palau* (CVE-122) maneuvering offshore on May 23, 1948, five Marine helicopters transported 66 troops to Camp Lejeune, North Carolina. Because the small HO3S helicopters could carry only three

that the use of a mix of two different ship types — specifically a helo transport and troop transport — was unsound because of the time needed to transfer troops to the helicopter carrier for the actual assault. The board recommended converting CVE-55 series escort carriers to specialized amphibious ships in conjunction with the new HRS and large HR2S helicopters.

More boards and reports followed during the early 1950s, against the background of the Korean War, 1950-53, which saw the first extensive use of helicopters in a wide variety of roles, although *not* in amphibious operations. (There was only one large-scale amphibious assault during the war, at Inchon in September 1950; see Chapter 16.)

A January 1951 proposal, developed at Marine Corps Headquarters, detailed future concepts for amphibious operations: the helicopter should be considered as a major participant in such operations and recommending the development program for ship-to-shore troop movement using the unique capabilities of the helicopter. The proposal suggested that it would be, "prudent, practical and timely to provide within the fleets the capability to land by helicopter the assault elements of one Marine division in continuous echelons."[6]

Besides the development of helicopters, during this period General Clifton B. Cates, Commandant of the Marine Corps, proposed building a class of dedicated helicopter ships which could carry 1,500 assault troops and eighteen 36-man helicopters. The ship's flight deck would be large enough to accommodate ten of the big helicopters to load troops and equipment.

It was an ambitious, far-seeing request and the Navy in essence went along with it. However, the Navy was not certain that the current state of development of the helicopter warranted such optimistic plans. The best the Navy would recommend was further investigation and experiment prior to any real construction of either helicopters or ships.

NEW AMPHIBIOUS SHIPS

The Marines had been dissatisfied with developments in amphibious ships for several years, even before they proposed the use of the helicopter and helicopter carriers. In April 1951, shortly before General Cates's proposal, the Marines had indicated the need for the helicopter carriers at a lower level, with the joint Navy-Marine aviation community. With the Korean War raging, new ships were being funded but it was unlikely that an untried concept such as helicopter assault would receive major support for a new, specialized carrier. Rather, the conversion of existing carriers appeared more reasonable.

Although initial Navy response to this request was cool, the Chief of Naval Operations, in October 1951, decided to allow the points raised by the Marine proposal to be evaluated by the U.S. Atlantic Fleet. In reality, the concept of moving troops from ships by helicopters had already been successfully demonstrated. However, not until 1955 was such a conversion undertaken – nine years after General Geiger's warning that the atomic bomb demanded such an approach to amphibious assault.

In May of that year the mothballed escort carrier *Thetis Bay* (CVE-90) was towed to the Philadelphia Naval Shipyard for conversion. The *Thetis Bay*, one of 50 jeep carriers built in record time by Kaiser industries, had been completed in April 1944. She was employed during the war to carry aircraft equipment, and troops, and not as an operational CVE. Displacing some 10,000 tons full load, and 512 feet long, the ship was in the yard just over a year, being recommissioned on July 20, 1956. Berthing was provided for a 1,000-man battalion as well as a Navy complement of 40 officers and 500 men. Cargo elevators and hoists were installed, but the after end of flight deck was cut away to facilitate moving large helicopters between the flight and hangar decks. Thus rebuilt, she was designated CVHA-1, for aircraft carrier (CV), helicopter (H), assault (A).

The *Thetis Bay* would normally operate twenty HRS-type helicopters. After exercises off the California coast, the new helicopter carrier began a series of periodic deployments to the Far East with other amphibious ships. She later operated with the Atlantic Fleet.

A much larger escort carrier, the *Block Island* (CVE-106), was to be converted starting in 1957. The *Block Island*, 24,000 tons and 557 feet long, had been commissioned in December 1944 and she too was mothballed after the war. She operated in the Atlantic-Mediterranean during the Korean War, and was brought into the Philadelphia Naval Shipyard for conversion to a helicopter assault ship. Her designation was to be LPH-1, as the Navy changed all large amphibious ships to an "L" prefix to avoid confusion with real aircraft carriers and auxiliary ships. The letter "P" indicated a troop (personnel) ship and the "H" helicopter capability.[8] The designation of the *Thetis Bay* was also changed from CVHA-1 to LPH-6. But the *Block Island* would never serve in an amphibious assault role. Her conversion was halted as an economy measure and she was scrapped in 1960.

Instead, available funds were being put into new construction LPHs. The Marines had won their case for a truly specialized ship and, on April 2, 1959, construction began on a series of purpose-built helicopter carriers of the *Iwo Jima* (LPH-2) class. Displacing 18,000 tons full load and 592 feet long, the *Iwo Jima* was the largest amphibious ship ever built when she was commissioned on August 26, 1961. She could embark 2,000 troops – a heavily reinforced battalion – and up to 30 HRS-type helicopters.

While the *Iwo Jima* was under construction, there was an immediate need for helicopter carriers to support the U.S. military posture in the Far East. Three of the war-built fleet carriers of the *Essex* (CV-9) class were hastily modified for helicopter operations: the *Boxer* (CV-21) became the LPH-4, the *Princeton* (CV-37) became the LPH-5, and the *Valley Forge* (CV-45) became the LPH-8. The *Tarawa* (CV-40) of this class briefly operated Marine helicopters in the late 1950s, but was not reclassified as an

Below: The U.S. Navy's first specialized helicopter carrier was the *Thetis Bay* (CVHA-1, formerly CVE-90). The escort carrier was modified to carry 1,000 troops plus helicopters, with a large elevator fitted to the after end of her flight deck to accommodate troop-carrying helicopters. Her career was short-lived as the Navy was able to convert larger ships to this role and build new helicopter carriers. (U.S. Navy)

Left: The *Iwo Jima* (LPH-2) was the world's first purpose-built helicopter carrier. The ship is intended to carry 2,000 troops and more than twenty helicopters. In this view the 18,300-ton, 592-foot ship has UH-1 Huey and CH-46 Sea Knight helicopters forward and Sea Knights and a CH-53 Sea Stallion aft. There is one elevator on each side to move helicopters between the hangar and flight decks. (U.S. Navy)

Left: The *Boxer* (LPH-4, ex-CV 21) as a helicopter assault ship with a reinforced Marine battalion mustered on her flight deck together with HRS (CH-34) and HR2S helicopters. These carriers, although expensive to operate because of their crew requirements, were highly successful in the LPH role. The battalion's vehicles are parked alongside the island structure. (U.S. Navy)

Left: The *Carronade* (LFS-1, later LFR-1) was the only fire support ship built for the U.S. Navy after World War II despite several studies and proposals to construct ships of this type. The *Carronade* had ten automatic launchers for 5-inch rockets plus a single 5-inch gun mount. She and three LSMRs were used in the fire support role during the Vietnam War. (U.S. Navy)

LPH. These *Essex*-ships, at 42,000 tons, could also embark up to 30 HRS-type helicopters and carry some 1,700 troops. They were very inefficient in the LPH role and had large crew requirements. Even with only half of their eight-boiler/four-turbine propulsion plant being manned they still required about 1,000 crewmen, almost twice the number of a purpose-built LPH.

The *Essex*-class carriers were retained in the LPH role into the early 1970s, when sufficient ships of the *Iwo Jima* class became available. Seven of these ships were completed up to 1969, providing the fleet with a major vertical assault capability.

The Korean War did stimulate the construction of new amphibious ships of a more conventional design. Larger, more capable tank landing ships (LST) and dock landing ships (LSD) were built to supplement the large number of World War II-built ships that were still available. Although the U.S. Marine Corps was committed to vertical assault, on a practical basis assaults would still be carried out by Marines coming ashore in landing craft and amphibious tractors, moving the few miles from ship to surf at perhaps ten and eight knots, respectively.

Later, three postwar-built Mariner-class cargo ships were converted to amphibious ships: the *Tulare* (AKA-112), *Paul Revere* (APA-248), and *Francis Marion* (APA-249). These ships, and scores of war-built APAs and AKAs, plus five *Charleston* (AKA-113)-class ships constructed for the purpose in the late 1960s, demonstrated the continued need for bulk cargo-carriers for landings, even in the era of vertical assault.

To supplement the remaining LSMR rocket support ships, a new, more efficient inshore fire support ship, the *Carronade* (IFS-1) was built. With the availability of cruisers and battleships plus the LSMRs for fire support, the IFS was never put into production.

Also notable during this period was the fact that interest in employing submarines in the cargo and transport role continued. After World War II the Marines looked at the potential of submarines for the amphibious role, and were supported by the Navy's submarine leaders who were seeking new roles for undersea craft following the war. Several configurations were tried for the troop transport/commando mission (designated SSP, later ASSP and then LPSS) and to carry cargo to the assault area (SSA, later ASSA). The transport submarines were most useful for delivering Navy swimmers (UDT) and commandos rather than in more conventional amphibious tactics. These submarines had a hangar for rubber landing craft, and experiments were conducted carrying a small amphibious tractor in the hangar, with some operations conducted with helicopters lifting troops off the submarines.

SUEZ: THE FIRST VERTICAL ASSAULT
In the summer of 1956, the long-simmering dispute between Egypt on the one side and Britain and France on the other boiled over. Egyptian leader Gamal Abdel Nasser nationalized the Suez Canal. Both Great Britain and France viewed the takeover as a threat to their international commitments and began planning a joint operation to seize the Canal. French military assistance to Israel led to that nation's making a pre-emptive strike against Egypt, giving Britain and France the excuse needed to intervene. (Egypt had denied passage of Israeli ships through the canal and had taken other actions to force the Israeli assault.)

Already involved in a bitter guerrilla war in Algeria – whom she already suspected of receiving support from Egypt – France was not ready for another conflict. And Britain, having oriented defense policy toward nuclear weapons for deterrence, had only a limited number of troops and warships to commit to the operation, codenamed "Musketeer." The inability of the French and British to launch their attack quickly, when surprise and world opinion would have been on their side, led to postponement of the Anglo-French operation until October 1956.

Shortly after the Israeli attack, on October 31, British and French aircraft bombed Egyptian installations. Anglo-French air operations continued, but not until November 5 were combat troops committed, when there was a parachute drop by a combined Anglo-French assault forces of 1,100 men.

The Anglo-French seaborne assault force also approached the Egyptian coast belatedly. The naval force included one large carrier (British) and four light carriers (two British and two French) plus two helicopter ships, escorting surface warships, transports, landing ships, and the British light carriers *Ocean* and *Theseus*.

Neither of these light carriers, both completed in

Below: The British helicopter carrier *Theseus* approaches Port Said after the Egyptian port had been captured by Anglo-French forces. On her deck are Whirlwind helicopters (similar to the U.S. HO4S/H-19 series). The British helicopter assault was a most successful operation, especially in view of the limitations of the helicopters employed. (Courtesy *Globe and Laural*)

1944, were modified for helicopter operations. The *Ocean* had embarked the British Joint Experimental Helicopter Unit with six Whirlwind and eight Sycamore helicopters, and about half of a 600-man Marine commando plus some 600 RAF personnel. The *Theseus* carried ten Whirlwinds from the Navy helicopter squadron, the remainder of the Marine commando, and several hundred support troops. (The Whirlwind was the British version of the HRS/H-19; the Sycamore was a light helicopter able to carry only four passengers in addition to its pilot.)

The landing plan provided for two Royal Marine Commandos embarked in conventional transports to come ashore in landing craft; the commando embarked in the two light carriers was to serve as a mobile reserve to exploit the success of the paratroops or the Marines landed over the beach. This plan led to rejection of the opportunity for a daring and worthwhile exploitation of the helicopters under Allied-controlled skies.

On the morning of November 6 there was a brief shore bombardment by three destroyers. The use of larger warships, including the French battleship *Jean Bart*, had been dropped from the fire support mission to minimize possible civilian casualties. British and French carrier-based fighters provided air support for the landings which began with amphibious tractors bringing British Marines ashore at 6:45 a.m. The two commandos and a squadron of Army tanks came ashore against light Egyptian opposition.

An hour later, the first Whirlwind lifted off a helicopter carrier, flying-in the embarked commando's commanding officer, operations officer, and two radiomen. The intended landing zone was covered with smoke and the Whirlwind pilot sought a clear space. He came down in a sports stadium at Port Said. No sooner had the Marines jumped clear than it was found that the stadium was occupied by Egyptian soldiers.

Amidst a hail of gunfire, the helicopter's passengers clambered back aboard and the machine soared skyward. Its fuselage was holed by 22 bullets, its rotor blades were nicked, and the pilot was slightly wounded. A safe landing was made near the western breakwater of the port.

A short time later the troop-carrying helicopters began leaving the *Ocean* and *Theseus*. The Army Whirlwinds in the *Ocean* could each carry only five fully equipped Marines; the Navy Whirlwinds in the *Theseus* could lift seven; the Sycamores could transport three. Each Marine carried his own weapon, ammunition, rations, water canteen, gas mask, spare clothing, and ammunition for crew-served weapons – mortar rounds and 106-mm anti-tank rounds. Doors, windows, and seats were stripped from the helicopters to lighten them. A Marine stood in the doorway of each Whirlwind with a submachine-gun to give covering fire.

At thee-minute intervals the helicopters came down to hover within a foot or so above the ground while the troops jumped clear at a landing area near the de Lesseps statue in Port Said.

Right: The Suez operation saw the first large-scale use of helicopters to lift troops directly into combat. This painting by Admiralty artist William Herbert Lane shows Whirlwind helicopters landing Marines from the carriers *Ocean* and *Theseus* near the de Lesseps statue at Port Said. The senior British commander at Suez was overly conservative and did not properly exploit the capabilities of his helicopter and paratroops. (Royal Navy)

Below: Troops of No. 41 Commando of Royal Marines race for their Wessex (H-34 series) helicopters on the flight deck of the carrier *Albion*. The ship could operate some sixteen to twenty helicopters, with each Wessex able to lift twelve men and their gear. In this period all helicopters used aboard British ships were flown by the Royal Navy. (Royal Navy)

Below right: Royal Marines of 42 Commando climb up cargo nets onto the carrier *Albion* during exercises off the coast of Sabah. They are disembarking from a Westland SR.N5 hovercraft, one of several evaluated jointly by the British Army and Navy in the 1960s. They were not adopted by the British for the amphibious assault role. (Three of these craft – designated PACV for Patrol Air Cushion Vehicle – were evaluated by the U.S. Navy in the Vietnam conflict; they were later tested by the U.S. Coast Guard). The U.S. Navy and Marine Corps did adopt a larger, improved air cushion landing craft, for the amphibious role, two decades later. (Royal Navy)

The 22 helicopters landed a hundred Marines in history's first "vertical assault." One Marine was wounded as he landed and was flown back to the carrier, reaching the ship's sick bay just nineteen minutes after having left the flight deck.

Altogether, 415 Marines and 22 tons of ammunition and equipment were landed in an hour and a half. One helicopter ran out of fuel and ditched near the *Theseus*. A launch from the ship quickly rescued the pilot and three wounded men whom he was taking back to the carrier. Casualties among the Marines were light except for a tragic mistake. A carrier-based attack aircraft fired into a concentration of Marines, killing one and wounding almost a score. The error was caused by different maps being used by the fliers and lack of effective cooperation among various fire-control teams.

The total Royal Marine casualties in the Port Said landings were 9 killed and 60 wounded (total British losses at Suez were 22 dead and 77 wounded; the French lost ten dead, one missing, and 33 wounded in the assault). Casualties among the defending Egyptians were severe, at least 650 killed and 950 seriously wounded at Port Said. Once ashore, the Anglo-French force advanced rapidly and only the ceasefire demanded by the United States halted them at midnight on November 6–7.

The Suez Canal – the objective of Operation "Musketeer" – was not captured. The commanders had been too conservative, and had lost the opportunity of a rapid and successful operation.

The opportunity to exploit the helicopter in the amphibious assault had been missed.

The place of the helicopter in amphibious assault, however, was firmly established in the Royal Navy. The defense White Paper issued at the beginning of 1958 stressed the need for rapid intervention forces. Two light fleet carriers, the 27,000-ton, 736-foot carrier *Bulwark*, originally completed in 1948, and her sister carrier *Albion*, completed in 1947, were successively taken in hand for conversion.

As commando carriers the *Albion* and *Bulwark* would be similar to the U.S. Navy's LPH amphibious ships, but whereas the U.S. ships normally operate as part of an amphibious squadron with a variety of other amphibious ships, the British commando carriers were intended to operate independently of other "amphibs." Thus, they were provided with more extensive command and control facilities, could carry a more balanced landing force, and embarked landing craft as well as helicopters to put their troops ashore.

The *Bulwark* was recommissioned as the first commando carrier on January 19, 1960, and the *Albion* on August 1, 1962. To lift the Marines each ship carried sixteen Whirlwind helicopters, plus five spares.

The Korean War and the subsequent Suez landings had demonstrated beyond all question that amphibious landings still had a major place in the atomic age and that helicopters would be a key element of those landings.

16.
AMPHIBIOUS REJUVENATION

THE WRONG WAR

During the five years immediately following World War II there was a steady decline of U.S. amphibious capabilities as the Marine Corps struggled to simply remain alive. With the anticipated reductions in the armed forces that naturally follow a war, the Marines would be hard-pressed to survive. The whole question of the future need for amphibious landings against a hostile shore, the Air Force seeking a pre-eminent position in U.S. defense policy,[1] and the threat of the atomic bomb to amphibious task forces made the future of the Corps questionable.

Only through the direct intervention of Congress did the Marines survive in the 1945–50 period as an independent and viable service. Marine strength fell to about 67,000 by mid-1950, and the number of amphibious ships in active service fell precipitously with hundreds of ships being laid up in reserve or cut up for scrap. During this same period, however, the Marines were able to make significant strides, in collaboration with the Navy, in the fields of turbo-jet aircraft and helicopters.

The outbreak of the Korea War changed the situation with respect to the decline of U.S. amphibious forces. In the early hours of Sunday, June 25, 1950, the North Korean Army thrust south across the 38th Parallel dividing North and South Korea. The attack caught the South Koreans by surprise.

President Truman directed U.S. naval forces in the Far East to support the South Koreans while U.S. Army occupation troops in Japan hastily prepared to enter Korea. The South Korean troops were finally able to secure a small perimeter around the port of Pusan.

The first U.S. combat unit sent to Korea from the United States was the 1st Provisional Marine Brigade comprised of the 5th Marine Regiment, a battalion of the 11th Marines, three aircraft squadrons, and supporting troops – a total of 6,500 men. The troops boarded available transports and set course for the Far East.

Even while the surviving South Koreans and the available U.S. soldiers were fighting to hold the Pusan perimeter, and the 1st Brigade was at sea, General of the Army, Douglas MacArthur, the U.S. commander in the Far East, asked the Joint Chiefs of Staff for the entire 1st Marine Division to strike in an amphibious assault on the west coast of Korea, at Inchon. The port city was 25 miles from Seoul, the capital of South Korea, and close to the 38th Parallel. MacArthur explained, "If I only had the 1st Marine Division under my command again, I would land them here [Inchon] and cut the North Korean armies attacking the Pusan perimeter from their logistic support and cause their withdrawal and annihilation."[2]

The Joint Chiefs of Staff were apprehensive about committing a Marine division to a hastily conceived amphibious landing. Of particular concern was MacArthur's proposed landing site: there was no beach at Inchon, only piers and seawalls. Currents ran as high as eight knots and the tidal range, among the highest in the world, was 32 feet! The assault channel to the landing sites was narrow and could be easily mined or blocked by a sunken ship. Further, the troops would have to land directly into the city, with little room to maneuver.

But MacArthur was adamant. To pour troops into the Pusan perimeter and have them fight their way out and then push the North Koreans back up the length of the peninsula would be a long, costly campaign, in some ways similar to the costly campaigns in France during World War I.

Although MacArthur had hoped to hold the 1st Brigade in Japan until the remainder of the division could assemble for a September 15 landing – the

Below: The docking well of the landing ship *Cabildo* (LSD-16) is a beehive of activity as Marines stand by their LVTs in preparation for a landing on the Korean peninsula. LSDs and their successors, the LPDs, have a considerable degree of versatility for amphibious operations. (In the 1950s they were planned for modification to support flying-boats, but that program was aborted.) (U.S. Navy)

optimum tidal date to permit landing craft to cross the harbor's mud flats – he was forced to send the Marines into Pusan to help save the perimeter. The brigade landed at the port on August 3, with the escort carrier *Sicily* (CVE-118) standing offshore with Marine F4U Corsairs to provide close air support.

The Marines fought hard at Pusan, while stateside the Marine reserves were called to the colors to restore the 1st Marine Division rapidly to its wartime establishment of 240,900 plus the supporting 1st Marine Aircraft Wing with another 4,000 men. Marines from the 2nd Division at Camp Pendleton on the East Coast were shifted to the 1st Division, and the 1st Korean Marine Regiment was assigned to give the division four infantry regiments (one already fighting in Korea). However, only the U.S. 1st and 5th Marine Regiments would actually make the Inchon assault. Two jeep carriers, the *Sicily* and *Badoeng Strait* (CVE-116), would provide Marine-piloted Corsairs for close air support.

Major General Oliver P. Smith took command of the division. Under the Seventh Fleet, the U.S. afloat command in Far Eastern waters, Amphibious Group 1 under Rear Admiral James H. Doyle would undertake the Inchon landing.

The first objective would be the island of Wolmi-Do in Inchon harbor. This was a cave-infested island, connected to the mainland by a 600-yard causeway. About 2,200 North Korean troops were in Inchon and on the island. Another 21,500 troops, of relatively high quality, were in the Seoul-Kimpo area and could be moved into Inchon at short notice.

The planned landings would be supported by approximately 230 ships, mostly U.S., but a few British and other allied navies were also represented. Three *Essex*-class carriers provided air support with the two escort carriers ready to give the assault troops close air support.

The plan was to assault Wolmi-Do on the morning tide of September 15 with the 3rd Battalion, 5th Marines and then *wait all day for the evening tide before landing the rest of the two regiments at Inchon with only 99 minutes of daylight remaining!*

On the morning of September 13, the Gunfire Support Group moved up the narrow Flying Fish Channel toward the harbor to begin the pre-invasion bombardment. The ships discovered a newly laid minefield which was destroyed by automatic weapons fire. For two days there were air and gunfire strikes on Wolmi-Do and other strong points in the area.

In the pre-dawn darkness of September 15, the amphibious ships carefully threaded their way up the channel toward Inchon. On board the amphibious flagship *Mount McKinley* were General Smith, Admiral Doyle, *and* General MacArthur. At 5:45 a.m. the cruisers and destroyers opened a barrage, followed by Corsair strikes. (The one battleship in commission, the *Missouri*, was firing her 16-inch guns at Samchok in a diversionary operation.) As the landing craft approached Wolmi-Do, the LSMRs began firing their barrages of 5-inch spin-stabilized rockets.

The first assault wave hit Green Beach on Wolmi-Do at 6:33 a.m. In 30 minutes the Marines had captured the island. As the main assault force waited for the flood tide, the planes and ships continued to bombard Inchon. By early afternoon, the transports and LSTs were moving up Flying Fish Channel to get into position for the assault.

At 5:30 p.m. the main assault began. The U.S. commanders believed that the enemy, now alert to the invasion, would offer stiff resistance. The main seawall at the harbor was the primary target of the assault, euphemistically divided into the two "Beaches," Red and Blue. Red and Blue were hit simultaneously. LVTs landed on Red Beach in 23 waves with the eight LSTs coming in behind them.

The lead LVTs carried scaling ladders which, in some cases, were too short for the seawall. The Marines vaulted over the wall. But the second and third waves began taking fire as they approached their beach, the LSTs being singled out for special attention. In the smoke and confusion, they made the beach. The *LST-973* was hit by a mortar shell while the *LST-914* was hit by gunfire and began to burn. The fire was quickly extinguished. Two other LSTs were also hit.

The scene on Blue Beach was much the same, with LVTs and LCVPs rammed against the seawall, their Marines struggling ashore. Vice Admiral Arthur D. Struble, the Seventh Fleet commander, was anxious to see the progress of the assault. His barge approached a section of the seawall where dynamite had been planted to blast openings. Only the alert call from a Marine sergeant warned the Admiral's barge off in time.

Below: Four LSTs unload men and equipment during the difficult but highly successful landing at Inchon in September 1950. The Navy-Marine assault team, at General MacArthur's direction, was able to undertake this operation less than three months after the start of the Korean War. Left to right can be identified the *LST-611*, *LST-845*, and *LST-715*. In 1958, the 158 remaining LSTs were given names of American parishes and counties. (Civilian-manned LSTs used for cargo operations were not named.)

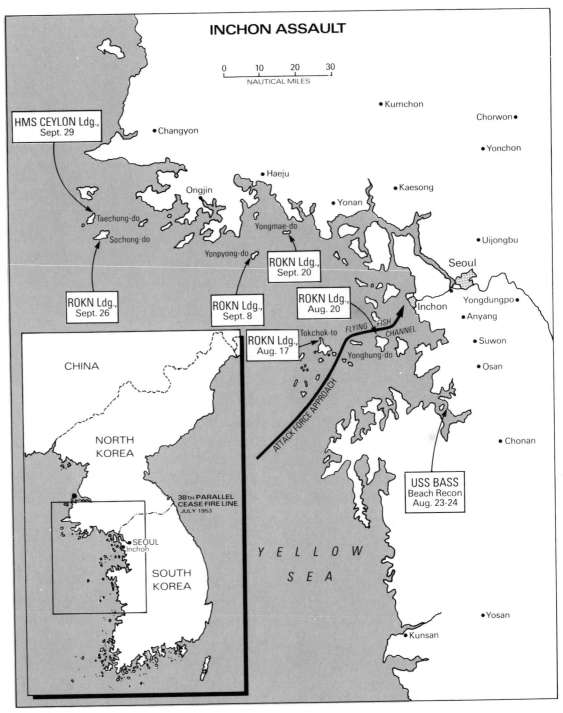

The assault proceeded brilliantly. On the morning of the 16th the first eight LSTs, which had spent the night beached, were withdrawn and nine more took their place. On the evening tide most of those were withdrawn and another six put in. By that time, the evening of the 16th, there were some 15,000 troops ashore with 1,500 vehicles. Within a day of the landing all major objectives had been taken. Marine casualties were extremely light – 22 killed and 174 wounded. General MacArthur signalled from his flagship: "The Navy and Marines have never shown more brightly. . . ."

At 6 p.m. on the 16th, General Smith assumed command of the Marines ashore. The Army's 7th Infantry Division began landing at 2 p.m. on September 17. That night the Marines captured Seoul's Kimpo airfield. The Marines were now a part of the land campaign. Operations along the coast, such as crossing the Han River, were undertaken by Marines in amtracs, at times with gunfire support from cruisers and destroyers offshore.

Success was due, in large part, to luck, fortuitous events, and, to some extent, the intelligence collection begun in July. But most of all, Inchon took place and was a success because of the brilliant plan conceived by General MacArthur and ably executed by the Navy and Marines.

The Inchon landings had the desired effect, turning the North Korean flank, throwing their troops into disarray, and permitting U.S. and South Korean forces to go on the offensive.

Following the success at Inchon, another amphibious assault was planned, this to be at Wonsan on the western coast of North Korea. The 1st Marine Division was again to make the landing. However, upon arrival at Wonsan the Navy found that more than 2,000 Soviet mines had been laid by the North Koreans, and South Korean troops were already in the city. The Marines could not land until October 26, when they came ashore to find not only South Koreans and U.S. soldiers, but also a Bob Hope USO show.

The Marines and ground forces continued to move northward, toward the Korean border with Chinese-controlled Manchuria. Signs of Chinese entry into the conflict were ignored or mistaken. When the Chinese went on the offensive in November 1950 the Marines and soldiers began falling back. General Smith declared, "We are not retreating. We are just attacking in a different direction."

AMPHIBIOUS EVACUATION AND RAIDS

Semantics aside, the Marines and soldiers fell back before the human waves of Chinese attackers. U.S. close air support was limited by bad weather, while the withdrawal was hampered by the need to evacuate wounded, freezing weather, snow, and shortages of supplies and munitions as air drops were increasingly difficult to undertake. At the port of Hungnam on the eastern coast, at almost the narrowest point of the peninsula,

landing ships took off several thousand troops in a Dunkirk-type operation during December, and then blew up the port. The scope of the amphibious-operation-in-reverse was impressive: 105,000 U.S. and Korean troops, 91,000 refugees, 17,500 vehicles, and thousands of tons of cargo. The evacuation force consisted of six APAs, six AKAs, 81 LSTs, eleven LSDs, thirteen troop transports, and 76 chartered merchant ships, most of which made two trips.

The first six months of the Korean War had demonstrated the efficacy of amphibious operations – in both directions. During the next two and a half years of fighting on the Korean peninsula there were no major amphibious operations, but several amphibious raids were carried out by U.S. and British Marines.

Probably the first British effort came on the night of September 12–13, 1950, as a diversion for the Inchon landings. Six Royal Marines and a naval petty officer landed on a beach south of Inchon as did a U.S. Army company of Rangers to plant decoy reconnaissance gear to mislead the Koreans.

These Marines were from the British Far East Fleet. British raids were soon being conducted by the newly raised No. 41 (Independent) Commando, the Marines being armed and equipped by the United States. In late September 1950, 67 of the Royal Marines went aboard the U.S. submarine Perch (SSP-313), a specially configured transport submarine, to blow up North Korean railroad tracks about 100 miles south of the Soviet port of Vladivostok.[3]

North Korean patrol boats were observed near the first landing site and the mission was shifted to another target. On the night of October 2 the Marines and a U.S. Navy UDT section came ashore

Right: The high-speed transport *Begor* (APD-127, former DE-711) stands by to load the last U.S. troops leaving the Korean port of Hungnam as explosions rip harbor installations. Navy amphibious forces were able to evacuate large numbers of troops, civilians, and material during the retreat from North Korea after the entry of Communist Chinese forces into the conflict. (U.S. Navy)

Left: Marine HRS-1 helicopters land a 4.5-inch rocket-launcher unit during operations in Korea in August 1952. The Marines and Army made extensive use of helicopters in the Korean War, but not for assault from the sea. Until recently the Marines normally used the same aircraft as did the Navy. (U.S. Marine Corps)

Centre left: The *Perch* (SSP-313) was one of several post-World War II transport submarines employed by the U.S. Navy. Here the *Perch* has a watertight cargo hangar aft of her conning tower from which this tracked amphibious vehicle has just emerged. The Navy used transport submarines extensively during the Korean and Vietnam Wars, in the former with British commandos. (U.S. Navy)

Below left: A Marine HRS-2 helicopter over the escort carrier *Sicily* (CVE-118) heads ashore with cargo slung beneath it during an amphibious exercise. Another HRS is picking up cargo from the carrier's flight deck, with another helicopter parked forward. Several CVEs were operational in the Korean War with Marine F4U Corsairs used for close-air support operations. (U.S. Navy)

Opposite page, top left: The transport submarine *Sealion* (SSP-315), without a cargo hangar, is shown during an exercise with an HRS helicopter on her after deck while Marine raiders paddle away from the submarine. The midships "bulges" indicate storage areas for rubber raiding rafts. (U.S. Navy)

Opposite page, top right: The *Sealion* uses the more prescribed method of launching rubber craft – simply submerging from under them. In this view the *Sealion* still mounts a 5-inch deck gun (forward of the conning tower) as well as 40-mm guns on conning tower "steps." The 5-inch gun was removed soon after this photograph was taken. The transport submarine *Tunny* (APSS-282) used her 40-mm guns during Vietnam operations. (U.S. Marine Corps)

Opposite page, bottom left: Marines are brought up on a flight deck elevator to their waiting HRS helicopters on an escort carrier. This and many other exercises in the late 1940s and 1950s helped the Marine Corps to develop vertical assault tactics and techniques. Just forward of the elevator are arrestor cables for fixed-wing aircraft operations. (U.S. Navy)

Opposite page, bottom right: Marines paddle a rubber raiding craft away from a PBM Mariner flying-boat. Although the flying LST concept was cancelled earlier than this 1955 exercise, the Marines continued to use seaplanes for carrying small raiding parties for several more years. This concept was not used by U.S. Marines in combat. (U.S. Marine Corps)

in ten rubber boats towed by a motor launch carried in a hangar on the *Perch*'s deck. The landing, planting of explosives, and withdrawal was a success.

Farther down the Korean coast, Royal Marines landed the same night from the high-speed transports *Horace A. Bass* (APD-124) and *Wantuck* (APD-125). This raid was also successful, as was another launched by the APDs the following night. But in the latter operation one Marine was killed as the commandos withdrew under fire.

A major British operation was carried out on April 7, 1951, when 250 Marines in the dock landing ship *Fort Marion* (LSD-22) and a U.S. Navy UDT detachment in the high-speed transport *Begor* (APD-127) undertook a raid near Songjin to destroy coastal railroad lines. With a cruiser-destroyer covering force, the UDT beach reconnaissance was undertaken, followed by the Marines coming ashore in LVTs. The line was

destroyed, but the mission was irrelevant, the line having been abandoned some months before.

Several more raids were carried out by the 41 (Independent) Commando before it was withdrawn from the Korean war zone in December 1951. Most were successful, and helped to both keep the North Koreans and their Chinese allies concerned that the raids were a prelude to a major landing, and helped interdict coastal rail traffic, especially at locations that could not be easily attacked by aircraft or naval gunfire.

LEBANON, 1958

Since the late 1940s, the U.S. Navy has maintained a continuous deployment of warships and support units in the Mediterranean as the Sixth Fleet. A reinforced Marine battalion was embarked in amphibious ships to operate in the Med as a component of the fleet. (At the outbreak of the Korean War the afloat battalion sailed through the

Suez Canal and crossed the Indian Ocean to join the Marine buildup in the Far East.)

The battalion in the Med regularly made exercise landings, often with allied Marines or as part of larger, multi-service exercises. The first landing in a potential combat environment occurred in 1958 in Lebanon.

Largely unopposed, the Marine landing at Beirut in July 1958 was undertaken as an indirect result of the Soviet effort to establish a political base in the volatile Middle East in 1956. The President of Lebanon, Camille Chamoun, had closely aligned his country with NATO, bringing down the wrath of the Egyptians and the Syrians who were locked in their own power struggle against Jordan and Iraq. Syria began sponsoring a rebellion in Lebanon. On July 14, 1958, Arab nationalists seized the Iraqi government, killing the king and his prime minister.

The Lebanese President, fearing a major escalation of Syrian intervention in his country, called for U.S. assistance. President Eisenhower responded immediately and ordered the Sixth Fleet's Marines to go ashore in an operation named "Bluebat." At that time there were three amphibious squadrons in the Med, each with a battalion of some 1,800 Marines. Two battalions were ordered ashore, to land north and south of Beirut.

The United States was not prepared to support a major landing in the Middle East. The Air Force aircraft designated to support such an operation were in the United States. (Aircraft based at NATO installations in Turkey could not participate in a Middle East crisis because of political considerations.) There were two Navy attack carriers in the Med plus an anti-submarine carrier. No amphibious helicopter carriers were present.

The order to land was given on the 15th. At the time only one battalion was in position to comply; the other two would arrive off the Lebanese coast two or three days later. On July 15, just after 3 p.m., and preceded by a flyover of aircraft from the carrier *Essex*, a battalion of Marines came ashore four miles south of Beirut, half a mile from Beirut International Airport. A second took place the following morning, with a third battalion coming in on the 18th.

The bemused Marines came ashore meeting no opposition except the clusters of sightseers and Lebanese vendors, and girls in bikinis. (It was a scene to be duplicated seven years later and half a world away in South Vietnam.) Overhead, aircraft from the *Essex* flew patrol. They were unneeded. For the first time in two months, Beirut passed the night in relative calm. There was a rebel group of 2,000 men in the area, there was some question of how the Lebanese Army would react to the landing, and Syrian armored forces were three hours away by road. But there was no movement against the Marines, U.S. resolve carrying the day.

More Marines were flown in from the United States to join the three battalions who had come ashore from the Sixth Fleet. The U.S. buildup reached 6,000 Marines and 8,000 soldiers. By September, the situation was sufficiently quiet for the Americans to withdraw. By mid-month the American troops had departed. Vice Admiral James L. Holloway, Jr., Commander in Chief, Special Command Middle East, noted, "None of the death, destruction, hunger and disease that are normal results of warfare were left in our wake. A new government had been formed; a condition of reasonable stability and relative freedom from external threat prevailed; and the independence and territorial integrity of Lebanon had been secured." (The irony of his statement would surface nearly 25 years later.)

Only the Marines in the Sixth Fleet's amphibious squadrons were able to respond to President Eisenhower's directive within a matter of hours.

CUBA, 1962

What could have been a major U.S. amphibious assault into Cuba did not transpire. U.S. troops had landed in Cuba in 1898 to push out Spanish forces during the Spanish-American War. Afterwards Marines had been dispatched to Cuba to help maintain order, while the U.S. naval base at Guantanamo had long had a Marine guard detachment.

Evidence of Soviet installation of intermediate-range ballistic missiles and nuclear-capable strike aircraft being brought into Cuba precipitated a face-off between the United States and the Soviet Union in the fall of 1962. President John F. Kennedy instituted a naval blockade around Cuba, and the world watched as the two superpowers moved their cautious way around the possibility of nuclear war.

While U.S. Navy dependents were evacuated from the Guantanamo base, more Marines were flown in from Camp Pendleton and Camp Lejeune. An expeditionary brigade was embarked in amphibious ships on the Pacific coast and sailed through the Panama Canal and into the Caribbean to join with Atlantic FMF units in preparation for an assault on Cuba.

A number of military options were being considered by the White House: a naval blockade, a

Below: LCVPs from the attack transport *Rockbridge* (APA-228) bring Marines ashore during the 1958 landings in Lebanon. A civilian photographer stands among troops of the 3rd Battalion, 6th Marine Regiment. Farther inland are bikini-clad tourists and ice-cream vendors – a very different situation from what the Marines were to encounter at Beirut 25 years later. (U.S. Navy)

"surgical" air force strike against the missiles and bombers should they be landed, or a full-scale invasion. The decision was blockade. The Marines returned to their bases.

FROM INDO-CHINA TO VIETNAM

Shortly after World War II, Communist rebels struck the old city of Tourane (later called Da Nang). The French, who had always had close dominion over South east Asia, found themselves fighting a frustrating war. While they secured Tourane, the French began a series of amphibious operations to recapture territory held by the rebels, the Viet Minh.

Between January 18 and 21, 1947, French troops landed at various inland targets, followed by an assault by troops in ten landing craft on February 4 from the water approaches to the old city of Hue. Connecting with Army troops, the landing force eventually recaptured Hue by February 9.

Additional amphibious operations continued for the next two months, with landings south of Tourane. The operation on March 16, using the aircraft aboard the escort carrier *Dixmunde* (formerly HMS *Biter*/AVG-3) for close air support, marked the first combat operations for French aircraft carriers.

The initial effect of these amphibious assaults in the coastal and delta regions of Vietnam was to repel the rebels, sending them inland to regroup and build strength. The French also believed that small-scale amphibious raids against rebel supply points along the coast would reduce their offensive capabilities. The French established a monitoring operation along the coast, using surface and air assets. The concept was close to the American surveillance programs 20 years later.

French operations against the growing strength of the Viet Minh continued into the early 1950s. In December 1953, the French planned the first phase of an offensive against Tuy Hoa, a coastal town midway between Tourane and Saigon. With an amphibious assault by Army and Navy troops in LSTs and merchant ships on January 20, 1954, the town was under French control by the end of

the day. Heavy artillery was landed from the ships on the 23rd.

Partitioned in 1954, Vietnam dissolved in a long, bloody civil war with the Soviet Union and Communist China helping their client state, North Vietnam, while the United States desperately tried to support its weak ally, South Vietnam. The United States offered help to the French in evacuating people who did not wish to remain in the north after the ceasefire and division of the country. Rear Admiral Lorenzo S. Sabin, Commander Amphibious Force, Western Pacific and Commander Amphibious Group 1, flew to Haiphong in North Vietnam to finalize arrangements with French Navy officials. The French Army would embark the refugees in American LSTs, while the French Navy would provide harbor pilots.

Following initial beach surveys by frogmen of UDT-12, the refugees boarded the attack transport *Menard* (APA-201) on August 16. Eventually 1,900 people made the three-day voyage to Saigon. After this trial run, other lifts followed using various types of U.S. amphibious ships.

The partition of Vietnam led to more fighting and increased Communist activity throughout Southeast Asia. In response to a crisis in Laos – Communist-supported insurgents, the Pathet Lao, had greatly increased their pressure on the anti-Communist government – and to reassure the neighboring Thai government, the Amphibious Ready Group (ARG) of the U.S. Seventh Fleet entered the Gulf of Siam in May 1962. Additional Marine units, including two A-4 Skyhawk attack squadrons, began arriving in Thailand a week later.

A 1,500-man Marine Battalion Landing Team (BLT) and a CH-34 helicopter squadron were unloaded from their ships at piers in Bangkok, and waited to be joined by additional BLTs being ferried into Thailand by Air Force cargo planes. When the units had all arrived in Thailand they formed the 3rd Marine Expeditionary Brigade. This show of strength and support for American allies in the region helped ease the Laotian Crisis, and by late June, most of the U.S. combat forces, including the 3rd Brigade, had departed.

Below: During the Vietnam War the Navy and Marine Corps continued to conduct amphibious landing exercises in the Atlantic-Mediterranean areas as well as in Southeast Asia. Here the attack transport *Chilton* (APA-38) is circled by landing craft preparing to form up into assault waves. Despite the extensive investment in helicopters, the United States continues to make large-scale use of landing craft and amphibious tractors. (U.S. Navy)

DIRECT U.S. PARTICIPATION

Following the Gulf of Tonkin Incident of August 2 and 4, 1964, which led the United States into open combat against the Communists, a major influx of men and matériel began pouring into South Vietnam. Air Force and Marine tactical aircraft squadrons began to arrive on a regular basis in 1965, while offshore the Seventh Fleet's carrier task forces patrolled up and down the Vietnamese coast.

Part of the Marine contribution included the 9th Marine Expeditionary Brigade, elements of which

bedecked the "invaders" with garlands of welcoming flowers.

On May 7, Brigadier General Marion Carl, the first Marine fighter ace (having flown at Midway and Guadalcanal), led his 3rd Brigade ashore in an unopposed landing at Chu Lai, 55 miles southeast of Da Nang. By May 12, the Chu Lai landings were complete, and the 3rd Brigade became part of the III Marine Amphibious Force (MAF), which ultimately became the largest Marine organization in South Vietnam, providing most of the Marines who subsequently fought the long, bloody ground

Above: Marine HUS (CH-34) helicopters lift off from the helicopter carrier *Princeton* (LPH-5, former CV-37) during the landing at Chu Lai in South Vietnam. Amphibious capabilities permitted the United States to move troops up and down the coastal area of Vietnam with ease. However, there were no assaults against major Viet Cong opposition. (U.S. Navy)

came ashore from amphibious ships at Da Nang on March 8, 1965. The American military leadership wanted the Marines at Da Nang to secure the large, and growing, air base, as well as to release South Vietnamese units for field combat. Growing attacks by U.S. Navy and Air Force aircraft against enemy positions indicated that Communist attention against the land bases from which many of the aircraft flew would not be long in coming.

The 9th Brigade landed at Red Beach Two, on the southern shore of the Bay of Da Nang. Battalion Landing Team (BLT) 3/9 (3rd Battalion, 9th Marine Regiment) began landing at 9 a.m., and the last wave was ashore by 9:18. BLT 1/3 was flown from Okinawa to Da Nang in Marine KC-130 transports, and arrived at 11 a.m. There was now a full brigade of Marines ashore in South Vietnam.

Except for occasional Viet Cong fire, which scored a few hits on the KC-130s, the Marines encountered no opposition at the airfield. On the beach at Da Nang, the only people the assault teams met were friendly, waving South Vietnamese who

war in the first four years of direct American involvement in South-east Asia.

The Chu Lai landings were meant to secure the property for an airfield to be constructed in time for flight operations to begin on June 1. Solving considerable terrain problems, such as the soft clay in the area, the Navy and Marine construction teams met the deadline. The first Marine A-4 Skyhawks arrived to inaugurate the Chu Lai strip at 8 a.m. on June 1, 1965, and began flying combat missions shortly after 1 p.m. the same day. Chu Lai became an important airfield in the south, supplying close air support services to allied ground units throughout South Vietnam.

Eventually the III MAF moved into offensive, seek and destroy missions, far inland. American amphibious capability gave a huge flexibility for moving troops around a very long country. But most of the Marines' amphibious landings in Vietnam were "administrative" or against light opposition. Amphibious warfare consists of trained troops and specialized ships and landing craft. In Vietnam many of these trained amphibious troops were used as ordinary infantrymen, such as deploying the 1st Marine Division inland in the I Corps area which included the important northern sectors of South Vietnam, from Chu Lai and Da Nang to the border with North Vietnam. This was, in many respects, a misuse of specially trained troops, who were poorly equipped and had inadequate logistic elements for sustained combat in an inland area.

While most of the Marines in Vietnam fought a ground war in I Corps, some of their compatriots

The area south of the South Vietnamese capital of Saigon was known as the Mekong Delta, and it provided the Viet Cong with a haven for many years. Many of the residents of the Delta alternated their allegiance between the Communist rebels and the South Vietnamese and their American allies. Thus, the Delta became a region of "little wars" characterized by attempts of the Americans and South Vietnamese to halt the flow of arms and men from North Vietnam to the insurgents in the south. The intricate series of rivers and tributaries of the Mekong Delta became a complicated battle-

Above: Marines come ashore without opposition during an exercise southeast of Danang, South Vietnam, in October 1965. These LCMs are from the attack cargo ship *Seminole* (AKA-104). All the Marines have M14 rifles, a weapon that never achieved the popularity of its predecessors, the M1903 and M1, or its successor, the M16. (U.S. Navy)

were involved in a more direct form of amphibious operation in support of Operations "Game Warden" and "Market Time."

"GAME WARDEN" AND "MARKET TIME"

Prior to the Gulf of Tonkin Incident in August 1964, the South Vietnamese Navy and its Marine component had carried out an amphibious landing on the Ca Mau Peninsula, at the confluence of the South China Sea and the Gulf of Siam. The area was a hotbed of Communist insurgent activity and would remain so throughout the entire Vietnam War. Following the resolution of internal disputes concerning who had control of the landing forces – ultimately it was decided to use the American method of passing control to the Marine or Army commander only when the assault force had established its beachhead – the South Vietnamese landed on January 1, 1963, together with their American advisers. However, the Viet Cong forces, apparently alerted to the landings, had fled and the landing was unopposed.

ground where forces of varying size faced each other in a cat-and-mouse game.

The United States began a long-range operation called "Game Warden" to try to stem the flow of weapons to the Viet Cong. "Game Warden" included riverine forces with patrol boats, landing craft, and helicopters. Both Army and Marine units were assigned to work with the "Game Warden" craft. Immediately north of the Delta lay the Rung Sat Special Zone, 400-square-miles of tortuous jungle and swamp. Previous attempts to clear the Rung Sat had been inconclusive. By January 1966, however, growing Viet Cong activity necessitated a more intense campaign.

Navy Captain John D. Westervelt, Commander, Amphibious Squadron 1 and Commander, Amphibious Ready Group, and Colonel J. R. Burnett, commanding the Marine Special Landing Force, began gathering intelligence in preparation for the amphibious campaign, codenamed Operation "Jackstay," aimed at ridding the area of the Viet Cong and the flow of supplies in the Rung Sat.

Above: The landing ship *Garrett County* (LST-786) was one of several LSTs employed in Vietnam as support ships for coastal and riverine forces. In this view there are PBR riverine patrol craft alongside while Navy UH-1B Huey helicopters use the ship as a floating base. Used in the Mekong Delta, this World War II-built ship has a tripod mast and heavy boom fitted aft. She retains 40-mm guns. (U.S. Navy)

assault force met no opposition, except for crudely lettered signs exhorting the local villagers not to follow the Americans and to beware of Viet Cong-placed booby-traps. "The booby-traps are used to kill the Americans. The soldiers who kill U.S. Army love their country."[4]

The Marines spent the day bringing supplies and vehicles ashore, preparing for subsequent operations up-river. U.S. Coast Guard patrol boats guarded against Communist attacks from along the coast. Operating from this base, "Jackstay" gathered momentum during the first week as Marine teams spread out to attack Viet Cong enclaves. Additional landings had brought more companies of Marines to Red Beach. Various seaborne raids, using LCM landing craft on the rivers and helicopters to airlift troops over the dense jungle, kept the Marines in contact with the enemy.

On March 31 an assault began against a major Viet Cong stronghold on the Vam Sat River. The carrier *Hancock* sent A-1 Skyraiders and A-4 Skyhawks against the suspected enemy positions, while the *Washoe County* (LST-1165) and *Henry County* (LST-824) contributed their own 40-mm gunfire support aimed at the riverbanks to kill any hidden Viet Cong. A combined 18-boat U.S.-South Vietnamese boat convoy entered the Vam Sat with the troops keeping up an intensive fire at suspected hostile positions along the river banks. This procedure was called "reconnoitering by fire," and was meant to elicit response from any enemy troops in hiding. No opposition was encountered as the Viet Cong again melted back into the jungle.

Although initial Viet Cong reaction to the "Jackstay" landings seemed minimal, it soon became clear that the landings were having some effect when caches of food and ammunition, and jungle arms factories were discovered by the U.S. and South Vietnamese troops.

These highly modified amphibious landings of "Jackstay" contributed significantly to the larger "Game Warden" operation, and eventually led to the well-known riverine warfare, characteristic of the Vietnam War. It made use of the traditional implements of amphibious operations, the close air support from carriers, as well as the wide variety of special ships and smaller boats.

It was found that the standard U.S. landing craft – the LCVP, LCPL, LCM, and LCU types – were not well suited for such operations in the Delta, and many modifications were made, including the addition of armor and heavy weapons. "Jackstay" ended on April 7, 1966, after little more than a year's duration. During that period the Marines suffered only five men killed in action and 24 wounded, while the Viet Cong body count was 63 killed and five captured. The enemy casualties were light by Marine standards, but the area was largely denied to Viet Cong forces during the period.

Various amphibious ships and craft were moved off the Vietnamese coast to within helicopter striking range of the area. In addition, arrangements were made for close air support from Seventh Fleet carriers standing farther offshore.

The large group of men and ships, as well as the supporting units, finally came together, and on March 26, 1966, the first "Jackstay" mission entered the operating area near Red Beach on the Long Thanh Peninsula. The large helicopter carrier *Princeton* stood offshore to control the day's operations. After an initial reconnaissance by UDT-11, the Marines came ashore at 7:15 a.m. While planes from the carrier *Hancock* flew overhead, the *Princeton*'s helicopters were delayed by a fast-developing thunderstorm. When launched some 35 minutes late, the helicopters and landing craft brought in their Marines. The

Right: The CH-46 Sea Knight (designated HRB prior to 1962) has served as the U.S. Marine Corps' medium transport helicopter since the mid-1960s. Almost three hundred of the twin-engine, tandem-rotor helicopters are in Marine service, with the Navy flying several in the logistic support role. Normal capacity is 26 troops. (U.S. Navy)

Right: The CH-53 Sea Stallion served as the U.S. Marine Corps' heavy lift helicopter from the late 1960s until the early 1980s, when it was redesignated a medium-lift helicopter (at that time the three-engine CH-53E Super Stallion entered service). In Marine service the CH-53A/D models can lift 38 troops. (U.S. Navy)

"DECKHOUSE" LANDINGS

During and after the conclusion of "Jackstay," most Marine amphibious activity centered around the series of coastal landings collectively named "Deckhouse". These were generally multi-battalion search-and-destroy missions into South Vietnam coastal areas. By 1967 the Marine landing operations were centered on I Corps in attempts to flush the Viet Cong from their jungle camps and staging areas. "Deckhouse V" from January 6 to 15 involved a lift from the helicopter carrier *Iwo Jima*, as well as seaborne assault, but netted few results.

Rough seas on January 4, the original D-Day, created problems for the amphibious ships and even on January 6 the seas were such that the Vietnamese marines could not transfer safely from transports to their LCMs. They had to be taken back to Vung Tau, their staging point, and reloaded on larger LPDs and LSDs which had protected well decks. The operation was further hampered by South Vietnamese intelligence leaks, and flooded rice paddies restricted the combined U.S.-Vietnamese mobility. Again, little was accomplished.

"Deckhouse VI," the final operation in the series, began on February 16, 1967, and continued to March 3. After the normal bombardment by rocket-firing landing ships and supporting surface ships, the *Iwo Jima* sent helicopters out in conjunction with a seaborne company in LVTs.

This time Viet Cong opposition was moderate. Sporadic but occasionally intense Viet Cong firing during "Deckhouse VI" resulted in six Marines being killed and another 80 wounded. The enemy death toll was estimated at 280, the largest number of the entire "Deckhouse" series.

Other amphibious search-and-destroy operations kept the Marines busy throughout 1967. A major problem with the airlift capability arose when all the CH-46A Sea Knight helicopters, the Marines' basic troop carrier, were grounded after a series of fatal crashes. The III MAF relegated the CH-46 to emergency use until the cause of the mishaps could be determined and fixed. Of note, helicopters provided the Marines (as well as U.S. and South Vietnamese soldiers) with unprecedented mobility, close air support, and medical evacuation capabilities.

The Marine amphibious force ended 1967 on a sour note when the initial landing of Operation "Ballistic Arch" ran into heavy surf due to faulty Intelligence. The amphibian tractors bringing the troops ashore could barely cope with the pounding waves, and at times, the troops hung on inside the tractors knee-deep in water. The landing proved to be unopposed, although heavy contact with Viet Cong forces had been forecast.

It was typical of the many frustrations of amphibious operations during the American phase of the Vietnam War.

SUBMARINE OPERATIONS

After World War II the U.S. Navy's submarine force found itself in search of a mission. The Soviet Navy had a small, obsolete surface fleet and virtually no merchant marine. Thus, a new *raison d'être* for submarines was being sought. The U.S. Navy in the late 1940s and 1950s looked into a variety of roles for undersea craft – special anti-submarine configurations, cruise missile launchers, minelayers, submarine tankers, cargo submarines, and transport submarines.

The last were intended, as were their World War II predecessors, to land reconnaissance troops, saboteurs, and raiders behind enemy lines. When the United States became involved in Vietnam the transport submarine *Perch* (APSS-313) was based at Subic Bay in the Philippines and was

conducting training operations on a regular basis with various U.S. and British special forces. The *Perch* was a World War II-built submarine, which had been modified to carry troops and could stow a motor launch in a deck hangar; she was used for commando raids during the Korean War.

As part of "Jungle Drum III," a multi-nation exercise in the spring of 1965, the *Perch* landed 75 Marine reconnaissance troops on the Malay Peninsula. That August and September she conducted search and rescue operations off the coast of Vietnam, one of the few U.S. submarines directly involved in the conflict.

Subsequently, beginning in November the *Perch* landed Marine "recce" troops and Navy UDT personnel on the coast of South Vietnam, in areas held by or suspected to be under Viet Cong control. Often these landings were in preparation for landings by Marines from the Seventh Fleet's amphibious ready group.

In this period the *Perch* carried an armament of two 40-mm deck guns plus machine guns that could be mounted on the conning tower. During Operation "Deckhouse III" in August 1966, while men from UDT-11 were conducting a beach reconnaissance, Viet Cong began firing at the beach party. The *Perch* answered with cannon and machine gun fire. Similarly, when a South Vietnamese unit working on the beach in conjunction with the UDT was threatened by Viet Cong, the *Perch* anchored 500 yards offshore to provide gunfire support if required. Again the submarine's deck guns were ordered into action. The next morning the *Perch* took the 85 Vietnamese troops off the beach and, with several refugees, transported them out of the area and transferred them to patrol craft.

On another occasion during "Deckhouse III" the *Perch* called in air support and A-1 Skyraiders added their ordnance to the submarine's gunfire

Below: The *Grayback* (LPSS-574) was the U.S. Navy's last conventionally propelled transport submarine, her successors being nuclear-propelled. A former cruise missile submarine, the two forward missile hangars were retained to carry landing craft or to "lock out" submersibles and swimmers while submerged. The three fins on her deck are AN/BQG-4 fire control sonar domes. (U.S. Navy)

Above: Swimmers handle a rubber boat on the deck of the *Grayback*. Note the size of the hangar doors. The tracks in the deck are for safety lines for men working on deck in rough seas. (U.S. Navy)

against Viet Cong positions near the beach. This marked the last time a U.S. submarine used a deck gun in combat, with the *Perch* being the last such craft to have guns.

Through August 1966 the *Perch* on several occasions landed UDT personnel on South Vietnamese beaches, usually in support of amphibious operations – "Double Eagle" and the "Deckhouse" series. These operational missions were interspersed with training operations in the Philippines and off Taiwan. Finally, in October 1966 the *Perch* headed east, for the United States and service as a reserve training submarine, ending more than two decades of active service.

Her successor as the Navy's transport submarine was the USS *Tunny* (APSS-282), a modified World War II-built submarine, and the *Grayback* (LPSS-574), a postwar submarine that had been constructed specifically to launch the Regulus land-attack cruise missile. The *Tunny*, converted in 1966, began operations. She served in Southeast Asia in the transport role only until October 1968. Two missions proposed for the *Tunny* were stillborn: After the capture of the U.S. Intelligence ship *Pueblo* (AGER-2) by North Koreans it was proposed that the *Tunny* carry Navy commandos into Wonsan Harbor to blow up the ship; that plan was vetoed by senior U.S. commanders. Another plan called for the *Tunny* to carry commandos to a point off Haiphong Harbor to attack a major target near Hanoi; that plan was also vetoed.

The *Grayback*, converted in 1968–69, had two ex-Regulus missile hangars faired into her forward hull. These could carry self-propelled swimmer delivery vehicles and rubber rafts. She picked up the special operations role in Vietnam during 1970–72, operating with Navy UDTs and commandos (SEALs).[6]

THE MARINES LEAVE VIETNAM

Throughout 1968 the afloat Marines of the Seventh Fleet's amphibious groups continued combined helicopter and seaborne assault missions along the coast, particularly in the active areas of Quang Tri Province just below the border between North and South Vietnam. By 1969 the U.S. government had decided to withdraw much of the massive military presence in Vietnam and return the responsibility of actual fighting to the South Vietnamese. The process was called "Vietnamization," and together with a bombing halt over much of North Vietnam, it was hoped that the withdrawal would eventually bring the Communists to the peace table and end the war.

The withdrawal of Marines from Vietnam was slow but by December 1970, the 1st Marine Division had shrunk to 12,500 men (its strength a year earlier had been more than 28,000). On February 8, 1971, South Vietnamese troops entered Laos in Operation "Lam Son 719." It was the first example of an all-Vietnamese effort. No U.S. units crossed the border, although U.S. aircraft, including the 1st Marine Aircraft Wing, flew sorties to support the South Vietnamese.

Four days later, on February 12, an amphibious ready group arrived off the southern coast of North Vietnam in an effort to dissuade the North Vietnamese from responding to the "Lam

Son 719" operation. It was thought that Marines might have to make a landing at the Communist city of Vinh because they were practising daily amphibious exercises outside the 12-mile territorial limit to divert attention from the Laos invasion. The amphibious force departed the area on March 6.

The North Vietnamese monitored the Marine exercises, noting in a history of "Lam Son 719," published in 1971, that the U.S. Seventh Fleet "kept North Vietnam under constant threat of invasion by several thousand Marines on board American ships cruising off the Vietnamese shore."[5]

On April 7, President Nixon announced additional U.S. troop withdrawals from South Vietnam and by April 14 the III MAF had departed. Its departure led to the reactivating of the 3rd Marine Expeditionary Brigade to direct remaining Marine activities. But this brigade's existence was brief. Its aviation element, the 1st Marine Aircraft Wing, sent most of its squadrons to bases in California, Hawaii, or Japan. Marine ground elements continued to maintain a presence, conducting reduced firing against enemy positions, but generally preparing for withdrawal.

The final 3rd Brigade operations began on May 1. Operations ceased on the 7th, effectively ending Marine combat activity in South Vietnam. On June 25 the remaining Marines embarked in the USS *Saint Louis* (LKA-116) and departed Da Nang, leaving only a few support and staff personnel to clean up. On June 27 the brigade was deactivated.

With the Paris peace accords of 1973 the Americans withdrew most of their combat units from South Vietnam. With U.S. troops gone and American public opinion against further involvement in Southeast Asia, the North Vietnamese began their final drive in January 1975. They overran Cambodia in March and then thrust deep into South Vietnam. By April 21, South Vietnamese President Thieu had resigned, and the capital lay open to the North Vietnamese.

Operation "Eagle Pull" had evacuated the Cambodian capital of Phnom Penh before the Communists took over, using Marine helicopters from the Amphibious Ready Group Alpha including the *Okinawa* and Navy helicopters from the carrier *Hancock*. "Eagle Pull" went off as planned on April 12, 1975.

Three weeks later, plans for the evacuation of Saigon were implemented as Operation "Frequent Wind." A large evacuation group of ships waited offshore to receive the shuttle of helicopters carrying American citizens and their dependents from the doomed city of Saigon. On board amphibious ships was the 9th Marine Expeditionary Brigade, ready to go ashore and bring out the remaining Americans if a military presence were needed.

The frenzied panic that characterized the final evacuation of Saigon belied the relatively smooth though lengthy flight operations of "Frequent Wind" begun shortly after noon on April 29. The Marine brigade commander, Brigadier General R. E. Carey, flew from the amphibious command ship *Blue Ridge* (LCC-19) to Tan Son Nhut air base near Saigon to set up his command post. His two Marine CH-46 squadrons began the shuttle to get the ground security force into position at the American Embassy, and begin the shuttling of evacuees to the ships.

Flight operations continued into the darkness and by 8 a.m. on April 30 the last eleven Marine guards were airlifted from the roof of the American Embassy, leaving Saigon and its citizens to their fate.

Opposite page, top: The docking well of the *Vancouver* (LPD-2) shows M48 tanks and a jeep in an LCU (foreground) with another M48 tank and other vehicles on the garage deck. There is a tracked cargo handling system in the overhead to move supplies into landing craft. (U.S. Navy)

Opposite page, bottom: The largest amphibious ships to have been constructed are the U.S. Navy's LHA/LHD-series helicopter carriers. Led by the *Tarawa* (LHA-1), these ships displace 39,300 tons and are 820 feet long. Carrying some 2,000 troops and approximately 30 helicopters, they differ from the smaller LPHs by having a large docking well for landing craft. The five ships of the *Tarawa* class are being followed by the similar *Wasp* (LHD-1) class, with the lead ship completed in 1988. The *Tarawa* has a large stern elevator and a deck-edge elevator on the port side. (U.S. Navy)

Above: The *Newport* (LST-1179), completed in 1969, introduced a radical new design to tank landing ships. The traditional bow door arrangement was abandoned to provide a pointed bow for achieving 20 knots. Vehicles are unloaded over a ramp positioned by the large derrick arms forward. There are two, asymmetrical funnels, davits amidships for small craft, and a helicopter landing deck amidships. A stern door permits direct access to the tank deck; the twenty ships of this class are able to launch amphibious tractors while underway. (U.S. Navy)

Below: A Marine M103 tank prepares to go aboard the *Newport*. The ship's unusual bow configuration is shown here with the bow sections open and the ramp lowered from the derrick arms. The arms give the 8,340-ton ship an overall length of 562 feet (522⅓ feet hull length). Diesel propulsion is provided. (U.S. Navy)

17.
THE OTHER NAVIES

THE SOVIET EXPERIENCE[1]

Since the end of World War II, several other navies have maintained significant amphibious assault capabilities, particularly that of the Soviet Union.

In 1939, the 1st Separate Naval Infantry Brigade was established in the Baltic Fleet to fight in the war against Finland (1939–40). By mid-1941, when the Soviet Union entered World War II, there were 25 individual naval rifle brigades and twelve artillery brigades under the aegis of the Red Fleet.

As the war continued, a total of 40 brigades, six independent regiments, and several separate battalions of naval infantry were formed. They varied in composition, with most having organic artillery units and two of the Baltic Fleet's brigades having tank battalions. (These two brigades, the 2nd and 5th, fought as ground troops and were not used in landing operations.) When the war ended there were almost 500,000 sailors fighting ashore, some in what were called Naval Rifle units and others in army units. Some naval troops assigned to the fleet were still called Naval Infantry.

There were several significant amphibious operations during the war. The approximately 100,000 naval troops that remained under fleet and flotilla control were used to defend naval bases and islands as well as to carry out amphibious landings, often in conjunctions with army troops.

The Soviet Navy made 114 amphibious landings during World War II. Some were quite small – essentially raids of platoon size. But four of the landings, two at Kerch-Feodosya, one at Novorossisk on the Black Sea, and one at Moon Sound in the Baltic, each involved several thousand troops. According to Soviet sources, of the

114 landings, 61 were planned and organized in less than 24 hours! In all, the Navy landed some 330,000 troops during the war, soldiers as well as marines. Most of the landings were short-range operations, across straits, bays, and large rivers, and several were made in coordination with paratroops, especially those along the North Korean coast in August 1945 during the brief Soviet campaign against the Japanese.

Several important Soviet officials were associated with amphibious operations during the war. Admiral S. G. Gorshkov, Commander-in-Chief of the Soviet Navy from 1956 until 1985, had directed landings in the Black Sea-Azov-Danube campaigns; Leonid Brezhnev, head of the Soviet government from 1964 until his death in 1982, was a political officer with the 18th Assault Army during landings on the Black Sea coast, where he received a minor wound; and Marshal V. F. Margelov, commander of Soviet airborne forces from 1954 to 1974, served in the Naval Infantry during the war. (Margelov changed the uniform of airborne troops to include the blue-striped T-shirt of the Navy as a symbol of the specialized nature of paratroops, who could also "cross seas" to carry out an assault.)

After the war the Naval Infantry was disbanded for almost two decades. Apparently, Soviet observations of U.S. and British Marines in the postwar period, and the Soviets' own analyses of their requirements as naval operations expanded, led to the decision to reinstitute a Marine force. The Soviets publicly acknowledged the existence of Naval Infantry units on July 24, 1964, when, in conjunction with the traditional Navy Day, a front-page pictorial in the military newspaper *Krasnya Zvezda* (Red Star) showed Marines

Below: The Soviet Ropucha-class LST is one of the more attractive Soviet amphibious ships. Like most Soviet "amphibs" the nineteen Ropuchas were built in Poland. The 3,200-ton, 370²/₃-foot ship can carry 25 armored personnel carriers or a lesser number of tanks plus 230 troops. Like the later U.S. LSTs, the Soviet ships have both bow and stern ramps. There are twin 57-mm guns forward and aft of the superstructure. (U.S. Navy)

Right: The largest Soviet amphibious ships are the multipurpose *Ivan Rogov* (shown here in the Baltic Sea) and the *Aleksandr Nikolayev*. They displace 13,000 tons full load and are 518¼ feet long, with a speed of 23 knots. Capable of carrying ten light or medium tanks plus 30 armored personnel carriers and some 550 troops, the ships have bow doors for access to their tank decks, a docking well for landing craft, and two helicopter landing areas (connected by a tunnel through the superstructure). (West German Navy)

Right: During the past decade the Soviets have led the world in the development of high-speed, air cushion landing craft. The Aist craft shown here can move two medium tanks plus 220 troops at speeds of 60 knots for 350 nautical miles; later vehicles are larger and more capable. This type displaces 250 tons loaded. Two gas turbines turn four aircraft-type propellers plus two lift fans.

coming ashore in amphibious personnel carriers. It was announced that these newly formed units conducted amphibious maneuvers during joint operations with other Warsaw Pact forces. Naval Infantry – about 500 Marines from the Baltic Fleet – participated in the Moscow parade on November 7, 1967, commemorating the October Revolution, the first time such a body had marched in Red Square since World War II.

Marine units were soon built up in the various fleets until, by the 1970s each of the fleets had a regiment of some 2,000 Marines. By the early 1980s the Pacific Fleet was increased to a Marine brigade. Subsequently, each of the three European fleets' Marines were increased to brigade size and the Marines in the Pacific Fleet were enlarged to a division. The brigades now have 3,000 to 4,000 men, and the single division some 7,000 Marines.

Under current Soviet doctrine, Naval Infantry units used to strike at hostile shores come ashore primarily from amphibious personnel carriers, supported by amphibious tanks. Troop-carrying helicopters and air cushion vehicle landing craft are also used, but these can be carried in only a few naval and merchant ships.

The large Aist, Lebed, and Pomornik classes of air cushion landing craft have ranges of sev-

eral hundred miles. Thus, they can carry several hundred Marines for strikes against targets in the regional seas surrounding the Soviet Union. The latest Soviet amphibious platform is the Wing-In-Ground (WIG) effect craft, which resembles a large flying-boat. Reminiscent of the U.S. Navy's R4Y "flying LST," the Orlon-class WIGs can skim over the water, come down offshore and, driving up *onto the beaches*, deliver their cargoes of assault troops and light vehicles.

The air cushion landing craft and WIGs help to compensate the shortfall in large landing ships. In 1987 the Soviet Navy had an estimated 74 landing ships – 39 LSMs of the *Polnocny* class, 33 LSTs of the *Alligator* and *Ropucha* classes, and two multi-purpose ships of the *Ivan Rogov* class (completed in 1987 and 1982). Only the 13,000-ton *Rogov*s have a docking well, used for carrying air cushion landing craft.[2] A bow ramp permits the ships to unload heavy vehicles onto the beach and two helicopter decks and a hangar permit the operating of four Ka-25 Hormone-C troop helicopters.

Shortly after the Naval Infantry branch was re-established in the early 1960s Marine units began periodic deployments aboard amphibious ships. These troop-carrying "amphibs" have operated on a regular basis in the Mediterranean since the mid-

Right: The Soviet Aists and other air cushion landing craft provide the Soviets with a highly effective short-range assault capability. Here a PT-76 amphibious tank rolls off an Aist, which can carry four such vehicles. Note the rapid-fire cannon mounts forward and the fire control radar above the bridge. The air cushion vehicles can carry troops and tank up onto the beach and across swamps and flat terrain.

Right: The Wing-In-Ground (WIG) effect vehicle may be the "ultimate" amphibious assault craft. This is an artist's concept of the Orlan WIG, now operational in the amphibious role with the Soviet Navy. The WIG is a seaplane-like craft that flies low over the water. In the amphibious role the turboprop-powered Orlan can run up onto the beach, with the bow opening to unload troops and light vehicles. Its striking range is at least several hundred miles.

Opposite page, top: The Royal Navy and Marines have, like the U.S. Navy, continued to emphasize helicopter assault for amphibious operations (unlike the Soviet navy, which has fostered air cushion and WIG vehicles). In this view of the helicopter carrier *Bulwark*'s flight deck in 1973, Marines wait for Wessex (U.S. HSS-1/H/34) helicopters to carry them ashore for a NATO exercise at Vieques Island, Puerto Rico. (U.S. Navy)

Opposite page, bottom: The *Bulwark* was typical of the light fleet carriers begun by Britain during World War II that served effectively as helicopter carriers from the early 1960s. The *Bulwark*'s sister ship *Hermes* saw combat as a helicopter/VSTOL carrier in the 1982 Falklands War. In this view the *Bulwark* has a Royal Marine Commando's artillery and vehicles on her after flight deck (after lift is lowered to the hangar deck). (Royal Navy)

1960s. The first amphibious ship deployment to the Indian Ocean (from the Pacific Fleet) took place in 1968, and from 1970 amphibious ships with Marines on board have been observed on deployments off the western coast of Africa (Angola) as well as other areas. The periodic amphibious landings in the fleet areas have been supplemented by larger landings in the *Okean* '70 and '75 exercises, as well as by a landing by Naval Infantry on the coast of Syria and the practice amphibious assault near the Polish border (*Zapad* '81), both in 1981, and a later exercise landing on the Vietnamese coast.

In some exercises the initial assault by Marines is followed by ground forces being landed, coming ashore from amphibious ships or merchant ships. Also, the Soviets appear to plan to use airborne assaults with its seven Soviet airborne divisions in coordination with amphibious forces against key coastal objectives.

SCALING DOWN THE ROYAL NAVY

In 1966 Britain's Labour government – forced to reduce budget expenditures – made the decision to withdraw major military forces from east of Aden. This decision would lead to the elimination of Britain's conventional aircraft carriers. For the forseeable future the Royal Navy would concentrate on NATO commitments in the North Atlantic, primarily anti-submarine warfare.

As part of the new defense policy, the planned CVA.01, to have been an advanced, 53,000-ton warship, was cancelled in 1966. The existing conventional aircraft carriers would be phased out of service, the last, HMS *Ark Royal*, leaving service in 1978. Helicopters and possibly, in the future, Vertical/Short Take-Off and Landing (VSTOL) would constitute the Royal Navy's sea-based aviation component. It was envisioned that land-based RAF aircraft could provide all of the at-sea support that the fleet would require.

Significantly, the British government laid great emphasis on amphibious forces. The two helicopter or commando carriers *Albion* and *Bulwark* continued in service. They were supplemented by two new LSDs, the 12,120-ton *Fearless* and *Intrepid*, completed in 1965 and 1967, plus a series of landing ships logistic (LSL) of 5,675 tons, with the lead ship, the *Sir Bedivere*, completed in 1967.

When the conventional carrier *Hermes*, 28,700 tons full load, was phased out as a fixed-wing aircraft carrier in 1970 she became a commando carrier, replacing the *Albion*. The *Bulwark* and *Hermes* were briefly resuscitated as ASW carriers (with Sea King and Wessex helicopters). Meanwhile, the Royal Navy was able to begin construction of a series of three small carriers, originally designated by the euphemism "through-deck cruisers." These would be 19,500-ton ships, 677 feet long, with gas turbine propulsion providing a maximum speed of 28 knots.

These ships had a full flight deck with a long, starboard island structure. Their normal aircraft capacity was to be fourteen – nine Sea King ASW helicopters and five of the new Sea Harrier VSTOL light attack aircraft.[4] For short periods, a Marine commando could be embarked and the regular aircraft offloaded in favor of troop carriers. The first of the through-deck cruisers, HMS *Invincible*, was commissioned on June 11, 1980.

When the *Invincible* joined the fleet, with two sister ships scheduled to follow in 1982 and 1985, the British government was undergoing another cost-cutting exercise. The Royal Navy felt the sharp end of the axe, the reductions coming about in large part because of the government's decision made in 1980 to replace the Polaris deterrent force with new, more costly Trident submarines.

Under the reductions, the two LSDs, *Fearless* and *Intrepid*, were to be discarded, as would the *Hermes* as soon as a second through-deck cruiser or "VSTOL carrier" was completed in late 1982. Even the three new VSTOL carriers were not safe, as the decision was soon made to sell off the second ship to a foreign navy, keeping only two VSTOL carriers in the British fleet.

Accordingly, in mid-1982 the Royal Navy's conventional forces consisted of the small VSTOL/helicopter carriers *Hermes* and the new *Invincible*, two LSDs, six LSLs, and a flotilla of destroyers and frigates (some quite capable), nuclear-propelled and diesel-electric attack submarines. Within two years the fleet would be even smaller, with the *Hermes* replaced by a still-smaller sister to the *Invincible*, and with the LSDs and some of the destroyers and frigates probably discarded.

The British assault capability was vested in three highly trained Marine Commandos, Nos. 40, 42, 45, each with some 600 men, plus several squadrons of Sea King and Wessex assault helicopters.

There was no plan to reduce this force.

The year 1982 saw the Royal Navy and Royal Marines go to war.

THE SOUTHERNMOST ASSAULT

Britain and Argentina fought a three-month war which took the world by surprise in one of the most unlikely arenas, the South Atlantic – a winter war in an area cold, forbidding and totally inhospitable to naval activities. The dispute arose from the long-time claims by the Argentine government to the small islands known as the Falklands, 400 nautical miles east of Argentina, inhabited by some 1,800 British citizens, and the island of South Georgia, almost 800 nautical miles farther east. In 1982, the Argentine dictator, General Leopoldo Galtieri, facing major political unrest at home, decided to strike out to capture the Falklands – called the "Malvinas" by Argentinians – to divert attention from problems at home and garner popular support.

British forces in the Falklands region consisted of the ice patrol ship *Endurance*, armed with two 20-mm guns and carrying two helicopters (also to be discarded in 1982); a Royal Marine detachment of some 30 men, with an additional twelve Marines on South Georgia, who had been landed from the *Endurance*.

Argentina could muster a considerable force to capture the Falklands, which were within striking distance of land-based aircraft on the mainland. The Argentine Navy in 1982 could count one ex-British light carrier (20,000 tons), one ex-U.S. light cruiser, eight destroyers and three frigates, some with Exocet anti-ship missiles, four diesel submarines, and an amphibious lift of two LSTs, one LSD, and several lesser ships plus a number of merchant ships.

The Argentinian Army had 130,000 men, mostly conscripts and of limited quality, and there was a Marine force of 10,000 men. The latter, organized into five infantry battalions, one commando battalion, and one amphibious battalion plus support units, was highly capable. Carried in amphibious ships, they could come ashore in a score of LVTP-7 amphibious tractors (of the type then used by the U.S. Marine Corps).

General Galtieri and his military junta had planned to "recapture" the Falklands on April 1, 1982. Bad weather delayed the invasion by 24 hours. The assault force consisted of most of the Argentine Fleet. The carrier *25 de Mayo* carried eight A-4Q Skyhawk attack aircraft and four S-2E Tracker ASW aircraft, plus a few Sea King and Alouette helicopters. The carrier also had Army troops embarked.

At 3 a.m. on April 2 the Argentine submarine *Santa Fe* landed twenty Marine frogmen in rubber boats to secure a beachhead near the capital of Port Stanley on the easternmost island of the Falklands. At 6:30 another 80 Marines came ashore in rubber boats from the missile destroyer-flagship *Santissima Trinidad* to assault the Royal Marines barracks and Government House. The main force of Marines then came ashore in nineteen or twenty LVTs from the LST *Cabo San Antonio* to seize the airfield and harbor areas. Nearby was the light carrier *25 de Mayo* with 1,500 army troops embarked, with more soldiers being flown in by C-130 Hercules transports, which began landing at the captured airfield at 8:30 a.m.

Forewarned of the approach of Argentine ships, the British Marines were deployed in defensive positions. When Argentine commandos attacked the barracks with automatic weapons and grenades they inflicted no casualties as the Royal Marines had already been deployed.

For two hours the Argentinians attacked Government House. The Marines resisted, killing two of the attackers in a two-hour exchange of fire. Also, one landing craft was hit by a British anti-tank rocket. But as reinforcements poured ashore, the decision was made to surrender the Falklands. The Royal Marines had suffered no casualties in their brief resistance.

On April 3 a small Argentine force approached the British settlement of Grytviken on South Georgia. A frigate had about 40-odd Marines on board while a polar support ship carried an Alouette light helicopter and a Puma troop helicopter.

At midday after a helicopter reconnaissance of the settlement, the Puma lifted fifteen Marines to the island. The second load of Marines was being landed when the dozen Royal Marines on the island, under Lieutenant Keith Mills, opened fire. The Puma was hit by small arms fire. It managed to lift off only to crash. The accompanying Alouette landed nearby and its Navy crew pulled the survivors from the Puma. Two Marines were killed and the helicopter destroyed.

At the same time, the Royal Marines opened fire on the frigate *Guerrico* in the harbor. The ship, hit by three anti-tank rockets and more than 1,200 rounds of small arms ammunition, was forced to withdraw while firing on the British with her 100-mm gun. One sailor was killed on the ship.

The Argentine Marines engaged the British force for two hours. Four of the invaders were killed (for one Royal Marine wounded) before the British surrendered. The Falklands (now Malvinas) and South Georgia were firmly under Argentine control.

In late March, British intelligence sources (and Argentinian public announcements) had made it obvious that an assault on the Falklands was in the offing. On March 29 the British Admiralty directed the nuclear-propelled submarine *Spartan* to embark stores and weapons at Gibraltar and deploy immediately to the South Atlantic. More nuclear

Right: Preparing for war: Argentine Marines and their amphibious tractors return to the LST *Cabo San Antonio* after an exercise with U.S. forces in 1981. The following year the LST and the Marines were landing in the Falklands. The 8,000-ton ship was built to a modified U.S. design. She carries 23 medium tanks and 700 troops. (U.S. Navy)

attack submarines would follow as soon as possible.

With news of the actual landing and fall of the Falklands, a major task force was made ready in Britain with destroyers and frigates already at sea being ordered to affect a rendezvous. Rear-Admiral John F. (Sandy) Woodward, at sea in command of a exercise in the eastern Atlantic, was ordered to assume command of the forces being assembled for the recapture of the Falklands – Operation "Corporate."

The Falklands are 7,100 miles southwest of Great Britain. The closest base to the Falklands available to the British was the airfield on Ascension Island, about half that distance. Any direct air support for Operation "Corporate" would have to come from the ships of the British force.

On April 5 the VSTOL carriers *Hermes* and *Invincible* departed Portsmouth amid cheers from the throng of people lining the waterfront. The *Hermes* had twelve Sea Harrier VSTOL aircraft, nine Sea King ASW helicopters, and nine Sea King transports; the *Invincible* had eight Sea Harriers and eleven Sea King ASW helicopters – a total of 49 aircraft at the end of a 7,100-mile supply line. With the force were four civilian-manned LSLs, carrying most of the 1,500 available Marines, including Special Boat Squadron personnel. The overall ground force commander would be Major-General Jeremy Moore, RM. The landing would be directed by the 3rd Commando Brigade Headquarters under Brigadier Julian Thompson, RM. The main assault force would eventually consists of the three Marine commandos, the 2nd and 3rd Battalions of the Army's Parachute Regiment, plus several lesser combat and support units – a total of 10,000 men who would have to be carried to the Falklands and supported at the end of a long, vulnerable supply line.

With the ships at sea, 66 Special Air Service (SAS) "raiders" plus support personnel were flown to Ascension with their special gear to meet the task force. Similarly, spare parts and other gear as well as some personnel who had been too late to be embarked in the ships, were also flown to the remote island.

While the ships were steaming south, the dockyard at Gibraltar and yards in Britain were taking in hand a variety of merchant ships – Ships Taken Up From Trade (STUFT) – for modification to military missions. These included the luxury liners *Queen Elizabeth II* and *Canberra*. Some ships were rapidly fitted with troops berths; almost all with helicopter platforms, satellite communications gear, and light anti-aircraft guns. One small liner was converted to a hospital ship. As they became available, these ships would steam south bringing more gear and troops. A total of 45 merchant ships participated in the STUFT program, being modified in remarkably short time.

THE BRITISH LANDINGS

The retaking of South Georgia was the first phase of the British counterattack. In addition to the political aspects of retaking the island, it could serve as an advanced base for the British force, i.e., only 780 miles from the Falklands.

The British assault force consisted of a destroyer and a frigate, a fleet tanker, and the patrol ship *Endurance*. A company of Marines from 42 Commando plus several SAS personnel embarked, with the ships carrying one ASW helicopter, two troop helicopters, and three light Wasp helicopters.

Dubbed Operation "Paraquat," this part of the Falklands campaign started badly as an SAS team was landed on South Georgia to undertake a reconnaissance of the Argentine positions. The SAS had badly underestimated the winter conditions on the island. Needing evacuation, they called in helicopters. Two of the Wessex helicopters were lost on April 22 to the "white out" phenomena. The third Wessex, piloted by Lieutenant Commander Ian Stanley, was able to extract the team and crews of the two crashed helicopters in a remarkable flying feat. Subsequently, SAS and SBS teams went ashore by helicopter and rubber boats in a more hospitable area of South Georgia.

Another frigate, with two Lynx ASW helicopters embarked, was dispatched to join the South Georgia operation. On April 25, as the British force closed on Grytviken, the Argentine submarine *Santa Fe* was sighted on the surface, carrying supplies to the garrison.

British ship-based helicopters depth-charged and then attacked the submarine with rockets. She was severely damaged and sunk within the harbor, a demoralizing sight for the Argentine defenders.

British Marines came ashore by helicopter while the warships fired 235 rounds of 4.5-inch ammunition in a demonstration bombardment (these were the largest guns in the British fleet). The Argentine troops at Grytviken surrendered on the 25th and those at the settlement of Leith the following day.

British troops of the 5th Infantry Brigade, carried south in the liner *Queen Elizabeth II*, would be shifted to other, less politically important ships at South Georgia. The British would also establish an afloat repair facility there.

In the Falklands proper the Argentinian troops continued to prepare for the coming assault. Light attack aircraft in the islands and squadrons in Argentina made ready to strike the British task force. Also, two Argentine naval forces were at sea – the light cruiser *General Belgrano* with two destroyers, the latter carrying Exocet anti-ship missiles, and a small carrier force centered on the *25 de Mayo*, which carried several A-4Q Skyhawk attack aircraft as well as ASW aircraft and helicopters. Also at sea were two small Argentine submarines.

On May 2 the *Belgrano*, while several hundred miles south of the British forces, was torpedoed and sunk by a British nuclear submarine. The destroyers sped away unharmed, leaving the cruiser's survivors struggling in the water. (After this there was no further threat to the British from the Argentine carrier group.)

Not only did the two surface groups threaten Admiral Woodward's force, but so did the two German-built Type 209 submarines.[3] If either British VSTOL carrier had been lost or severely damaged by Argentine air or submarine attacks, or through an operational accident, the entire Falklands operation would have had to have been cancelled. (The second *Invincible*-class carrier was completed in June 1982, just after the conflict was over.)

As the main British force arrived off the Falklands the ships were soon brought under air attack, principally by aircraft based in Argentina. The British were handicapped by lack of radar warning aircraft and true fighter-interceptors. Using shipboard radar and Sea Harriers (each carrying two Sidewinder missiles plus 30-mm cannon), the British rapidly developed air defense tactics.[4]

Several Argentine ships in the area were attacked by the Harriers and by missile-carrying helicopters. And, on a continuous basis, strong ASW patrols were carried out with innumerable contacts attacked in the relatively shallow, difficult waters off the Falklands. But the major threat was from air attack. On May 4, Argentinian Super Etendards attacked the destroyer *Sheffield* with Exocet missiles. The warship was hit by a single missile, whose 350-pound warhead did not explode. However, fires, fed by the missile's unexpended fuel, burned out the ship and she later sunk while under tow. Another destroyer was damaged by an Exocet missile fired from shore. Other British warships were damaged by bombs in this pre-landing period.

In preparation for the main landings, British SAS and Special Boat Squadron (SBS) personnel began landing in the Falklands to collect intelligence and attack Argentine positions. On May 11, SAS teams and gunfire from British warships destroyed eleven Argentine aircraft in the Falklands, an ammunition dump, and radar. Following this raid the Argentinians did not base aircraft in the Falklands, requiring all strikes against British ships to be flown from the mainland. (In another, little publicized operation, an SAS team of eight men flew into Argentina in a Sea King launched from the *Invincible*, steaming west of the Falklands. The team reported on Argentine air operations until the campaign was over, and were then taken off by submarine. The helicopter was left in Chile and burnt by its crew when bad weather prevented them from returning to the *Invincible*.)

The British amphibious ships, troop-carrying merchant ships, and cargo ships came together in the South Atlantic on May 17 and began "cross decking" men and equipment. Helicopters had to shift troops and their gear, as the ships had been hastily loaded, not necessarily in the order that men and equipment would be landed. On the night of May 18 while transferring men between the ships, a Sea King HC.4 helicopter crashed at sea in a gale. Only nine of the thirty men on board were saved. (An ASW version was also lost during this phase after mechanical problems; its crew were saved.

The Argentinians had expected the British to come ashore near the capital of Port Stanley, on the east coast of the Falklands. Most of their troops were deployed to resist such an attack, and mines were laid offshore. Instead, the British made the decision to enter San Carlos Water, the channel between the major islands – a relatively vulnerable position – and assault Port Stanley from the *west*, across the mountains.

British amphibious ships and several merchant ships entered San Carlos Water on the night of May 20–21. D-Day was early on the 22nd. The landing force consisted of the assault ships *Fearless* and *Intrepid*, the troop-carrying liner *Canberra*, and five of the LSLs with an escort of six frigates and one destroyer. One frigate went into the channel with the amphibs; the other warships formed a protective line at the entrance, ready to engage attacking aircraft with their guns and missiles.

The Marines and "paras" began landing in darkness, at 3:40 a.m. Sixteen landing craft brought the troops ashore while a variety of helicopters lifted in the heavy weapons and equipment, a reversal of the usual landing technique. There was little Argentine ground opposition because of the location chosen and diversionary actions by SAS and SBS personnel. In addition to providing anti-air and anti-submarine defense, the warships stood ready to provide gunfire support. (For the entire Falklands campaign there were fourteen ships available with a total of twenty-one 4.5-inch guns; they fired approximately 7,900 rounds in shore bombardment operations.)

With the daylight, mainland-based Argentine aircraft began attacks against the amphibious force in the restricted San Carlos Water. These attacks were by bomb-carrying A-4 Skyhawks.[5] Despite intensive anti-aircraft fire from the ships and interceptions by the carrier-based Sea Harriers, Argentine bombs sank one British frigate and seriously damaged two other warships. Two other ships were hit by bombs that did not explode because they had been released too low, before their fuzes could arm. Fifteen Argentinian aircraft were lost during the day.

While the beachhead was being established near San Carlos, the carrier-based Sea Harriers flew almost continuous daylight combat air patrol with two aircraft normally airborne and two on each of the carriers on standby. This was the combat debut for VSTOL aircraft.

The first British troops to go ashore were the 2nd Parachute Battalion and 40 Commando, followed by 45 Commando and light tank, engineer, and other specialized Army and Marine units. During D-Day (May 22) more than 3,000 troops and 1,000 tons of supplies were brought ashore. By the 25th, 5,500 troops and 5,000 tons of supplies were ashore. These were remarkable numbers in view of the limited unloading capabilities of the British force, the shortage of heavy-lift helicopters, and the periodic attacks by Argentinian aircraft.

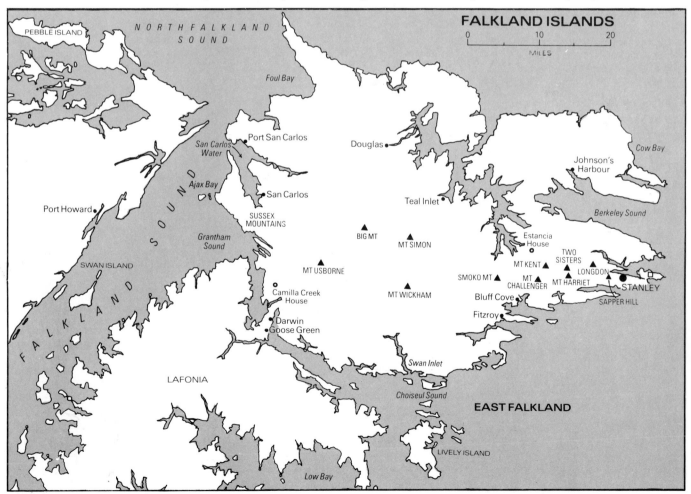

No amphibious tractors or other advanced landing craft were available to the British.

Once ashore, the British troops expanded their beachhead in the vicinity of San Carlos. Engineers began assembling matting to permit Harriers to operate ashore and Rapier air-defense missiles were sited.

Argentine air attacks against the beachhead resumed on May 23. Skyhawks and Mirages damaged one frigate in return for seven aircraft lost. The next day the frigate *Antelope* blew up and sank during an attempt to disarm a bomb which had lodged in the ship's engine room during the May 23 raids.

On the 24th more Argentine aircraft attacked. Two landing ships were damaged, with eight aircraft reportedly shot down.

On the 25th the attackers returned. The container ship *Atlantic Conveyor*, being employed as an aircraft transport, was struck by two Exocet missiles launched by Super Etendard aircraft. The STUFT ship had sailed south from Britain with a load of eleven helicopters, including four large Chinook cargo helicopters, eight Navy Sea Harriers and RAF Harriers. Most of the aircraft were flown off before the ship was struck by the Exocet missile, which started fires that eventually burned her out and sank the ship. Three of the four Chinooks as well as six Wessex were destroyed and twelve men died as the ship was burned out and sank. The one Chinook that had flown ashore would achieve a remarkable record in transporting troops and supplies, flying 109 hours in combat conditions during the campaign, carrying up to 80 armed troops in a single lift.[6]

The RAF Harriers transported in the *Atlantic Conveyor* had already been flown to the carriers, from which they operated until several began flying from the advanced bases set up ashore.

After consolidating their positions ashore, the paratroopers advanced on the Argentine positions at Darwin and Goose Green, while the Marines set off for the capital of Port Stanley. The British attacked the Argentinians on the 28th, achieving victory after almost twelve hours of combat despite four-to-one odds – 450 against 1,600. Harriers provided close air support in addition to their air-defense missions. However, the British battalion commander, Lieutenant-Colonel Herbert Jones, VC, was killed, his place being taken by Major Christopher Keeble.

The Marines had had a long, arduous, overland trek. Each man carried at least 100 pounds of weapons, ammunition, clothing, provisions, and water. They captured Mount Low, overlooking Stanley airfield on June 7. In a flanking action, two of the LSLs steamed to the eastern side of the islands with the Army's 5th Infantry Brigade. On arrival at Fitzroy, south of Port Stanley, the British commanders delayed unloading the two landing ships and they were caught by Argentine A-4s on June 8. Both the *Sir Galahad* and *Sir Tristram* were struck by bombs and badly damaged, and abandoned. The former was

Below: The *Hermes* in her Falklands configuration, operating Sea Harrier VSTOL fighter-attack aircraft and Sea King ASW helicopters. In the Falklands she served in a variety of roles in heavy seas and against intensive Argentine air and submarine attacks. Note the ship's ski-ramp to permit launching heavily loaded Sea Harriers. (She also flew RAF Harriers during the conflict.) (Royal Navy)

scuttled. Fifty men lost their lives in this attack, among them 32 from the 1st Welsh Guards Battalion embarked in the *Sir Galahad*. This was the worst single loss for the British during the entire campaign. (This was also the last British ship loss in the campaign – previously two destroyers, two frigates, and the *Atlantic Conveyor* had been sunk by Argentine bombs and missiles; several other destroyers and frigates were heavily damaged.)

On June 13 the "paras" and Marines began their major attacks against the Argentinian positions around Port Stanley. After some fighting, at 10 p.m. on June 14 the Argentinians surrendered. There were approximately 12,000 Argentine troops in the Falklands. Most were soldiers who had been poorly trained and poorly led; the 1,000 Argentine Marines were excellent troops.

The British assault was well planned and innovative, and the British troops were well trained, well motivated, and generally well led. Their losses were relatively small, with total military and civilian casualties being 255 killed and a further 777 injured. (The only numbers announced by Argentina were 652 men dead and missing.) A leading journalistic account of the war concluded:

> "The overwhelming burden of the land war fell upon Brigadier Julian Thompson and his brigade staff, whose achievement is hard to overstate. Thompson found the long weeks at sea – lacking a firm directive and faced with political and service liaison issues of a kind that few officers of his rank are asked to undertake – very difficult indeed. Once ashore in command of his [Marine] brigade, he was in his element. 'The brigadier is splendid – so straightforward and philosophical,' one of his commanding officers wrote of him. 3 Commando Brigade, and the country, were lucky to have Thompson."[7]

British forces were successful despite the lack of air superiority at the outset of the invasion and the lack of sufficient amphibious ships for the assault. The Harriers proved to be highly successful, with a remarkable availability rate (over 90 per cent) while the two VSTOL carriers proved most flexible.[8] The STUFT program provided the necessary shipping to complement the few British amphibious ships, while naval auxiliaries and merchant ships transferred thousands of tons of fuel, munitions, provisions, and spare parts to the warships. RAF transport aircraft flying from Ascension regularly parachuted high-priority supplies and personnel to the task force.

As the official British report summarized:

> "In the space of seven weeks a task force of 28,000 men and over 100 ships had been assembled, sailed 8,000 miles, effectively neutralized the Argentinian Navy and fought off persistent and courageous attacks from combat aircraft which outnumbered its own by more than six to one. This in itself was no mean feat, but the task force then put ashore 10,000 men on a hostile coast while under threat of heavy air attack; fought several pitched battles against an entrenched and well supplied enemy who at all times outnumbered our forces; and brought them to surrender within three and a half weeks."[9]

The Falklands assault was a remarkable amphibious campaign.

THE ISRAELI EXPERIENCE

While world attention was focused on the war in the South Atlantic, in the summer of 1982 the Israelis undertook a major amphibious operation in the eastern Mediterranean. Shortly after declaring its independence in May 1948 and winning the war for survival, the Jewish state established a small naval force which was to meet with several surprising successes over the next thirty years.[10]

The Israelis made extensive use of seaborne raiders in various wars, mostly small groups in rubber boats launched against hostile Arab neighbours from submarines or motor torpedo-boats. On one occasion Israeli raiders came ashore in Lebanon in rubber boats to find commercial rent-a-cars waiting on the beach road. After the operation, the departing raiders left the cars on the beach road, the return forms properly filled out with appropriate credit card data.

Prior to 1982 the Israeli Navy had conducted only three amphibious landings under combat conditions. In the Six Day War of 1967, Israeli motor torpedo boats landed commandos at Sharm el-Sheikh at the Red Sea entrance to the Gulf of Aqaba. When helicopters landed the assaulting paratroops they found the Israeli flag flying over the former Egyptian positions.

During the War of Attrition (1969–70) a small Israeli force landed on the island of Ras Abu-Darj at the mouth of the Gulf of Suez. The third landing was to help rescue a missile boat stranded on the Saudi Arabian coast. In order to salvage the ship, bulldozers were brought in by landing craft.

By 1982 the Israeli Navy had, in addition to submarines, missile boats, and patrol craft, the 328-foot, Dutch-built cargo ship *Batsheva*, which had been converted to a landing ship with a 2,000-ton capacity, and the 200-foot tank landing craft *Ashdod*, *Ashkelon*, and *Achziv*. A few smaller LCTs were also available.

On June 6, 1982, as part of the invasion of Lebanon – Operation "Peace for Galilee" – rubber boats carrying Israeli commandos came ashore north of the coastal city of Sidon, some 35 miles north of Israel's border with Lebanon, on Awali beach. The Israeli Army was moving up the coastal road, approaching the city from the south.

The commandos intercepted two vehicles carrying terrorists toward the city. Meanwhile, more rubber craft arrived carrying paratroops ashore. These troops, in turn, prepared a beachhead for the largest Israeli amphibious operation ever attempted, employing the *Batsheva* and two of the larger LCTs. Loaded into the ships were more paratroopers, tanks, armored personnel carriers, and engineering equipment. Accompanying the landing craft were several missile and patrol boats, to protect the landing from possible Syrian intervention, and tugs for assisting ships damaged by enemy attack.

During the next few days, landing craft brought ashore paratroops, engineers, armored units, and support troops, with the intention of rapidly cutting off Sidon and the Palestine Liberation Organization (PLO) terrorists in the south of Lebanon from the northern area of the country. As a result of the landing, according to some reports, 1,000 PLO were trapped inside Sidon.

A second landing was carried out to the south of Sidon on June 9. Troops and vehicles were shut-tled south to the second landing area (Zaharani) following a commando landing to clear the area.

Although the PLO had considerable artillery (up to 100-mm size) in the Sidon area, which could have engaged the landing forces, and the beachhead was within range of Syrian aircraft and missile boats, there was no significant opposition to the landings. Some PLO artillery fire into the landing area was recorded, but no damage was inflicted.

The Falklands and the Lebanon landings both demonstrated the value of amphibious assaults. Today, in addition to the United States, several other nations maintain significant amphibious assault capabilities. The word *significant* is imprecise. Innovation, the elements of surprise, good planning and leadership, the use of merchant ships and submarines, and many other factors can provide a meaningful capability.

Right: Israel is one of several smaller nations to make use of amphibious assault capabilities. Here the LCT *Achziv*, a 730-ton, 205½-foot craft loads troops and armored personnel carriers at Awali after the 1982 invasion of Lebanon. Israel now has six LCTs plus a 1,150-ton landing ship in service. (Israeli Navy courtesy *IDF Journal*)

Right: An Israeli LCT and, in the background, the larger *Batsheva* during the 1982 invasion of Lebanon. Amphibious landings were used to block PLO attack and withdrawal routes to complement the land invasion – a traditional role for amphibious forces. The Israeli censor has removed the number from the LCT, a sister ship of the *Achziv*. The Israelis have also used torpedo and missile craft and submarines to land raiding parties along Arab coasts. (Israeli Navy courtesy *IDF Journal*)

18.
FUTURE CONCEPTS
AND REQUIREMENTS

A CHANGING ROLE

Throughout the Vietnam War, the United States continued to keep battalions of Marines forward deployed in amphibious ships in the Mediterranean and in the Pacific-Indian Ocean areas. These Navy-Marine amphibious units were small in size (about 2,000 troops) and in capability (only five tanks and six howitzers), but were a clear symbol of U.S. presence and the Marines could be moved to a crisis area and maintained offshore almost indefinitely. Because of their limited combat capabilities, these battalions could be put ashore in only benign or very low-level threat situations.

In the 1980s, the U.S. Marine Corps numbered almost 200,000 men and women – larger than the British Army. These men and women were exceedingly well trained and, in most respects, well equipped. In reality, however, the Marines were "light infantry," lacking personnel carriers, anti-aircraft and anti-tank weapons, and other equipment necessary for sustained combat against heavily armed opposition.

Two major changes in U.S. Marine Corps posture and roles occurred in the 1980s. First, during the Carter Administration (1977–81) there was a shift in U.S. military interests from a world-wide, multi-area capability to an emphasis on a NATO-Warsaw Pact conflict in central Europe. The principal roles for the Navy-Marine amphibious team in such a conflict appeared to be supporting the flanks of NATO, with landings in Norway and possibly Denmark and in northern Mediterranean countries to help resist Soviet advances.

The result was a "heavying up" of Marine units. The new M198 155-mm towed howitzer entered Marine service, the weapon being so large that only the (relatively few) CH-53E Super Stallion helicopters could lift it. On the ground the gun is too large to be manhandled or even moved by the familiar 2½-ton cargo truck common to U.S. military units. Similarly, the decision was made to procure the new M1 Abrams tank in place of the M60 series, requiring more space aboard ship, more maintenance, and more fuel. At the same time, a "family" of light armored vehicles was ordered, again requiring additional space aboard amphibious ships, and suitable for helicopter lift only by the CH-53E.

These and other developments by the 1980s were restricting the mobility and flexibility of the Marines. Further, the added firepower – necessary in view of the reduced numbers of men in Marine units – would not enable them to fight first-line Soviet or surrogate units effectively.

Second, in this period the Marines received a new forward-deployment role following the capture of the American Embassy by Iranians in late 1979. The loss of potential bases in Iran and increasing threats to Western interests (mostly oil) in the Persian Gulf led to the so-called Rapid Deployment Force (RDF) program. Under this concept, weapons, munitions, vehicles, and provisions for a Marine amphibious brigade (16,000+ men) were placed aboard modified merchant ships and anchored off Diego Garcia in the Indian Ocean.[1] In a crisis period, the ships – operated by

civilian seamen – would sail to an allied port in the Gulf area while the Marines would be flown to the port to "marry up" with their equipment.

While this force would *not* have an amphibious assault capability, and a secure port/airfield would be needed, it did provide a means for the movement of a combat force from sea to land. The program was soon expanded to provide a brigade-sized set of equipment on merchant-type ships in the Marianas, another set on merchant-type ships in the eastern Atlantic, and a fourth set pre-positioned ashore in Norway. This pre-designation of units further restricted the flexibility of the Marines.

At the same time that brigades – reinforced regiments – were designated to join this pre-positioned

material, the Marines continued to provide afloat battalions in the Mediterranean and Pacific-Indian Ocean areas.

The Vietnam conflict had, like the Korean War, aroused a new interest in amphibious ship construction. Although often criticized for his anti-navy attitudes, Secretary of Defense Robert McNamara (1961–68) did approve the construction of a large number of naval ships, including new classes of amphibious ships. The five *Tarawa* (LHA-1)-class ships were the "ultimate" amphibious ship design, with a full load displacement of 39,400 tons, making them the largest combatant ships built by the U.S. Navy since World War II apart from aircraft carriers.

The LHA design was an enlarged LPH helicopter

Right: The amphibious assault ship *Wasp* (LHD-1) is shown about to be "launched" by the lowering of the platform onto which she has been moved at the Litton/Ingalls Shipyard in Pascagoula, Miss. The LHD series is the latest and largest version of the amphibious helicopter carrier, whose origins date to the immediate post-World War II period. In this view the stern gate to the docking well and the starboard deck-edge aircraft elevator are lowered (a second elevator is on the port side). Note the large island structures of the LHA/LHD designs. In wartime these ships may be impressed for operating mine countermeasure and anti-submarine aircraft in place of their assault helicopters and Harrier VSTOL aircraft. (Litton/Ingalls Shipbuilding)

ship, with accommodations for almost 2,000 troops and space for 35 helicopters and, subsequently, VSTOL aircraft. The ships also had a large docking well and vehicle storage decks. The well could hold four 135-foot LCUs (formerly LCTs) or seventeen LCMs or 45 amphibious tractors.

Also constructed under the Kennedy-McNamara amphibious buildup were five attack cargo ships of the *Charleston* (AKA-113) class, fifteen amphibious transport docks (LPD), five dock landing ships (LSD), and twenty tank landing ships (LST). The LPDs were a development of the LSD with a smaller docking well but more space for troops and more decks for vehicles and cargo.

All these ships had a sustained speed of 20 knots and would be provided with helicopter landing

decks. To achieve 20 knots the *Newport* (LST-1179)-class ships have a ship-like bow design with large derrick arms projecting over the bow to lift a 112-foot ramp over the bows for unloading onto pontoon bridges. The LSTs have a large deck structure with a drive-through corridor for vehicles to move between the forward and after maindeck areas. A stern ramp permits unloading of landing craft into the water while the ship is underway (or loading when moored stern-to a pier).

These 50 amphibious ships, plus two purpose-built command ships, provided the U.S. Navy with a modern amphibious force from the 1970s until the end of the century.

The third post-World War II amphibious construction program was undertaken in the early 1980s during the Reagan Administration, spurred on by Secretary of the Navy, John F. Lehman, Jr. (1981–87). Actually, during the previous Carter Administration Congress had forced initiation of a new LSD class over the president's protests. But it was for the Reagan-Lehman program to provide the next generation of amphibious ships: the *Wasp* (LHD-1)-class helicopter assault ships, *Whidbey Island* (LSD-41) class, and air cushion landing craft – the LCAC series.

The *Wasp* is virtually identical with the previous *Tarawa* class, with minor modifications increasing the displacement to 40,530 tons full load. A major change is the redesign of the docking well to provide for carrying three air cushion landing craft. (The *Wasp*-class LHDs will replace the seven *Iwo Jima*-class LPHs from the early 1990s.)

The U.S. Navy had experimented with three British-developed SR.N5 air cushion vehicles or "hovercraft" in the mid-1960s, employing them in Vietnam for patrols in marshy areas. They were not evaluated in the amphibious assault role, as the British had evaluated them. In 1977 the Navy took delivery of two prototype air cushion landing craft, designated Jeff-A and Jeff-B. These were of competitive designs, and after evaluation a program began to in the early 1980s to produce 107 of them (later cut to 90, with even that number in doubt in the post-Reagan period).

These LCACs have a loaded weight of 200 tons and can carry one main battle tank or several smaller vehicles at speeds up to 40 knots, with a 50-knot maximum when empty. The first LCAC was delivered in December 1984. The LCACs permit the high-speed movement of troops and vehicles to the beachhhead, with a strike range of 50 miles. Their use, of course, is dependent upon many other factors, such as gunfire support and helicopter assault range.

The Reagan-Lehman naval program has also included the reactivation of the four mothballed *Iowa*-class battleships, the world's last operational dreadnoughts. The four ships had served in the Korean War, being decommissioned and laid up in reserve in 1955–58. The *New Jersey* was reac-

1.

2.

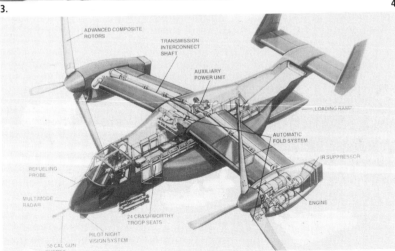

3.

4.

tivated for gunfire support in the Vietnam War in 1968–69. Subsequently, in partial response to the Marine Corps' need for amphibious gunfire support, all four of the *Iowa*-class ships have been recommissioned, the *New Jersey* in 1982, the *Iowa* in 1984, the *Missouri* in 1986, and the *Wisconsin* in 1988.

Another significant amphibious-related program of the Reagan-Lehman period is the MV-22 Osprey, a high-speed, rotary-wing aircraft, being developed primarily for the Marine Corps to replace the CH-53A/D and CH-47 in the amphibious assault role. The Marines plan a near-term procurement of 500 MV-22s with the Navy, Air Force, and Army also intending to procure small numbers.

The V-22 design, developed from the Bell XV-15A technology-demonstration aircraft, has twin rotor-engine nacelles mounted on a connecting wing; the nacelles rotate to a horizontal position for conventional aircraft flight and are vertical for vertical take-off and landing or hover. Maximum speed will be about 275 mph, or some 100 mph faster than helicopters. The aircraft will have an internal cargo capacity of 24 troops or 10,000 pounds and an external (slung) capacity of 15,000 pounds. Rolling take-offs and landings are the

1. The so-called Jeff-B prototype of the U.S. Navy/Marine Corps Air Cushion Landing Craft (LCAC) moves at high speed in the Gulf of Mexico while carrying an M60 main battle tank and a jeep utility vehicle. The craft rides on a cushion of air, created by gas turbine engines and trapped by a rubberized "skirt." Gas turbine engines also provide thrust through aircraft type propellers, mounted in shrouds. The craft have small bow and stern ramps with a drive-through configuration. Soviet air cushion landing craft are considerably larger. (U.S. Navy)

2. Three production LCACs operated by the Marine Corps maneuver at high speed. Note the propellers mounted in shrouds, each with twin "rudders." The LCACs can deliver troops and cargo up onto the beach, and can easily traverse swamps and other marsh areas. While the LCACs provide considerable mobility and lift capability, their demands for shipboard space, maintenance requirements, and need for integration into overall amphibious assault techniques have raised many questions, few of which have been answered realistically. (Textron Marine Systems)

3. The MV-22 Osprey tilt-rotor aircraft will replace the CH-47 and CH-53A/D helicopters in U.S. Marine Corps service during the 1990s. The tilt-rotor design combines the features of a helicopter and a conventional, turboprop-powered aircraft. In this artist's concept an MV-22 pulls away from a helicopter assault ship with landing gear retracted and engine nacelles in the horizontal position for conventional flight. The Osprey provides a new degree of amphibious strike mobility. (Bell Helicopter Textron)

4. This cutaway view of the MV-22 shows the large cargo cabin that can accommodate 24 troops, unloaded through a stern ramp. The two engine nacelles rotate to a vertical position for hover and VSTOL operations. Aboard ship the wing-engine structure rotates to a position parallel with the fuselage and the rotors fold for handling and stowage. In this drawing a .50-caliber multi-barrel (Gatling) gun is provided in the nose; a gunship variant has been proposed. (Bell Helicopter Textron)

normal operating mode, although vertical take-off and landings are possible. Thus, the design has the advantages of both a conventional aircraft and helicopter. (The production aircraft are being produced by a Bell-Boeing team.)

ACTION IN THE MEDITERRANEAN: LEBANON

The constantly simmering turmoil in the Middle East erupted once more in June 1982, when Israeli air and ground forces thrust deep into beleaguered Lebanon. The campaign was an attempt to confront the numerous factions of the Palestine Liberation Organization (PLO) which controlled most of Lebanon, providing a base for terrorists to raid into Israel. After a rapid but bloody campaign, which ended with a decisive Israeli victory over the PLO and its Syrian sponsors, a ceasefire provided for an Israeli and Syrian withdrawal from Lebanon in early September. The ceasefire would be administered by a United Nations force.

Included in this multi-national peacekeeping group were Marines of the U.S. 32nd Marine Amphibious Unit (centered on the 2nd Battalion, 6th Marine Regiment). In late August 1982, some 800 of these Marines came ashore at Beirut as part of the international force and established themselves around the airport and nearby shoreline.[2] Like the 1958 landing, this operation was unopposed, although the atmosphere during the coming months would be considerably more tense and confused. The Marines became involved in several fire-fights with the Moslem rebels situated in the mountains ringing Beirut.

The Marines returned to their ships after most of the PLO troops and leaders had left Lebanon. But the Marines were again landed, on September 29, as the situation deteriorated. The 1,200-man Marine amphibious unit (reinforced battalion) again took up positions at the Beirut airport. French and Italian contingents followed. This time the Marines suffered several casualties, most from PLO and possibly Shi'ite Moslem gunfire. Periodically U.S. warships offshore fired on PLO and Shi'ite positions, and U.S. carriers flew an unsuccessful air strike against mountain positions.

On May 30, 1983, the 24th Marine Amphibious Unit under Colonel Tim Geraghty came ashore, relieving the previous unit. The situation was deteriorating and a second amphibious unit – from the Pacific Fleet – was ordered to steam through the Suez Canal and take up station offshore. Then, on the morning of October 21, an explosives-laden truck was driven into the Marine compound by a Shi'ite driver. Ineffective defenses – the Marine sentries did not have magazines in their rifles – failed to stop the truck, which crashed into the building used as a barracks. In the ensuing explosion, 220 Marines, 18 sailors, and 3 soldiers were killed; many others were injured. (Elsewhere in Beirut, another suicide truck crashed into the French barracks killing 56 troops.) On November

Right: In 1982, U.S. Marines maintain a security position near the Beirut airport while an LST and LPD rest at anchor off the coast of Lebanon. The Marines now faced a very different task and a different kind of enemy than they had in the 1958 landing in Lebanon. In 1982 the Marines were ill-prepared for fighting terrorists, especially in the confused political situation of the time. (U.S. Marine Corps)

19 the battered 24th Marine Amphibious Unit was relieved by the 22nd, which had just completed the assault on Grenada (see below). Marines remained ashore in Beirut until February 1984, when they clambered back aboard their ships. The Marine presence in Lebanon ended.

The Marines had suffered a major loss and there had been little to show for their occupation of a small sector of strife-torn Lebanon. The role and value of the Navy-Marine amphibious presence was in question.

ACTION IN THE CARIBBEAN: GRENADA

Just as the Marines were reeling from the Beirut bombing, U.S. forces of all services became involved in combat much closer to home. The unlikely scene for the fighting was the small Caribbean island of Grenada, with an area of barely 133 square miles. In March 1979, the island had been taken over by a reformist government under Maurice Bishop.

Increasing Communist influence in the government alarmed U.S. and other Caribbean leaders. Torn between trying to placate American interests and pleasing his Communist Cuban masters, Bishop was arrested and executed on October 19, 1983, by more ardent Communist supporters. Grenada's airport and shops were closed and the radio station went off the air. Mounting concern for 600 U.S. citizens on the island, mostly students at St. George's Medical College, prompted the U.S. government to propose an invasion of the island, codenamed "Urgent Fury."

On the island were the Grenadian People's Revolutionary Army of some 500 to 600 men plus about 2,500 militia; the Cubans had 784 men on the island, mostly construction workers, with about one-quarter of them regular military, and there were about 100 advisers and technicians from North Korea, Libya, East Germany, and Bulgaria on the island. There were plenty of small arms and automatic weapons available, including a dozen ZU-23 (23-mm) anti-aircraft gun mounts.

The 22nd Marine Amphibious Unit – based on the 2nd Battalion, 8th Marines – and the Marine helicopter composite squadron were at sea in ships of the Navy's Amphibious Squadron 4, which was bound for the eastern Mediterranean and duty in Lebanon. The Marines were under the command of Colonel James P. Faulkner. The amphibious squadron consisted of the helicopter carrier *Guam* and the landing ships *Barnstable County* (LST-1197), *Manitowoc* (LST-1180), *Fort Snelling* (LSD-30), and *Trenton* (LPD-4).

The large aircraft carrier *Independence* (CV-62) and her air wing formed the main aerial contingent of the assault, while Army and Air Force units from the United States would also be flown to Grenada to participate.

PhibRon 4 departed from Norfolk, Virginia, on October 17 and on the 21st was diverted to

Opposite page, top: A Marine CH-53 Sea Stallion helicopter unloads troops in the vicinity of Pearls airport on Grenada. The troops and "chopper" are from the helicopter carrier *Guam*, the flagship of the amphibious squadron that led the assault on Grenada. The embarked Marines were supplemented by Army troops flown from the United States. The Navy-Marine amphibious team continues to provide a mobile, effective assault capability for landings against objectives that offer limited opposition. (U.S. Department of Defense)

Opposite page, centre: A Marine CH-53 Sea Stallion hovers near a CH-46 Sea Knight at Point Salines in Grenada during the 1983 landings on the Caribbean island. The Marines undertook a classic helicopter/amphibious tractor assault – twice. The second effort was to help our Army troops who had become bogged down. The landings were highly successful against Cuban construction troops with limited military opposition to the Americans. (U.S. Navy)

Opposite page, bottom: This is the command version or LVTC-7/AAV-7C. Used by battalion and higher level commanders, the vehicle is fitted with several radios. Note the door in the rear door/ramp. The vehicle, which weighs 25 tons loaded, has a land speed of 40mph maximum and a water speed of eight mph. (U.S. Marine Corps)

Right: The latest U.S. amphibious assault vehicle series was the LVTP-7, redesignated as the amphibian assault vehicle (AAV-7) in the early 1980s to give the craft a more "sexy" name. Subsequent efforts to develop improved vehicles have foundered on costs and lack of Navy and Defense Department support. Instead, the AAV-7 vehicles are being modernized. (U.S. Navy)

the Caribbean for Operation "Urgent Fury." Vice Admiral Joseph Metcalf III, commander of the Second Fleet and Joint Task Force Commander (JTF-120), would direct the landings.

In darken ship conditions, the task force approached Grenada, arriving on station at 2 a.m. on October 25. The *Fort Snelling* put Navy SEAL commandos into the water to reconnoiter the beaches off Pearls airfield. An hour later the SEALs reported that surf conditions were unfavorable for the planned assault. (Four SEALs were lost in the operation, apparently all in the surf.) The decision was made to mount an air assault on the airport and the town of Grenville.

The *Guam* launched the first assault helicopters laden with Marines at 4 a.m. on the 25th, while steaming off the eastern side of Grenada. CH-46 Sea Knights touched down at Pearls airport at 5:20, and ten minutes later a second assault landed Marines in Grenville. The few Cuban troops in the area fired at the Marines in Grenville with small arms, and the Marines called in fire support from waiting AH-1T Cobra gunship helicopters off the *Guam*. The Cobras quickly silenced the guns. By 7:30 the first two objectives were secured.

While the Marines hit Pearls, U.S. Army Rangers parachuted into Point Salines airfield in the southern area of the island, jumping from C-130 Hercules at an altitude of only 500 feet. The first major opposition, largely from Cuban construction workers employed in building the airfield, complicated the assault. U.S. Air Force AC-130 gunships were called in to deliver fire support for the Rangers. By 10:28 a.m. the Rangers had secured the airfield and the True Blue Campus of the medical college, rescuing the trapped students.

Heavy Cuban resistance momentarily pinned down the Army troops and to relieve the pressure the Marines were directed to mount a night amphibious assault on Grand Mal Beach, north

of the capital city of St. George's. While the *Trenton* held station on the eastern side of Grenada, the rest of the amphibious force moved to the southern end to support this second Marine landing.

Thirteen amphibian tractors and five tanks came ashore at Grand Mal. By first light on October 26 there were 250 Marines ashore with the LVTs while another company of Marines was lifted by helicopter from Pearls airfield to a landing zone north of the beach. The two companies joined up and proceeded to rescue the island's British Governor-General and his staff, who were in the Governor's mansion surrounded by hostile troops.

Two Marine Cobra gunship helicopters tried to make suppression runs for the U.S. troops advancing on the Governor's mansion. Cuban anti-aircraft guns brought down one AH-1T, seriously wounding the pilot. The gunner dragged the pilot from the wreckage and ran for help, but was cut down by Cuban gunfire. The second helicopter was also shot down trying to protect the crew of the first helo. Both Marine crewmen in the second Cobra were killed.

At this time Army Rangers and troops from the 82nd Airborne Division struck at the Cuban and Grenadian positions around St. George's. These troops had been ferried across the island by Marine CH-46s from the *Guam*. More medical students were rescued at Grande Anse Beach, south of St. George's. Again, Marine helicopters airlifted Rangers to carry out the rescue under Cuban fire.

For the next few days the Marines and soldiers continued to secure the remaining towns of Grenada. On October 30 a Marine company conducted a mechanized reconnaissance along the western coast of the island, being carried in LVTs escorted by an LCM, LCU, and LST, with Cobra gunships providing aerial support. Captain Carl R. Erie, commander of the amphibious squadron, lat-

er wrote, "This innovative use of seaborne assets in direct support of tactical troop movements ashore proved very effective as only light resistance was encountered."[3] Another Marine landing, on the island of Carriacou, fifteen miles north of Grenada, was planned for November 1. SEALs had already landed early on the 31st to reconnoiter the beach and landing conditions.

At 5:30 a.m. two Marine companies landed, one by helo from the *Guam* and one by LVT from the *Manitowoc*. Encountering no resistance, the Marines quickly secured the local Communist headquarters and arms cache. By 8:20 the island was declared secured. The Marines were relieved by troops from the 82nd Airborne.

"Urgent Fury" completed, the Marines returned to their ships, which belatedly headed for the Mediterranean and a planned afloat deployment with the Sixth Fleet of six months' duration.

Captain Erie wrote: "Operation 'Urgent Fury' was a very fast moving tactical situation. Limited planning was the rule. There were six operations conducted using seaborne assets; four . . . in the first 36 hours . . . three of the four were at night."

Of the lessons of "Urgent Fury," he concluded:

"The use of armor . . . proved to be very effective . . . . Once the Grenadian forces realized the Marines were ashore with armor they quickly broadcast [the news] . . . it was all over.

Conducting amphibious assaults in the dark was very effective. Night assaults should be the desired option whenever feasible.

Grenada demonstrated that a Navy-Marine ATF [Amphibious Task Force] is capable of fast, flexible combat operations in support of joint task force operations."[4]

U.S. casualties in the Grenada operation – Marines, Rangers, and SEALs – totalled eighteen killed and 116 wounded. Of the Cubans on the island, 25 were killed and 59 wounded (all survivors were returned to Cuba). Twenty-four Grenadians were also killed – 21 in the accidental U.S. bombing of a mental hospital adjacent to an anti-aircraft site.

These Marines – like their British cousins in the Falklands – again demonstrated their great flexibility and the continued need for specialized amphibious forces.

Below: The Harrier VSTOL aircraft, a British design, proved in the Falklands conflict and in various exercises to be an excellent close support aircraft for amphibious operations. The Harrier is capable of "living aboard ship" and, for brief periods, on unimproved positions ashore, as shown by these U.S. Marine-piloted Harriers taxiing on a road at Quantico, Va. This AV-8A variant is carrying Mk-77 napalm bombs and pods of 4-inch Zuni rockets; a 30-mm gun pod is faired under the fuselage. (U.S. Marine Corps)

Right: The LVTP-7/AAV-7 has a rear door/ramp for debarking the 25 troops. While the LVT was developed to carry Marines up onto the beach, the vehicles are now being used as armored personnel carriers to transport troops ashore. The LVTs, however, suffer from poor tracks for land movement, high profile, and lack of armor. (U.S. Navy)

Right: U.S. amphibious forces took on a new role in the 1980s, in response to the many crises in the Persian Gulf area and elsewhere, with the formation of the rapid deployment forces. Here the civilian-manned, Navy vehicle cargo ship *Mercury* (T-AKR 11) loads Marine vehicles and equipment at a U.S. port prior to being forward deployed in the Indian Ocean. When necessary, the ships would sail to a friendly port where Marines flown in would "marry" with the equipment. (U.S. Navy)

Right: The U.S. Navy utility landing craft *LCU-1665* filled with troops and cargo trucks enters the docking well of an amphibious ship during a U.S.-South Korean exercise. Despite the development of air cushion landing craft and helicopters, the U.S. Navy-Marine amphibious team still relies heavily on conventional landing craft and amphibious tractors for landing operations. This reliance severely limits the potential effectiveness of future assault landings. (U.S. Navy)

NOTES

CHAPTER 1

1. Robert K. Massie, *Peter the Great* (New York: Alfred A. Knopf, 1981), p. 586.
2. Sir Henry Bunbury, *Narratives of Some Passages in the Great War with France (1799–1810)* (London: Peter Davies Ltd., 1927), pp. 35–36.
3. E. B. Potter and Fleet Admiral Chester W. Nimitz, USN (eds.), *Sea Power, A Naval History* (Englewood, N.J.: Prentice-Hall, Inc., 1960), p. 141.
4. British Marines were given the prefix "Royal" in 1802 as a reward for their loyalty in mutinous times.
5. Francis Whiting Halsey, *History of the World War*, Vol. VIII (New York and London: Funk & Wagnalls, 1920), pp. 106–107.
6. An outstanding popular account of the Dardanelles campaign is Alan Moorehead, *Gallipoli* (New York, Harper & Row, 1956).
7. Winston S. Churchill, *The World Crisis, 1911–1918*, Vol. III (London: Odhams Press, Ltd [n.d.]), p. 899.
8. *Ibid.*, Vol. IV, p. 1212.

CHAPTER 2

1. Operations Plan 712. One of the best published descriptions of the evolution of Marine amphibious doctrine can be found in Peter A. Isely and Philip A. Crowl, *The U.S. Marines and Amphibious War* (Princeton, N.J.: Princeton University Press, 1951). Ellis died mysteriously in the Japanese-held Palau Islands in 1923.

CHAPTER 3

1. The U.S. submarines in the Pacific were unable to undertake effective operations against the Japanese because of faulty torpedoes. This problem was not fully solved until mid-1943.
2. Quoted in Lieutenant Colonel R. D. Heinl, Jr., USMC, *The Defense of Wake* (Washington, D.C.: Headquarters, U.S. Marine Corps, 1947), p. 22.
3. Japanese Demobilization Bureaux Records, *Reports of General MacArthur – Japanese Operations in the Southwest Pacific Area*, Vol. II, Part I (Washington, D.C.: Government Printing Office, [1966]), p. 95.
4. There was one benefit to the United States from the Aleutian landings. A Japanese pilot was forced to land his A6M Zero fighter on an island; his plane flipped over and his neck was broken. Americans found this aircraft virtually intact and obtained their first look at the remarkable Zero (called "Zeke" in the U.S. code scheme for Japanese aircraft).

CHAPTER 4

1. "Preparations for the Invasion of England" Directive No. 16, July 16, 1940. Quoted in Anthony Martienssen, *Hitler and His Admirals* (New York: E. P. Dutton & Co., 1949), p. 69.
2. Telford Taylor, *The Breaking Wave* (New York: Simon & Schuster, 1967).
3. Martienssen, p. 70.
4. Winston S. Churchill, *Their Finest Hour* (Boston: Houghton Mifflin Co., 1949), p. 330.
5. Grand Admiral Erich Raeder, *My Life* (Annapolis, Md.: U.S. Naval Institute, 1960), p. 331.
6. The full Churchill memorandum is reproduced as Appendix A.
7. Correspondence dated September 3, 1937, in Drax papers at the Churchill College Archives.
8. The use of these designated rescue craft for combat operations was a violation of the Geneva Convention.
9. Correspondence dated September 7, 1939, in Keyes papers at the Churchill College Archives.
10. See Chapter 7 for a description of the "Glen"-class LSI(L) transports.
11. Quoted in Captain Stephen Roskill, RN, *Churchill and the Admirals* (New York: William Morrow & Co., 1978), p. 176.

CHAPTER 5

1. Marine regiments are referred to as the 1st Marines, 2nd Marines, etc., without the designation "regiment." The suffix regiment is generally used in this book to avoid confusion with Marine divisions.
2. Donovan instead became the director of the Office of Strategic Services (OSS) in World War II, the U.S. operational Intelligence force.
3. Four Marine raider battalions were established during the war, with two Raider regiment headquarters being established in 1943. All Raider units were abolished in January-February 1944. Similarly, four parachute battalions were established, as well as a Parachute regiment headquarters (in 1943). These units were also abolished in January-February 1944. The parachute units made no combat drops during the war because of the assault distances involved in the Pacific, the small size of most atoll targets, and the shortage of suitable transport aircraft.
4. These were some of the longest combat missions of the war for single-engine fighters. At that time the A6M Zero (U.S. codename Zeke) was probably the world's only single-engine warplane that could fly a mission of that duration.

CHAPTER 6

1. The Battle of the Atlantic against the German U-boat fleet was not won by the Allies until the critical convoy battles of March 1943.
2. Designated the P-51 in U.S. service, the Mustang fighter was built in the United States by North American Aviation and would become one of the outstanding fighters of the war. The ability of the Mustang to escort B-17 and B-24 heavy bombers from bases in Britain to targets in Germany would permit the resumption of daylight bombing after the disastrous B-17 losses of 1944.
3. Capt. S. W. Roskill, RN, *The War at Sea*, Vol. II (London: HMSO, 1956), p. 251.

4. Ronald Lewin, *Churchill as Warlord* (New York: Stein & Day, 1973), p. 139.

5. General of the Army Dwight D. Eisenhower, USA, *Crusade in Europe* (Garden City, N.Y.: Doubleday & Co., 1948), p. 90.

6. The *Argus*, begun as an Italian passenger liner, was launched in a British shipyard in 1917 and completed as a carrier. She had twelve Seafire fighters on board for "Torch." This was the first combat operation for this navalized version of the famous Spitfire.

CHAPTER 7

1. Peter A. Isley and Philip A. Crowl, *The U.S. Marines and Amphibious War* (Princeton, N.J.: Princeton University Press, 1951), p. 48.

2. In her new role the *Manley* was originally classified as a miscellaneous auxiliary (AG-28) but changed to high-speed transport (APD-1) in 1940.

3. Quoted in Lieutenant Colonel Frank O. Hough, USMCR, *et. al.* (Washington: Government Printing Office, 1958), p. 27.

4. Quoted in General H. M. Smith, USMC, *Coral and Brass* (New York: Simon & Schuster, 1949), p. 95. In addition to the Higgins landing craft, the U.S. Navy procured 225 Higgins-designed motor torpedo (PT) boats during the war.

5. Winston S. Churchill, *Closing the Ring* (Cambridge, Mass.: Houghton Mifflin, Co., 1951), p. 217.

6. Winston S. Churchill, *Their Finest Hour* (Cambridge, Mass.: Houghton Mifflin, Co., 1949), p. 252.

7. James L. Mooney (ed.), *Dictionary of American Naval Fighting Ships*, Vol. VII (Washington, D.C.: Government Printing Office, 1981), p. 569.

8. John C. Niedermair, "As I Recall . . . Designing the LST," U.S. Naval Institute *Proceedings* (November 1982), p. 58.

9. Churchill, *Closing the Ring*, p. 514.

10. Prime Minister's Personal Minute, September 9, 1944, in Churchill Papers 20/153 [Top Secret].

11. The Navy designation AGC technically indicated miscellaneous auxiliary (AG) – communications (C).

12. Rear Admiral Samuel Eliot Morison, USNR, *Aleutians, Gilberts and Marshalls*, (Boston, Mass.: Little, Brown & Co., 1962), p. 207.

13. Memorandum from Chief of Naval Operations to Commander, Amphibious Training Command, U.S. Atlantic Fleet; subject: CGC *Duane* – Status of, March 13, 1944 [Confidential].

CHAPTER 8

1. Rear Admiral Samuel Eliot Morison, USNR, *History of United States Naval Operations in World War II*, Vol. IX *Sicily-Salerno-Anzio* (Boston: Little, Brown & Co., 1964), p. 209.

2. Meeting of Prime Ministers, May 1, 1944, Cabinet papers 99/28.

CHAPTER 9

1. General Marshall quoted in Forrest C. Pogue, *George C. Marshall, Organizer of Victory 1943–1945* (New York: Viking Press, 1973), p. 321.

2. General of the Army Dwight D. Eisenhower, USA, *Crusade in Europe* (Garden City, N.Y.: Doubleday & Co., 1948), p. 207.

3. Some official British sources cite the *X-20* and *X-24* as the midgets participating in "Neptune-Overlord." However, the second craft was the *X-23*.

4. Prior to D-Day, General Patton was publicly acknowledged as Commander of the First U.S. Army Group. This was a phantom formation created in England to persuade the German high command that an assault force was being readied in England to cross the Channel to the Pas-de-Calais *after* the initial Normandy landings. ("Fortitude" was the codename for this successful deception.)

5. In the authors' opinion, the only other modern amphibious assault approaching this complexity was the much smaller landing at Inchon, South Korea, in September 1950.

6. Russell F. Weigley, *Eisenhower's Lieutenants* (Bloomington, Ind.: Indiana University Press, 1981), pp. 77–78.

CHAPTER 10

1. The *Argonaut* carried the designation of submarine minelayer (SM-1) until September 22, 1942, when she was reclassified as a transport submarine (APS-1). After her conversion the *Argonaut* retained a torpedo attack capability.

2. These 6-inch guns were the largest ever mounted in U.S. submarines; British and French submarines carried larger deck guns.

3. After resigning from the Marine Corps, in 1939, Carlson was in China and observed troops of the Communist Eighth Route Army. Impressed by the stamina and dedication of the Chinese, he subsequently re-joined the Marine Corps and applied some of the techniques he observed to the 2nd Raider Battalion when he returned to active duty. Carlson also adopted the term "gung ho," which loosely translated as "work together," to help instill spirit in his troops. (The term was later used as a title for a John Wayne movie about the Makin raid.)

4. General Holland M. Smith, USMC (Ret), *Coral and Brass* (New York: Scribner's Sons, 1949), p. 132.

5. The *Argonaut* was sunk by Japanese surface ships in the Solomon Islands area on January 10, 1943, with the loss of 105 crewman – the heaviest toll of any U.S. submarine sinking in the war.

6. From about 1946 the SBS was an all-Royal Marine unit, being formally designated Special Boat Squadron in 1975.

CHAPTER 11

1. Action report of Headquarters New Georgia Air Force (Forward Echelon 2nd Marine Aircraft Wing), June 29, 1943–August 13, 1943; quoted in Robert Sherrod, *History of Marine Corps Aviation in World War II* (Washington, D.C.: Combat Forces Press, 1952), p. 151.

CHAPTER 12

1. Allan R. Millett, *Semper Fidelis: The History of the United States Marine Corps* (New York: Macmillan Publishing Co., 1980), p. 401. The statement probably stemmed from the confusion at the reefs which, combined with heavy surf and the inexperienced coxwains driving the LVTs, caused many of the amtracs to founder, some with inoperative pumps. The anger and frustration of the Marines at this dangerous point in the landing can be appreciated.

2. Mountbatten, formerly Chief of Combined Operations, was appointed to the joint Southeast Asia command in August 1943 with the rank of acting admiral. He was fully supported for the position by U.S. military leaders and by President Roosevelt, all of whom were greatly impressed by him.

CHAPTER 13

1. The most-recent analysis of the significance of – and the battle for – Peleliu

is Harry A. Gailey, *Peleliu 1944* (Baltimore, Md.: Nautical & Aviation Publishing Co., 1983).

2. Robert Sherrod, *History of Marine Corps Aviation in World War II* (Washington, D.C.: Combat Forces Press, 1952), p. 290.

CHAPTER 14

1. H.M. Smith and P. Finch, *Coral and Brass* (New York: Scribner's, 1949), p. 243-4.

2. The Marine Corps structure at the end of the war consisted of three amphibious corps with six divisions and four aircraft wings plus support units. At that time the U.S. Army (including the Army Air Forces) numbered just over eight million men and women and the Navy just over three million.

3. Some B-29s made multiple landings on Iwo Jima. One B-29 crew landed on the island five times during its eleven combat missions.

CHAPTER 15

1. Major Perry McCoy Smith, USAF, *The Air Force Plans for Peace 1943–1945* (Baltimore, Md.: Johns Hopkins Press, 1970), p. 49. He returned as a major general.

2. A camera photographed flying fragments of the *LSM-60*, and a very few fragments fell on nearby target ships. Scores of other amphibious ships participated in the Bikini tests – Operation "Crossroads." Some, mostly war-damaged, were used as targets and others as support ships for the tests' command and support staffs. The *Mount McKinley* (AGC-7) served as the test commander's flagship at Operation "Crossroads," with the command ships *Appalachian, Blue Ridge* (AGC-2), and *Panamant* (AGC-13) also participating.

3. Major General Leslie M. Groves, USA (Ret), *Now It Can Be Told* (New York:

Harper, 1962), p. 384.

4. Geiger, Commanding General FMF Pacific, wrote the letter on August 21, 1946. He died in January 1947, at the age of 61. Congress promoted him posthumously to four star rank, the first Marine aviator to attain such status.

5. DCNO(Ops) Memo to DCNO(Air), 6 May 1947, Subject: Employment of Helicopters in Amphibious Warfare.

6. In the context of naval aviation, "H" indicates a helicopter squadron, "M" Marine, and "X" experimental. However, HMX-1 is officially designated simply Marine Helicopter Squadron 1. It still serves as a development unit and provides helicopter transport for the President.

7. The studies are summarized and cited in Lieutenant Colonel Eugene W. Rawlins, USMC, and Major William J. Sambito, USMC (eds.), *Marines and Helicopters 1946–1952* (Washington, D.C.: Headquarters, U.S. Marine Corps, 1976).

8. Contrary to periodic accounts, LPH *never* indicated "landing platform helicopter"; the "L" stands for amphibious.

CHAPTER 16

1. The U.S. Air Force was established as a separate service in 1947.

2. Quoted in Colonel Robert Debs Heinel, Jr., USMC, *Soldiers of the Sea* (Annapolis, Md.: U.S. Naval Institute, 1962), p. 539.

3. The post-war transport submarines carried several designations:

The designation APSS was used during the *Grayback*'s conversion, but she was designated LPSS prior to commissioning.

4. Lieutenant Commander Robert E. Mumford, Jr., USN, "Jackstay: New Dimensions in Amphibious Warfare," in Frank Uhlig, Jr. (ed.), *Naval Review, 1968* (Annapolis, Md.: U.S. Naval Institute, 1986), p. 77.

5. *From Khe Sanh to Chepone* (Hanoi: Foreign Languages Publishing House, 1971), quoted in Marine Corps, History and Museums Division, *U.S. Marines In Vietnam: Vietnamization and Redeployment, 1970–1971* (Washington, D.C.: GPO, 1986), p. 209.

6. The Navy's Sea-Air-Land (SEAL) teams were established during the Vietnam War as commando-type units. SEALs operated in several areas of South Vietnam during the war and, apparently, made limited incursions into North Vietnam, usually operating from motor torpedo boats in the latter activities.

The SEAL organization later subsumed the Navy's UDT units.

CHAPTER 17

1. This section has been adapted from Chapter 9 of "Naval Infantry, Coastal Missile-Artillery, and Spetsnaz Forces" in *Guide to the Soviet Navy*, 4th edition (Annapolis, Md.: Naval Institute Press, 1986); also see Lieutenant Colonel Louis N. Buffardi, USA, *The Soviet Naval Infantry* (Washington, D.C.: Defense Intelligence Agency, April 1980), and Rear Admiral K. A. Stalbo, "The Art of Naval Landings of the Great Patriotic War,"

Morskoy Sbornik (No. 3, 1970), pp. 23–30.

2. Displacements for post-World War II ships are given in terms of full-load displacement. The *Rogov*'s standard/full load displacement is similar to that of a World War II-era cruiser.

3. Unknown at the time to either the Argentinians or British, the fire control consoles of the two Type 209 submarines were improperly wired, preventing their torpedoes from being accurately aimed. One boat is believed to have gained an attack position on one of the British VSTOL carriers.

4. Variants of the Harrier design also entered service with the RAF, Spanish Navy, Indian Navy, and the U.S. Marine Corps, designated AV-8 in U.S. service.

5. The A-4 Skyhawk (formerly A4D) is a carrier-based strike aircraft, originally developed by Douglas for the nuclear strike role from U.S. aircraft carriers. The aircraft has been adapted for conventional light attack missions with Skyhawks subsequently being transferred to several other nations. (The Skyhawk has been phased out of U.S. Navy attack squadrons and is being retired from U.S. Marine attack squadrons in favor of the AV-8B)

6. The Chinook, designated CH-47 in U.S. service, is similar to the U.S. Navy-Marine Corps H-46 Sea Knight series. It has a lift capacity of 8½ tons.

7. The British lost 37 aircraft in the Falklands campaign:

	Enemy action	On board ship	Operational
Sea Harriers	2	–	4
Harriers (RAF)	3	–	1
Helicopters	7	13	7

Submarine	to SSP	to APSS	to LPSS
SS-315 *Sealion*	Nov. 2, 1948	Oct. 24, 1956	Jan. 1969
SS-313 *Perch*	Jan 19, 1948	Oct.24, 1956	Aug 22, 1968
SS-282 *Tunny*	1966	Feb 1967	Jan 1, 1968
SSG-574 *Grayback*	–	–	Aug 30, 1968

Argentinian aircraft losses totalled 103 plus another 14 probable losses to British action (including 31 destroyed on the ground in the Falklands by special forces and naval gunfire).

8. Max Hastings and Simon Jenkins, *The Battle for the Falklands* (London: Michael Joseph Ltd., 1983), pp. 362–363.

9. H.M. Government, Secretary of State for Defence, *The Falklands Campaign: The Lessons* (London: HMSO, December, 1982), p. 6.

10. For example, in 1956 Israeli naval forces captured an Egyptian destroyer approaching Haifa to bombard the Israeli port, while in the 1973 war the Israeli Navy sank thirteen Egyptian and Syrian missile boats with no Israeli losses or damage in history's first missile-versus-missile naval engagements.

CHAPTER 18

1. The term Marine Amphibious Brigade for a reinforced regiment, with air support (i.e., a composite aircraft group) came into vogue in the 1970s. Similarly, a reinforced Marine battalion plus a composite aircraft squadron was designated as a Marine Amphibious Unit; a reinforced Marine division plus aircraft wing would be designated as a Marine Amphibious Force. In early 1988 the Marine Corps redesignated these formations as Marine Expeditionary Brigade, Marine Expeditionary Unit, and Marine Expeditionary Force, respectively.

2. Approximately 400 French and 800 Italian military personnel also entered Beirut along with a British armored car unit.

3. Unpublished letter to the editor of the *Naval War College Review*, July 5, 1984.

4. *Ibid.*

APPENDIX A

The following is the memorandum from Winston Churchill, as Prime Minister, to his chief staff officer, General Hastings Ismay, written shortly after the evacuation of the British Army from Dunkirk.

4 June 1940

We are greatly concerned – and it is certainly wise to be so – with the dangers of the German landing in England in spite of our possessing the command of the seas and having very strong defence by fighters in the air. Every creek, every beach, every harbour has become to us a source of anxiety. Besides this the parachutists may sweep over and take Liverpool or Ireland, and so forth. All this mood is very good if it genders energy. But if it is so easy for the Germans to invade us in spite of sea-power, some may feel inclined to ask the question, "Why should it be thought impossible for us to do anything of the same kind to them?" The completely defensive habit of mind which has ruined the French must not be allowed to ruin our initiative. It is of the highest consequence to keep the largest numbers of German forces all along the coasts of the countries they have conquered, and we should immediately set to work to organise raiding forces on these coasts where the populations are friendly. Such forces might be composed of self-contained, thoroughly equipped units of say one thousand up to not more than ten thousand when combined. Surprise would be ensured by the fact that the destination would be concealed until the last moment. What we have seen at Dunkirk shows how quickly troops can be moved off (and I suppose on) to selected points if need be. How wonderful it would be if the Germans could be made to wonder where they were going to be struck next, instead of forcing us to try to wall in the island and roof it over! An effort must be made to shake off the mental and moral prostration to the will and initiative of the enemy from which we suffer.

APPENDIX B

The following memorandum from Winston Churchill, as Prime Minister, to his chief staff officer, General Hastings Ismay, demonstrates his views of how Operation "Round-Up," the planned 1943 cross-Channel invasion of France, should be executed.

15 June 1942

For such an operation the qualities of magnitude, simultaneity, and violence are required. The enemy cannot be ready everywhere. Six heavy disembarkations must be attempted in the first wave. The enemy should be further mystified by at least half a dozen feints, which, if luck favours them, may be exploited. The limited and numerically inferior air force of the enemy will thus be dispersed or fully occupied. While intense fighting is in progress at one or two points, a virtual walk-over may be obtained at others.

2. The second wave nourishes the landings effected, and presses where the going is good. The fluidity of attack from the sea enables wide options to be exercised in the second wave.

3. It is hoped that "Jupiter" [operations in northern Norway] will already be in progress. Landings or feints should be planned in Denmark, in Holland, in Belgium, in the Pas-de-Calais, where the major air battle will be fought, on the Contentin peninsula, at Brest, at St. Nazaire, at the mouth of the Gironde.

4. The first objective is to get ashore in large numbers. At least ten armored brigades should go in the first wave. These brigades must accept very high risks in their task of pressing on deeply inland, rousing the populations, deranging the enemy's communications, and spreading the fighting over the widest possible areas.

5. Behind the confusion and disorder which these incursions will create, the second wave will be launched. This should aim at making definite concentrations of armour and motorised troops at strategic points carefully selected. If four or five of these desirable points have been chosen beforehand concentrations at perhaps three of them might be achieved, relations between them established, and the plan of battle could then take shape.

6. If forces are used on the above scale the enemy should be so disturbed as to require at least a week to organise other than local counter-strokes. During that week a superior fighter air force must be installed upon captured airfields, and the command of the air, hitherto fought for over the Pas-de-Calais, must become general. The R.A.F. must study, as an essential element for its success, the rapid occupation and exploitation of the captured airfields. In the first instance these can only be used as refuelling grounds, as the supreme object is to get into the air at the earliest moment. Altogether abnormal wastage must be expected in this first phase. The landings and installation of the flak at the utmost speed is a matter of high consequence, each airfield being a study of its own.

7. While these operations are taking place in the interior of the country assaulted, the seizure of at least four important ports must be accomplished. For this purpose at least ten brigades of infantry, partly pedal-cyclists, but all specifically trained in house-to-house fighting, must be used. Here again the cost in men and material must be rated very high.

8. To ensure success the whole of the above operations, simultaneous or successive, should be accomplished within a week of zero, by which time not less than four hundred thousand men should be ashore and busy.

9. The moment any port is gained and open the third wave of attack should start. This will be carried from our Western ports in large ships. It should comprise not less than three hundred thousand infantry, with their own artillery, plus part of that belonging to the earlier-landed formations. The first and second waves are essentially assaulting forces, and it is not until the third wave that the formations should be handled in terms of divisions and corps. If by zero [D-Day plus] 14 seven hundred thousand men are ashore, if air supremacy has been gained, if the enemy is in considerable confusion, and if we hold at least four workable ports, we shall have got our claws well into the job.

10. The phase of sudden violence, irrespective of losses, being over, the further course of the campaign may follow the normal and conventional lines of organisation and supply. It then becomes a matter of reinforcement and concerted movement. Fronts will have developed, and orderly progress will be possible. Unless we are prepared to commit the immense forces comprised in the first three waves to a hostile shore with the certainty that many of our attacks will miscarry, and that if we fail the whole stake will be lost, we ought not to attempt such an extraordinary operation of war under modern conditions.

11. The object of the above notes is to give an idea of the scale and spirit in which alone they can be undertaken with good prospects of success.

APPENDIX C
Amphibious Warfare Ships and Craft
(Anglo-American Designations)

Ship Designations during World War II

AGC	amphibious force flagship (later LCC)	APD	high-speed transport (later LPR)
AKA	attack cargo ship (later LKA)	APM	mechanized artillery transport (later LSD)
APA	attack transport (later LPA)	APS	transport submarine
		ATL	Atlantic tank lighter (later LST)

LSC   landing ship carrier
LSD   landing ship dock
LSF   landing ship fighter direction
LSG   landing ship gantry
LSH   landing ship headquarters
LSH(L)   landing ship headquarters (small)
LSI(H)   landing ship infantry (hand-hoisted)
LSI(L)   landing ship infantry (large)
LSI(M)   landing ship infantry (medium)
LSM   landing ship medium
LSM(R)   landing ship medium (rocket)
LSP   landing ship personnel
LSS   landing ship stern-chute
LST   landing ship tank
LST(H)   landing ship tank (hospital)*
LST(M)   landing ship tank (mother)*
LSV   landing ship vehicle

*Unofficial designation.

Landing Craft Designations during World War II

DUKW   amphibian truck
LBE   landing barge emergency repair
LBF   landing barge flak
LBK   landing barge kitchen
LBO   landing barge oiler
LBV   landing barge vehicle
LBW   landing barge water
LC(FF)   landing craft (flotilla flagship)
LCA   landing craft assault
LCA(HR) landing craft assault (hedgerow)
LCC   landing craft control
LCE   landing craft emergency repair
LCF   landing craft flak
LCG(L)   landing craft gun (large)
LCG(M)   landing craft gun (medium)
LCH   landing craft headquarters
LCI(G)   landing craft infantry (gunboat)
LCI(L)   landing craft infantry (large)
LCI(S)   landing craft infantry (small)
LCM   landing craft mechanized
LCN   landing craft navigational
LCP   landing craft personnel
LCP(L)   landing craft personnel (large)
LCP(M)   landing craft personnel (medium)
LCP(N)   landing craft personnel (nested)
LCP(R)   landing craft personnel (ramp)
LCP(S)   landing craft personnel (small)
LCP(SY) landing craft personnel (survey)
LCP(U)   landing craft personnel (utility)
LCR   landing craft rubber
LCR(L)   landing craft rubber (large)
LCR(S)   landing craft rubber (small)
LCS(L)   landing craft support (large)
LCS(M)   landing craft support (medium)
LCS(R)   landing craft support (rocket)
LCS(S)   landing craft support (small)
LCT   landing craft tank
LCT(E)   landing craft tank (emergency repair)
LCT(R)   landing craft tank (rocket)

LCV   landing craft vehicle
LCVP   landing craft vehicle and personnel
LCW   landing craft air propelled
LCT(A)   landing vehicle tracked (armored)
LVT   landing vehicle tracked

Post-World War II Ship Designations

AKSS   cargo submarine
APSS   transport submarine (later LPSS)
CHVA   assault helicopter carrier (later LPH)
DEC   control escort vessel
IFS   inshore fire support ship
LCC   amphibious command ship
LFR   inshore fire support ship
LFS   amphibious fire support ship
LHA   amphibious assault ship (helicopter carrier)
LHD   amphibious assault ship (helicopter carrier)
LKA   amphibious cargo ship
LPA   amphibious transport
LPD   amphibious transport dock
LPH   amphibious assault ship (helicopter carrier)
LPSS   transport submarine
LPR   amphibious transport (small)
LSD   dock landing ship
LSI(L)   infantry landing ship (large) (former LCI(L))
LSM   medium landing ship
LSMR   medium landing ship (rocket)
LSS(L)   support landing ship (large) (former LCS(L))
LST   tank landing ship
LSU   utility landing ship (former LCT(6))
LSV   vehicle cargo ship
LSV   vehicle landing ship
PCC   submarine chaser control
PCEC   submarine chaser escort control
SCC   submarine chaser (wood) control
SSP   transport submarine (later APSS)

Post-World War II Landing Craft Designations

AALC   amphibious assault landing craft
AAV   amphibian assault vehicle
LCA   landing craft assault
LCAC   landing craft air cushion
LCC   landing craft control
LCM   landing craft mechanized
LCPL   landing craft personnel, large
LCR   landing craft rubber
LCR(L)   landing craft rubber (large)
LCR(S)   landing craft rubber (small)
LCSR   landing craft swimmer reconnaissance
LCU   landing craft utility
LCVP   landing craft vehicle personnel
LVT   landing vehicle tracked
LVT(A)   landing vehicle tracked (armored)
LVT(H)   landing vehicle tracked (howitzer)
LVTC   landing vehicle tracked command
LVTE   landing vehicle tracked engineer
LVTP   landing vehicle tracked personnel
LVTR   landing vehicle tracked recovery
LVT(U)   landing vehicle tracked (utility cargo)
LVW   landing vehicle wheeled
LWT   amphibious warping tug
SLWT   side loading warping tug

SELECTED BIBLIOGRAPHY

BOOKS

AMPHIBIOUS OPERATIONS

Brigadier General G. G. Aston, Royal Marine Artillery. *Letters on Amphibious War.* London: John Murray, 1910.

John Cresswell. *Generals and Admirals: The Story of Amphibious Command.* London: Longmans, 1952.

Colonel Robert Debs Heinel, Jr., USMC. *Soldiers of the Sea.* Annapolis, Md.: U.S. Naval Institute, 1962.

Bernard Ferguson, *The Watery Maze.* New York: Holt, Rinehart and Winston, 1961.

Harry A. Gailey. *Peleliu 1944.* Annapolis, Md.: Nautical & Aviation Publishing Co., 1983.

A. Cecil Hampshire. *The Secret Navies.* London: William Kimber and Co., 1978.

Max Hastings. *Overlord, D-Day, June 6, 1944.* Annapolis, Md.: Naval Institute Press, 1984.

— and Simon Jenkins. *The Battle for the Falklands.* London: Michael Joseph, Ltd., 1983.

Peter A. Isley, and Philip A. Crowl. *The U.S. Marines and Amphibious War.* Princeton, N.J.: Princeton University Press, 1951.

Robert Rhodes James. *Gallipoli.* New York: Macmillan Co., 1965.

James D. Ladd. *SBS, The Invisible Raiders.* London: Arms & Armour Press, 1983. [History of the Royal Marines' Special Boat Squadron.]

Ronald Lewin. *Churchill as Warlord.* New York, N.Y.: Stein & Day, 1973.

John Lodwick. *The Filibusters.* London: Methuen & Co., 1947. [SBS operations in the Mediterranean in World War II.]

Allan R. Millett. *Semper Fidelis, The History of The United States Marine Corps.* New York: Macmillan Publishing Co., 1980.

Allan Moorehead. *Gallipoli.* New York: Harper & Row, Publishers, 1956.

Gerald Pawle. *The Secret War, 1939–1945.* New York: William Sloane Associates, 1957. [Efforts of the Admiralty's Department of Miscellaneous Weapons Development – many of which were oriented toward amphibious operations.]

Rowena Reed. *Combined Operations in the Civil War.* Annapolis, Md.: Naval Institute Press, 1978.

General H. M. Smith, USMC. *Coral and Brass.* New York: Simon and Schuster, 1949.

Telford Taylor. *The Breaking Wave.* New York: Simon and Schuster, 1967. [German plans for invading England in the summer of 1940.]

OFFICIAL HISTORIES AND REPORTS*

Lieutenant Colonel Louis N. Bulffardi, USA. *The Soviet Naval Infantry.* Washington, D.C.: Defense Intelligence Agency, April 1980.

Chief of Combined Operations [UK]. *Combined Operations, The Official Story of the Commandos.* New York: Macmillan Co., 1943.

Vice Admiral George Carroll Dyer, USN (Ret). *The Amphibians Came to Conquer, The Story of Admiral Richmond Kelly Turner.* 2 vols. Washington, D.C.: GPO [1971]. [A subjective view of the senior U.S. amphibious force commander of World War II.]

James A. Field, Jr. *History of United States Naval Operations Korea.* Washington, D.C.: GPO, 1962.

From Khe Sanh to Chepone. Hanoi: Foreign Languages Publishing House, 1971, quoted in Marine Corps, History and Museums Division, *U.S. Marines In Vietnam: Vietnamization and Redeployment, 1970–1971.* Washington, D.C.: GPO, 1986.

General Staff [of General Douglas MacArthur]. *Reports of General MacArthur, The Campaigns of MacArthur in the Pacific.* Washington, D.C.: GPO, 1966.

—. *Reports of General MacArthur, Japanese Operations in the Southwest Pacific Area.* 2 vols. Washington, D.C.: GPO, 1966. [Compiled from Japanese Demobilization Bureaux Records.]

H.M. Government, Secretary of State for Defence. *The Falklands Campaign: The Lessons.* London: Her Majesty's Stationery Office, December 1982. [Reprinted in part as "The Falklands Campaign." USNIP [Naval Review] (May 1983), 118–139.]

Lieutenant Colonel John Hixson, USA, and Doctor Benjamin Franklin Cooling. *Combined Operations in Peace and War.* Carlisle Barracks, Penna.: U.S. Army Military History Institute, 1982.

Lieutenant Colonel Frank O. Hough, USMCR, Major Verle E. Ludwing, USMC, and Henry I. Shaw, Jr. *Pearl Harbor to Guadalcanal* in *History of U.S. Marine Corps Operations in World War II.* Washington, D.C.: GPO, 1958.

James L. Mooney (ed.). *Dictionary of American Naval Fighting Ships*, vol. VII. Washington, D.C.: GPO, 1981. Appendix "Tank Landing Ships (LST)" lists and provides brief histories of LSTs No. 1 through No. 731 (569–731).

M. M. Postan. *British War Production*. London: HMSO and Longmans, Green & Co., 1952.

Charles R. Smith. *Marines in the American Revolution, 1775–1783*. Washington, D.C.: GPO, 1975.

Lieutenant Colonel Eugene W. Rawlings, USMC, and Major William J. Sambito, USMC (eds.). *Marines and Helicopters 1946–1962*. Washington, D.C.: Headquarters, U.S. Marine Corps, 1976.

Captain S. W. Roskill, RN. *The War at Sea*, 3 vols. London: HMSO, 1954–61. [Official history of the Royal Navy in World War II.]

Royal Navy, Naval Staff History. *Submarines*, vol. II. *Operations in the Mediterranean*. London: Admiralty Historical Section, 1955.

Lieutenant Colonel Ronald H. Spector, USMCR. *U.S. Marines in Grenada 1983*. Washington, D.C.: Headquarters, U.S. Marine Corps, 1987.

Charles L. Updegraph, Jr. *U.S. Marine Corps Special Units of World War II*. Washington, D.C.: Headquarters, U.S. Marine Corps, 1972.

U.S. Navy, Bureau of Ships. *Ships' Data, U.S. Naval Vessels*. Vol. II, *Mine Vessels, Patrol Vessels, Landing Ships and Craft* [April 15, 1945]. Washington, D.C.: GPO, 1946.

— Director of Naval Intelligence. *Allied Landing Craft of World War II*. London: Arms & Armour Press, 1985. [Reprint of 1944 publication *Allied Landing Craft and Ships*.]

— Office of the Secretary of the Navy. *Lessons of the Falklands, Summary Report*. Washington, D.C.: Department of the Navy, February 1983.

GENERAL HISTORIES

Winston S. Churchill, *The Second World War*. 6 vols. London: Cassell & Co. Ltd., 1948–1954.

— *The World Crisis 1911–1918*, 4 vols. London: Odhams Press, Ltd. [n.d.]

General of the Army Dwight D. Eisenhower, USA. *Crusade in Europe*. Garden City, N.Y.: Doubleday and Co., 1948.

Robert H. Ferrell (ed.). *The Eisenhower Diaries*. New York: Norton, 1981.

Martin Gilbert. *Road to Victory, 1941–1945*. vol. VII of *Winston S. Churchill*. Boston, Mass.: Houghton Mifflin Co., 1986.

Eric J. Grove. *Vanguard to Trident*. Annapolis, Md.: Naval Institute Press, 1987. [British naval policy since World War II.]

Major General Leslie M. Groves, USA (Ret). *Now It Can Be Told*. New York: Harper, 1962.

Francis Whiting Halsey. *History of the World War*. 10 vols. New York and London: Funk & Wagnalls, 1920.

Frederick C. Lane. *Ships for Victory*. Baltimore, Md.: Johns Hopkins Press, 1951. [U.S. Maritime Commission programs of World War II, which included all U.S. LSTs and most AGC/AKA/APA series amphibious ships.]

Rear Admiral Samuel Eliot Morison, USNR. *United States Naval Operations in World War II*, 15 vols. Boston: Little, Brown, 1947–1962.

Norman Polmar. *Aircraft Carriers*. New York: Doubleday & Co., 1969.

Forrest C. Pogue. *George C. Marshall, Organizer of Victory 1943–1945*. New York: Viking Press, 1973.

A. Terry Rambo. "A Preliminary Analysis of Naval Conventional Warfare." [Study for Office of Naval Research.] McLean, Va.: Human Sciences Research, Inc., February 1966.

Terence Robertson. *The Ship With Two Captains*. London: Evans Brothers Ltd., 1957. [An excellent account of the exploits of HM/submarine *Seraph*.]

Captain Stephen Roskill, RN. *Churchill and the Admirals*. New York: William Morrow & Co., 1978.

Major Perry McCoy Smith, USAF. *The Air Force Plans for Peace 1943–1945*. Baltimore, Md.: Johns Hopkins Press, 1970.

Russell F. Weigley. *Eisenhower's Lieutenants, The Campaigns of France and Germany 1944–1945*, 2 vols. Bloomington, Ind.: Indiana University Press, 1981.

REFERENCE WORKS

James C. Fahey. *The Ships and Aircraft of the U.S. Fleet*. Annapolis, Md.: Naval Institute Press, various editions 1939–1965. [Reprints of the original Fahey works.]

Jane's Fighting Ships. London: Jane's Publishing Co. (and predecessors), various editions.

H. T. Lenton and J. J. Colledge. *British and Dominion Warships of World War II*. London: Ian Allan, 1964.

Jurg Meister. *Soviet Warships of the Second World War*. London: Macdonald and Janes, 1977.

Norman Polmar. *Guide to the Soviet Navy*, 4th ed. Annapolis, Md.: Naval Institute Press, 1986.

— *The Ships and Aircraft of the U.S. Fleet*. Annapolis, Md.: Naval Institute Press, 1978, 1981, 1984, 1987 editions.

J. Rohwer and G. Hummelchen. *Chronology of the War at Sea 1939–1945*. 2 vols. London: Ian Allan, 1972, 1974. [Translated from German.]

ARTICLES**
VARIOUS ARTICLES IN:
Globe and Laurel (UK, monthly)
Marine Corps Gazette (USA, monthly)
Morskoy Sbornik [Naval Digest] (USSR, monthly)
The Gator (Amphibious Force U.S. Atlantic Fleet, weekly)
The Naval Review (UK, quarterly)
U.S. Naval Institute *Proceedings* (USA, monthly)
U.S. *Naval War College Review* (USA, bi-monthly)

Warship International (USA, quarterly)

SPECIAL ARTICLES

Glen St. J. Barclay. "'Butcher and Bolt': Admiral Roger Keyes and British Combined Operations, 1940–1941." Naval War College *Review* (March–April 1982), 18–29.

Lieutenant J. Hollis Bower, Jr., USN. "In Defense of the Large Slow Target." USNIP (January 1970), 128–130.

Lieutenant Colonel Michael J. Byron, USMC. "Fury From the Sea: Marines in Grenada." USNIP [Naval Review] (May 1984), 118–131.

Richard A. Cahill. "The Significance of Aboukir Bay." USNIP (July 1967), 79–89.

John B. Dwyer. "Surface Action, Submarine Support Special Ops." *Soldier of Fortune* (May 1987), 44–47, 111.

Captain Mike Eldar, Israeli Navy (Res.). "The Amphibious Assault at Sidon." *IDF Journal* (Summer 1986), 47–51.

Major General J. L. Moulton, RM. "The Marine as an Instrument of Sea Power." USNIP (November 1975), 28–36.

Lieutenant Commander R. E. Mumford, Jr., USN. "Jackstay: New Dimensions in Amphibious Warfare," in Frank Uhlig, Jr. (ed.), *Naval Review 1968.* Annapolis, Md.: U.S. Naval Institute, 1968, 68–87.

John C. Niedermair. "As I Recall . . . Designing the LST." USNIP (November 1982), 58–59.

Lieutenant William H. Poe, USN. "Another Task for the LST." USNIP (February 1969), 130–133.

Dr. Robert L. Scheina. "The Malvinas Campaign." USNIP [Naval Review] (May 1983), 98–117.

Cornelius C. Smith. "Our First Amphibious Assault." *Military Review* [U.S. Army Command and General Staff College] (February 1959), 18–28.

Rear Admiral K. A. Stalbo. "The Art of Naval Landings of the Great Patriotic War," *Morskoy Sbornik* (No. 3, 1970), 23–30.

David Syrett. "The Methodology of British Amphibious Operations during the Seven Years and American Wars." *Mariner's Mirror* (August 1972), 269–280.

Dr Dov S. Zakheim. "The Role of Amphibious Operations in National Maritime Strategy." *Marine Corps Gazette* (March 1984), 35–39.

*GPO = U.S. Government Printing Office.
**USNIP = U.S. Naval Institute *Proceedings.*

INDEX

Ranks shown are highest used in text.
  Abbreviations: Brit., British; Fr., French;
  Ger., Germany; Japn., Japanese; U.S.,
  United States

Abercromby, Lt.-Gen. Sir Ralph, 9, 10, 20
Aboukir beach, landings, 10
Achziv (Israeli), 169–170
Adak, Japanese landings, 28–29, 96; U.S.
  landings, 93, 96–97
"Adlerangriff" (Eagle Attack), 32
Adirondack (U.S. AGC-15), 70
Air cushion landing craft
  Aist class (Soviet), 161–162
  Jeff-A and Jeff-B (U.S.), 173–174
  LCAC series (U.S.), 173
  Lebed class (Soviet), 161
  Pomornik class (Soviet), 161
  SR.N5 (Brit.), 141, 173
Akitsu Maru (Japn.), 23
Aland Islands, landings, 9
Alaska (U.S.), 17
Albion (Brit. battleship), 13
Albion (Brit. aircraft carrier), 141, 163
Aleksandr Nikolayev (Soviet), 161
Aleutian Islands, Japanese landings, 28–29,
  96; U.S. submarine landing, 93; U.S.
  landings, 96–97
Alexander, Gen. Harold, 72, 90
Alfred (U.S.), 16
Allen, Maj. Gen. Terry, 53
Alligator class (Soviet), 161
Amphibious command ships/flagships,
  development, 69–71; post-World War II
  construction, 157
Amphibious ships, see landing ships and
  craft; designations, 185–186
Ancon (U.S. AGC-4 ex-AP-66), 70, 84
Anderson, Lt.-Gen. Kenneth, 51
Antelope (Brit.), 168
Anthony (Brit.), 48
"Anvil" ("Dragoon"), 89; also see Southern
  France landings
Anzio, landings, 61, 71, 76–78, 81
Appalachian (U.S. AGC-1), 70
Apraxin, Gen.-Adm. Fedor Matveevich, 9
Argonaut (U.S. SM-1 ex-SS-166), 91–93
Argus (Brit.), 50, 51
Arkansas (U.S. BB-33), 86
Ark Royal (Brit. aircraft carrier, 1938), 36
Ark Royal (Brit. aircraft carrier, 1955), 162
Armada, Spanish, 8, 32
Ashdod (Israeli), 169
Ashkelon (Israeli), 169
Ashland (U.S. LSD-1), 68
Atlantic Conveyor (Brit.), 168–169
Atomic bombings of Japan, 131
Attu, Japanese landings, 28–29, 96; U.S.
  landings, 93, 96–97
Augusta (U.S. CA-31), 53, 69
Australian-New Zealand Corps (ANZAC),
  11–14
Autogiro, U.S. Marine interest, 133
"Avalanche," 75–76

Bachaquero (Brit.), 48, 53, 60
Badoeng Strait (U.S. CVE-116), 143
"Ballistic Arch," 153–154
Barbey, Rear Adm. D. E., 115, 117
Barham (Brit.), 35, 36
Barnegat (U.S. AVP-11), 71
Barnstable County (U.S. LST-1197), 176
Baruka, landings, 97
Batsheva (Israeli), 169, 170
Beirut, landings, see Lebanon
Begor (APD-127 ex-DE-711), 145, 146
Bernadou (U.S. DD-153), 51–52

Betio, landings, 103–107, 112
Biak, landings, 115
Bikini, atomic bomb tests, 133
Biscayne (U.S. AGC-18 ex-AVP-11), 70, 71
Bishop, Maurice, 176
Biter (ex-U.S. AVG-3); see *Dixmude*
Bladensburg, battle, 17
Block Island (U.S. LPH-1 ex-CVE-106), 137
Blue Ridge (U.S. LCC/AGC-20), 157
Bolulo (Brit.), 69, 87
"Bonus," 48
Bougainville, landings, 98–99, 102
Bourne, Lt.-Gen. Alan G., 35,
Boxer revolt, 18
Boxer (Brit. LST), 60, 70
Boxer (U.S. LPH-4 ex-CV-21), 137–138
Boyington, Maj. Gregory, 101
Bradley, Gen. of the Army Omar, 7, 70, 80,
  82, 88
Breconshire (Brit.), 67
Brezhnev, Leonid, 160
Britain, Battle of, 32
Brodie launching system, 62, 131
Broke (Brit.), 54
Brooke, Field Marshal Sir Alan, 79
Brunbury, Sir Henry, 9–10
Bulwark (Brit.), 141, 162–163
"Buccaneer," 108
Buckner, Lt. Gen. Simon B., 126, 128
Burma, planned Allied landings, 121
Burnett, Col. J. R., 151

Cabildo (U.S. LSD-16), 142
Cabo San Antonio (Argentine), 164–165
"Cactus" (Guadalcanal airfield), 40, 113
Calpe (Brit.), 45
Ca Mau Peninsula, landings, 151
Canberra (Brit.), 165, 167
"Capital," 121
Carey, Brig. Gen. R. E., 157
Carl, Brig. Gen. Marion, 150
Carlson, Lt. Col. Evans F., 92–93
Carriacou landings, 178
Carronade (U.S. LFR/IFS-1), 138–139
Carter administration, 171, 173
Castiglione, landings, 54
"Catchpole," 107
Cates, Gen. Clifton B., 136, 137
Catoctin (U.S. AGC-5), 71
Celebes, landings, 23, 26
Centurion (Brit.), 82
Chamoun, Camille, 147
Charleston (U.S. AKA-113), 139, 172
Chenango (U.S. CVE-28), 53
"Cherryblossom," 99
Chiang, Generalissimo Kai-Shek, 108
Chilton (U.S. APA-38), 149
China, Japanese operations, 23–24
Christie, J. Walter, 22, 55
Churchill, Winston S., in World War I, 10,
  11, 14, 15; in World War II, 32, 34, 35, 37,
  46, 47, 49, 59, 60, 61–62, 69, 72, 74, 77, 78,
  79, 82, 108; 1940 memorandum on landing
  operations, 183; 1942 memorandum on
  landing operations, 183–184
Civil War (U.S.), 18
Clark, George Rogers, 17
Clark, Lt. Gen. Mark, 50, 70, 75, 76, 94–95
"Claymore," 37
"Cleanslate," 97
Clemens, Martin, 41
Coastwatchers, in Solomons, 21–22
"Co-Prosperity Sphere," 121
Cole (U.S. DD-155), 51
Columbus (U.S.), 16
Combined Operations established, 34–35
Combined ships, development of, 69–71;

post-World War II construction, 157
Coningham, Air Marshal Arthur, 75
Conolly, Rear Adm. Richard L., 107, 113
Coral Sea, battle, 28, 29, 38, 96–97
Corfu, landings, 9
Coronado (U.S.), 17
"Coronet," 130–131
"Corporate," 165–169
Corry (U.S. DD-463), 87
Courbet (Fr.), 82
Cowie (U.S. DD-632), 73
Crerar, Lt.-Gen. H. D. G., 46
"Crusader," 94
Cuba, 1898 landings, 18; planned 1962
  landings, 148–149
Cuban missile crisis, 148–149
Culebra, landings, 55–56
"Culverin," 108
Cunningham, Adm. Sir Andrew Brown, 49,
  51, 54, 72, 80
Cunningham, Vice Adm. J. H. D., 35
Curacao, landings, 17
Currin, Lt. Col. Mike, 97

D-Day, see Normandy landings
Daffodil (Brit.) 69
Dakar, landing attempt, 6, 35–36, 69, 70
Da Nang, landings, 150–151
Dardanelles landings, 6, 7, 10–13, 15, 20,
  55, 105;
  casualties, 14
Darlan, Adm. of the Fleet Jean, 53
Davis, Jefferson, 18
"Deckhouse", 153–154, 155
de Gaulle, Gen. Charles, 35, 36
Dempsey, Lt.-Gen. Sir Miles, 82, 83
Denmark, landings, German, 31
"Detachment," 122
Devonshire (Brit.), 35
Diahatsu (Japn.), 23
Dieppe landings, 6, 45–46, 54, 89
Dill, Gen. Sir John, 47
dive bombing, development of, 22
Dixmunde (formerly HMS *Biter*/AVG-3),
  149
Doolittle, Lt. Gen. James, raid Tokyo, 28; in
  Italy, 75
Donovan, Col. William, 5–7, 40
"Double Eagle", 155
Doyle, Rear Adm. J. H., 143–145
"Dracula," 121
Drake, Sir Francis, 32
Dreadnought (Brit.), 12
Duke of York, 10
Duncan, Adm. Lord, Adam, 9–10
Dunkirk, evacuation, 14, 145, 183
Durban (Brit.), 82

"Eagle Pull," 157
Egypt, British 1801 landings, 10; Anglo-
  French 1956 landings, 139–141
Eichelberger, Lt. Gen. Robert L., 100, 114–
  115
Eisenhower, Gen. Dwight D., 95; command
  of North Africa invasion, 49, 50, 54, 94;
  command of Normandy invasion, 79–80,
  114; invasion of Sicily, 72
Eldorado (U.S. AGC-11), 70, 132
Ellis, Maj. Earl H., 20, 115
"Elkton", 97, 98, 101
Eniwetok, landings, 107–108
Endurance (Brit.), 164, 165
Enterprise (U.S. CV-6), 39, 41
Erie, Capt. Carl R., 177–178

Ernest-Ernie-Plunkett-Drax, Adm. Sir Reginald, 34
Erskine, Lt. Gen. Graves B., 135
Essex (U.S. CV-9), 109, 134, 139, 143–144, 148
Estes (U.S. AGC-12), 70
Eureka, 57
"Extended Capital," 121

Falklands, Argentine landings, 164–165; British landings, 6, 7, 165–169, 178
Faulkner, Col. James P., 176
Fearless (Brit.), 163, 167
Fedala, landings, 51–53
Feldt, Comdr. Eric, 21–22
Fisher, Adm. Sir John, 14
"Flagpole," 94
Fleet Marine Force, U.S., established, 20, 22
Fletcher, Vice Adm. Frank Jack, 43
"Flintlock," 106
"Flying LST," see Tradewind (R3Y) aircraft
"Forager," 109–114
Forrestal, James V., 123, 125, 132
Fort Marion (U.S. LSD-22), 146
Fort Snelling (U.S. LSD-30), 176–177
France, 1798 quasi-war with, 17; 1944 southern landings, 62, 71
Francis Marion (U.S. APA-249), 139
Fredenhall, Maj. Gen. Lloyd, 50
"Frequent Wind," 157

Galbreath, Lt. (jg) John H., 124
Gallipoli, see Dardanelles landings
Galtieri, Gen. Leopoldo, 164
"Galvanic," 102–106
"Game Warden," 151–152
Garrett County (U.S. LST-786), 152
Geiger, Lt. Gen. Roy, 113, 114, 126, 128, 133
General Belgrano (Argentine), 166
George II (King of England), 8
George VI (King of England), 69
Geraghty, Col. Tim, 175
German landing craft, 32, 34
German, plans for invading Britain, see "Sealion"
Gerow, Maj. Gen. Leonard T., 84
Ghormley, Vice Adm. Robert L., 41
Gilberts, Japanese landings, 28; U.S. landings, 18, 91–93, 96, 102–106, 107, 108, 109
Giraud, Gen. Henri H., 95
Glen-class ships (Brit.), 37
Glenearn (Brit.), 67
Glengyle (Brit.), 37, 66, 67
Glenroy (Brit.), 67
Goering, Field Marshal Hermann, 22
Gold Beach, landings, 82, 86–87
"Goodtime," 99
Gooseberry-Mulberry projects, 82, 83, 87
Gorshkov, Adm. of the Fleet of the Soviet Union S. G., 160
Grayback (U.S. LPSS-574), 154–155
Grenada landings, 6, 7, 176–178
Groves, Maj. Gen. Leslie, 133
Guadalcanal, landings, 36–44, 91, 97
Guam, Japanese landings, 24–25; U.S. landings, 109, 112–113
Guam (U.S. LPH-9), 176–178
Guerrico (Argentine), 164

Hall, Rear Adm. J. L., 84
Halsey, Adm. William F., 28, 110, 115, 117, 131
Hamilton, Gen. Sir Ian, 14
Hancock (U.S. CV-19), 152, 157
Harold (King of England), 8
Harris, Maj. Gen. F., 135–136
Harris (U.S. APA-2), 112
Hastings, battle of, 8
Hatteras Inlet, landings, 18
Hayate (Japn.), 25
Helicopter carriers, U.S. development, 137–139, 172–173; British development, 139–140, 141, 163
Helicopters, development for amphibious assault, 133–140
Helicopters, early U.S. Marine interest, 133–136
Henry County (U.S. LST-824), 152
Hermes (Brit.) 162–163, 165, 168
Hewitt, Rear Adm. H. Kent, 69, 70
Higgins, Andrew J., 42, 56–57
Hill, Rear Adm. Harry W., 103, 104
Hiryu (Japn.), 25

Hitler Adolf, 31, 32, 33, 34, 38, 76–77, 83, 88
Hollandia, landings, 114–115
Holloway, Vice Adm. James L. Jr., 148
Homma, Lt. Gen. Masaharu, 26, 27
Hope, Bob, 145
Horace A. Bass (APD-124 ex-DE-691), 146
Hosogaya, Vice Adm. Boshiro, 29
Hughes-Hallet, Capt. John, 45, 46, 82
Hungnam evacuation, 145–146
"Husky," 72-75, 95

I-175 (Japn.), 102
"Iceberg," 126–128
Illustrious (Brit.), 48
Implacable (Brit.), 12
Inchon, landing, 7, 120, 136, 142–145
Independence (U.S. CVL-22), 102, 109, 176
Independence (U.S. CV-62), 176
Indochina, landings, 149; also see Vietnam
Indomitable (Brit.), 48
Ionian Sea islands, landings, 9
Iowa (U.S. BB-61), 174
Iphigenia (Brit.), 15
"Ironclad," 48
Ismay, Gen. Hastings, 183
Ivan Rogov (Soviet), 161
Intrepid (Brit. 2nd class cruiser), 15
Intrepid (U.S. CV-11), 107
Intrepid (Brit. assault ship), 163, 167
Invincilble (Brit.), 163, 165–166
Irwin, Maj. Gen. Noel M., 35, 69
Israeli landings, 169–170
Iwo Jima, landings, 70, 71, 121, 122–126, 132
Iwo Jima (U.S. LPH-2), 137–139, 153, 173

"Jackstay," 151–153
Japanese home islands, planned Allied assault, 130–131
Jean Bart (Fr.), 50, 52, 53, 140
Jewell, Lt. N. L. A., 94–95
Jones, Lt. Col. H. J., 168
"Jubilee," 45–46
"Jungle Drum III," 154
Juno Beach, landings, 82, 86–87
"Jupiter," 183

Kaiten manned torpedoes, 30
Kajioka, Rear Adm. Sadamichi, 25
Keeble, Maj. Christopher, 168
Kennedy, John F., 148; administration, 173
Kerch-Feodosya landings, 160
Kesselring, Field Marshal Albert, 76–77, 78
Keyes, Lt. Col. Geoffrey, 37, 94
Keyes, Adm. Sir Roger, 15, 35, 36, 37
King, Adm. Ernest J., 39–40, 41, 47, 50
Kinkaid, Vice Adm. Thomas C., 96, 117
Kirk, Rear Adm. Alan G., 70
Kiska, landings, 29; also see Aleutian Islands
Komandorski Islands, battle, 96
Korea, 1871 landings, 17; Korean War, 7, 136, 137, 141, 142–148, 172, 174
Koryu midget submarines, 30
Kreuger, Gen. Walter, 131
Kwajalein, landings, 106–107, 132

"Landcrab," 93, 96
Lafayette Escadrille, 53
Lake Erie, battle, 17
Lake Michigan (Brit.), 12
landing craft, see landing ships
landing ships and craft, British and U.S. development of
APD, 56
LB (K), 81
LCA, 58
LCG, 63
LCI, 62–63
LCVP, 57–58
LCT, 59
LPD, 63
LSD, 23, 68
LSM, 63
LSMR, 63, 66
LST, development, 59–62; carrier modifications, 90, 131; comments by Winston Churchill, 6, 59, 61–62; losses, 62 see also helicopter carriers and landing vehicles. designations, 185–186
landing ships, Japanese development of,
APD, 30
LSD, 23
LST, 30
landing ships, Soviet development of, 161

landing vehicles, development of,
DUKW, 68, 72, 73
LCAC, 173–174
LVT, 22, 55, 58–59; first uses, 41, 44
SR.N5, 141
LB(K).1 (Brit.), 81
LCA 403 (Brit.), 76
LCA 446 (Brit.), 76
LCG(L)-939 (Brit.), 65
LCI(L)-326 (U.S.), 62
LCI(L)-522 (U.S.), 89
LCI(L)-769 (U.S.), 62
LCT-199 (U.S.), 86
LCT-555 (U.S.), 86
LCT-638 (U.S.), 86
LCT(A) (5)-2421 (Brit.), 86
LCT(R)-125, 77
LCU-1481 (U.S.), 68
LCU-1665 (U.S.), 179
Lawford (Brit.), 87
Lebanon, 1958 landings, 147–148; 1982 landings, 175–176
Lee, Gen. Robert E., 18
Lehman, John F. Jr., 173–174
Leigh-Mallory, Air Chief Marshal, 46, 80
Lejeune, Gen. John A., 20
Lemay, Lt. Gen. Curtis, 131
Lewin, Ronald, 47
Lexington (U.S. CV-2), 38
Leyte, landings, 117–119
Leyte Gulf, battle, 117, 119
Liddell-Hart, Sir Basil Henry, 6
Liscombe Bay (U.S. CVE-56), 102
Lloyd, Air Marshal Hugh, 75
Lloyd (U.S. APD-63 ex-DE-209), 57
Lofoten Islands, landing , 37
Long Thanh Peninsula, landings, 152
LSM-44 (U.S.), 65
LSM-60 (U.S.), 133
LST, development, see landing ships and craft
LST-1 (U.S.), 61
LST-4 (U.S.), 81
LST-16 (U.S.), 90
LST-21 (U.S.), 62
LST-229 (U.S.), 61
LST-282 (U.S.), 89
LST-357 (U.S.), 75
LST-359 (U.S.), 75
LST-263 (U.S.), 98
LST-507 (U.S.), 81
LST-531 (U.S.), 81
LST-776 (U.S.), 131
LST-611 (U.S.), 143
LST-715 (U.S.), 143
LST-845 (U.S.), 143
LST-914 (U.S.), 143
LST-973 (U.S.), 143
LST-983 (U.S.), 90
LST-1179 class, see *Newport*
LST-3033 (Brit.), 62
Lucas, Maj. Gen. John P., 77
Luftwaffe, failure to defeat Royal Air Force, 31–33
Luzon, landings on, 1941, 27; 1945, 119–120
Lybecker, Gen., 9

MacArthur, Gen. Douglas A., in World War II, 7, 27, 28, 39–40, 49, 79, 97, 100–101, 103, 114–120, 130, 131; in Korean War, 142–145
MacNamara, Robert S., 172
Madagascar, landings, 47–49
Makin atoll, Japanese landings, 27; U.S. submarine raid, 91–93, 102; U.S. landing, 102
Malcolm (Brit.), 54
Malvinas, see Falklands
Malaya, landings, 26
Manitowoc (U.S. LST-1180), 176–178
Manley (U.S. APD-1 ex-DD-74), 56
Maracaibo-class LSTs (Brit.), 53, 59–60
Marathon, landing, 8
Margelov, Marshal V. F., 160
Marianas, landings, 108, 109–114
Marianas Turkey Shoot, see Battle of the Philippine Sea
Marines
British, established, 8, development, 34
Dutch, established, 8
Russian, established, 9
U.S., established 16; Fleet Marine Force established, 20, 22; first division formations, 40; first amphibious corps, 44
"Market Time," 151–152

Marshall, Gen. George C., 6, 39–40, 46, 47, 49, 61; considered for command of the Normandy landings, 79
Marshalls, landings, 70, 106–108
Martin, Maj., see "Mincemeat"
Mason, Paul, 42
Maryland (U.S. BB-46), 103, 104
Massachusetts (U.S. BB-59), 51, 52, 53
Massie, Robert K., 9
Matthews (U.S. AKA-96), 66
"Menace," 35–36
Menard (U.S. APA-201), 149
Mercury (U.S. T-AKR 11), 179
Meredith (U.S. DD-726), 87
Messina, German-Italian evacuation, 74
Metcalf, Vice Adm. Joseph III, 177
Mexican Civil War, 22
Mexican War of 1847, 18
Midway, battle, 28, 38, 96, 109
Midway Island, Japanese landing attempt, 6
"Mincemeat," 95
Mindoro, landings, 117, 119
Missouri (U.S. BB-63), 143, 174
Mitscher, Vice Adm. Marc A., 122, 126
"MO" (Moresby), 38
Moon Sound landings, 160
Montgomery, Gen. Bernard L., 73, 80, 82, 88
Moore, Maj.-Gen. Jeremy M., 165
Moore, Maj.-Gen. Sir John, 10
Morgan, Lt.-Gen. Frederick E., 79, 80
Morison, Rear Adm. Samuel Eliot, 70, 74
Morocco, landings, see Operation "Torch"
Morotai, landings, 115
Mountbatten, Adm. Lord Louis, 37, 46, 108, 121
Mount McKinley (U.S. AGC-7), 143
Mount Whitney (U.S. LCC/AGC-19), 157
Mulberry-Gooseberry projects, 82, 83, 87
Mulcahy, Maj. Gen. Francis P., 98, 126
Murphy, Robert, 50, 54
Musashi (Japn.), 117
"Musketeer," 139–141
Mussolini, Benito, 72, 75
MV-22, see Osprey aircraft

Napoleon (Napoleon Bonaparte), 10, 32
Narwhal (U.S. SS-167), 91, 93
Nashville (U.S. CL-43), 119
Nassau (U.S. CVE-16), 96
Nasser, Gamal Abdel, 139
Nautilus (U.S. SS-168), 91–93
Nelson, Viscount Horatio, 32
"Neptune," 81; see "Overlord"
New Britain, landings, 97, 100–101
New Georgia, landings, 97–98
New Guinea, landings, 6, 100–101, 102, 114, 130
New Jersey (U.S. BB-62), 174
New Mexico (U.S. BB-40), 128
New Orleans, battle, 17
Newport (U.S. LST-1179), 159, 172–173
New Providence, landing, 16–17
Nicholas, Capt. Samuel, 16–17
Niedermair, John, 60
Nigitsu Maru (Japn.), 23
Nimitz, Adm. Chester W., 10, 38, 39–40, 41, 106, 112, 114, 115, 122, 125, 130
Nixon, Richard, 157
Noemfor, landings, 115
Norman landing, 8
Normandy, German defenses, 83–86
Normandy, naval forces, 88, 95
Normandy, naval losses, 87
Normandy, landings, 6, 47, 61, 62, 70, 72, 75, 77, 78, 79–88, 89, 108, 109, 110; ships participating, 61, 88, 95
North Africa landings, 49–54, 69, 72, 89, 94–95
North Holland, landing, 9
Norway, German landing, 31
Novorossiysk, landings, 160

Ocean (Brit.), 139–141
Okean exercises, 162
Okinawa, landings, 71, 93, 108, 121, 122, 126–130
Okinawa (U.S. LPH-3), 157
"Olympic," 130–131, 132
Omaha Beach, landings, 82, 83–86
Operations, see specific code names
Orlon-class (Soviet), 162
Osprey (V-22) aircraft, 174–175
Ostend, raid, 15
"Overlord" (Normandy landings) 6, 47, 61, 62, 70, 72, 75, 77, 78, 79–88, 89, 108, 109, 110; ships participating, 61, 88, 95

Palaus, landings, 114–116
Palau (U.S. CVE-122), 135
"Paraquat," 165
Patrol Boat No. 32 (Japn.), 25
Patrol Boat No. 33 (Japn.), 25
Patton, Gen. George S., 50, 51, 52, 53, 72, 73–74, 78, 82, 88
Paul Revere (U.S. APA-248), 139
Pavuvu, landings, 97
PC-2161 (U.S.), 87
"Peace for Galilee," 169
Pearl Harbor, Japanese attack, 24, 25, 28, 38, 49, 75, 103, 109, 113
Peleliu, landings, 115–116
Pennsylvania (U.S. BB-38), 113
Perch (U.S. APSS/SSP-313), 145, 146, 148, 154, 155
Pershing, Gen. John, 20
Pétain, Marshal Philippe, 54
Peter the Great, 8–9, 10, 20
Peters, Capt. T. A., 101
Philippines, 1898 landings, 18; Japanese landings, 26–28; U.S. landings 1944–1945, 93, 108, 116–121, 122, 126, 130
Philippine Sea, battle, 10
Piasecki, Frank, 133
Plataea, battle, 8
Polnocny class (Soviet), 161
Port Said, landings, 140–141
Port Stanley, Argentine landings, 164; British landings, 168–169
Potter, Prof. E. B., 10
Price, Capt. Martin, 48
Prince of Wales (Brit.), 26
Princess Iris (Brit.), 69
Princeton (U.S. LPH-5 ex-CV-37), 137, 150, 152
Providence (U.S.), 16
Pueblo (U.S. AGER-2), 155
Pyle, Ernie, 128

Queen Elizabeth II (Brit.), 165, 166

R3Y, see Tradewind aircraft
Raeder, Grand Adm. Erich, 32, 33
Raleigh (U.S. LPD-1), 157
Ramillies (Brit.), 48, 49
Ramsay, Adm. Sir Bertram, 80
Ranger (U.S. CV-4), 53
Rangoon, planned Allied landing, 121
Rapid Deployment Force (U.S.), 171
Reagan, Ronald, 173; Reagan administration, 173–174
"Reckless," 115
Regulus missile submarines, 155
Rendova, landings, 97
Repulse (Brit.), 26
Resolution (Brit.), 36
Rhodes, proposed Allied assault, 78
Richelieu (Fr.), 35, 36
Ridgeway, Maj. Gen. Matthew B., 76
River Clyde (Brit.), 11–14, 55, 62
Roberts (Brit.), 75
Roberts, Maj.-Gen. H. F., 45, 46
Rockbridge (U.S. APA-228), 148
Rocky Mount (U.S. AGC-3), 70
Roebling, Donald, 22, 58
Roi-Namur, landings, 107
Roosevelt, Brig. Gen. Theodore, 53
Roosevelt, Col. Theodore, 18
Roosevelt, Franklin D., 40, 46, 47, 49, 52, 69, 71, 72, 74, 79, 108, 117, 130
Roosevelt, Maj. James, 92
Rommel, Field Marshal Erwin, 76, 83, 94
Roskill, Capt. S. W., 46, 88n.
Rosenthal, Joe, 125
Row, Brig. R. A., 99
Rupertus, Maj.-Gen. William H., 101
Russell Islands, landings, 97
Ryujo (Japn.), 26, 27
Ryder, Maj.-Gen. Charles, 50

Sabin, Rear Adm. Lorenzo S., 149
Safari (Brit.), 95
Safi (Fedala), landings, 51–53
Saint Louis (U.S. LKA-116), 157
Saipan, landings, 109–112, 114
Sakaguchi, Maj. Gen. Shizuo, 27
Salamis, battle, 8
Salerno, landings, 61, 70, 71, 75–76
Samuel Chase (U.S. APA-26), 81

San Carlos Water, landing, 167–168
Santa Fe (Argentine), 164, 166
Santissima Trinidad (Argentine), *164*
Saratoga (U.S. CV-3), 39, 41
Savo Island, battle, 43
"Sealion," 6, 31–33, 34, 88
Sealion (U.S. SSP-315), 146
Secretary class (U.S.), 71
Seminole (U.S. AKA-104), 151
Seraph (Brit.), 50, 94–95
Shakespeare (Brit.), 95
Sheffield (Brit.), 166
Shepherd, Brig. Gen. Lemuel C., 113
Sherwood, Robert E., 100
Shibasaki, Rear Adm. K., 106
"Shingle," 77
Shinshu Maru (Japn.), 23
Ships taken up from trade, 165–166
"Shoestring," 41
Shoho (Japn.), 38
Shoup, Lt. Col. David M., 103, 105
Sicily, landings, 61, 71, 72–75, 81, 95, 108
Sicily (U.S. CVE-118), 143, 148
Sikorsky, Igor, 133
Sino-Japanese conflict, 23–24
Sir Bedivere (Brit.), 163
Sir Galahad (Brit.), 168–169
Sir Tristram (Brit.), 168
Six Day War (1967), 169
"Sledgehammer," 47
Slim, Lt.-Gen. Sir William, 121
Smith, Lt. Gen. Holland M., 57, 92–93, 102–106, 109–112, 114, 122, 132
Smith, Lt. Gen. Walter Bedell, 80
Smith, Maj. Gen. J. C., 102–106
Smith, Maj. Gen. Oliver P., 116, 143–145
Smith, Maj. Gen. R. C., 102–106, 111–112
Smith, Maj. Perry McCoy, 132
Solomons, Japanese landings, 39; U.S. landings, 97–99, 130
Soryu (Japn.), 25
Southern France, landings, 81, 89–90
South Georgia, see Falklands landings
Soviet amphibious operations, 160–162
Spaatz, Gen. Carl, 130
Spanish-American War, 18, 40, 148
Spartan (Brit.), 165
Spotswood, Col. Alexander, 8
Spruance, Adm. Raymond A., 109, 110, 112, 114, 122, 126, 131
"Stalemate," 115
Stalin, Joseph, 78, 108
Stanley, Lt. Cmdr. Ian, 166
Strasser, Maj. Heinrich, 51
Struble, Vice Adm. Arthur D., 119, 143
Sturges, Maj.-Gen. Robert, 48
submarines, in landing operations, British, 37, 50, 81–82, 93–95; British commandos from U.S. submarines, 145–146; U.S., 91–93, 139, 145–146, 154–155
Suez, landings, 139–141
Sumatra (Dutch), 82
Sumatra, 1830s landings, 18; planned Allied landings, 108
"Super Gymnast," see "Torch"
Sword Beach, landings, 82, 83, 86–87
Swordfish (U.S. SS-193), 93
Sybil (Brit.), 95
Syfret, Rear Adm. E. N., 48
Syria, landings, 37, 94

T-101 (Japn.), 29
T-131 (Japn.), 30
T-137 (Japn.), 30
T-138 (Japn.), 30
T-149 (Japn.), 26, 30
T-151 (Japn.), 29
T-172 (Japn.), 30
Talisman (Brit.), 94
tank laning ships, see landing ships and craft
Tarawa, Japanese landing, 28; U.S. landings, 93, 102–107, 123, 132
Tarawa (U.S. CV-40), 137
Tarawa (U.S. LHA-1), 7, 159, 172–173
Taylor, Telford, 31
Tedder, Air Chief Marshal Arthur W., 49–50, 54, 72, 79, 80
Tennessee (U.S. BB-43), 126, 128
Texas (U.S. BB-35), 51, 52, 86
Theobold, Rear Adm. R. A., 96
Themistocles, 8
Theseus (Brit.), 139–141

Thetis (Brit.), 15
Thetis Bay (U.S. LPH-6/CVHA-1 ex-CVE-90), 137
Thieu, Nguyen Van, 157
Thompson, Brig. Julian, 165, 169
Thurston (U.S. AP-77), 86
"Tiger," 81
Tilton, Capt. McLane, 17
Tinian, landings, 109–112
Tojo, Hideki, 111
Torbay (Brit.), 94
"Torch," 49–54, 69, 72, 89, 94–95
"Tokyo Express," 44, 118
Tradewind (R3Y) aircraft, 134, 161
Treasury Islands, landings, 99
Trenton (U.S. LPD-14), 157, 176–177
Troubridge, Rear Adm. Thomas H., 89
Trieste, planned Allied landings, 90
Tripoli, 1801 war, 17
Truman, Harry S, 57, 130, 131
Tulagi, landing, 41
Tulare (U.S. AKA-112), 139
Tunny (U.S. APSS-282), 146, 155
Turnage, Maj. Gen. Allen, 113
Turner, Vice Adm. Richmond Kelly, 41, 42, 43, 70, 110, 112, 122, 126
25 de Mayo (Argentine), 164, 166

Udet, Ernst, 22
"Urgent Fury," 176–178
Ushijima, Gen. Mitsuru, 128
Utah Beach, landings, 82, 83–86

V-22, see Osprey aircraft
Valley Forge (U.S. LPH-8 ex-CV 45), 137
Vancouver (U.S. LPD-2), 159
Vandalia (U.S.), 18
Vandegrift, Gen. Alexander A., 40, 41, 44, 99, 108, 133
Vangunu Island, landing, 97
Vietnam War, 66, 141, 146, 149–157, 171, 172
Vindictive (Brit.), 15

Wainwright, Maj. Gen. Jonathan M., 28
Wake Island, landings, 25
Wantuck (U.S. APD-125 ex-DE-692), 146
War of Attrition, 169
War of 1812, 17
Warspite (Brit.), 87
Washington, Gen. George, 16, 17
Washington, Lawrence, 8
Washoe County (U.S. LST-1165), 152
Wasp (U.S. CV-7), 39, 41
Wasp (U.S. LHD-1), 172–173

"Watchtower," 36–44
Weigley, Russell, 88
Westervelt, Capt. John D., 151
Whidbey Island (U.S. LSD-4), 173
William the Conqueror, 8
Wilkinson, Vice Adm. Theodore S., 117
Wilson, Brig. Gen. Thomas, 107
Wilson, Capt. Louis H., 113
Wingate, Brig. Orde, 121
Wing-In-Ground (WIG) effect vehicles (Soviet), 161–162
Wisconsin (U.S. BB-64), 174
Woodward, Rear Adm. J. F., 165, 166
Wonsan, landing, 145
Wright, Capt. Jerauld, 94–95

X-20 (Brit.), 81–82, 95
X-23 (Brit.), 81–82, 95
Xerxes, 8

Yamato (Japn.), 38, 117
Yamamoto, Adm. Isoroku, 28
Yorktown (U.S. CV-5), 38
Yubari (Japn.), 25

Zapad '81 exercise, 162
Zeebrugge, raid, 15, 35